Introduction to Computer Music

Introduction to Computer Music

Nick Collins

University of Sussex, UK

A John Wiley and Sons, Ltd, Publication

This edition first published 2010
© 2010 John Wiley & Sons Ltd

Registered office
John Wiley & Sons Ltd, The Atrium, Southern Gate, Chichester, West Sussex, PO19 8SQ,
United Kingdom

For details of our global editorial offices, for customer services and for information about how to
apply for permission to reuse the copyright material in this book please see our website at
www.wiley.com.

Library of Congress Cataloging-in-Publication Data
Collins, Nick (Nicholas)
    Introduction to computer music / Nick Collins.
        p. cm.
    Includes bibliographical references and index.
    ISBN 978-0-470-71455-3 (pbk.)
1. Computer music–Instruction and study. I. Title.
    MT723.C63 2009
    780.285–dc22
                                                                    2009026525

A catalogue record for this book is available from the British Library.

ISBN 9780470714553 (pbk.)

Set in 10/12pt Garamond by Sunrise Setting Ltd, Torquay, UK.
Printed and bound in Great Britain by TJ International, Padstow, Cornwall.

In memory of Drew Gartland-Jones

Contents

About the Author

Dr Nick Collins is a composer, performer and researcher in the field of computer music. He lectures at the University of Sussex, running the music informatics degree programmes and research group. Research interests include machine listening, interactive and generative music, audiovisual performance, sound synthesis and music psychology. He co-edited the *Cambridge Companion to Electronic Music* (Cambridge University Press), and is fond of the non sequitur. He is an experienced pianist and computer music performer, and active in both instrumental and electronic music composition. He has occasionally toured the world as the non-Swedish half of the Swedish audiovisual laptop duo 'klipp av'. Sometimes, he writes in the third person about himself, but is trying to give it up. Further details, including publications, music, code and more, are available from http://www.informatics.sussex.ac.uk/users/nc81/

Preface

HOW TO USE THIS BOOK

This preface sets out possible ways to approach the text depending on a few common backgrounds from which you might encounter computer music. We'll also set out some conventions used in the book.

The natural constituencies for this text are musicians who are learning about new technologies which support musical activity, and technologists who want to engage with the rich world of music.

You might have knowledge and practical experience in music theory and music making, perhaps in a number of different musical traditions such as Western classical, popular music, jazz, Hindustani, Carnatic, gamelan, gagaku and many more that may be experimental, functionally constrained and commercial to various degrees. You probably already recognize that boundaries blur and musical styles and genres are as much temporary talking points or pliable historical labels as anything else; you may already have come into contact with electronic music in various ways. It is hard to have escaped the central role of the recording in much current musical practice, for example!

Most people already have general computer literacy as far as some social technologies go (email, setting up a MySpace page, networking via Facebook), and you may be familiar with some of the standard types of computer music software for general use, such as sequencers, sound editors and trackers. But perhaps you have little or no prior experience of computer programming itself, and may not have an extensive background in mathematics.

This book has its challenges, for in places we must deal with certain points which are motivated by mathematical and programming considerations. I ask you to consider that you can always skip over any mathematics that alarms you; you can always return to it later, and I will always endeavor to provide written language explanations alongside any equations I introduce. To avoid the equations entirely would be to avoid some of the richness of this field, and many readers will find that the equations and algorithms will enhance their understanding. Whilst I will do my best to explain important algorithmic ideas in computer music, there is not room in this book itself to provide a full explanation of any one particular programming language. To keep coverage wide ranging, and avoid committing to any one technology when a multiplicity of software is on offer, pseudocode has been used at points in the book to outline a few algorithms, rather than giving them in a particular language. Nevertheless, various languages will be mentioned in due course, and the best advice is to try them all out, see how you get along and find your favorites!

Despite any danger of obsolescence, I've not shied from linking in to current developments in computer music. This book has its own role to play in the historical record, and I shall not be embarrassed to have featured some systems which fell by the wayside.[1]

You may be a student on an established course, or an independent artist. There is something for everyone within this book, with a number of levels and ways in which the book can be used depending on your background and preferences. But ultimately it doesn't matter whether you consider yourself to be more experienced in music, or in computers, or, indeed, in archaeology.

The chapters in this book are all highly interlinked, and highly interdisciplinary. If you understand the origins of a sound, you will do better at recreating that sound, and processes which modify sounds are intimately linked to creating new sounds, and are of great importance to musicians and composers .... So chapters on analysis, synthesis, processing, interaction, composition and more are all tied together. Indeed, one of the most difficult things to decide on was the ordering of the chapters. The decision was to put analysis–processing–synthesis in the order in which they conventionally appear in a signal chain. Yet, in the end, it is up to readers to choose the path that works best for them. If you can't wait to find out about laptop orchestras, you can go directly to the networks chapter. If some of the material is a bit challenging, feel free to skip it and come back to it later. What matters is that this is your book, to be read in any manner you choose.

CONVENTIONS

This book is laid out to help people learn. Each chapter begins with an outline of major themes to be covered, and ends with a short summary of important points. Along the way some additional information has been provided in side panels. In a number of cases this is to separate off a few more mathematical expositions from the main flow of text. Each chapter closes with a set of exercises meant to test knowledge gained during the chapter and promote wider thinking about the issues therein. There is nothing patronizing intended about any of this; ignore any exercises and summary points you have no use for, and leave them to those who find such materials helpful to their own learning.

This book uses standard academic conventions, such as referencing. When you see a citation in the text like this [Scheirer, 1998] you can look up the full reference in the back of the book and follow up further information there. Providing these references is essential to the book's utility as a survey of the field, introducing many fascinating projects. So whilst they sometimes break up the flow of the text for the reader (until you learn to read with them

---

[1] If by some miracle you are reading this a hundred years hence, I promise you I've tried my hardest to get all the dates correct and not to unduly misinform you. You might find many of my speculations rather of their time; apologies. You might be an artificially intelligent reader rather than a human; how wonderful!

there), their benefits outweigh this. Each chapter also has its own set of further reading resources.

For reasons of space, and for practicality, only discrete equations and operational algorithms are presented. This sometimes means overlooking some continuous, infinite equations which can aid full mathematical exposition, but errs on the side of practical computer music. You are directed to further reading for additional coverage. The notation $x(n)$ appears for a function which is accessed at integers n. Although in signal processing textbooks you may see $y[n]$ used for a discrete function of time, I follow the convention of previous computer music textbooks in using simple parentheses. However, within psuedocode algorithms, $y[n]$ is used for accessing an array y at index n just as in Java or C programming code. It is also helpful to be familiar with the basic convention for a sum in mathematics using $\sum$; $\sum_{n=0}^{9} x(n)$ would be the sum of the values of x at the first ten non-negative integers.

So with that out the way, I hope you find the material useful and enjoyable, and we can now proceed.

Acknowledgments

I hassled many good people in the preparation of this manuscript, including researchers who clarified their work, image contributors, and my own students who provided honest advice and feedback. At Wiley, I owe a debt of gratitude to the various teams involved in all stages of book production, and specifically to Jonathan Shipley, Georgia King, Emma Cooper and Nicole Burnett. Wiley also commissioned peer reviews on the initial proposal and the first set of chapters drafted for the book; thanks in particular to Robert Rowe, Peter Freeman, Miroslav Spasov and Marc Estibeiro for extremely helpful review materials as part of that process. In addition, I personally solicited reviews from the computer music community for each chapter. For proof reading, and many wonderfully helpful comments, many thanks in reverse alphabetical order to Sarah Woodall, Matthew Woolhouse, Scott Wilson, Bob Sturm, Stefania Serafin, Meg Schedel, Julian Rohrhuber, Martin Robinson, Josh Reiss, Marcus Pearce, Thor Magnusson, Chris Kiefer, Anna Jordanous, Andrew Hugill, Tom Hall, Jason Freeman, Julio d'Escriván, Michael Casey and Torsten Anders. I should also thank all the mailing lists I've ever asked questions of . . . ; the remaining errors are my own.

Finally, apologies to family and friends for any unhealthy obsession with completing this book that has overtaken me in the last year.

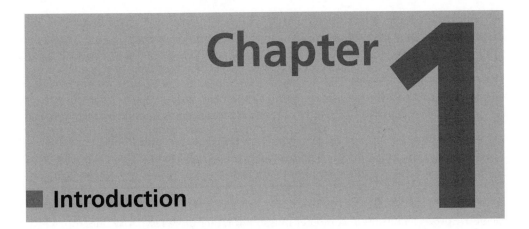

Chapter 1

Introduction

'Some digital techniques are little more than precise versions of previous mechanical and analog processes. But precision is not the most important attribute of the computer. What the computer offers the composer is programmability – the extension of functionality in any direction.'

Curtis Roads [Roads, 1985a, p. xiii]

OBJECTIVES

This chapter covers:

- the definition of computer music, how computer music relates to music in general, and why we should pursue it;
- a quickstart guide and a summary of the important concepts;
- the history of computer music.

1.1 WHAT IS COMPUTER MUSIC?

Computer music could be most generally defined as *music that involves a computer at any stage of its life cycle*. This encompasses a very wide variety of musical activities, even if 'unplugged' acoustic music and electric (e.g., amplified) music without microprocessors are excluded. We are not yet at the stage where singing to yourself in the shower is automatically accompanied by computers, though this may well change in an era of smart homes. We are, however, in a digital era[1] where as soon as music is recorded computers tend to become intimately employed in the service of sound, and music is also produced directly from computer music software. The reader is no doubt already familiar with many cases of computers in music, whether using a virtual recording studio on a laptop, running a score-editing program, or using the massed ranks of computers making up the Internet. Perhaps less traditional examples of computing stations are provided by mobile phones, personal digital assistants and handheld games consoles, and most new electronic appliances for our homes now have embedded microprocessors (even if not all of them sing). The predominant type of music technology for convenience and price is now digital gear, so that even most hardware boxes lurking within our music stores (synthesizers, fx pedals, mixers) turn out to be computational devices with embedded software.

There are other definitions of computer music, and rather more restrictive ones too, which consider only music that is entirely created on a computer, relies centrally on computer technology for the artistic conception, and cannot have any independent existence. But the working definition in the previous paragraph is a useful talking point to get us started, and this book will cover all manner of roles for computers in musicking.

To define music itself, by the way, would be to get ourselves into all sorts of semantic difficulties at an early stage. Suffice to say that since music is so vital a human activity, it is best to leave as much scope as possible for people to disagree on its definition. So this book will not restrict itself to music that fits clear models of Western concert music, but will cover much alternative work, such as sound installations and other sound art. We must always be conscious of the many and rich circumstances of music making throughout the world; certainly, Common Practice Music Notation written for conservatoire-trained musicians is not the only valid way of going about matters.

With music varying widely in its intended function and setting, it may be spontaneous or require intensive planning, may be pre-composed or improvised within different parameters, and may be disseminated through various routes including community participation, performers touring, record stores or broadcast technology. We shall explore many different ways in which computational technology intersects with musical practice. Where computers have thoroughly inserted themselves throughout society, they are naturally to be found as central tools in music production and performance. The convenience of much modern music making tends to rely on the substantial editing capabilities of computers, and many musical developments are now absolutely dependent on them.

In one ironic work conceived by Reinhold Friedl, however, 'computer music' was produced by drumming on old Atari computer shells (Peter Hollinger was the percussionist at the

---

[1] This is not the forum to consider any solutions to the disparity in wealth and opportunity around the world that undermines any over-optimistic recognition of a universal 'digital age'. Computers are predominantly the preserve of richer countries, and though initiatives like the One Laptop Per Child project are to be welcomed as increasing accessibility, clean drinking water and other more fundamental concerns take precedence over the relative luxury of computer music in the grand scheme of things. Nevertheless, you probably have access to computers – otherwise you wouldn't be interested in this book – and you probably fall into the 20% or so of the world population with access to the Internet; and on this basis we proceed.

premiere performance in Berlin, for the International Computer Music Conference in 2000). This example shows how easy it is to undermine any 'canonical' definition with counter examples and borderline cases, and perhaps indicates why we need to be careful in general. What is music, after all, but a social construction, and why separate computer music from it? Mainly because categories are sometimes useful for partitioning knowledge for the purposes of reasonable learning, but not because we have to take the borderlines too seriously; we shouldn't worry if we find ourselves straying across them.

Computer music is an interdisciplinary pursuit, at the intersection of the arts and the sciences. All sorts of disciplines inform it: music, computer science, psychology, physics (acoustics), engineering (signal processing, electronics) [Moore, 1990, p. 24]. It is important to realize that academic disciplines are themselves just categories of convenience, and there is no cause for any sort of inferiority complex just because computer music is a younger one. We can take any results from whichever field can help us in our quest. We can walk a line between the arts and the sciences and jump off in whatever direction our investigations take us. So it is perfectly possible for a physicist and a composer to collaborate; they might even be the same person, such as the 'composer–scientist' Bob Sturm, one of whose works is evocatively entitled *50 Particles in a Three-Dimensional Harmonic Potential: An Experiment in 5 Movements* (1999)!

1.1.1 Some Examples of Computer Music

The provisos in the previous section have shown that we must be careful with categories, which, if too quickly taken as real, highly constrain our ability to survey matters. As the artificial intelligence guru Marvin Minsky has pointed out, musical style only really means anything with respect to a vast field of examples [Minsky and Laske, 1992]. A data-driven approach constructs models from a host of examples, and it is healthy to use examples always to clarify points. In this spirit, some central exemplars of computer music are now listed, as a prelude to the many fascinating inventions and explorations detailed in this book. These examples are not in any way meant to encapsulate the field, but to pique your curiosity.

An early example of writing a computer program to generate music is the *Illiac Suite*, named after the University of Illinois Automatic Computer (hence, Illiac), by the musical chemists Lejaren Hiller and Leonard Isaacson, which was first performed on 9 August 1956. This painstakingly crafted work is described in great detail in their book *Experimental Music: Composition with an Electronic Computer* from 1959, and collects various musical experiments from species counterpoint to serialism. Yet they weren't the only ones to investigate the potential of computer-assisted composition at the time; an unsuccessful attempt on the pop charts was made in 1956 by Douglas Bolitho and Martin Klein with the song *Push Button Bertha*! In truth, only the song's melody line had been composed following machine instructions, and a lyricist, Jack Owens, was brought in to anthropomorphize the Datatron computer on which the program had run [Ames, 1987]. Contemporary manifestations of computer-generated music include the Koan software, MadPlayer portable music hardware, RjDj for the iPhone, and many more, where we really have become used to receiving new music composed and played back on demand at the touch of a button.

John Chowning adapted the frequency modulation (FM) technique that underpins FM radio into an algorithm for digital sound synthesis in 1967. It took until 1983 for this work to be taken up by a mass audience, in what remains the biggest-selling synthesizer of all time, the Yamaha DX7. The technique has gained the status of a classic method of sound synthesis, capable when carefully handled of some realistic sounds as well as empowering new soundscapes, and was used in countless 1980s records as well as in Chowning's own 1970s computer music compositions. It has been the subject of many implementations, from mobile phone soundcards to virtual emulations of the original hardware DX7. The Fall 2007 edition of the Computer Music Journal pays homage to Chowning's *Stria* (1977), promoting this FM composition to the status of a modern classic.

We are now used to computers which can record and process many channels of sound in realtime. But before the 1990s typical computers were too slow to allow such manipulation (particularly at higher sound quality), and often confined themselves to sending control messages. Analog synthesizers were preferred by musicians in the 1960s and 1970s because they responded immediately. One pragmatic use of computers was to send control information for synthesis hardware rather than directly synthesize everything virtually. In the 1980s MIDI (Musical Instrument Digital Interface) was the control messaging standard of choice, but it is worth featuring one earlier system. Max Mathews's GROOVE (Generated Realtime Operations On Voltage-controlled Equipment), in operation from October 1968 [Mathews and Moore, 1970], employed a DDP-224 computer as the control engine for an array of analog synthesis equipment. This allowed complex musical time functions far beyond the basic existing analog step sequencer. Laurie Spiegel further adapted this set-up to create VAMPIRE (Video And Music Program for Interactive Realtime Exploration/Experimentation, extant 1974–9) [Spiegel, 1998], an early live audiovisualizer. There are deep historical precedents to the current fascination with live audiovisuals in club and cinema contexts.

One recurrent dream in computer music is the creation of a virtual performer. The idea of a machine musician has a long history in human thought, and has heady implications in artificial intelligence. It is a fascinating endeavor, to shape a system that will become an independent musical agent, and, hopefully, sufficiently adept and interesting even to promote new modes of interaction. To mention one computerized twist on this tale, the trombonist George Lewis created a famous system called Voyager (the system has been around under this name since 1985, though there are earlier experiments). Voyager is a highly personal creation, a complex system with a wide scope in live improvisation. It can play with multiple human players, typically utilizing pitch-to-MIDI convertors to track notes. Digesting this information, and forming multiple statistical representations of the state of play, the system willfully interjects and responds. Lewis isn't seeking to make a deterministic system by any means, but an independent-minded and stimulating equal participant in music making.

We are becoming accustomed to having access to new sound synthesis, analysis and processing possibilities, and they can change musical culture. Auto-Tune[2] is a plug-in of great popularity with producers, primarily used for correcting a singer's wobbly intonation (most notoriously when that singer is rather untalented to begin with). The realtime digital signal processing first attempts to find the pitch of an input audio signal, and then if this is mistuned with respect to a template (e.g., notes in the current key of a song), carries out a subtle resynthesis to ensure the pitch is appropriate. The effect can also be applied in a less subtle way quite deliberately, for example by setting the pitch correction speed too fast for the processor to cope. This was famously used by the producers Mark Taylor and Brian Rawling for Cher's 'Believe', released in November 1998 [Sound, 1999], and by Nigel Godrich and Radiohead on the *Kid A* album from 2000.

We could go on, through musical computer games, musical robots and mobile phone orchestras. The rest of this book should provide plenty of further examples.

1.1.2 Sociable Computer Musicians

Music is a social art, at least outside the musician's preparation time for practicing and composing. Music can be the social glue which binds human gatherings together, and is often highly participatory for all involved, even if some settings, such as classical concertizing, can harbor a more one-way transmission process from stage to audience. For a musician, social networking is a central part of the business, and most music making is a collaborative pursuit, even if ensembles vary in the degree of hierarchy they contain.

In computer music, the same eventual social outcomes and negotiations must be borne seriously in mind. Though the lone bedroom producer or the late-night coder are stereotypes which sometimes seem to deny this, online digital music releases are certainly intended for other ears. Indeed, computers as a communication tool enable many new forms of social interaction (the popularity of social networking sites like MySpace and Facebook attest to this). Yet computer technology also has many parts to play within more traditional musical settings, and a sympathy for and understanding of the social values of music making can ease engagement between the acoustic and the digital worlds. We will also come to explore many new ensembles empowered by computers, from the laptop orchestra to mobile phone groups, and see how network music brings a new vitality to musical networking!

New communication systems tend to impact in a major way on society, and the Internet has been no exception. Musical distribution models have been revitalized, and intellectual property laws challenged in many ways. Economics and legislation are lagging behind the wave of experimentation, but new music in the Internet age is in rude health. The explosion of downloadable media content, popularly invoked by mention of such brands as MP3, iPod/iTunes and YouTube, is a major factor in the reconfiguration of the music industry in the current era. Later parts of this book will tackle this online music presence, and explore

---

[2] www.antarestech.com

new technologies intended to automatically keep abreast of the voluminous data available, under the theme of 'music information retrieval'.

It seems unfair to pick any one example amongst many, and thus perhaps to further a viral campaign, but let's point to Buraka Sound System. Whether they are still there when you read this can be determined by checking the validity of this web link (http://www.myspace. com/burakasomsistema). The popular YouTube video for 'Sound of Kuduro' features the odd glimpse of a laptop screen, but also promotes the essential human presence in music making and enjoyment (http://www.youtube.com/watch?v=4CkXhtw7UNk). I wouldn't have found out about them and obtained their first album, *Black Diamond* (2008), had it not been for the rapidity and ease of online promotion that bypasses conventional media. Musicians actively explore any new technology that helps them to reach other people.

1.1.3 Why Investigate Computer Music?

There are many practical benefits that digital technology, and particularly computers, have brought to music, which will be explored at length in this book. These often have the form of convenient storage and editing capabilities, as in the use of computers for audio recording and score typesetting. The transformative powers of computer algorithms to modify and tweak sound, and generative prowess in the creation of new sounds and music, will also be discussed.[3] We shall see many analytical tools for music which are only available by employing computers. Moore [1990, p. 4] notes that computer music offers new standards of 'temporal precision' and 'precise, repeatable experimentation with sound'.

The notion of experimentation is further exemplified by the natural employment of computers in the modeling of music, for multifarious purposes including acoustics, music analysis, psychology and, not least, composition. It is natural to seek computer assistance in exploring novel musical systems and theories. The computer can be a laboratory to try out alternative tunings, or new esoteric twists on serialism. Whilst Iannis Xenakis began his work in stochastic music in the 1950s manually, by 1962 he had turned to the computer to automate the hard work of using probability distributions. The Autechre album *Confield* (2001), a powerful abstract electronica somewhere between skewed electronic dance music and club-tinged electroacoustics, is the result of intense experimentation with computer generation of music.

Let us consider a clear example of the use of the computer as a basic labor-saving device. In order to compose *Music of Changes*, a work for piano from 1951, John Cage literally spent six months throwing coins. The Book of Changes is the Chinese *I Ching*, a system of 64 hexagrams, and Cage was mapping from the hexagrams to parameters of piano music. He wanted to give up certain compositional decisions to the oracle of the *I Ching*. The saving of time must have been a great relief to him when Lejaren Hiller, the computer composer and a close collaborator of his (for example on *HPSCHD* from 1969) wrote a computer program

---

[3]'Unlike real oscillators, computer-simulated oscillators can produce low frequencies with ease and precision' [Mathews, 1969, p. 53].

to 'roll the dice' on his behalf. Long printouts of psuedorandom numbers so generated could be provided for Cage to work from. Divination had been automated.

It is interesting to consider the gap between production and perception. There are undoubtedly sequences of actions which no individual human player could accomplish, impossible synchronizations that no human ensemble could navigate with or without conductor and click track, which can be programmed with a computer. In some cases these are still perceptible, despite being beyond the means of human players to enact. In terms of sound itself, there are regions of timbre denoting truly novel electronic sounds which nonetheless remain clearly audible. In this sense, there is leeway between our evolutionary capacities to perceive structure and to act in the environment, even though it is hard to deny close links between the two in biological heritage. We may interpret novel sounds through various glasses, from basic auditory mechanisms to cultural acceptability, and computers allow us to hit some new spots in this domain. It is useful, though, to be aware of the psychological factors which ultimately constrain those musical structures that can have a practical effect. To this end, the reader is encouraged to read and take inspiration from the psychoacoustic and music psychology literature [Moore, 2004; London, 2004]; [Moore, 1990, pp. 10–11].

Computers can replace human performers to allow the production of new sounds or hyper-precise actions. Introducing mechanical means of performance is not new in itself; for example, the Mexican-American composer Conlon Nancarrow was hammering out a series of glorious studies for player piano from the 1950s (prompted himself by Henry Cowell), and anticipated many of the later possibilities of sequencer music. The roll of honor here might go on to mention Frank Zappa's *Jazz From Hell* (1986) composed with Synclavier, Alistair Riddell's computer-controlled piano works, or Vidovsky's music for MIDI Piano, but the rigid metronomic virtuosity of electronic dance music is perhaps the most public manifestation of tight mechanical specification. Music for computer offers the most perfect control of any desired aspect, whether it be pitch, timing, timbre, space or any other. Sometimes, particularly in earlier non-realtime works for tape, this power comes at the price of losing the human performance element (some composers might also call this a benefit, as they escape the additional intermediacy of interpretation). As Paul Lansky has written of tape music, 'You are no longer scripting a performance' [Lansky and Roads, 1989, p. 41], but fashioning a finished opus, give or take the act of diffusing it in playback. There are also, however, many works which seek to integrate computer resources with human players at the time of performance, and these can still exploit inhuman transformations enabled by computer as long as the computer is somehow aware (through human action, or clever algorithms) of when to act.

1.2 QUICKSTART GUIDE TO COMPUTER MUSIC

Most people have a horror of reading manuals closely. You already understand that you can skip around this book as you need and pick out the sections that interest you. But if you are a newcomer to this field, you will find there are some important concepts to 'get your head around'. So, to help you move quickly to the outcomes that most interest you, some core ideas are introduced here in the manner of a 'quickstart' guide. These provide a central basis for computer music which should help your explorations, though it may repeat things you already know; just skim to where you feel you have something to gain.

1.2.1 Sound Waves and the Brain

Sound waves propagate in air as changes in pressure, essentially by air molecules bashing against each other, forming regions of higher (compression) and lower (rarefaction) density. So the more air molecules are crammed together, the higher the density and pressure. The branch of physics known as acoustics describes such phenomena, and sound waves can actually propagate in any state of matter. You may have seen reports from astronomers about (very low frequency) sound waves in interstellar gas clouds, or have heard sound underwater where the waves propagate four times faster, enabling you to hear more distant objects. There are even underwater concerts, though none yet in interstellar gas clouds to my knowledge, but as humans are most usually making music on land, air molecules seem to be what we're most used to.

Yet, once the sound waves reach our eardrums, they are translated through a number of other mediums, such as a solid, the tiny bones in the middle ear, and a liquid, the fluid-filled cochlea. An incoming sound eventually ends up as electrical signals in the brain, produced by the electrochemical triggering of the hair cells by the motion of the basilar membrane. The physiology of this transduction process is fascinating, and well worth further study [Pickles, 1988; Moore, 2004], but for now you should simply be aware that the domain of physics at the point of intersection with human audition becomes psychophysics, or more specifically psychoacoustics. And once on the auditory pathways of the central auditory system in the brain, sound becomes a subject for neurobiology and eventually at the highest level cognitive psychology. Science has penetrated many of the mysteries concerning how humans perceive sound, but much work remains to be done, and it would be misinformation to say that human hearing was a solved problem. Neuroscience is a fascinating discipline, but cannot yet provide a full working model of auditory cognition, despite some incredible successes in probing human capacities.

Where does this leave us? Results from acoustics will be used when modeling sound with computers. Results from psychoacoustics inform computer models of human hearing. The psychology of music is an active research field, with many overlaps with computer music.

1.2.2 The Time Domain

There are two main ways to plot sound that crop up sufficiently often to make explaining them an important part of this introductory chapter. Before either is discussed, please bear in mind that human auditory perception itself is the best judge we have of sound *as an experience*; nevertheless, using graphical plotting methods to explore sound has many benefits and can provide great insights.

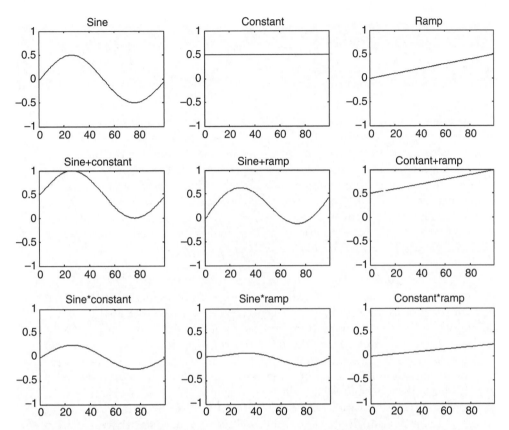

Figure 1.1 Basic signal operations in the time domain. The three signals on the top row are combined by addition in the middle row and multiplication in the lowest row. The signal operations act pointwise over time. The 'constant' signal is also called a DC (direct current) offset. When it is added to another signal, it offsets that signal; when it multiplies, it scales the range.

Pressure waves can be measured at a single point in the air; just put a microphone there! An electrical analog, such as changing voltage, can be measured across a component in a circuit. The time-varying value so gained is a **signal**. At this point, the first plot we shall explore is that of signal strength on the y-axis against time on the x-axis. This is the **time domain**, and the signal is also called the **waveform** (some example time-domain diagrams appear in Figure 1.1). The signal strength is measured with respect to some baseline, typically the zero line on the graph. For instance, in air, the pressure is measured with respect to baseline atmospheric pressure, and will be positive if there is greater pressure (density of air molecules) and negative if there is reduced pressure (density). Signal strength goes by the special name **amplitude**. It is possible to convert to a measure of signal **power** (capacity to do work, energy available) by squaring the amplitude. Most signals are not a simple

Linear and Logarithmic

Consider the sequence 1, 10, 100, 1000, ... Each number is formed by adding another zero at the right, effectively multiplying the previous number by 10 – equivalent in the decimal system to shifting the 1 across the columns to the left. Since these numbers otherwise will span a very large range, they can most conveniently be compared simply by noting the number of zeroes in the written expression. 1, 10, 100, 1000, ... is replaced by the sequence of **exponents** 0, 1, 2, 3, ... The original numbers can always be recovered by taking 10 to the **power** of a given exponent; that is, multiplying 10 by itself as many times as the exponent asks ($10^0 = 1, 10^1 = 10, 10^2 = 100, 10^3 = 1000, ...$).

The operation described in the previous paragraph is a transformation of ordinary numbers into an alternative domain, that of **logarithms**. A logarithm always acts with respect to some base; for our convenience, 10 is the base used here. The logarithmic domain is a much improved vantage point from which to survey a wide range of numbers. This is the motivation for using decibels as a measurement of signal strength instead of basic amplitude. The human auditory system can cope with a range from 10^{-12} to 1 watt per square meter of power, from the threshold of hearing to the threshold of painfully intense sounds. The ratio of quantities here, comparing painfully loud to vanishingly soft, is 1 followed by 12 zeroes to one; the logarithmic domain gives a better handle on such a wide range. **Exponentiation** allows the recovery of normal numbers again.

Evolution has equipped us to be sensitive to the log (logarithm) of quantities in many instances, rather than the linear scale. Logarithms are used often with musical quantities, for instance in the perception of pitch as well as loudness, but are also useful, for example, in modeling sensitivities to light or to pressure on the skin.

constant direct current, but alternate around the baseline; even though signal strength could be positive or negative, power (the square of amplitude) remains positive. Power can also be measured as an average over a stretch of time, giving rise to a well-defined statistical average amplitude such as the **root mean square**.

For audio signals dealt with by computer software, the range of amplitude is typically normalized to floating point values between −1.0 and 1.0.

We shall deal with signals throughout this book. As a warning at this stage, it is interesting to note how they can be combined. It is possible to talk of scaling a signal (multiplying all its values by a constant) or offsetting (adding a constant signal). These operations are fundamental for mapping signal values to other number ranges, required as the preconditions of later processing. Be forewarned that the mathematics of combining signals can be disconcerting; to multiply two signals, each a function of time, $a(t)$ and $b(t)$ to form a new signal $c(t) = a(t) * b(t)$ is to multiply together the instantaneous values of a and b at each moment of time. Figure 1.1 illustrates this for three basic signals. There are some important consequences of multiplying signals in the time domain, but we shall return to this point later once we have more machinery to deal with it.

Human hearing is approximately logarithmic (see sidebar) over much of its scope. For this reason, it is convenient to convert amplitude to units known as **decibels**.[4] The standard equation for this is:

$$\text{value in decibels} = 10 \log_{10} \left(\frac{\text{input power}}{\text{reference power}} \right) \qquad (1.1)$$

where the power of a signal is the square of the amplitude, and $\log_{10}$ is used for logarithms to base 10. To work with amplitude directly:

$$\text{value in decibels} = 20 \log_{10} \left(\frac{\text{input level}}{\text{reference level}} \right) \qquad (1.2)$$

The logarithm must be taken to a base, 10 in this case, and the measurement of decibels is always with respect to a reference level. If we imagine signals within the range -1 to 1, we could set a reference level at full power of 1, or make it very small, perhaps 10^{-12} watts per square meter (this latter case is often denoted by dB SPL, which stands for sound pressure level). In the first case, full amplitude would be 0 dB and all lesser amplitudes would be represented by negative numbers of decibels. In the second, 1 would be 120 dB ($10 \log_{10} 1/10^{-12}$) relative to the reference. In both cases, an amplitude of zero would be negative infinity, since that is the logarithm of zero. You may have seen audio software and hardware meters using various conventions here; a mixer's working scale could be from $+9$ dB down to infinity, allowing some 'headroom' rather than immediate overloads. I have also skipped a couple of technicalities – for example, taking an average measure of amplitude during some time span – here for the sake of the exposition [Loy, 2007a, Chapter 4].

Just a word or two of warning: decibels are useful since they are more perceptually relevant than amplitudes. But loudness as a psychoacoustic phenomenon is still more complicated than this. Also, the logarithmic scale should not be used in exactly the same way as the original values – do not add decibels together as if this added the associated

---

[4]Some authors write deciBel to respect the human surname Bell, and this also explains the standard abbreviation dB. Lower case is used in this book for decibel, as it is for amp, voltage etc.

signals' amplitudes. For such operations, it is necessary to return to the amplitude domain. However, certain rules of thumb are applicable: for example, doubling the amplitude of a signal is equivalent to a decibel increase of 6 dB. Successive gain operations, each of which multiplies the amplitude of a signal, can be dealt with by adding decibels, since they are multiplications rather than additions in the original amplitude domain.

1.2.3 Periodicity

We are sensitive to any object which vibrates in a repetitive manner at sufficient rate. The object follows the same physical pattern over and over again, many times per second, an **oscillation**. For example, in speech or singing, when you produce a vowel sound, the vocal folds in your larynx are set into oscillation, passing through puffs of air at a steady rate to create a periodic source. Periodic vibration is characterized by the **period**, measuring the length of an individual repetition in seconds, or the **frequency** of vibration, the number of repetitions per second, measured in **Hertz** (abbreviated Hz). These two quantities are inversely related to one another, so that a 100 Hz oscillation has a period of $1/100 = 0.01$ seconds, or one centisecond.

Figure 1.2 depicts two periodic signals. One looks wobblier, with more peaks than the other, but both repeat once per second (since the reciprocal of one is one, the period is one second and the fundamental frequency is 1 Hz). In some sense that we must unpack, the smooth-looking function here is much simpler and more basic than the wobbly function.

A periodic wave will play back in a loop, but there is always a choice of where to start it from when first setting it in motion. The starting position within a single cycle is the **phase**. You will also see phase referred to as the instantaneous position within a period at a given time.

It is necessary at this stage to introduce one method for analyzing sound which is particularly applicable to periodic signals. This method is Fourier analysis, a theory that allows any perfectly periodic sound to be broken down into the simplest possible basic oscillations. To find what these most basic periodic signals are, we can consider the simplest physical system with a periodic solution, as described by a mass solely under a linear restoring force, such as a mass on a spring without any friction. The solution to this system is the pure sound known as the **sine** (also called a sine tone or sine wave, or more generally a sinusoid or sinusoidal oscillation; you may also be aware of the dual function known as the cosine, a sine function shifted along a bit, which is also a sinusoid). The sound of this waveform is similar to that of a tuning fork, and some electronic tuners or alarm beeps; older analog music studios often had dedicated sine tone generators. It is easily produced on a computer from its basic equation. It sounds, well, plain, and has in some sense the simplest sound color, because if there were a simpler periodic sound, we could decompose the sine in turn into simpler entities yet; but in fact the sine is the end of the line.

Having introduced the sine, we can use it. The Fourier theory states that a perfectly periodic signal can always be analyzed in such a way that it is broken down into sine

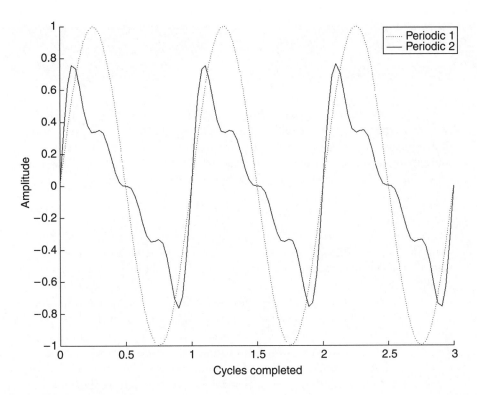

Figure 1.2 Periodic waveforms.

components. Each sine component can be described by a frequency and a phase, though the phase is often less important in perception for periodic sounds, as well as an amplitude weighting to say how strongly that component is present. Further, given the period of the signal to be analyzed, the lowest frequency component which can appear will correspond to this **fundamental frequency**. All other sine components will have frequencies which are at the possible integer multiples of this fundamental frequency, the spacings of a **harmonic series**. So if the fundamental frequency was 100 Hz, the components would have frequencies of 100, 200, 300, 400 and so on. Such multiples are termed **harmonics**, numbered from the fundamental as the first harmonic, or **overtones** when numbered such that the second harmonic (double the fundamental frequency) is the first overtone. Not all these components will necessarily have the same strength in the mixture which recreates the original signal; some frequencies may not be present at all.

Now, it is a short step from mentioning frequency to invoking the word 'pitch', but we must be careful. **Pitch** is a psychoacoustic attribute of sound in which the brain tries to find a explanatory fundamental frequency as if an incoming sound were periodic and its components followed a harmonic series. Since many independent sounds can arrive at once,

Sinusoids

A mathematical description of the sinusoid must take account of the natural unit of angle in trigonometry, the radian. The sine function is periodic, with a period of 2π radians. It is always possible to 'run through' a period at faster speed by multiplying the 2π by a frequency f, to form an angular velocity $2\pi f$, usually denoted by the Greek letter ω. We can formulate a general sinusoid as

$$\sin(\omega t + \phi) \tag{1.3}$$

where ϕ is a phase offset, since it is possible to start off this function at any point in its cycle. From trigonometry, we know that a cosine wave is a sine wave shifted in phase by $\frac{\pi}{2}$ radians. The phase offset allows the expression of a linear combination of sine and cosine waves ($\sin(A + \phi) = \sin(A)\cos(\phi) + \cos(A)\sin(\phi)$; thus, since ϕ is a fixed angle, it determines the coefficients of combination), which reduces to a pure sine for $\phi = 0$ and a cosine for $\phi = \frac{\pi}{2}$ (remember, a cosine is a sine advanced in phase by $\frac{\pi}{2}$ radians). Because of the duality of sine and cosine, it would have been possible to start from cosine waves instead of sines; hence the more general term sinusoid (when speaking informally, sine is often used instead of sinusoid). Note that the only two parameters of the function are the frequency and the phase.

By scaling the output, it is possible to add a third parameter for the amplitude of the signal, but since this could be done with any signal, it is not presented here as part of the equation for a sinusoid itself.

and not all sounds approximate a harmonic series, this is in general a rather hard problem, and we shall return to consider it in more detail in Section 3.5.1.

As a demonstration, the more complex periodic sound (periodic 2) from Figure 1.2 is broken down into sinusoidal components in Figure 1.3. Figure 1.4 then demonstrates a short-cut version, called a **line spectrum**, which shows the different harmonics and their respective strengths in the mix, though discarding any phase information. Because the exact mixture is known in this example, the diagram shows perfect identification of the components; but in general, as we shall next investigate, finding the constituents of a complex sound can be a little more tricky.

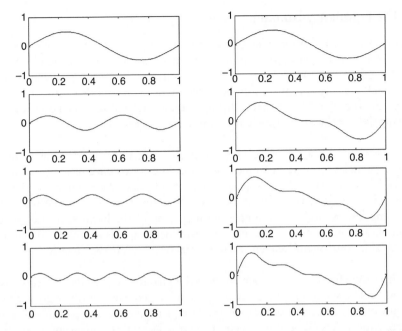

Figure 1.3 Sinusoidal components of a periodic sound. The left column shows each individual sine component (they vary in their amplitude). The right column gives the mix so far at each stage, as the sines are added together down the page.

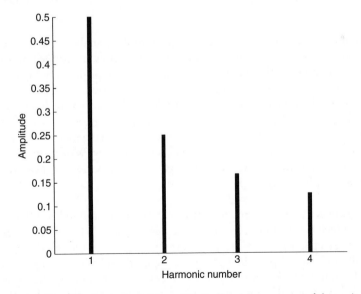

Figure 1.4 Line spectra. The frequency and amplitude of each component of the periodic sound are indicated (though phase information is dropped).

1.2.4 The Frequency Domain

We are not always in a position where we have a perfectly periodic sound of known period. We may not know the period of a sound in advance; we may have a sound which varies its period (a glissando, for instance), or a noise source which is not periodic at all. Many musical sounds are only at most psuedo-periodic (there is some subtle fluctuation of period), and the period is only relatively stable during a **steady state** of sustained oscillation, rather than during the fast-changing **transient** beginning of the sound.

In the physical world, a vibrating object can simultaneously oscillate at a number of different frequencies to make a complex vibration (the coexistence of multiple frequencies is described by the principle of superposition in physics). Depending on the material properties of the object, the relation between different excitable frequencies, also often known as **modes**, can follow the simple linear spacing of the harmonic series, or take on more complicated inharmonic patterns. The term 'harmonic' is not applicable in the latter case if analyzing component frequencies, so **partial** or mode are the preferred general terms.

Despite this failure for sounds in general to be well-behaved and periodic, it is still possible to measure whether a sound has energy at any particular frequency during a given time. Note that because of the dual nature of time span and frequency, the accuracy of this measurement in frequency must depend on how much of the period is taken into account. In principle, though, you might imagine 'testing' a sound beginning at one point in time, for a certain duration for each frequency you want to measure. By carrying out a succession of these tests at different starting points, it is possible to make a map of a sound's frequency content across time.

This process of measurement is a particularly useful tool for analyzing sound, and the most common form of this analysis employs the Fourier analysis mentioned above. Whilst it would be possible in principle to try and measure every frequency starting at every point, a computer only has finite memory and finite processing resources. A compromise to allow for practical constraints is to use a large basic period (relative to most frequencies we want to study), and carry out a Fourier analysis *as if the signal were periodic during that segment of time*. As long as the audio signal doesn't change too much during this period, we will obtain measurements for all the harmonics of the analysis frequency. Whilst this doesn't get us a measurement for every frequency, we at least gain a useful subset of measurements (I am skipping a few complications for the time being).

The **spectrogram** is a plot over time indicating the energy in a sound at different frequency components (which are the multiples of the analysis frequency). One Fourier analysis is carried out for each step in time; these steps are evenly spaced out, though the analysis regions might partially overlap. Typical figures on a computer might be an analysis fundamental frequency of around 43 Hz, and 86 analysis **frames** per second (so the Fourier analysis regions overlap by one half). Figure 1.5 shows a spectrogram obtained in this way. The shade plotted at a particular (time, frequency) point is a logarithmic power measurement (essentially, decibels). The three-dimensional graph (shade here substitutes for seeing the

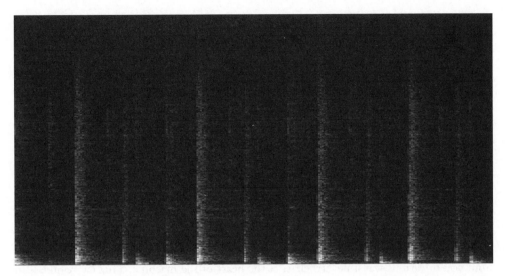

Figure 1.5 Spectrogram view of a drum loop. The percussive strikes are visible as (noisy) vertical bands. Noise sounds tend to be broadband, having energy at all frequencies.

third dimension directly) is best thought of for now as a grid, a time-frequency plane of cells, each of which is an energy measurement at a particular time and frequency.

There is a lot more to say concerning such analysis, and Chapter 3 will take up these issues, including the mathematics. For now, it is important to recognize that the **frequency domain** provides an alternative viewpoint on sound to the time domain. You will also see references to the **spectrum** of a sound, as an energy distribution over frequencies.

Fourier analysis has been used here to break all sounds down in terms of sines. However, this does not mean that the description is necessarily compact for all sounds. White noise is the most brutish form of noise; it has equal energy at all frequencies on the average over time. A Fourier analysis, even with a tiny fundamental frequency of analysis, will only pick up this mean flat spectral distribution. So for noisy sounds, the spectrogram can be a rather inefficient descriptor. The separate modeling of noise components in a sound is an issue for Section 3.2.4.

The frequency decomposition view of sound is of central importance, and evolution has not missed out on this good trick. The cochlea in your inner ear is at heart a frequency analyzer, with 3500 or so inner hair cells strung out on the basilar membrane and differentially sensitive to incident frequencies [Moore, 2004, p. 33].

I have already warned of the complexities of the psychoacoustic attribute of loudness. The dynamic range of the ear varies with frequency, and a set of contours can be experimentally established which describe how different amounts of power at different frequencies equate. These **equal loudness contours** (also called Fletcher–Munson curves) show that it takes substantially more pressure at bass frequencies for us to react, and that we are particularly sensitive to areas of the spectrum associated with speech, peaking at around 3500 Hz, the resonant frequency of the auditory canal before the eardrum. This frequency-dependency also means that the same music played back at different overall volumes automatically has a different equalization (EQ). Some hi-fis attempt to compensate for this to some extent (e.g., boosting bass at low overall volume), but it is an important warning to mix engineers.

1.2.5 Digital Audio

The computer has to deal with ones and zeroes. Whilst friendly software might hide this from you in various ways, nevertheless, at the heart of the machine, a binary regime is in play, and the computer is manipulating **bits** (**binary digits**, in other words, which have the value 0 or 1). But how can the real world, where movement is smooth and apparently continuous, be digitized? The first thing to realize is that the computer doesn't have to store a number into just one of two values, but can use a succession of bits to represent a given number. For instance, eight bits is one **byte**, and binary arithmetic tells us that we could represent 2^8 or 256 different values by using one byte. By using 256 different values we can obtain a much better approximation to the instantaneous value of a continuous sound than we could with two!

Computers have to digitize, to turn continuous **analog** values into **digital** ones. The process implies some loss of information; but, importantly, by increasing the **bit resolution** we can have as high an accuracy as desired, and our approximation gets better by a factor of two with every bit we add.

This is not the only approximation; we must also digitize time itself. We cannot store a value as if there were an infinite number of instances per second, for this would require infinite storage. So we must select a **sampling rate**, often denoted by R or f_s in mathematical notation. A typical sampling rate would be 44 100 Hz, that is, measuring a value, taking a sample, 44 100 times per second. As these sampling instances are equally spaced in time (driven by an accurate clock) there is one value sampled every $1/44\,100 \approx 0.0000226757$ seconds. The sampling of an input waveform in time and amplitude is represented in Figure 1.6 by the grid, and the diagram also demonstrates the **quantization** that must take place, rounding off signal values when captured to the nearest grid levels on the y-axis.[5]

---

[5]The term quantizing recurs in sequencing, where it refers to forcing the start time values of events to comply with a grid.

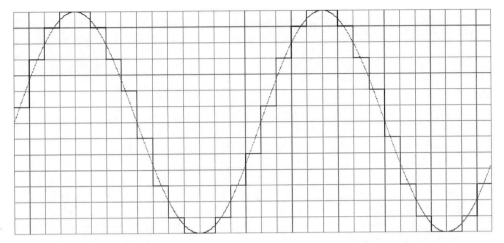

Figure 1.6   Continuous function sampled onto an underlying grid. Note that the values at each sampling step have been quantized to the nearest grid line on the y-axis to give the step function.

The digital sine

For a digital system, it is only possible to deal with discrete samples of time n; with a sampling rate of R per second, time passes such that sample n occurs after n/R seconds. For a sine, the distance traversed in the angular domain of the function input is time $*$ angular velocity $= \omega n/R$, and we can formulate a general sinusoid as

$$\sin(\omega n/R + \phi) \qquad (1.4)$$

Computer music will always remain dependent on some form of microphone and loud-speaker if interfacing with the outside sound world. Note that there is simply no way to get audio into and out of a computer without an ADC (analog to digital convertor) and a DAC (digital to analog convertor).

Digital audio is supported by a mathematical theory which supplies conditions on the reproduction capabilities of the sampling process [Loy, 2007b; Watkinson, 2001; Pohlmann, 2005]. The **sampling theorem** is the essential statement of the reproducible bandwidth, that

Proof of Aliasing

A trigonometric derivation of aliasing, due to Richard Hamming [Hamming, 1989, pp. 22–24], is presented here for mathematically inclined readers. Consider the cosine form of a general sinusoid: $\cos(2\pi f n + \phi)$ where f is the frequency as a proportion of the sampling rate and n is the sample index, $n = 0, 1, \ldots$. Thus a frequency of 1/2 in this case would correspond to the Nyquist rate, and a frequency of 1 to the sampling rate. The number f can always be broken down into an integer and a fractional part (there will only be integer parts involved for frequencies at the sampling rate and above). So taking the integer part as m and the fractional part as a we obtain $\cos(2\pi(m + a)n + \phi)$. Because of the cosine periodicity, and since n is always an integer, the $2\pi m n$ in the argument can be removed. We are left with $\cos(2\pi a n + \phi)$ where a is known to be fractional. If a is less than 1/2, we are done, because our original cosine was equivalent to a sampled cosine at a frequency under Nyquist. If a is greater than 1/2, write $a = 1 - b$; then we have $\cos(2\pi(1 - b)n + \phi)$. The $2\pi n$ drops out again, and because a cosine of a negative angle is the same as that of a positive, and a phase shift does not affect frequency, $\cos(-2\pi b n + \phi) = \cos(2\pi b n - \phi)$. So all frequencies f reduce to frequencies within the range 0 to 1/2, and aliasing is inevitable when sampling.

is, exactly which frequencies can be represented by a digital system. As you might suspect, the higher the sampling rate, the better the range of representable frequencies. The critical boundary is the **Nyquist limit**, which is at half the sampling rate. No frequency above Nyquist can be represented by a digital system. To restate this in another way, there must be at least two samples per period if a sine tone is to be accurately stored.

What happens to any higher frequency? The digital system will attempt to store such frequencies, but will end up recording an alias, that is, another frequency below the Nyquist limit, instead. This gives rise to **aliasing** distortion, also called **foldover** – basically, misrepresented frequencies.

In order to avoid this happening, which would cause audible noise, an ADC is always preceded by a low-pass filter, which makes sure that there is no energy in the input at frequencies over half the sampling rate to cause aliasing. The DAC also makes use of a low-pass filter, as the final reconstruction step from the sampled digital values to the smooth waveform of the continuous analog signal.

The computer can only run at a certain clock speed, so it has a maximum rate at which it could ever sample time. Measuring devices are also only accurate to a certain resolution. Yet the approximation is sufficiently good with high sampling resolution and bit resolution, and, critically, high-quality convertors, to convince even golden ears. Engineers now have many decades of experience in the design of the conversion process between analog and digital, now favoring one-bit oversampling convertors which neatly sidestep some of the difficulties of designing appropriate low-pass filters (with additional benefits). Older arguments about the quality of digital audio, which was admittedly a little shakier when first commercially available due to inferior convertors, have little credibility now. And the versatility of computer-based production for audio, as well as perfect copying fidelity with error correction, are too useful to permit a move back to analog. Digital file management is easier, allows random access and takes up less space; multiple generations do not build up noise, avoiding compromises in the process of recording. Of course, some analog recording formats are still commonly available, and valued for their own characteristics (and their own recording quirks such as print-through, wow and flutter), but digital audio is king [Watkinson, 2001; Pohlmann, 2005].

There is one more restriction of a digital audio system to relate, which is that bit resolution is intimately related to dynamic range. The rule of thumb is that one bit corresponds to six decibels of range. Since all rooms (even recording studio control rooms) have a background noise floor of at least 20 dB SPL, the approximately 98 dB range of 16-bit audio [Pohlmann, 2005, p. 37] can bring us close to the ear's own dynamic range at its most sensitive frequency region.[6] The dynamic range of digital audio far surpasses the 55–65 dB standards for commercial analog audio, or even 80 dB for high quality professional tape machines [Roads, 1996, p. 40]. 24-bit digital audio has a potentially better dynamic range than the human ear, across the spectrum (in practice, conversion issues may restrict this a little). Whilst 32-bit (even 64-bit!) floating point audio is often used internally in software, the quality is dependent on the original bit resolution of the ADC used to get the analog data into digital format (there are 32-bit digital signal processor (DSP) chips, however).

Whether recording engineers in certain styles of music really use the available dynamic range or not is another issue, with a backdrop of a 'loudness war' in marketing and broadcast. Many mastering engineers, dance producers and noise musicians deliberately compress music to compete with each other for maximum playback volume; they should note that compression makes music tiring to listen to relatively fast, destroys ambience except for an ambience of onslaught, and has other implications on quality of playback and presentation of mix [Katz, 2007].

1.2.6 Filters

A filter is any sound processor which affects different frequency components of a sound in different ways. The filter might be used to inject or attenuate energy at different points

---

[6]We must cover 120 dB, so we take a new reference level for our digital system at the noise floor of 20 dB SPL, assuming that sound below this level (which the digital system cannot represent) would have otherwise been masked. This is not quite true in practice, due to nonlinear masking effects and frequency content of the noise floor, but does as a rule of thumb. Note that resetting the reference level is not breaking the 'don't add decibels' rule.

across the spectrum. Some filters (all-pass filters) do not affect energy at all, but introduce different delays at different frequencies. Indeed, this disturbance of the phase relationships in a signal is another basic characterization of a filter; cancellations and reinforcements are set up by combining the original signal with time-delayed versions of itself, which usually has the effect of changing the energy at particular frequencies [Roads, 1996, pp. 19–20].

There are certain basic filter types that frequently occur. Figure 1.7 details four basic types and their effect on the magnitude spectrum. Filter diagrams should not be idealized; in practice, filters have non-trivial stop bands, regions of transition between passing and blocking frequencies. They may not be perfectly flat, with some ripple providing additional coloring. The effect of a filter on magnitude is only one part of the story, and the effect on phase (frequency-dependent time delay) is also of note.

In general, an arbitrary filter can have a complicated effect upon the spectrum. Filters are of basic utility in modeling real sounds. The body of an acoustic instrument can be considered to be a filter which gives flavor to the timbre of a sound. A violin body is well coupled to the air (the strings are not) and colors the raw string vibrations. By changing the shape of your mouth and throat, you filter the air stream to produce different vowel sounds and consonants.

It is possible to view a spectrogram as a bank of filters; each frequency measurement is the output of one band-pass filter. The cochlea is also essentially a filter bank, with each inner hair cell a distinct band-pass filter only responsive to components of incident sound within a particular frequency range.

1.2.7 Timbre

Timbre might be described as a means of differentiating sound sources, which takes into account aspects of their acoustical production, even when controlling for certain common features. For instance, imagine a piano, a clarinet and a trumpet all playing a 261.626 Hz fundamental at 90 dB SPL in an anechoic chamber (so that there is no reverberation to complicate matters, the walls being lined with fully absorbent material). You would still hope to tell them apart, despite the common period and intensity.[7] This image of instruments actually seems to propose rather static sounds with perfectly fixed frequency and amplitude, when in reality all sounds are time varying. And indeed, the changing character over time of features of the sound, including the envelope (time-function) of pitch and loudness, is an essential part of this differentiation. Applying knowledge of the spectrum of a sound, periodic sounds might be told apart by the way in which different harmonics fluctuate in amplitude, or more generally, for non-periodic sounds, by the time-varying energy exhibited in the spectrum. Periodic sounds still tend to begin with a noise-like transient, so different physical regimes can be passed through in succession. All of this

---

[7]This definition paraphrases the American Standards Association who placed timbre in negation as the attribute of sound which isn't pitch or loudness!

Filter Mathematics Part 1

Warning: the mathematics here is summarized for brevity. More technical detail is available in Roads [1996], Loy [2007b] and the signal-processing books referenced particularly in Chapters 3 and 4.

The next output sample is calculated as a linear combination of current and past inputs and feedback from past outputs. Conventionally, $x(n)$ is the value of the input and $y(n)$ is the value of the output at step n. Past values are indexed as $x(n-k)$ or $y(n-k)$ for k samples back in time. Note that to convert to time in seconds, rather than indexing directly in samples, the index would be multiplied by the sampling period $1/R$ (R is the sampling rate). But we do not need to worry about this purely on a sample processing level.

The (causal) linear time-invariant general filter equation is then

$$y(n) = \sum_{k=0}^{M} a(k)x(n-k) - \sum_{k=1}^{N} b(k)y(n-k) \qquad (1.5)$$

where the $a(k)$ are $M+1$ feedforward coefficients and the $b(k)$ are N feedback coefficients. If all the feedback coefficients are zero or $N=0$, removing any feedback, the digital filter is called a **finite impulse response** (FIR) filter. If there is any feedback, energy can theoretically recirculate forever (even if in practice on a computer there is a limit based on the number precision) and the filter is called an **infinite impulse response** (IIR) filter. The impulse response describes what happens to a single sample of one followed by all zeroes (i.e., $1, 0, 0, \dots$) when passed through the filter.

More complex responses for general sequences are formed from many scaled and delayed copies of the impulse response through a process called convolution; but we will return to this in Chapter 4.

By the way, just as with feedback from microphone and mixer, if the recirculating energy is too great it may continue to build up, causing a blow-up – an unstable filter. Since they have no feedback, however, all FIR filters are stable.

The general filter equation can be more profoundly analyzed to explore the spectral consequences of the filter on a signal. The full mathematics of filters is only recommended for the mathematically literate reader. Nevertheless, we shall return to this in due course in Chapter 4, and try to say more about it intuitively, too.

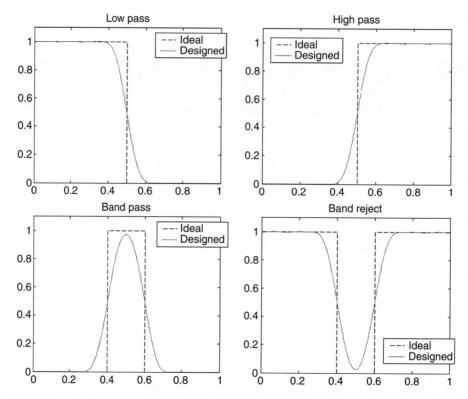

Figure 1.7   Four basic filter types. Magnitude spectra illustrate the frequency responses for four standard filter types. The band-reject filter is also often called a band-stop or notch filter. Each plot shows the frequency response for an ideal filter, and the actual frequency response for some real finite impulse response filters approximating the ideal specification. In this diagram, the x-axis is marked in terms of 'normalized frequency', with a reference of the Nyquist rate, so 0 = 0 Hz and 1 = half the sampling rate. This makes the diagram independent of the sampling rate.

adds up to a complex sound-description that is the timbre of the sound, and requires a multi-dimensional property list, a particular model of sound analysis, to outline.

Psychological studies of timbre have investigated what properties are *most* important in differentiating sounds [Risset and Wessel, 1999; Beauchamp, 2007a]. The findings do not always agree, and are of course rather dependent on the stimuli (orchestral instruments often being the subject matter) [Bregman, 1990, pp. 122–126]. Whilst some features are peculiar to certain investigations, others do tend to recur, including the spectral centroid[8] and the attack envelope, which correlate well with the physical properties of struck objects. Through experience, even instruments which have distinct qualities of sound in different

---

[8]In this case a measure of the centre of mass of the spectral energy averaged over time.

portions of the range (such as the clarinet's chalumeau, clarino and altissimo registers) are perceived as coming from a common source, no doubt assisted by additional spatial and visual cues. In electronic music, which allows many novel timbres, this viewpoint on physical production is suddenly absent. It is likely that evolved mechanisms play a large part in deciphering and categorizing new timbres for a listener [Windsor, 2000], though humans are also undoubtedly adaptable learners when exploring new territory.

Western classical music before the 20th century only really confronted timbre in terms of orchestration. The increased emphasis on dazzling instrumental effect in the music of Debussy, Stravinsky and their peers began to set timbre apart, and Schoenberg's daring musical line constructed from timbre changes ('Farben', the third movement of his *Five Orchestral Pieces* of 1909) brought timbre to centre stage. An overt treatment and hunt for timbral resources became a feature from the mid 20th century, becoming associated both with contemporary classical music (e.g., the sound masses of György Ligeti's *Atmosphères* from 1961) and with the explicit sound manipulation of electronic music (e.g., Pierre Schaeffer's 1948 *Étude aux Chemins de Fer* and Bernard Parmegiani's 1975 *De Natura Sonorum*). However, the expressive carrying potential of timbre has a healthy reality in the beating of partials of metallophones in the Indonesian Gamelan, the ornamental instructions of Japanese Gagaku and the husky flow of Australian Aboriginal music, to name but three examples which substantially predate Western music's own preoccupations.

1.2.8 Space

Another important aspect of sound, particularly in electronic art music and film music production, is space. We speak of **spatialization** as the act of rendering a sound in space. The perceptual side of the coin is **localization**, the perceived location of a sound for an observer. Most prosaically, acoustic instrumentalists (or mobile phone speakers!) are naturally heard as emitting sound from their current positions, but virtual sound sources can also be evoked by configurations of loudspeakers and more complicated rendering strategies. Environmental acoustics also play a part. Within enclosed rooms, reflections from the walls lead to reverberation alongside the sound traveling directly from the source to your ears. Reverberation can add to the sense of liveness of a sound, as well as obstructing some cues to localization. Architectural acoustics, surround-sound set-ups, compositional and mixing strategies in the treatment of space and more can all interact in the portrayal of space in music.

The site of presentation of music, whether delivered within an enclosed chamber of particular reverberant characteristics, or even outside or underwater, has always been recognized by musicians as a major practical factor in performance. Space on human scales is unavoidable in music, since with a speed of sound of around 340 meters per second in normal temperature and altitude conditions, the wavelengths of pressure waves become comparable to room sizes (20 Hz has a wavelength of 17 m!). Space has been employed as a compositional factor [Brant, 1998], from antiphonal practice in church music (such as J. S. Bach's *St. Matthew Passion* (1727) setting for two offset choir and orchestra groups), to offstage musicians for timbral effect (trumpets, horns and percussion in Mahler's Second Symphony) and deliberate placement of musicians in space to make dense counterpoint more discernible (Henry Brant's *Antiphony I* (1953) for five orchestral groups). Recorded music, however, brings the issue of space to the fore at the point of playback; schemes must be devised to compensate for the potential unnaturalness of loudspeaker reproduction. In the extreme, with the challenge of evoking virtual acoustics, it is probably with electronic music that the issue of space has become most intensely a compositional concern in and of itself.

Aside from earlier investigations into stereo that date back as far as 1881, a brief history of spatial experimentation might mention Moholy Nagy's *Stage Scene – Loud Speaker* (1924–6) a loudspeaker placed on a bidirectional revolving table, an art project that anticipates Stockhausen's famous circular sound distribution method for the quadraphonic *Kontakte* (Contacts, 1958–1960). Fantasound, an adaptable multichannel configuration used for the film *Fantasia* in 1940 anticipated later surround-sound experiments in the film industry.[9] The *Pupitre d'Espace* (Space Console, 1951) of Jacques Poullin allowed the live diffusion of *musique concrète* within a four-speaker set-up of front-left–front-right–rear–overhead, by a human controller gesturing within this special music stand's induction coils. January 1953 saw the creation of the first octophonic (eight-channel) piece, John Cage's *Williams Mix*, this four-minute-fifteen-second work only realized after a lengthy project of analog tape splicing from a 192-page score. Space has continued to exert fascination as an important aspect of electroacoustic music, from loudspeaker orchestras (the first being the Gmebaphone in 1973) to purpose-built venues. The latter include temporary demonstration housings such as the 425-speaker Philips Pavilion (1958) or the German Pavilion at the Osaka Expo in 1970, as well as new sound systems for theatres, cinemas and planetariums! Whilst quadraphonic sound was an unsuccessful commercial experiment in the 1970s, cinema standards, especially supported by the popularity of DVDs and computer games, have helped to bring at least 5.1 (left–centre–right, back-left–back-right and '.1' subwoofer) to many homes.

The psychoacoustics of spatial hearing and different multichannel formats will be investigated more thoroughly, starting in Section 2.5.

1.2.9 Patching, Signal Flow and Unit Generators

Dedicated items of equipment for particular audio tasks often come as black boxes, where the inner workings are concealed, but the expected inputs and outputs are carefully specified in the manual. Consider the more traditional recording studio, with many racks of esoteric gear lining the walls, and the problem of plugging one unit into another as amplified over all the available equipment. You may have seen dedicated patch bays in such studios which help to avoid running long wires everywhere. Imagine a behemoth of a modular analog synthesizer, perhaps with a 'Battleships'-like pin matrix, or more untidily, wires strung from one side of the beast to another to connect up its many modules. Even the sound from a

---

[9]Because of the limitations of the cinemas of the day, the full Fantasound release of *Fantasia* was only shown at a few venues, reproduced over many loudspeakers; later general release was mono.

humble electric guitar might be passed through a series of effects pedals prior to reaching the amp. It is clear that **patching** is central to electronic music, and may become arbitrarily complex the more components are available to be plugged together.

Modularity can be a healthy sign of careful design: a particular functionality is encapsulated in a single module. A module can just be considered as a black box, with the fine details of its working concealed from view. The module is still perfectly usable as long as the expected inputs and outputs are known and appropriate values are therefore passed in and extracted. This encapsulation of functionality is useful in software as in hardware, and carries across from the physical world of real wires to the virtual world. A network of boxes can itself be considered a single black box (see Figure 1.8). This is useful to gradually build up a more and more complex system, with each stage of the design carefully delineated.

In computer music, Max Mathews named useful basic modules in sound synthesis software **unit generators** [Mathews, 1969, p. 35]. A unit might be a sine generator or a noise generator, or act as a processing unit of some form. In each case, the nature of the inputs and outputs to that unit vary based on the functionality encapsulated. But each unit is a ready-made module, easily employed as a building block to create complex patches for musical tasks.

A **signal** can be generally defined as any transmission of information, and in computer music typically refers to a time-varying value. This might be the alternating current output by a microphone, or the succession of sample values obtained by an analog to digital convertor. Electronic music involves many signals being routed between different sources and destinations. Establishing how information propagates is crucial to designing a computer music system.

To depict this we can draw a block diagram, showing which units plug into which, but with a notion of **signal flow**. The set of units and their connections is a processing graph demonstrating how the system deals with information; that is, how signals flow through the system and what processes them on their way. The system must start somewhere and end up with some final output (or else nothing will be observed to happen!). Typically, there might be an input from the outside world (a microphone plugged into the ADC for the computer) and a final output back to the outside world (the DAC).

These signal flow networks can support multiple sampling rates in one graph. In general, there is no overall rule as to when changes occur in signals, so that values end up being updated at different rates, and the limiting case is a constant which remains fixed. You may see reference to different official rates in computer music systems, including **audio rate** (sometimes a-rate), corresponding to the sampling rate of a digital system and **control rate** (sometimes k-rate), typically being a slower and more efficient update rate for control signals. There are various forms of message which are singular data sent when cued at a particular time. There is even an initialization rate (i-rate), namely a constant starting value, as the constant limiting case.

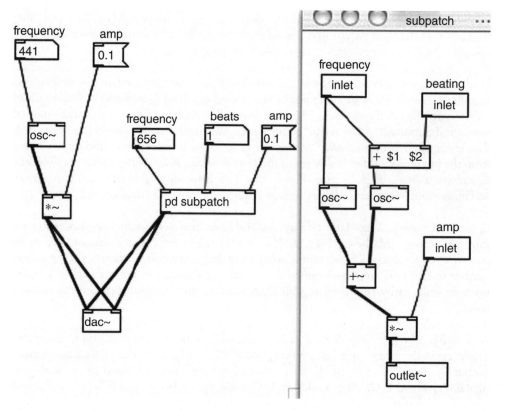

Figure 1.8   Patching in Pd. This screenshot from the Pd software package shows the boxes and wires of a patching network, with a subpatch abstraction (itself explicated in the right-hand window). The patch adds one sine oscillator at 440 Hz to a beating oscillator (two sines close together in frequency) at 656/657 Hz. Each box is specialized by the text inside it. The ~ sign and thicker wires in Pd mark out audio signal flow rather than control messages. Other systems might differentiate boxes more by the graphical icon.

The idea of units and patching is a standard paradigm, and the block diagrams describing how modules plug together have often formed the basis for graphical user interfaces (GUIs) in computer music software. Table 1.1 lists a selection of standard software that has this kind of front end; Figure 1.9 provides another graphical example, from Ross Bencina's AudioMulch software. Much other software also employs it, though in a more implicit manner; for instance, some text-based systems allow you to plug unit generators together by specifying the graph with program code, rather than drawing it out visually.

1.2.10 Computer Music Software

You have probably already been confronted by the dazzling and bewildering array of available computer music software. Software goes in and out of fashion, commercial imperatives

Table 1.1 A selection of modular patching environments for computer music.

Program	Availability	Description	Reference
'Max' paradigm family	Commercial and FOSS variants	Max/MSP, Pd, jMax visual programming languages	Puckette [2002]
Reaktor	Commercial (Native Instruments)	Toolkit to build your own software synthesizer	http://www.native-instruments.com
AudioMulch	Commercial (Ross Bencina)	Software for building your own signal processing network	http://www.audiomulch.com/
OpenMusic	FOSS (IRCAM)	Computer composition software with a graphical patching front end (Lisp under the surface)	http://sourceforge.net/projects/ ircam-openmusic/
Logic environment	Commercial (Apple)	Processing graph can be customized from a patching interface (similar facilities exist in some other studio environments, such as Cubase, and the virtual patchcords are explicit on the back panel in Reason!)	http://www.apple.com/logicstudio/ logicpro/
Tassman	Commercial (Applied Acoustics Systems)	Sound synthesis environment where an acoustic model is built up from components	http://www.applied-acoustics.com/tassman.htm
Bidule	Commercial (Plogue)	Patching environment for sound synthesis and processing	http://www.plogue.com/

drive a constantly shifting backdrop of operating systems, and even free software offers the perpetual opportunity for upgrades and also for discontinuation of a favorite package. Even a brief look at the history of computer systems will reveal an abundance of different machines with a panoply of software; museums and other archives are fighting a losing battle just to hold onto a fraction of these systems over time.

Fortunately, software doesn't change so fast as to make all advice untrustworthy, and there is much venerable and proven computer music software. If you are taking a course, your tutor may be expecting you to learn some particular packages, or you may be wondering what to try next. As you progress through this book you will see a variety of software featured. Since no one application can possibly cover all desirable goals, exploring a variety is healthy. So I present here two warnings, in the form of two aspects of software you should be aware of. I shall provide a few examples but not an exhaustive survey, and other packages crop up throughout this book.[10]

---

[10]If some of these are historical by the time you read this, as is very likely in this fast-paced world, at least I've provided a flavor of the era I live in!

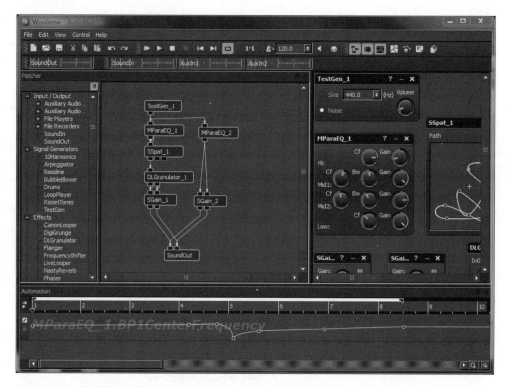

Figure 1.9   Patching in AudioMulch. This screenshot shows the AudioMulch 2 application, with a central patching view for plugging many generators and processing units together; control GUIs for the individual units can be seen on the right. Reproduced by permission of Ross Bencina, audiomulch.com.

First, some software is commercial and some is free. Neither implies superior quality; some of the most powerful sound synthesis environments are open-source software, for example, and so are free to use and extend (for example, Pd, Csound and SuperCollider). The abbreviations FOSS (for Free and Open-Source Software), and also FLOSS, with the addition of a Libre for good measure, often appear. On the other hand, a number of commercial packages are established in the music industry, and even if they have free clones or rivals, their staying power and market share is often related to being professional, reliable and well-documented products (examples are Pro Tools, Logic Audio, Cubase, Digital Performer, Sibelius and Finale). Demo versions (with limited use time or with disabled saving functionality) are often available to 'try before you buy'. Whilst there are some standards for exchanging data between packages, there are many issues of compatibility between different ones, and commercial software often uses proprietary file formats and protocols which make it more difficult to exchange data.

Second, different software takes different amounts of effort to learn. This may seem a truism, but you must appreciate that it is not just due to problems of design in the software and its documentation. A more significant underlying reason is the tradeoff between the learning curve for a program and the degree of customization achievable with it. This means, essentially, that you can find programs that are straightforward to use because they have few options. They seem powerful at first, but quickly pale as you reach a point where you see the design limitations (examples might be drawn from many effects plug-ins). On the other hand, there are programs which require a great investment of your time, even to get quite limited results at first. Yet they significantly reward long-term work, eventually repaying your apprenticeship and allowing fundamental experimental investigations. This is really also just the choice between immediate results and deferred reward. Either type of software could eventually become a standard part of your armory: a sound editor or sequencer can be relatively easy to learn to use, and yet be a reliable tool for standard tasks; a complex sound synthesizer might provide interesting compositional stimulus for you each time you employ it.

The best advice is to learn a variety of software, and not just that which is easy to pick up. You tend to understand less about the underlying processes if you only use packages on the surface level, and deeper understanding is a positive contribution to computer music composition and research. Knowing a wider variety of tools also supports more informed choices when judging the needs of computer music projects. Ultimately, use whatever gets the job done quickly and well, and always bear in mind the artistic and scientific outcomes above the implementation; it is easy to be distracted by technical issues from real aims.[11]

1.2.11 Programming and Computer Music

Programming is an essential skill for the computer musician who wants to investigate new sound worlds, and perhaps be first to set foot in them. It is always possible to rest comfortably behind the bleeding edge using whatever systems are made available by other explorers (some commercially minded). And much interesting music can still be made this way, even with facilities that the designers of software have overlooked or discounted (think of the glitch movement in electronica). Yet the truly interesting new possibilities, and the repurposing of technology to individual projects, ultimately require the facility to build new software.

No one would seriously claim that everything should be coded from the ground up; aside from some aesthetic tinkerers, building your own operating system before you make computer music is probably an indirection too far. It is typically good practice to make use of any existing code you can, to spend your time concentrating on the truly original aspects of your project. To assist this, there are many extension libraries for well-known general-purpose programming languages. For efficient audio signal processing code, C remains a popular choice. Yet there are many other computer music tasks, such as

---

[11]Kyle Gann's rant and the comments following on from it are an enlightening read in this regard (see http://www.artsjournal. com/postclassic/2006/05/postsemester_rampage_electroni.html).

algorithmic composition, which can be profitably pursued using any favorite language, and are also supported by many third-party libraries. There are also some scientific modeling environments which are often used by researchers for prototyping, such as MATLAB and GNU Octave, again with plenty of third-party extensions.

There are specialized programming environments explicitly for computer music which might rest upon a standard language such as Java or Lisp, or even be new languages in their own right, even if they bear a family resemblance to prior work (for example, SuperCollider is a descendent of Smalltalk and C which also explores syntactical tricks from more esoteric languages [McCartney, 2002]). There are also scripting languages integrated into particular software, such as the scripting language available in Sibelius, the Nyquist language now integrated into the free Audacity audio editor, or the use of JavaScript in Max/MSP. Operating systems themselves often provide the facility to script instructions for applications, and may have extensive command-line facilities for scripting processes. The latter might be useful, for example, if building a computer-controlled installation which has to be started up by a gallery curator each day with the minimum of fuss (turning the power on) and automatically set itself up.

Table 1.2 lists a selection of some popular options for computer music programming at the time of writing. I have not attempted to collect together all the third-party libraries available, but will mention a few useful ones at other points in this book. There are many historically important computer music languages as well [Loy, 1989a; Roads, 1996; Lyon, 2002]. It should also be noted that many of these systems support arts computing beyond sound alone, having facilities for audio and visuals, and helpful functionality for interfacing to all types of controllers and information beyond the computer itself. In this situation, systems like Processing or Flash, which have increasing amounts of audio support, and may be very well suited to building web applications, can also be helpful.

Programming itself is not taught in this book, and I have chosen to provide pseudocode for algorithms rather than concentrate on any one language, because of the wide range of options available. It is not especially difficult to come to terms with the syntax of a particular language, but it can take a substantial investment of time to explore the associated libraries of available functions. In these cases, the best documentation is usually that which provides plenty of real examples, such as those with which major computer music systems like Max/MSP, Csound and SuperCollider are replete. These make the learning of such systems much more fun and immediate than the study of dry textbooks for general-purpose languages like C. Modern development environments compile code very quickly, or the languages are interpreted, so that the response to running a command can seem to be immediate. Allied to realtime audio synthesis, the facility for fast feedback is now the norm, and development usually has few of the frustrating waits that were historically associated with programming activity.

Table 1.2   A selection of popular computer music programming languages.

Program	Availability	Description	Reference
Pd	Mac/Linux/PC (FOSS)	Pure Data, a popular visual programming language for audio	Puckette [2007]
Max/MSP	Mac/PC (commercial, Cycling74)	Visual programming language with JavaScript scripting, a distant commercial cousin of Pd	Winkler [1998]; Zicarelli [2002]
SuperCollider	Mac/Linux/PC (FOSS)	Draws on Smalltalk and C, but is its own interpreted language. Optimized for realtime audio synthesis and smoothly combines algorithmic composition and synthesis	McCartney [2002]
Csound	Mac/Linux/PC (FOSS)	Contemporary descendent of the historic MusicN series. Old school syntax, but now with integrated Python scripting. Includes a rich catalogue of sound synthesis and analysis methods	Boulanger [2000]
Common Music	Mac/Linux/PC (FOSS)	LISP/Scheme-based, interpreted system for musical algorithm design supporting many output formats from MIDI to Csound	Taube [2004]
ChucK	Mac/Linux/PC (FOSS)	Novel computer music language exploring notions of concurrency, with the colorful Audicle programming environment	Wang [2008]
Impromptu	Mac (free)	Scheme-based, interpreted system which can act as an AudioUnit plug-in host	Sorensen [2005]

1.2.12 Representing Music on a Computer

I have already cautioned that there are many different musics in the world, and it would be surprising if 'one sound fits all' were true. Whilst common practice notation and 12-tone equal temperament have been very successful musical memes in terms of the volume of music dependent on them, they are not the last word on the representation of music. The interfaces of software often make rather constrained decisions about what music typically consists of, tied to the culture being serviced by the product, and this is another reason to have the ability to create or adapt your own software if need be. In general, it befits enlightened musicians to be as aware as possible of the assumptions underlying their musical practice. This critical facility may even lead to the recognition of genuine new musical possibilities.

Representation cannot be escaped; whenever creating music, we are forced to choose our theories and tools (because we get a choice: there is no one music theory, and no one best tool). But computers in particular are so stubborn in their insistence that every detail must be specified that they bring home the need to create explicit well-formed theories of music in an unavoidable way. There can be no woolliness and appeals to irrational philosophy, at least in the operation of the computer itself (wherever decisions are deferred to human minds, well, here anything can happen!).

A prominent theme in electronic music is the 'sound object', an extended concept of musical materials, respecting the continuous transformation of sound in high-dimensional spaces of timbral description [Landy, 2007; Wishart, 1996]. The sound object can encompass a musical note, but also treats interconnected sequences of notes with portamento, environmental sounds, richly synthesized spectral complexes, and many other transformational possibilities.

Henkjan Honing has stated that there is no great justification for the note event as the founding concept in music cognition [Honing, 1993]; but here is a riposte from more than twenty years earlier, from Max Mathews:

> The final principle for specifying sound sequences is the *note concept*. Sound exists as a continuous function of time starting at the beginning of a piece and extending to the end. We have chosen, for practical reasons, to chop this continuous sound into discrete pieces, called notes, each of which has a starting time and a duration time. This division is admittedly a restriction on the generality of sound synthesis, but one we are not brave enough to avoid. Needless to add, notes have been around for some time. [Mathews, 1969, p. 36]

The ease with which we slip into thinking of notes will recur in this book (soon, in the context of MIDI, for example). What is really going on is the choice of the timescale and sonic features for description. Music is a time-based artform, but quite what the best vantage point in time is may depend on who is doing the analysis, and much composition takes place 'out of time'. Of course, ultimately in presentation music is bound by the speed with which the brain can process and handle the 'perceptual present'. There are certain conveniences to the segmentation of music into events which may have great benefit from an evolutionary perspective. The way in which we comprehend complex musical textures is related to the way our marvelous auditory systems let us break down complex scenes in the environment, whether on the savannah or at cocktail parties [Bregman, 1990]. There are many theories as to how the information processing takes place and what is broken down when analyzing an auditory scene. Again, we shall come back to this.

The chief point for now is that we may extract musical information at a number of timescales and viewpoints. In a digital system, the lowest level consists of the samples themselves. Music in conventional understanding is a much higher-level process, whose entities operate over longer timescales; nevertheless, computer music gives us the opportunity to specify individual samples on the way to building up a larger-scale picture. It will be convenient at points to looks at **blocks** of samples, say 64 at a time, or larger **frames**,

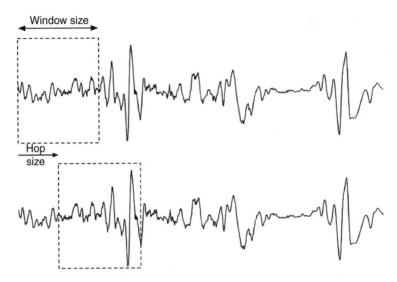

Figure 1.10 Sliding window. Two frames are separated by *hop size* samples; each frame manipulates the samples in a window (shown outlined by the dashed box). A single feature value might be obtained that says something about the variation of the signal in the window, or a whole set of features might be extracted at once.

perhaps windows containing 1024 samples. Looking at a group of samples at once can be convenient for making statistics which describe longer-term motion, all in aid of working up to the higher-level musical descriptors. We shall encounter processes aimed at extracting particular summary features for successive windows of samples. Figure 1.10 demonstrates how this might work with a sliding window; two successive frames are depicted, separated by a hop of a number of samples.

Converting from analog signals, through digital samples, to more abstract layers of description has been called the **signal-to-symbol problem** [Matarić, 2007, p. 73]. An example would be trying to backwards engineer the notes of a classical score given only the audio signal of a clarinet, a problem which seems fair enough on the surface, but proves rather more complicated in practice. It is often convenient to use computers to treat symbols at a high level of abstraction, but computer systems may include a number of levels of description, and complete systems will incorporate both real-world and virtual spaces. With all of this understood as operating with respect to some model of what music is, the representation problem is not a trivial one, and underlies any modeling efforts in computer music.

1.3 A WHIRLWIND HISTORY OF COMPUTER MUSIC

At the time of writing (2008), computer music is 58 years old; that is, if we count the popular tunes played live via the warning hooter on the CSIR Mk 1 computer in Australia in 1951 [Doornbusch, 2004].[12] You might wonder how the computer forced a sound out of the hooter; essentially, by blasting out impulses (a one and then zeroes) repeating at a desired frequency, with no low-pass reconstruction filter. In the same year, the first (analog) recording of computer music was made, of popular tunes performed by the Ferranti Mark I computer following a program by Christopher Strachey, by a BBC unit visiting the 'electronic brain' in Manchester [Fildes, 2008].

These early mainframe computers were room-sized behemoths of the era before integrated circuits and the marvels of miniaturization. The first real computers, in the modern sense of electronic programmable data processing machines, only date to the 1940s, though there are many precedents in mechanical technology, from the Jacquard Loom of 1801 to Charles Babbage's plans for an Analytical Engine. Indeed, there are many musical precedents and anticipations of computer music, by people ranging from experimental music composers to mechanical instrument builders – sometimes the same individuals [Hugill, 2007]. As Moore [1990, p. 8] notes, 'human imagination is the driving force behind human technology'. Famous figures in computer science had anticipated the consequences for the arts, from Ada Lovelace's prescient remarks in 1843 on the Analytical Engine's potential for automated composition, to Alan Turing's theoretical and then practical involvement in the birth of computing. The history of the computer itself, then, is a prime driver of practical success, as what had only been imagined or theorized came to be engineered.

The year 1957 is a special point in our history. The first serious investigation of the potential of computer music is usually attributed to Max Mathews, sometimes dubbed the 'father' of computer music [Lyon, 2002, p. 21]. Having access to facilities at Bell Labs in 1957, and with the lenient and musically inquisitive research director John Pierce to support him, Mathews was instrumental in many computer music firsts. Rather than using an analog recording of a hooter, he was able to work with an early digital to analog convertor[13] and directly write programs whose output could eventually be transferred to magnetic tape. The earliest recording from this process was the 20-second *In the Silver Scale* composed by Newman Guttman, premiered on 17 May 1957. The work immediately showed the potential of the computer by utilizing alternative tunings, rather than the standard equal-tempered scale. In order to create the piece, Mathews wrote the first computer music programming language, Music 1, the first of a whole series usually described as **Music N**, and whose distant and powerful descendants such as Csound are perfectly usable today. Along the way, Mathews originated the Unit Generator concept, was involved in early experiments in the synthesis of

---

[12] http://www.csse.unimelb.edu.au/dept/about/csirac/music/
[13] Perhaps the only set-up available in the world at that point, it was held by another company across the other side of town!

singing, and explored alternative interfaces such as graphical input and a radio conductor's baton.

From a few pioneers, engagement in computer music has rocketed in parallel with the massive reduction in space and costs of digital technology and electronic computers, and at the same time the marvelous acceleration of processor speeds. The computer music literature is replete with excitable citations of Moore's Law, as slow non-realtime rendering has given way to faster-than-realtime calculation. The power for significant realtime audio processing at CD quality has been available on standard home computers since around 1996. Whilst there are always ways to demand too much of whichever machine you have, it is no longer necessary to gain access to a few select institutions to explore computer music.

Really widely available and affordable home computers are traced to the beginning of the 1980s, era of the Commodore 64 and ZX Spectrum, though some musicians had begun early with the Kim-1 and its ilk in 1975. These early microcomputers had rather constrained sound chips, but this didn't stop the creation of some fantastic eight-bit music for computer games and the first tracker programs. Later revivals of those challenging compositional constraints are perhaps more familiar to some readers than the original, and there are thriving eight-bit music and demo scenes today. The take-up of the MIDI control protocol from 1982 led to many MIDI recording and generating computer music programs. By the 1990s, the typical home computer was powerful enough to run multichannel audio recording, processing and synthesis in realtime; there are also many precedents in the 1980s [Yavelow, 1989; Leider, 2004]. We shall survey these developments in Chapter 2.

Whilst there are many musical precedents, from Kraftwerk to hiphop, the explosion of electronic dance music with the rave era (1988 as the Second Summer of Love) saw frequent computer performances at raves. Many an Atari ST or Amiga was run on a dodgy electrical supply in a field, playing back new tracks via sequencer or tracker software! The now-familiar laptop performer became an increasingly common sight in the 1990s. By the new millennium many festivals seemed overrun with computational devices at centre stage, the operators often rather muted physical presences somehow making huge noises. But diversity is paramount in healthy musical scenes, and in a physical backlash there are now equally many alternative interface devices, handheld computers, self-built controllers and the like to offer plenty of movement potential, even where the sounds themselves are often so much larger than an acoustic musician alone could summon.

The computer became part of the arsenal of any popular musician and home recordist, alongside the computer music researchers and ostensibly serious composers. Conservatoire musical education is in no way a necessary qualification for computer music work; autodidact amateurs can easily find themselves become professionals, learning as they go (Autechre spring to mind). Whilst the grand *musique par ordinateur* institution IRCAM has been guilty at times of propagating a model separating engineers and composers, many of today's computer music pioneers are equally at home with technical issues in either domain. Though no one human being can be expert in all facets of a rapidly advancing field, musical curiosity will drive many musicians deep into the heart of machines, whilst many supposed engineers have found their artistic expression fulfilled via computer music.

So we live in a time of unadulterated activity, with relatively portable, powerful and affordable machines (we'll get to mobile phones and personal digital assistants later, too). With so much resting on computers, whether they are centre stage or backroom devices, there is plenty to explore in this book.

1.4 SUMMARY

This chapter has set the scene for the book, covering issues of definition for the field of computer music, and providing some central examples. We have had a glimpse of the rich history of the field, which matches well that of advances in computers. Musicians were quick to exploit the potential of the new generalized calculating machines, and there are plenty of examples of early projects from the 1950s. Present-day activity in computer music is extensive and fast paced, enriched by the speed of communication of ideas and the realtime audio power of even portable machines. The chapter has also provided a quickstart guide to computer music. This was intended as an introduction to an introduction, a useful starting point; nevertheless, I cannot possibly cover in the space all aspects of further disciplines that impact on computer music, from acoustics to musicology. The coming chapters will probe much more into the varied and exciting technologies and projects within computer music as a field in itself.

1.5 EXERCISES

1. Write down your own definition for computer music. Extra groupwork: get a friend to make their own independent definition; then compare your work and discuss. Optional extra: if you have the opportunity, discuss your definition with at least one experienced musician and one experienced computer user. Was the musician *really* just experienced in pure music? Was the computer scientist only expert in computers? Perhaps boundaries are not as solid as you might think.

2. Write down a list of all the music software you can off the top of your head. Try to identify common functionality between different programs. Can you form a taxonomy of computer music software?

3. Create a sine tone in as many different ways as you can. Beyond trying various software packages, this might extend to finding an analog sine tone generator or tuning device .... You should try and produce different frequencies at different

amplitudes and phases. Be careful that you don't play anything at painful volumes, particularly over headphones, but probe the limits of your hearing. Can you hear a 16 kHz sine tone at both low and high amplitude?

4. Research the following three artists: Laurie Spiegel, Markus Popp (Oval) and George Lewis. What different roles have computers played in their work?

5. Calculate the root mean square amplitude for one cycle of a sine wave, for the cases where the period contains 2, 10 and 100 samples. Do the same for one cycle of a cosine wave. How do your results compare? Is there a limiting value as the number of samples increases?

6. You have one signal at −10 dB, and one at −6 dB (the reference level is 1). Add up their amplitudes. What is the final result in decibels?

7. Draw a patching diagram showing a white noise generator plugged into a low-pass filter, and from there to a DAC.

8. Draw a patching diagram showing two sine tone generators, the first with its frequency set to 440 Hz and its initial phase 0, and the second a 550 Hz tone with phase $\frac{\pi}{2}$. The output of the first sine generator is multiplied by a scaling factor of 0.5 and the second by 0.1, and the signals are then summed before going to a DAC.

9. Draw a patching diagram for the IIR filter which consists of feedforward coefficients $a(0) = 0.5$ and $a(7) = 0.2$, and feedback coefficient $b(1) = −0.1$. In order to represent the delays you will need a delay unit with a signal input and output, and a delay time control in samples. The filter should be processing input from an ADC and then sending the result to a DAC.

10. Use the Hamming derivation of aliasing to construct a diagram of the phenomena showing an original wave with frequency over Nyquist, and the alias that is actually heard to result. For convenience, you will probably want to work with normalized frequencies such that 1 is the sampling rate, and 1/2 is Nyquist.

1.6

FURTHER READING

No book is an island, and some complementary materials are suggested at the close of each chapter in addition to the in-text references. Reading multiple perspectives on a topic will help to consolidate your knowledge.

Acoustics, Psychoacoustics and the Psychology of Music

Campbell, M. and Greated, C. (1987). *The Musician's Guide to Acoustics*. Oxford University Press, Oxford.

Cook, P. R. (ed) (1999). *Music, Cognition and Computerized Sound*. MIT Press, Cambridge, MA.

Deutsch, D. (ed) (1999). *The Psychology of Music*, 2nd Edition. Academic Press, San Diego, CA.

Everest, F. A. (2001). *The Master Handbook of Acoustics*, 4th Edition. McGraw-Hill, New York, NY.

Hallam, S., Cross, I. and Thaut, M. (eds) (2009). *The Oxford Handbook of Music Psychology*. Oxford University Press, Oxford.

Moore, B. C. J. (2004). *An Introduction to the Psychology of Hearing*, 5th Edition. Elsevier, London.

Pierce, J. R. (1992). *The Science of Musical Sound*, Revised Edition. W. H. Freeman and Company, New York, NY.

Roederer, J. G. (1995). *The Physics and Psychophysics of Music: An Introduction*, 3rd Edition. Springer Verlag, New York, NY.

Sloboda, J. A. (1985). *The Musical Mind*. Oxford University Press, Oxford.

Thompson, W. F. (2009). *Music, Thought, and Feeling: Understanding the Psychology of Music*. Oxford University Press, New York, NY.

Yost, W. A. (2007). *Fundamentals of Hearing: An Introduction*, 5th Edition. Academic Press, Burlington, MA.

Mathematics and Music

Benson, D. J. (2007). *Music: A Mathematical Offering*. Cambridge University Press, Cambridge. http://www.maths.abdn.ac.uk/~bensondj/html/maths-music.html

Loy, G. (2007). *Musimathics* (Volumes 1 and 2). MIT Press, Cambridge, MA.

Digital Audio

Pohlmann, K. C. (2005). *Principles of Digital Audio*, 5th Edition. McGraw-Hill, New York, NY.

Watkinson, J. (2001). *The Art of Digital Audio*, 3rd Edition. Focal Press, Oxford.

Electronic Music History

Chadabe, J. (1997). *Electric Sound: The Past and Promise of Electronic Music*. Prentice Hall, Englewood Cliffs, New Jersey.

Collins, N. and d'Escriván, J. (eds) (2007). *The Cambridge Companion to Electronic Music*. Cambridge University Press, Cambridge.

Cox, C. and Warner, D. (eds) (2004). *Audio Culture: Readings in Modern Music*. Continuum, London and New York.

Emmerson, S. (2007). *Living Electronic Music*. Ashgate, Aldershot, Hampshire.

Holmes, T. (2008). *Electronic and Experimental Music*, 3rd Edition. Routledge, New York, NY.

Manning, P. (2004). *Electronic and Computer Music*. Oxford University Press, Oxford.

Norman, K. (2004). *Sounding Art: Eight Literary Excursions Through Electronic Music*. Ashgate, Aldershot, Hampshire.

Schrader, B. (1982). *Introduction to Electro-Acoustic Music*. Prentice-Hall, Inc., Englewood Cliffs, NJ.

Shapiro, P. (ed) (2000). *Modulations. A History of Electronic Music: Throbbing Words on Sound*. Distributed Art Publishers, Inc., New York, NY.

Computer Music Textbooks and Reference Texts

Brown, A. (2007). *Computers in Music Education*. Routledge, New York, NY.

Dean, R. (ed) (2009). *The Oxford Handbook of Computer Music*. Oxford University Press, New York, NY.

Dodge, C. and Jerse, T. (1997). *Computer Music Synthesis, Composition, and Performance*. Schirmer Books, New York, NY.

Hugill, A. (2008). *The Digital Musician*. Routledge, New York, NY.

Lincoln, H. B. (ed) (1970). *The Computer and Music*. Cornell University Press, Ithaca, NY.

Mathews, M. V. (1969). *The Technology of Computer Music*. MIT Press, Cambridge, MA.

Moore, F. R. (1990). *Elements of Computer Music*. P T R Prentice Hall, Englewood Cliffs, NJ.

Pope, S. T. (2008). *The Big MAT Book: Courseware for Audio and Multimedia Engineering*. Extensive online resources at http://heaveneverywhere.com/TheBigMATBook/

Puckette, M. S. (2007). *The Theory and Technique of Computer Music*. World Scientific Publishing Co., Inc., Hackensack, NJ. Available from http://crca.ucsd.edu/~msp/ techniques.htm

Roads, C. (1996). *The Computer Music Tutorial*. MIT Press, Cambridge, MA.

Roads, C. and Strawn, J. (eds) (1985). *Foundations of Computer Music*. MIT Press, Cambridge, MA.

Roads, C. (ed) (1989). *The Music Machine*. MIT Press, Cambridge, MA.

Chapter 2

Recording

'Digital recordings can be copied indefinitely without loss of quality. If you happen to be a sound engineer, this is heaven. If you are a record company executive you take another pill for blood pressure and phone your lawyer to see if you can have it stopped.'

John Watkinson [Watkinson, 2001, p. 8]

OBJECTIVES

This chapter covers:

- the history of recording;
- the MIDI specification;
- digital audio workstations and virtual studio software;
- audio file formats and streaming standards;
- multichannel audio and spatialization;
- sampling: history, copyright and practical issues.

In recording technology, particularly studio software and audio interfaces, computer music has perhaps its most commercial arm, catering to the music industry and many home hobbyists. Some systems have been adopted in enough studios to make the claim of being 'industry standards', for example Digidesign's Pro Tools (sold as a combined hardware and software solution) and the Logic software now only supported on Apple computers.[1]

---

[1] With business involvement extending to training, you can even get certification as an operator for these packages.

With commercial interests so involved, there are many different software packages, formats and standards to get to grips with. This book cannot hope to cover in intimate detail every package. Instead we shall cover important principles which transcend particular software, and survey the general scene.

2.1 RECORDING: A HISTORY

Sound reproduction technologies were first patented in the latter half of the 19th century. Édouard-Léon Scott de Martinville's *phonautograph* (1857) was a scientific tool for recording sound waves on paper, but it was unable to play back sound as such.[2] It is Charles Cros and Thomas Edison's co-invention of the phonograph (1877) that is commonly credited with establishing an age of sonic reproducibility. The early phonograph was of immensely poor quality compared with today's technology, recording onto the outer surface of cylinders that quickly wore out with repeated playback. Initially the device was just a novelty, and recognition of its full commercial implications took time. The principle eventually captured the public imagination with the more robust disc-playing gramophone, heralding a succession of marvelous devices. Table 2.1 provides a timeline of some landmarks in the intensive development of recording technology since then.

For our purposes, the most important historical era to describe is the transition from analog to digital recording – computers natively manipulating digital data. Section 1.2.5 already introduced the technical basis of digital audio. Although research efforts in digital audio can be traced much earlier in the 20th century, commercially available digital recorders date from the 1970s. Whilst the industry remained somewhat suspicious of digital audio for some time, the surefire advantages of cheapness and easy non-destructive editing were to win out, and, as we have reviewed, continual improvement in the quality of conversion back and forth between analog and digital has solidified digital audio's hold on the market. Even so, the early appearance of the Compact Disc standard in 1982 presaged a remarkable success story in consumer adoption.

We have seen that digital sound synthesis can be traced back as far as 1957 and Max Mathews' experiments at Bell Labs. Although the 1990s is associated with easy and inexpensive multichannel audio recording on home computers, there are many (far more expensive and often custom-built) precedents in digital audio from the 1970s and 1980s. A list might include the SoundDroid Workstation digital sound editing suite, Digidesign's Sound Designer II editing software (1985), and the Digi-Sound 16 external interface (1982) [Leider, 2004]. In the 1980s home computers' inbuilt sound chips allowed their use as (usually eight-bit) digital synthesis and sample playback machines, with a limited number of channels, for games and with the early sequencers called tracker programs. Yet home computers were

---

[2]Some cunning researchers at the Lawrence Berkeley National Laboratory in the present day have converted paper phonautograms back to sound using a computerized scanning system, thus posthumously releasing the earliest sound recording [Rosen, 2008].

Table 2.1 Overview of advances in recording technology.

Date	Event	Description
1857	Phonautograph	Léon Scott's apparatus for recording sound graphically
1877	Phonograph	Co-invented by Cros and Edison
1887	Gramophone	Invented by Emile Berliner (uses discs)
1898	Wire recorder	Magnetic patterns recorded onto steel wire by Valdemar Poulsen for the 'telegraphone' answering machine [Pohlmann, 2005, p. 179]
1905	Electrical amplification	Lee De Forest invents the triode (later a vacuum tube proper); originally called the Audion
1907	First 'sound on film' experiments	In 1919 De Forest patented an optical soundtrack method that used the edge of the film stock
1920s	First magnetic tape research	Commercially available by 1948
1947–8	First transistors	Extreme miniaturization of electronics eventually possible
1948	Multitracking	Les Paul adapts the newly available tape recorder. Paul had already been practicing overdubbing with mono discs, simultaneously with Pierre Schaeffer in Paris
1950s	Intensive digital audio research begins following Claude Shannon's information theory	First commercial products in the 1970s
1982	CD	16-bit 44.1 kHz digital audio quickly becomes a standard consumer format
1983	MIDI specification	Standard developed for interconnecting hardware synthesizers, which also enables computer control of them
1988	CD-R	Not readily available for home computer use until about 1996
1991	MP3	MPEG 1 Layer 3 becomes an industry standard, with associated patents (MPEG stands for Moving Picture Experts Group, an organization which has spearheaded many new formats)
1999	Napster	Illegal downloading becomes mainstream
2001	iPod	Along with the iTunes site, helped establish legal download routes
2003	Web 2.0	MySpace launched, one of many new social networking sites allowing musicians to (potentially) promote their music without intermediaries. Web 2.0 is a post-hoc label for a rather loose collection of new Internet facilities

most frequently employed as sequencers of control data (such as MIDI, to be discussed formally below) for external hardware, since processing many channels of high quality audio directly was beyond their capability. Hardware digital synthesizers (which are essentially themselves dedicated computers running embedded software) avoid taxing the computer with all synthesis calculations. Digital synthesizers such as the Synclavier (prototype 1975, released 1976), Samson Box (1977), Fairlight (1978/9, the first commercially available sampler) and Giuseppe Di Guigno's 4∗ digital synthesizers (4A, 1976 and 4X, 1981) can also be traced to the 1970s. Lower-cost hardware samplers and digital synthesizers (including the famous Yamaha DX7) made digital systems more widely available in the early 1980s. Nevertheless, many research prototypes and early commercial programs of higher quality audio editing software were devised for the Atari ST, Apple and similar machines. It would certainly be a mistake to think that all virtual studios date from the 1990s; Yavelow [1989] describes a cornucopia of early virtual synths, sound design software and multitrack audio mixing programs that were in existence circa 1987.

It was not until the late 1980s and early 1990s that digital audio interfaces for computers really caught on for commercial studio purposes, with computers powerful enough to take on all recording, synthesis and editing legwork; 1995–6 is sometimes identified as the critical juncture at which operating systems and microprocessors were first able to support virtual studios on standard home computers. Nevertheless, some systems continued to farm out much audio digital signal processing to specialized hardware rather than directly calculating all audio playback and effects in software alone (the Digidesign model for professional Pro Tools installations, for instance). Yet as the 1990s progressed computers took on a role as general-purpose engines for digital audio operations, and software became available for each specific synthesis, processing and recording task. The concept of a high-quality multichannel virtual studio free of external rendering gear not only became a reality, but became potentially available to all computer users. This fact, and the impact of the Internet on digital music distribution (to be further discussed in Chapter 7) has made computer music central to the recording practices of a large number of musicians. Whilst studios will retain some importance as isolated acoustic spaces dedicated to recording, the ease of using portable digital recorders on location, of building a portable studio around a laptop computer and audio interface, has transformed the industry.

2.2 MUSICAL INSTRUMENT DIGITAL INTERFACE

At face value, recording suggests the capture of raw audio data, but it is also possible to record and play back any form of control data. You could imagine capturing individual key-presses on a keyboard, or tracking the position of a mouse cursor at a low rate (say 100 Hz), since you can hardly move your hand at audio frequencies! As discussed in Section 1.2.12, music can be represented on many levels, and the use of a 'note'-based format rather than continuous samples provides a substantial compression of the amount of descriptive data required.

Musical Instrument Digital Interface (MIDI) [Loy, 1989b]; [Rumsey and McCormick, 2006, pp. 373–418] is by no means a universal solution able to represent all musical instruments and situations digitally, despite being originally proposed by Dave Smith in 1981 as a 'Universal Synthesizer Interface'. It was a standard introduced enthusiastically by manufacturers rather early on in the digital music era (discussions 1981–2, first synthesizers with MIDI early 1983), with an initial emphasis on the interconnection of different manufacturers' keyboard-based synthesizers. Highly successful according to the needs of the time, MIDI has retained popularity partly by dint of early adoption. Yet it has been the subject of much subsequent debate and various post-hoc revisions, some specific to particular companies and some designed by researchers [Selfridge-Field, 1997]. We shall explore its capabilities and its deficiencies here in equal measure.

There is a caricature of MIDI that sees it as fitting best the model of a piano. Here, the player simply imparts velocity to a levering key, and once the hammer is in motion, very little can be done to influence the forthcoming sound. In fact, as witnessed by an array of available controllers, MIDI also supports continuous control data. It is more in the amount of musical information that can be transmitted per second, in a unidirectional message-sending model,[3] and some rather Western mainstream assumptions about what music actually *is*, that MIDI falls down (these problems also being the subject of some extensions). It is notable, though, that MIDI exists at all, providing as it does a clear alternative to recording audio; instead, it is possible to record control data in the form of MIDI events that require far less storage space and processing to play back. This reduced requirement makes MIDI a very useful pragmatic choice in the control of dedicated external synthesizers, for example, rather than rendering all sound internally within a computer. It certainly suited the 1980s, when systems had so much less memory, hard drive space and processing power for audio signals.

MIDI was created to be cheap to run, so it operates over an asynchronous serial connection at a low bandwidth: according to the original specification one device can send at most 31 250 bits per second.[4] Each distinct type of MIDI message is composed of 10-bit words. Padded with start and stop bits, words reduce to (eight-bit) bytes; we shall examine below the basic types of MIDI message and their byte structure. When many messages must be sent to activate or modify musical events at one moment in time, the bandwidth restrictions, the serial reading of the information and the temporal resolution assumptions of MIDI are a potential source of latency. Nevertheless, in situations where a single MIDI line is not responsible for a complex multitracked sequence with rich control data, the delay is often perceptually negligible and the illusion of immediate control easily established.

---

[3] Two-way communication is possible by using multiple MIDI lines, but is more difficult to set up, particular for more complicated device topologies. MIDI messaging does not allow failure reports, so is more like UDP then TCP/IP messaging (see Chapter 7).
[4] With more recent Universal Serial Bus (USB) keyboards, or entirely virtual studios, for instance, MIDI cabling itself has been dropped, and devices conform to the MIDI messaging protocol even though they may operate at higher rates. At its standard rate, MIDI is definitely not suitable for cueing or controlling high temporal resolution audio signal processing operations.

Each MIDI message is usually[5] a one-, two- or three-byte (eight-bit) sequence. The use of bytes makes hexadecimal notation common. One hex (hexadecimal) digit can take on 16 possible values from 0 to F; this represents a four-bit 'nibble'. So each byte is of the form XX for two hexadecimal digits. An example would be 2F, where F represents 15, and the 2 actually means $2*16$ because of its position in the 16s rather than the units column; so 2F is actually 47 in decimal. The first word is always a status byte (the most significant bit is a one) and the other bytes are data (starting with a zero). Because of this, only seven bits are left to convey actual values. Various types of message are differentiated by different status bytes, including channel commands (80–EF), the system exclusive command (F0), system common commands (F1–F7) and realtime commands such as sequencer controls and timing clock messages (F8–FF). The seven possible channel commands include a MIDI channel from 0–15 in the status byte data in this form:

[1 (3 bits channel command type from 0 to 6) (4 bits channel number)]

Because data bytes are effectively seven-bit, values are restricted to the region of 0–127; this is also the origin of the MIDI note number pitch range in 12-note equal temperament (MIDI note 60 is middle C, and nine semitones above this is 69, a concert A). Table 2.2 outlines the standard set of MIDI channel commands most typically used in standard MIDI sequencing (also see [Loy, 1989b, p. 188]).

Since its introduction, MIDI has been the subject of various pragmatic revisions. For instance, as the table outlines, the note-off message is often dropped in favor of a note-on at a velocity of 0. General MIDI (introduced in 1991, with a further version 2.0 in 1999) establishes various minimal requirements for MIDI-controllable synthesizers (such as amount of polyphony and supported sounds), and conventions on control change and program change message types. Program change messages selecting among 128 sounds were fine when MIDI was introduced, but seem to restrict possibilities severely on modern synthesizers with large memories. One extension specifies 14-bit sound selection messages by combining two control change messages with controller types 0 (first byte) and 32 (second), circumventing the seven-bit resolution of program change in General MIDI, ostensibly to allow the easy sharing of MIDI files with common playback sound sets.[6] Further MIDI specification extensions have confronted such issues as the inherent standard 12-notes-per-octave equal-temperament bias in the original specification.

Alongside the standard MIDI specification, which is specialized to live performance,[7] MIDI files are a general way of storing and recalling sequences of MIDI data, each event being

---

[5]The only exception is the system exclusive message (beginning with status byte F0 in hexadecimal), which allows manufacturer-dependent extensions, and which can have an arbitrary number of data words after a manufacturer ID byte. The extensions offered by this message type have created a get-out clause for updating the specification: '*System exclusive* is the great escape hatch of MIDI' [Loy, 1989b, p. 186].

[6]To further guarantee equivalent reproduction on disparate machines, Downloadable Sounds (DLS) provides an additional sampling standard for sound sources, which we will discuss later in the chapter.

[7]In practical terms, the separation of note-ons and -offs is a constant headache. Now, it must be admitted that performers do not necessarily know in advance how long they will hold down a key, so this information is part of recording MIDI data. But once stored, internal representations in sequencers will seek to keep track of which off is connected to which on; in short, to represent a note with a known duration. Conversion back to ons and offs would take place only when playing out the data again.

Table 2.2 MIDI Specification 1.0: channel command types.

Event	Data bytes	Description
Channel commands	One or two	X is channel from 0–15 in the following. MIDI equipment will often show numbers from 1–16 for channels, or values from 1–128, to avoid confusing consumers with computer science counting
On (9X)	MIDI note number, velocity	The classic event trigger
Off (8X)	MIDI note number, velocity	Rarely used since a MIDI On message with a velocity of 0 can act as a surrogate
Polyphonic Pressure (AX)	MIDI note number, pressure value	Note-specific controller values; in the context of keyboard playing, dubbed 'aftertouch'
Control Change (BX)	Controller type, value	Support for continuous control data streams, with higher-resolution (14-bit values) possible by sending successive control change messages with related controller types
Program Change (CX)	Program number	Change synthesizer sound (among up to 128 presets) on a given channel
Pressure (DX)	Single data byte	Overall pressure controller for a given channel (the advantage over a control change is that this just requires a single data byte)
Pitch Bend (EX)	Data1, data2	Pitch bend wheel data (could be co-opted for another controller for non-keyboard synthesizer interfaces) at 14-bit resolution packed into the two data bytes

stamped with a 'delta time', the time interval since the previous event. Three types of MIDI file exist with only type 0 (single mixed-down track of all events for one song) and type 1 (multiple tracks preserved for one song to support the original multitrack structure) favored by the great majority of MIDI sequencer software (type 2 is equivalent to having multiple type 0 files, packed into one file). Particularly for integration amongst multiple sequencers, drum machines and other timekeeping devices, standard MIDI also allows for (master to slave) synchronization. In the basic specification are MIDI clock and playback control messages such as Song Position Pointers (expressed in beats rather than seconds, by default at 24 ticks per beat). The absolute time (hours, minutes, seconds) MIDI Time Code (MTC) is used for advanced synchronization tasks such as syncing to video [Rumsey and McCormick, 2006, pp. 411–414].

It has always been fashionable to criticize MIDI as a representation, though it has supported innumerable practical real-life projects. It was certainly a remarkable instance of inter-company collaboration when first formulated, even if weaknesses were subsequently revealed as computer processing increases outdid expectations. What doesn't MIDI store?

As discussed in articles on research extensions to the specification [Selfridge-Field, 1997], MIDI does not represent pitch spellings (i.e., whether MIDI note 66 is F♯ or G♭), nor many other fine points of Western music notation (such as a slur or hairpin carrying across many notes), let alone the written and aural qualities of musics from other cultures.

As Loy [1989b, p. 192] notes, 'When musicians are given computer control over synthesizers, the natural course of things is to require ever more control over ever more resources'. An open-ended specification and the separation of transport mechanism from protocol are more future-proof. This is the design strategy taken by Open Sound Control, an alternative messaging protocol for network music (see Section 7.1.1). Nevertheless, MIDI remains an essential standard to be aware of. It has substantially impacted on the music industry and beyond (e.g., the MIDI Show Control standard for theatrical lighting) and shows no sign of going away, with provision now being made for MIDI over Ethernet.

2.3 VIRTUAL STUDIOS

With the central role of a computer now thoroughly established in most studio set-ups, the studio engineer focuses on software programs rather than hardware modules for many tasks. Instead of spending so much time staring into small LED display panels on rackmount gear, the studio user can stare at much larger computer screens instead! Home and mobile recording set-ups have become so widespread as to undermine traditional studio recording for many forms of music. Specialized studio environments, however, can still offer treated acoustics and multichannel monitoring systems that may be unavailable elsewhere, as well as a focus for certain communities of users [Schedel, 2007].

A **digital audio workstation** (DAW) is a computer equipped with an audio interface (ADC and DAC), within which all signal recording, processing, mixing and mastering operations take place [Leider, 2004, pp. 45–49]. Audio recording and editing are tasks at which the computer, as general digital information processor, excels. The ease of non-destructive editing, and the processing resources – as many tracks and effects as CPU horsepower allows, as many undos as memory allows – significantly underline why older analog hardware gear has fallen by the wayside. Where previously an array of software applications were run to cover different sound engineering and composition tasks, today's DAW software integrates multiple functionalities into single packages with correspondingly large help manuals.

As will be further investigated in Chapter 6, the virtualization of virtual studios has limits. There is no replacement for microphones and speakers, and the necessity for audio interfaces cannot be circumvented. Tactile surfaces – such as a remote mixing desk, or a bank of MIDI controllers – can provide simultaneous control and feedback on many operations at once. For live mixing, a mouse, which only allows the click and drag of one graphical widget

Ardour

As an example of DAW software, Ardour is featured here. This program exemplifies the high-quality work that is available within open-source projects. It is maintained by a team of developers led by the original author, Paul Davis. It is free to download, and available for Linux and OS X (though contributions to development are always welcome, see http://ardour.org/). The screenshot in Figure 2.1 demonstrates the multitrack paradigm, with simultaneous horizontal tracks in the central audio region sequencer. Available audio data (imported files, recordings and splices) appear listed on the right under 'Regions'. Standard per track facilities such as mute and solo buttons, and displays of automation data such as volume control curves, are visible. The multitrack region editing view is accompanied amongst other views by a mixer window, where one channel strip is assigned to each track, with gain fader, input and output routing, auxiliary sends, plug-in inserts and more. The master channel strip in this mix window is just visible on the far right.

Figure 2.1   Screenshot from the Ardour DAW software.

at a time, is often insufficient. But it is also interesting to observe how GUIs often ape the physical layout of hardware audio interfaces such as mixing boards. Reason's virtual rack-mount modules and corresponding wired patchbay 'around the back' are a prime example.

At this point, having mentioned Reason, we might go on to list some other famous and commercially successful packages of the last twenty or more years. In no particular order, standard DAW software includes Digital Performer, Cubase, Pro Tools, Logic, Sonar and many more. There is an armada of shareware and freeware software, much of a quality to rival the mainstream commercial packages (one of these, Ardour, is featured in the sidebar). There are further variants such as live sequencers for realtime mixing and processing, as used for fast prototyping or for laptop concert performance (e.g., Ableton Live). These are the software packages most closely profiled in music technology magazines, and there are plenty of monthly columns and online help forums dedicated to particular applications. This book is not going to attempt to teach you how to use any specific software or DAW set-up; the best way to do that is usually just to figure it out for yourself with a copy of an instruction manual, a Dummies' Guide or one of the many other home recording and studio technology books. It is best to try to learn more than one, and to isolate the more general principles which such software tends to follow. Depending on which studio you enter, you'll have to pick up a range of new software with each project (despite Pro Tools's claims to ubiquity, it is not the end of the story).

Table 2.3 outlines some of the standard tasks and different musical viewpoints offered by applications, and bundled up within virtual studios. The technical basis of these operations will be covered in greater detail at different stages of this book. The mother studio software is typically extensible by hosting third party plug-ins, which conform to supported plug-in standards. These may be proprietary and restricted to one system (like TDM plug-ins, which can actually run on the Pro Tools Time Division Multiplexing signal-processing hardware), have been originally proprietary but later opened up sufficiently to become a general standard (i.e., Virtual Studio Technology plug-ins) or be offered by an operating system (for example, Direct X, Audio Units and the Linux Audio Developer's Simple Plug-in API). Writing audio software in a common plug-in format can promote the wide dissemination of that work, since it can be run within a number of popular software hosts.

2.4 FILE FORMATS AND AUDIO CODECS

Digital audio can be perfectly[8] replicated to create as many copies as desired, and stored indefinitely. Since the data may be passed around different computer systems, and even streamed live from one source to be immediately utilized at a second point, there are a number of container formats which have been designed. Various needs are present; the

---

[8]The actual error rate supported by error correction techniques is around 1 in 10^{12} or better, depending on the coding redundancy and other clever tricks [MacKay, 2003].

Table 2.3 A selection of standard virtual studio paradigms; many bulgingly featured packages take on all these different viewpoints and tasks in one piece of software.

Format	Comments
Multitrack sequencer	Timeline editor of multitracked musical data (audio, MIDI, control functions), with time on the vertical (list view, tracker) or horizontal axis
Mixer	Gain, spatialization, compression, EQ and further plug-in facilities for each track as well as master and auxiliary busses
Patchbay	Virtual studio equivalent of a central hub for connecting modules – sometimes manifested as a visual programming environment for controlling signal flow between devices
Sound editor	Digital audio editor for splicing and processing
Virtual synthesizer	Sound synthesis engine
Effects plug-in	Sound processing tool
Librarian	Set-up manager (also for external MIDI gear, for instance)
Score editor	Editing via the traditional Western score viewpoint, including typesetting for publishing scores

availability of storage, the time costs of compression, the ability to stream data (to read a file section by section whilst maintaining audio rate output), the quality of audio supported in terms of bit resolution and sampling rate and the number of channels of data allowed.

A perennial headache in the use of digital audio systems is the conversion of one file type to another; fortunately, most software helps deal with this dilemma, though the supported file formats for different packages can vary, requiring the use of supplementary software. If you program your own software, you may find yourself confronting various file formats more directly, though again various libraries are available to assist (e.g., Erik de Castro Lopo's libsndfile, libmad for MP3, and many more). File input and output is one of those necessary but dull administrative tasks in programming before you reach the interesting processing.

Even if there may seem to be a bewildering array of file formats for audio, in practice certain favorites have been selected by the popularity of particular operating systems, software and situations [Rumsey and McCormick, 2006, pp. 264–271]; [Leider, 2004, pp. 85–117]. Table 2.4 lists some standard audio file formats. Commercial pressures can lead companies to develop proprietary formats and lock consumers into them; open standards attempt to avoid this headache, and provide open specifications which are not held back by patents. Proprietary layers including Digital Rights Management can wrap any existing sound file.

An audio **codec** is a particular encoding–**deco**ding (alternatively **compression**-**deco**mpression) scheme for packaging up audio data efficiently. Both **lossless** and **lossy** formats aim to achieve smaller file or stream sizes through a variety of information

Table 2.4   A selection of standard audio file formats; the top section lists lossless schemes, the lower section lossy perceptual audio codecs.

Format	Comments
WAV	Wave, audio data held in a RIFF (Resource Interchange File Format) container
AIFF	Audio Interchange File Format (similar container to WAV)
AU	Sun Microsystems legacy format, .au and .snd extensions
SD2	Sound Designer 2 – legacy format for Digidesign's Sound Designer 2 sound editing software (introduced 1985 and market dominant for ten years)
FLAC	Free Lossless Audio Codec
MP3	MPEG 1 Layer 3 – you no doubt have at least one on your computer already!
AAC	Advanced Audio Coding, part of the MPEG-4 standard, a successor to MP3
Vorbis	Open standard perceptual audio codec held in the Ogg container format (hence sometimes known as Ogg-Vorbis)
WMA	Windows Media Audio codecs (standard version is a lossy perceptual codec; there is a lossless version too, and other variants)

theoretic and audio modeling encoding schemes. The two can be respectively distinguished as preserving a perfect copy of data, or as discarding (hopefully less important) elements of the data. The latter lossy option allows higher compression rates, and is thereby pertinent to transmission over lower bandwidth channels. The drive to compression is particularly important when distributing audio files online; the historic rise in popularity of MP3 is related to the typical 10:1 compression ratio allowed, therefore achieving a download time of 10% that of uncompressed audio.

The modeling of human auditory capabilities is often highly beneficial to computer music tasks. An immediate demonstration of this assertion is **perceptual audio coding**, where lossy compression schemes exploit knowledge of psychoacoustics. Such coding methods discard information which is simply not noticeable to the average ear. This saves on storage without compromising audio quality, within the limits of the accuracy of the model; quality gracefully degrades as the compression ratio is increased. The analysis chapter covers the technical aspects of this in greater depth in Section 3.4.3.

Through file headers, or other mechanisms for implanting additional data in files, **metadata** accompanies actual sound data. In the traditional sound file header, this might state sampling rate, number of channels, quantization encoding, or bit depth. Metadata also allows contextual data, such as the name of an author, artist, engineer or their pet dog. The ID3 tags in MP3 hold metadata, and similar facilities exist in other formats.

With many existing file formats not mentioned here, development ongoing, and with much contemporary work also taking in visuals and many other facets of multimedia computing, you are likely to encounter many more formats in your time.

2.5 SPATIALIZATION

Spatialization is the art of placing sounds in space, perhaps to evoke and reproduce the original acoustic at the site of a recording, or to perform within a given space by controlling the **localization** of sounds. There are various manifestations of spatial sound, or **surround sound** as it is commonly known in consumer settings, each with their own required technical configuration of playback equipment, including their own encoding format for the data. Most familiar is the case where sound is stored and transmitted as one or more **channels**, co-temporal signals meant for simultaneous playback over a certain configuration of loudspeakers.

We have two ears, and although early recording devices and telecommunications were predominantly one-channel **mono** (the standard telephone has never left this mould), two-channel **stereo** was demonstrated as early as 1881. The occasion was Clément Ader's premiere of his *Théâtrophone* at the World Expo, where listeners heard a live stereo broadcast transmitted from the Paris Opéra. The remote reproduction was effected by many stage-side receivers and ultimately in one telephone line to each ear for each observer.[9] Stereo only really became a standard option in the 1960s (the first commercial stereo long player record dates from 1958, the first radio transmission 1961).

Since you are probably already aware of such standards as 5.1, 7.1, 10.2, 47.3[10] and the like, you might be forgiven for wondering why we would ever need more than two channels. We must distinguish sound as injected directly into the auditory canals by headphones – **binaural** audio – from the transmission of sound over loudspeakers in a room. The latter can cater to many people at once, but the challenge is in creating an adequate reproduction of the original soundscape over a large enough field to take in all observers. There are various reasons why this is a difficult task, from facets of the multichannel signal and the loudspeakers to the room acoustics and the listeners' own bodies. We must also distinguish using loudspeakers as individual point sources, which is straightforward, from trying to create a virtual sound source through a convincing phantom image between speaker locations, which is much more challenging and the topic of various spatialization strategies.

Even the situation for binaural playback rather than open conditions is complicated. Headphones play sounds directly into the auditory canals, and when simply reproducing

---

[9] http://histv2.free.fr/theatrophone/theatrophone.htm
[10] Sorry, I couldn't resist making one up.

what would normally be sent to loudspeakers, play back music which is heard at the center of the head, rather than depicting a real sound scene. In order to convey a spatial image as a listener in another environment may have heard it, binaural microphones can be used in an original recording to capture sound as it arrives at the auditory canals. Otherwise, recordings made with a (much more reliably still) dummy head and shoulders in a particular acoustic can help to build a processing engine which can convey the sense of being in that acoustic for a third party. Such work acknowledges the need to simulate the incidence of sound onto a human body – bouncing from the shoulders, reflecting from the pinnae (external folds of the ears), the acoustic shadow of the head – and leads to the **head-related transfer functions** (HRTFs) as engineering the filtering effect on sound arriving at the auditory canals from particular directions.[11] Although home and mobile headphone listening is common, social music experiences have traditionally tended to avoid headphones, though more recently headphone festivals such as placard (www.leplacard.org) and headphone-based clubs like Silent Disco have brought back rooms recollecting Ader's 1881 Paris Expo exhibition.

In the following subsections we shall first review the psychoacoustics of spatial perception, the way in which humans make sense of auditory environments and locate sound sources in space. We shall then consider different multichannel formats that offer some sort of control over spatial reproduction and synthesis.

2.5.1 Spatial Hearing and Room Acoustics Primer

Table 2.5 gives the main principles affecting our sense of localization, in terms of identifying the distance to a sound source, its actual relative position to our own location, its movement, and the acoustics of the listening context [Gerzon, 1974; Moore, 1990; Begault, 1994; Blauert, 1997; Malham, 1998; Moore, 2004]. Brief mention is also made of computational processes that might allow the simulation of the acoustical or perceptual effect, which are expanded in technical terms in Section 4.3.3. The table deals with auditory information only, but visual information can also influence judgment, as in the 'ventriloquist effect' where the movement of the dummy's mouth whilst a ventriloquist speaks convinces an audience to assign a voice to that location.

Relative position is typically measured in a spherical coordinate system, as depicted in Figure 2.2. Ambiguous sound source locations can be evoked by some cues, such as equal intensity and time delay to both ears for sounds on the central front–back and vertical **median plane** through the middle of our heads equidistant between the ears.[12] We actively move our heads to disambiguate sources and keep track of locations. Elevation and front–back localization especially relies on the filtering characteristics of our pinnae, as well as the

---

[11]One problem with this approach is that human pinnae subtly vary. Using HRTFs derived from another individual's body measurements may degrade listening cues [Begault, 1994, p. 71]. It is also necessary to be careful that the pinnae only appear once in the playback chain; that is, either the recording including pinnae filtering is played back directly into the auditory canals, or over loudspeakers the pinnae filtering is left out or compensated, since your outer ears will provide their own contribution!

[12]Although they allow lateralization (identification of which side of the head a sound source is closer to), ITD and IID cues are actually ambiguous within a 'cone of confusion' taking in front–back and up–down positions at equal distances from the two ears [Begault, 1994, pp. 51–52].

Table 2.5 Aspects of the psychoacoustics of sound localization.

Cue	Description	Model
Distance		
Inverse square law	This is the default cue as the basis of a perception of distance, though psychoacoustic loudness rather than intensity may be more accurate. Amplitude change is inversely proportional to distance	Gain
Proportion of reverberation	More distant objects in an enclosed space are heard with a proportionally greater amount of reverberation to the direct signal	Ratio direct to reverb
Atmospheric effects	High frequencies are attenuated more when traveling in air (more distant sounds are low-pass filtered, lower detail). Sound waves are subtly distorted with distance due to differential pressure effects	Low-pass filter, nonlinearity
Location		
Interaural Time Difference (ITD)	The relative time of arrival of a sound is compared by signal phase difference between the ears. This typically functions for up to 690-microsecond delays, corresponding to a 23-cm distance of travel between the ears. The requirement to compare signal differences at precise times also makes ITD ineffectual as a cue above 1500 Hz (wavelength must be greater than the distance between the ears, or it is ambiguous)	Delay
Interaural Intensity Difference (IID)	The relative intensity of a sound is compared between the two ears; most effective over 500 Hz (wavelengths corresponding to head size or larger diffract without significant attenuation around the head, whilst smaller-wavelength sounds show the effect of head shadowing)	Gain, filter
Body filtering	Familiarity with sound archetypes and the filtering effect of your own body particularly assists with elevation and front–back judgment. Your pinnae (external ear folds) are biased to the front	Filter
Law of first wavefront, Haas effect or precedence effect	First arriving evidence of a sound takes precedence in determining source location (the evolutionary advantage is in suppressing confusion due to secondary reflections over direct signal). This is often used in public address to give the illusion of sound emanating from the speaker, by delaying any amplified signal	Delay
Head movement	Disambiguation is assisted by head movements; sounds in front and behind will pan in different directions when you move your head	Head tracking
Motion		
Doppler effect	A traveling sound source still emits sound at the speed of sound; wavefronts interact with the radial speed of travel relative to an observer to shift perceived frequency. Perceived frequency = emitted frequency $\left(\frac{s}{s+v}\right)$ where s is the speed of sound and v the relative radial velocity (positive when approaching, negative when receding)	Interpolating delay line
Parallax effect	A closer object moves faster across the field of hearing	Velocity
Room acoustic		
Early reflections	First reflections within 30–50 milliseconds after the direct signal give clues to room dimensions (and also source location within that room). Significant reflections (rather than diffuse general reverberation) outside of 30–50 milliseconds may be heard as distinct echoes	Multi-tap delay line
RT60	This is the reverberation time for the many diffuse reflections to die down by 60 dB relative to the original stimulus	All-pass and comb filters
Interaural decorrelation	A sound source is heard as more stimulating when the sound arriving at the two ears is subtly dissimilar; this favors longer (not wider) concert halls	All-pass filter

sense of sounds being external (this is why untreated audio played directly via headphones typically sounds as though it is inside the head). We are much less effective at localizing sound if we are unfamiliar with the identity of a sound, not having encountered that sound before in environmental contexts.

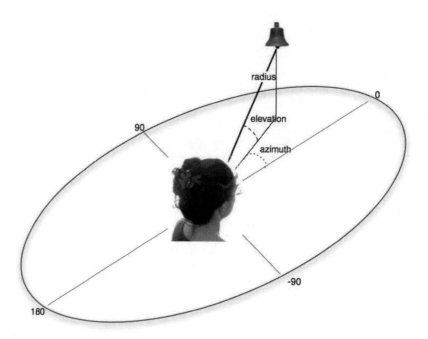

Figure 2.2   Spherical coordinate system for object positioning relative to the human head. The bell's position is determined by three parameters, the azimuth (angle of direction relative to face forwards on the flat horizontal plane at ear height, parallel to the ground), elevation (angle of elevation above or below your ear level) and direct (radial) distance to the object.

We can localize a fixed sound source or track a moving source. As you might suspect from the list of options in the table, there tend to be multiple cues with some redundancy, though not all spatial cues are equally effectively used by human audition, most being frequency dependent and degraded by certain environmental conditions like reverberation. Moore [2004, p. 266] notes that distance judgments are relatively inaccurate, with a 20% error rate for unfamiliar sources. There is also some (task-specific) evidence for binaural sluggishness [Moore, 2004, pp. 261–263], meaning that we are restricted in the speeds at which we can track moving objects. In ideal conditions our pinpointing of a source's direction on the horizontal azimuth plane can approach a minimum audible angle of 1° [Blauert, 1997, p. 39], but a moving source can only be tracked at 3° at most under optimal conditions [Begault, 1994, p. 50], with severe degradation based on the speed of the source (since this interacts with auditory integration times necessary to 'get a reading').

Room acoustics tend to come into play in most musical settings. Even outdoors, reflection from thermal layers of air, from the ground or water, from buildings and the natural landscape can have some effects upon auditory perception of sound location. The timescales of echoes tend to be much larger because of the greater distances involved, contributing to a sense of separate events rather than integrated reverberation. There is more open territory (free-field) within which to lose sound and thus faster dampening of sound energy. Reverberation is simply the reflection of pressure waves, and is most pronounced within an enclosed space. Each meeting of pressure wave and surface scatters sound waves, losing some energy in the collision each time (sounds don't reverberate forever outside of computer simulations). This is modeled by the frequency-dependent absorption coefficients of particular materials; essentially, how much like an open window the (perfect absorber) surfaces are. Stone tends to reflect a lot of sound energy, which is why cathedrals have long reverberation times of up to ten seconds or so. Optimum reverberation time varies for different musical tasks, from maximally damped anechoic chambers for pure acoustical tests, and the dry rooms of recording studio control rooms, up to the two-second or so reverberation times favored in concert hall acoustics (but not so conducive to comprehensibility of speech!). Plotting for a given sound source and observer the direct signal, isolated early reflections (under 100 milliseconds) and diffuse reverberation tail may require an involved geometrical computer model, such as a full sound wave tracing simulation. Or there are some simpler approximations using multi-tap delays and certain types of filter. Reverberation can interfere with exact localization cues even as it assists estimation of distance, and early reflections can be used in echolocation to identify obstacles and even their material properties. Multiple redundant cues, however, assist in localization even in the face of reverberant rooms or brief sounds [Moore, 2004].

2.5.2 Surround Sound Configurations and Multichannel Formats

Where speakers are simply localized point sources, we can use one channel of sound to drive each speaker. Certain computer-based musics are naturally sonified by available loudspeakers in this way, such as laptop or mobile phone speakers (both of which lack low-frequency reproduction), or other portable monitoring solutions.[13] Whether speakers adequately radiate sound waves into a room as if they were really natural acoustic objects coupled to the air, as we might desire in physical modeling of real instruments, is a further question. In this case, some special speaker designs, such as spherical and hemispherical speakers, can be brought into play [Roads, 1996; Trueman, 2007].

Otherwise, our dream might be to create virtual sound sources at arbitrary points in space, to command total control of a projection site, overcoming its own acoustic and substituting other spatial fields. This is easier said than effected. Table 2.6 lists some of the technological set-ups available in pursuing this goal. It is not an exhaustive list, but tries to indicate some of the chief options for spatialization. The ease of access to this technology varies;

---

[13] The discontinued Olympia SoundBug (released 2002) is attached to a surface, turning that surface into a soundboard when the bug vibrates. Sound quality is poor and dominated by the soundboard material, though there are newer variants such as the I-MU Vibro. It's difficult not to imagine applications in underground busking via the front plates of vending machines, or teledildonics.

wavefield synthesis in particular is an experimental system with a small number of current deployments. Nevertheless, whilst quadraphonic sound never caught on in the 1970s, the home studio of today could easily support the basic home cinema formats. An eight-channel output soundcard and eight monitors are enough to investigate most options in the table, though to gain any elevation, you will have to leave a horizontal plane . . . .

Table 2.6 Common spatialization technologies.

Scheme	Description
Monophonic (monaural)	Single channel – worked well enough for most people's experience of recordings and radio from 1876 to 1960 or so
Stereophonic	Two-channel playback, with a small sweet-spot stereo image (there are various further methods to try and widen the stereo image, or to simulate binaural cues without headphones)
Binaural	Two-channel signal for headphone playback; the effect of pinnae are already factored in, so the signal will not work naturally played back out loud as conventional stereo
Quadraphonic	Four channels: limited popularity in the 1970s
Octophonic	Eight channels surrounding an audience, a classic for electroacoustic music: typical arrangements are eight spaced on a circle by 45° (oriented with first speaker at 0° or at 22.5°), or the vertices of a cube to bring in a double quadraphonic set-up with elevation
5.1	The most famous cinema format, and popularly available on DVDs: five main channels at left, center, right, left surround and right surround, as well as one bass channel (the '.1'); suffers from poorer imaging at side and rear, since the two surround speakers span larger angles
Other cinema and theatre delivery standards	numspeakers.numsubwoofers including 6.1, 7.1, 10.2 and more; additional speakers may help with rear and side imaging – two subwoofers in 10.2 are intended to assist a feeling of envelopment
Game surround sound	Programming support for surround sound in games, often exploiting DSP chips on hardware soundcards, or low-level library code; audio engines include OpenAL, DirectSound3D, FMOD and more
Ambisonics	Speaker-independent encoding format for a 3D or horizontal sound field
Wavefield synthesis	Direct synthesis of sound wavefronts using hundreds of speakers: if you move, the sound image doesn't change location

The surround sound formats tend to require both a particular configuration of speakers (sometimes stipulated by standards bodies in terms of recommended angles and distances) as well as possible non-standard channel encoding and decoding for the signals. Although basic multichannel formats such as octophonic can be stored and played back using multiple mono or interleaved multichannel sound files, there are also alternative ways to encode signals for the sake of compression. In the **matrixing** method of the Dolby Surround home format unveiled in 1982, three or four speakers (left, right, optional center and rear) are driven from only two channels. The center channel is obtained as a scaled sum of the left and right; the rear is created from a scaled sum of opposing phase-shifted copies of the left and right.

It is also possible to make speaker-independent representations of sound adaptable to different speaker set-ups. Ambisonics[14] [Malham and Myatt, 1995; Fellgett, 1975; Gerzon, 1975] is one such system, encapsulating a three-dimensional sound field (there is a two-dimensional version as well). In the 'B-format', signals are encoded by the source mono signal W and the directional components on X, Y and Z axes giving the spatial orientation of a source at the receiver position. Decoding then allows this four-channel signal to be resolved into the available speakers, and can support accurate imaging over a large area of listeners. There must be at least four equally spaced speakers for horizontal reproduction and eight where elevation is also supported, but the rule of thumb for Ambisonics is that the more speakers that are available to be placed around the listening area, the better the reproduction. Ambisonics signals can be recorded directly, using the soundfield microphone, which combines an omnidirectional microphone with three directional cardioids, one for each of the front–back, left–right and up–down axes. Conversion of microphone output to other surround standards is also possible. Aside from the B-format WXYZ encoding, higher-order Ambisonics brings in additional encoding channels.

The cinema surround sound formats are by far the most popular options. Though they are non-uniform in their coverage of a sound field, our hearing is admittedly most sensitive at the front, and they arose in pragmatic circumstances of the demands of film, where dialog tends to trump spatial realism. The surround speakers in 5.1 usually just deliver effects to the side, rather than any convincing side or rear image. The possibility of rear imaging is only raised by the introduction of additional speakers, though again the configuration is biased to the front (see Figure 2.3). The .1 refers to the **low-frequency effects** (LFE) of the rumbling subwoofer. Our localization ability for low frequencies (under 100 Hz, which is .005 of 20 000 Hz rather than .1) is not good, particularly due to room modes, so the LFE channel speaker position is not critical. Cinema-derived surround sound formats are those most commonly supported in digital audio workstation software. For instance, specialized pan pots may allow the disposition of sound within the plane covered by the five full-range speakers in 5.1. DAW software is less comfortable with natively supporting encoded surround signals, but some translation plug-ins (such as Ambisonics Virtual Studio Technology (VST) plug-ins created at the University of York) are available to support work with other formats.

Different projects vary in their requirements for the quality of virtual acoustic space that can be conjured up, and may turn to different technical solutions. It is important to bear in mind the influence of human space perception, room acoustics, speaker design and configuration as well as the spatialization algorithms themselves. Not all systems can offer equally successful immersion across a large audience, and few cope naturally when audience

---

[14]The Latin root of this term literally means 'surround sound'.

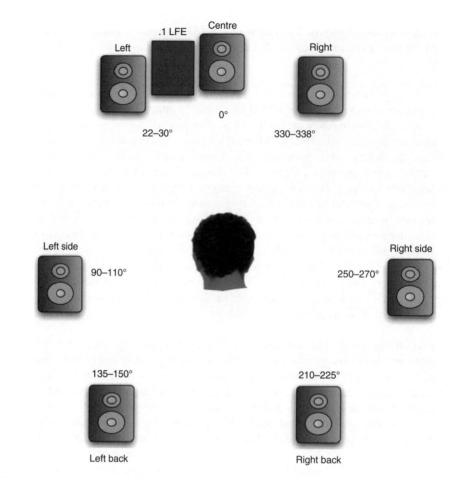

Figure 2.3   7.1 speaker configuration. The angles in degrees note the 'official' speaker positions relative to an observer in the sweet spot. The 5.1 configuration is the same, with the removal of the back speaker pair.

members move their heads. If delays are not carefully handled, the precedence effect is always a danger, where the nearest speaker tends to be assigned as a default location because the first direct sound arrives from that location. In some situations where microphones and speakers amplify instrumentalists or actors, the amplified signal can be delayed slightly so as to allow the first arriving sound waves to come from the original source. The electroacoustic rhetoric on the dream of flying sounds through space is partially undermined by results in perception that point to a less than acute tracking of a moving source in spatial hearing, which after all evolved in environments dissimilar to tightly controlled concert halls [Moore, 2004]. Manufacturers' claims for surround sound may often exceed reality, and psychoacoustic testing can hardly keep up with the proliferation of formats.

2.6 RECORDING TIPS AND TRICKS

This section is intentionally short, not just because there are innumerable other books which seek to teach you the art, but because it would be impossible to lay down a final list of strict instructions on how to record. Audio engineering is a creative task which fully engages the human auditory system. Most recordings take place in social settings, and are as bound to different cultural conventions as any music making. Sound engineering requires working within competing constraints, where there may be no ideal solution. Getting a good mix whilst a lead guitarist is breathing down your neck about the prominence of their fretwork is an exercise in patience!

We must also differentiate between at least four tasks in studio work, including recording of sound itself, studio experimentation and composition, mixing and mastering. Each has its own dangers. There are innumerable nuisances that waste time, from getting the perfect snare drum sound, effect or synthesis patch, to spending eight hours of a paid recording session fiddling with guitar tuning (an extreme but true example relayed to me by the producer Pat Collier). It is also easy to make your job more difficult at later stages in a recording chain by the attitude of 'fix it in the mix'. If you let through lower-quality materials early on it costs you time later, and in the worst cases the problem may not be solvable no matter how much AutoTune and hand splicing you throw at it.

There are some basic recording standards and principles that tend to operate in practice, such as:

- Keep a high signal to noise ratio. When you record, maximize the signal you can get without overloading; never record close to the noise floor. The more noise is around in your parts, the more is there to pile up when layering.

- Avoid digital distortion through overload; keep headroom at the top of the mix rather than risk hard clipping. Floating point audio in software helps avoid this danger, and judicious use of a limiter may guard against occasional peaks.

- Observe basic health and safety when dealing with electrical equipment, and continued noise levels. Take breaks for the sake of your ears; you should rarely be monitoring at high levels anyway, 85 dB SPL being a recommended reference level for 0 dB on your master fader.

- Be aware of basic principles of acoustics and psychoacoustics that impact on recording practice. These include room acoustics (for monitoring, and microphone placement) and equal loudness curves (for explanation of why mixes change at different playback levels, and why certain frequency regions of the ear are more sensitive to EQ).

- The more parts you are mixing, the more the competition for spectral space, and the greater the potential for one part to mask another. This can be alleviated somewhat when multichannel mixing is used, since auditory streams are well differentiated by spatial location (such benefits are lost in mono mixdowns, which is a reason to check your mix on multiple systems if it is meant for universal release). Another approach is to filter signals so that unimportant spectral components are hidden for each part, preventing the pile-up of spectral clutter.

For mixing in particular, I couldn't do better than paraphrase the advice of Leider [2004, pp. 170–186] some of whose chief principles I reiterate here:

- Use comparative mixing – check a reference mix in the style you are aiming for.

- Check on multiple monitor set-ups: high-quality flat EQ monitors for your main studio work, but lower-quality speakers to hear how it might sound in real-world situations!

- Don't overuse effects or pile up tracks for the sake of it; less is more.

- Consider the cognitive primacy of vocal parts.

- Apply equalizing by cutting frequencies, not boosting.

He discusses many further issues, such as noise gates, possible phase problems (the reason signal inversion is offered within systems, to stop destructive interference), spatial audio mixing and microphone placement. The Further Reading section for this chapter contains other references which will give you more material on these topics.

Recording work is prone to its own fads, with particular production styles becoming prevalent at particular times. Production style can involve choices both in the use of recording equipment and in the musical contribution of a producer to arrangement and composition. From Phil Spector's mono-radio-friendly Wall of Sound in the early 1960s to the skipping beats in Timbaland's R&B production in the 1990s, exciting production often combines musical innovations and studio wizardry; to summarize Brian Eno's position, the studio is an instrument in itself [Cox and Warner, 2004]. As already discussed in Chapter 1, a 'loudness war' in CD mastering and radio broadcast is one distraction from sensitive production in current popular music. Even electroacoustic art music has its own particular fetishes for desired listening qualities, and whilst there are many schools of thought, prior art and taste does tend to influence sound engineering as much as tenets of psychoacoustics. This is consistent with the higher-level content of music, after all.

2.7 SAMPLING

One of the most immediate and fun applications in computer music is the capture and manipulation of audio data. **Sampling** is the act of digitizing an analog signal, but also suggests the games that can be played once audio is in the form of digital samples. A sample technically refers to an individual number stored as part of a digital data stream, but colloquially it has come to mean a complete file of digital data ready for use. With so many files around, whole sample CDs' worth, uncounted web pages' worth, a mass of recordings in digital format indifferently await refashioning and repurposing. In short, any recording is up for grabs for audio collage. The ramifications for copyright are discussed below, as well as some of the history of sampling practice, and the associated technology.

2.7.1 A History of Sampling

The issue of recordings as musical material substantially pre-dates digital technology for audio. The popular turntable is a bona fide electronic musical instrument, treating vinyl as the source of sound to push and caress [Jordà, 2005].[15] Early experiments and recognition of record players, by such figures as Ottorino Resphigi, László Moholy-Nagy, Paul Hindemith and John Cage are well known [Cox and Warner, 2004]. An early school of recording manipulation which is often singled out is that of *musique concrète*, whose instigator Pierre Schaeffer and collaborators organized a concert entirely using turntables in 1948, demonstrating live mixing of sources. Having started the hard way with a disc cutter to record each new generation of sound manipulation, the French pioneers adopted the magnetic tape recorder in 1951 with, no doubt, some relief at the new convenience and precision of editing allowed! To focus on the turntable alone is thus to miss many other exciting movements. Halim El-Dabh's wire recorder experiments from 1944, Les Paul's pioneering of the overdub and multitrack, or early experiments with drawn sound on film stock in Russia, Canada and Germany demonstrate other musical innovations in the use of recording technology.

Schaeffer, in some of his *etudes*, dabbled in the manipulation of existing classical recordings. When sampling has allowed the capture and reuse of existing recordings, whose copyright owners have not necessarily given permission, controversy has arisen. The term sampling has become closely associated with such practices. A steadily increasing flow of examples of such exploration in processed sound can be acknowledged, and is summarized in Table 2.7. Whilst earlier experiments in art music did not raise great fuss, appearances of sampling in popular recording have been much more closely tracked, registering the greater sums of money involved. When 1970s DJs began to push the manipulation of recordings into a new vibrant cultural form in itself, particularly in hiphop originating from the Bronx, the controversy over reuse of other artists' materials was set to reach a wider stage. By the beginning of the 1990s the law suits had really started to kick in. The unrestricted sampledelica of De La Soul's *Three Feet High and Rising* (1989), to give one example, was to be reined in. Such a record, if intended for commercial release in the present time, would probably require so much copyright clearance as to seriously compromise its production!

Ironically, the point at which sample manipulation is most readily available to the greatest range of producers, the current era of computer-based virtual studios, sees the most sensitive

---

[15]Digital turntables have encroached a little here too, though the vinyl fetish may amuse the traditionalists indefinitely.

Table 2.7   Selected examples from the history of sampling.

Year	Artist	Release	Notes
1948	Pierre Schaeffer	*Étude aux Chemins de Fer*	Did the railway siding give permission?
1956	Buchanan and Goodman	*The Flying Saucer*	Novelty record licensed under radio laws of the time; combines a story about visiting UFOs with 1950s diner hits
1961	James Tenney	*Collage #1* ('Blue Suede')	Art music, so Elvis didn't notice!
1965	Daphne Oram	*Pulse Persephone*	Repurposes samples from world instrument recordings collection
1969	The Beatles	*Revolution 9*	Electroacoustic art music branded by the most popular group of the time
1981	Grandmaster Flash	*Adventures of Grandmaster Flash on the Wheels of Steel*	One-take demo of masterful mixing and scratching
1982	Afrika Bambaataa and the Soul Sonic Force	*Planet Rock*	Electro anthem, with thanks to Kraftwerk
1983	Double D and Steinski	*Lesson 1*	How to win a remix competition using classic hiphop materials
1989	John Oswald	*Plunderphonics*	All undistributed copies destroyed by the Canadian Recording Industry Association. Story and album available from www.plunderphonics.com
1990	Public Enemy	*Fear of a Black Planet*	BombSquad production makes extensive use of samples
2004	Danger Mouse	*The Grey Album*	'Cease and desist' orders soon follow if tampering with the Beatles canon and mixing it with Jay-Z's a cappella raps
2004	DJ Food (Strictly Kev and Paul Morley)	*Raiding the 20th Century*	Internet release; features many famous mash-ups. Available at http://www.ubu.com/sound/dj_food.html

restrictions on copyrighted material. This has not thwarted the many underground mash-ups, which twist together new combinations of existing songs in delightful inventions. The trick, possibly, is not to seek profit; beware of any situation where you find yourself able to pay lawyers' fees. Yet there are also cases of freely distributed material being the subject of destruction orders, such as the famous example of John Oswald's *Plunderphonics* album of 1989 [Cox and Warner, 2004; Landy, 2007].

2.7.2 Copyright

To begin with a caveat: since copyright laws vary from country to country and over time, this book seeks in no way to outline the current state of the law wherever you are reading this, nor to offer legal advice of any guaranteed validity.

Intellectual property (IP) rights are, in the most elevated sense, there to protect the creative output of inventors, artists and authors, particularly where rights to copy intellectual ideas underline or form the basis of trade. They are also the source of much controversy, pertaining to their interaction with commerce, their assignment and trading beyond the originators of ideas, the time duration of protection[16] and other legal complexities. It is tempting to always see them as an obstruction to new work, since they provide an additional layer of complication between inspiration and exploitation of an invention. The opportunity for individual artists or researchers to engage with materials within another's IP is usually mediated by some possibility of 'fair use' or 'fair dealing', almost always restricted to non-commercial research, teaching purposes or personal copying. Commercial release of copyright-breaching music is of course not to be undertaken lightly; IP is always most aggressively defended where larger sums of money are involved.

Copyright is a reality of current commercial musical practice, and has been most actively protected in Western culture for around two hundred years.[17] The chief expressions covered by musical copyright law are publishing rights, concerning sheet music or lyrics, the copyright of a particular recording, and performing rights for broadcast or public performance. Societies exist to administer the rights of registered copyright holders pertaining to these. Though official status can help to assert particular rights through legal channels, basic copyright is automatic in countries which subscribe to the Berne Convention of 1886.

Yet copyright has always had critics. John Oswald, the Canadian guru of sampling, is prominent amongst dissident voices in favor of fighting restrictions on sampling imposed by commercial music [Oswald, 2004]. As he has argued, 'if creativity is a field, copyright is the fence' [Cutler, 2004, p. 152].

Alternative licenses have been proposed, with varying restrictions, sometimes under the banner of **copyleft** as a play on copyright. Free software licenses including the MIT (X11) license and the BSD (Berkeley Software Distribution) licenses simply guarantee some minimal rights to keep library code available in the public domain, but not overly restrict its uses. Further schemes defend open-source software or products from commercial use, and allow the release of music where certain rights to remix and reuse are enshrined rather than

---

[16]This has steadily increased since 18th century laws. The Statute of Anne (1710) allowed for 14 years, with an optional extension of 14; the 1998 Copyright Term Extension Act in the United States increased an individual author's exclusive publishing rights to their lifetime plus 70 years!

[17]This is also the basis of an argument against copyright; since Shakespeare and Homer got by without copyright, why would creativity dry up if current authors were denied its protections? The more complicated financial, publishing and communications base of modern society might form the crux of a counter argument. I am not aware of case studies (perhaps undertaken in less legislated regions of the world) that probe these issues with real data; it is difficult just to turn off copyright for a year to see what effect that has!

discouraged. These include, for software, the famous GNU General Public License (GNU GPL), as well as, for recordings, the suite of Creative Commons (CC) licenses. Various other options exist for open-source movements and copyright activists to pursue in licensing. Few creators are so unconcerned for ego, plagiarism, or other appropriation as to anonymously release works without any license at all, as might be done in a spirit of immediately enabling all future human creativity.

Controversy in this field is pronounced for digital products, which are so easy to copy that copyright law has at times been left far behind. The unfettered swapping of MP3s online in the late 1990s led to a series of reactions from the music industry. One contemporary bugbear is Digital Rights Management (DRM), the imposition of additional protective layers on files which may even require the use of proprietary playback engines. Yet consumer distaste for DRM has often led to companies stepping down. This situation is analyzed more thoroughly when we explore digital music distribution later in the book (see Section 7.1.5).

The sampling war has already been waged, reaching its peak in late-1980s and 1990s legal judgments [Keller, 2008]. No permanent perfect line dividing fair use from exploitation could be drawn out, since social context shifts with time, and each new musical instance has its own uniqueness to argue. Yet the practical side is that copyright clearance must be obtained for any sample from an existing recording noticeable in your own works. Clearance should be obtained in advance of release, to avoid costly legal battles; since there are no consistent licensing prices, rerecording your own version of material may be cheaper than the fee you would be charged for using an original.

It will be extremely interesting to see what ultimate balance, if any, can be made in licensing recordings. Creative Commons is a proactive approach to the problem, but it is likely that there will continue to be an oscillation between business interests that favor tight licensing and the creative interests that cannot resist tinkering. In the long term (at least until lobbyists manage to make copyright perpetual) everything falls out of copyright, so if you have some particular composition of genius that uses uncleared samples, you could bury it for a hundred years or so and hope it will become popular (and relevant) then!

Distaste for commerce, and particularly larger-scale corporations, is intimately tied up with arguments against copyright. Making popular music inevitably leads to meeting corporate lawyers; making experimental music may just keep you below the radar.

2.7.3 Sample Playback

Having dealt with historical and legal issues, it is now time for the practical side. Sample playback is probably the most popular form of sound rendering, since it is highly efficient (just play back the original stored digital data) and as high quality as the original recording as long as we play back the samples at the original sample rate. You might wonder why we don't just use sample playback for everything. The reason is that the direct recall of sample data is not in itself a particularly flexible resynthesis method.[18]

Nevertheless, a digital sound recording can easily be played back at different rates from the original capture. This facility is at the expense of introducing amplitude distortion, aliasing and spectral envelope shifting which increases with the change of playback rate from the baseline. The most famous example of spectral change is the 'munchkinization' or 'chipmunk' effect as a vocal sample is played back faster, where the normal formants (spectral envelope peaks) of speech are shifted directly up in frequency until it no longer sounds natural. Intuitively, the spectral shift occurs because running through samples in a smaller time means reducing the period of any periodic sounds, hence increasing their frequency.[19]

To effect a playback rate change, we scan through the source data at a different rate, given by a ratio relative to normal playback [Puckette, 2007, pp. 32–36]. A ratio of one is equivalent to playback at the original sampling rate. In order to get through more of the source in a given time (faster playback) we would need to skip through the data faster, potentially missing out original samples. A playback ratio of two would mean twice as fast, equivalent to taking every second sample. For slower playback, we must read through the source samples at a slower rate, giving fractional ratios below one. Figure 2.4 depicts the idea of a read pointer, which increments with each output sample, in general by a non-integer amount; this increment *is* the playback ratio. Since the next value we need to output will not fall exactly on an original sample position, but between the samples, various schemes have been introduced to cope [Moore, 1990, pp. 164–165]. These include truncation (take the sample immediately before now), rounding (take the nearest) and interpolation using different degrees of polynomial, including first (linear), second (quadratic), third (cubic) and higher. Interpolation is the most expensive solution in computational cost, but gives the least amplitude distortion. As for aliasing, this is more noticeable for extreme ratios, especially where there is a lot of energy near the Nyquist frequency to begin with. There is an intimate connection here to the problem of resampling audio to run at different rates, as will be tackled in Section 4.1.1, and an appropriate use of an antialiasing low-pass filter based on the repitching ratio can avoid introducing aliasing distortion.

Sample-based synthesis exploits the ability to repitch by a change of playback rate, to create simulations of existing instruments from digital recordings. Because the artifacts of repitching are clear outside of small playback rate variations – as a rule of thumb, less than half an octave, though this is dependent on sound and interpolation scheme – multiple sources sampled at different pitches within an instrument's compass are used. In fact, in order to create high-quality models which reflect the change of timbre with amplitude and excitation mechanism, **multi-sampling** utilizes multiple source sounds even at a single

---

[18]That is, without further more advanced processing, which requires audio analysis; we shall get there in later chapters.

[19]For a more mathematical insight, consider the single digital sinusoid $\sin(\omega n/R + \phi)$. If the playback ratio is λ, then the change to the sine formula is to $\sin(\omega \lambda n/R + \phi)$ because at each sample we now move λn samples rather than n. This multiplies the sinusoid (angular) frequency by λ to $\omega \lambda$. Because all signals can be represented by a spectral decomposition of sines, the playback ratio will multiply all the frequencies of all the sines, shifting the spectral envelope by $\log_2(\lambda)$ octaves.

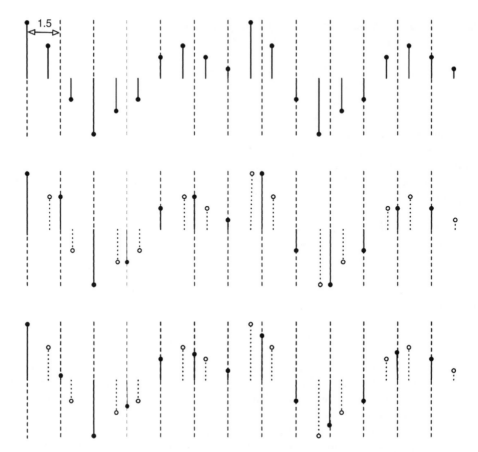

Figure 2.4 Digital audio data being played back at 1.5 times the original rate. The dashed vertical lines show the position of a read pointer which runs 1.5 times faster than the original source sample separation. The top chart shows the original signal overlaid with read pointer positions. The middle chart shows the effect of choosing the output sample values using truncation (take the previous sample). Output samples have filled heads, and the original samples are shown for reference as open circles with dotted tails. The bottom chart demonstrates linear interpolation: the output sample is halfway between the two flanking original sample values when the read pointer falls between original sample indices.

pitch. Software samplers can extend this to multi-sampled instruments limited in source data size only by RAM, and with streaming, local hard disk size or accessible network space.[20] By determining subtle loop points within a sample, saving on storage space and the modeling of user-controllable sustain is possible. In the typical MIDI sequencing paradigm, an individual MIDI note-on event triggers digital audio playback from the start of the sampled segment

---

[20]The patience of the recording engineer who prepares all the source data is perhaps an issue as well . . .

held in memory, which loops within markers until a MIDI note-off allows progression to the release portion of the sound.

Through such facilities, and buoyed by the basic efficiency of the mechanism, sampling has formed a standard source model for many digital synthesizers, from hardware synths to computer game audio engines. Amplitude envelopes, filters and other signal modifiers can be added to give additional musical control over the course of output sound. Source recordings also play a large part in other synthesis techniques, such as sample-based granular synthesis, which essentially forms large cloud sounds from many small 1–100 millisecond component extracts [Truax, 1988; Roads, 2001]. Rather than new forms made from many small parts, larger sources of the length of entire songs are also readily manipulable. The live playback of existing recordings, focusing on the mixing of multiple tracks with the addition of processing, is a mainstay of software for DJs and producers, such as the commercial Ableton Live and Traktor or the open-source Mixxx. Breaking long recordings down into component events more suitable for control in instruments is also a concern of much current software. This is most effective when applied to drum loops, as in Propellerheads' ReCycle. The processes by which digital audio data can be analyzed to effect beat matching, or to discover useful segments, will concern us in Chapter 3.

In sourcing digital audio data, there are a gazillion samples available on the Internet, though not all are in salubrious places. So let me start you off with a recent sample library initiative of great utility, created for the One Laptop Per Child project: http://wiki.laptop.org/go/Sound_samples. Another worthy project is the Freesound repository of Creative Commons licensed audio (www.freesound.org). DVDs stuffed with samples are often given away with home recording magazines, or can be purchased. Both open and more proprietary formats are around for the storage and transfer of sample data meant for hardware and software sampler instruments. The REX2 format for the aforementioned ReCycle stores entry points into isolated event segments in the data, as well as the sample data. Other formats support sample-based synthesis instruments ready for MIDI control, such as SoundFonts or Downloadable Sounds (DLS) [Rumsey and McCormick, 2006, p. 410]. Since such a common synthesis methodology is so widely supported, MIDI files can be shared with the sample-based instruments which allow their exact reproduction, circumventing issues of different implementations in General MIDI. This is the basis of the MIDI standard Extensible Music Format (XMF), but which itself merely imitates the general principles of the MOD (module) sequence+samples format established in the 1980s for tracker programs.

With so much digital audio data around, inventive ways of sourcing, repurposing and cataloging it remain a central concern of computer music and will continue to be confronted elsewhere in the book.

2.8 SUMMARY

This chapter has highlighted the central role of the computer in modern recording practice. Despite offering a few humble words of advice, my goal in this chapter has not been to influence every aspect of your recording work; there are a myriad of other texts to pursue here on the art of production, microphone technique, location recording and the like.

MIDI's persistence, despite its early adoption and manifest flaws, mean that it cannot be discounted in the present era. It is a legacy technology supported by reams of hardware, by some sensor interfaces, and as an internal representation in much software.

Digital audio workstations have transformed the world's studios, and many more bedrooms besides. Homes have become equipped with multichannel formats such as Dolby 5.1, and spatial audio has finally met some of its promise in the mass market, albeit skewed more by the imperatives of film over experimental music.

Sampled data is at the heart of the most common synthesis engines and an unavoidable basis of digital recording software. We have encountered the myriad audio file formats, and had a first glimpse of sound synthesis in the practices of sampling and sample-based instruments. Perfect reproduction has implications in society; we have strayed into the muddy fields of intellectual property. There may be no quick fix here to the present legal jumble, but a basic awareness of the vested interests is of some use, particularly in commercial work.

2.9 EXERCISES

1. Explore the speed limits of MIDI. If you have a multitimbral hardware synthesizer, you may be able to flood it with messages by very fast sequences of notes in multiple tracks. Virtual instrument plug-ins running entirely within a software sequencer may prove a little more robust since they can inherently overcome MIDI cabling transfer limits; your computer CPU might be more the issue. Nevertheless, probe the possibilities of sequences of MIDI notes and expressive controller information which far surpass human productive capability.

2. Choose a few different recordings of widely different production styles and genres. Taking care not to play things too loudly so as to disturb others and your own

hearing, try playing back each track at quiet, medium and loud volumes (70, 85 and 100 dB SPL). How does your perception of the mix change?

3. How large in megabytes is a quadraphonic recording that is four minutes and 32 seconds long, recorded at a sampling rate of 48 000 Hz and with a bit depth of 24?

4. How long in seconds is a 128 kilobits-per-second (mono) MP3 file which takes up 3.45 megabytes? Assuming the file was converted to a .wav file (16-bit, 44 100 Hz sampling rate), how much larger would it be?

5. Compare headphone listening with listening out loud, to the same track. In what ways do headphones lead to you hearing sound at the center of your head? If you were lucky enough to play binaurally prepared material, how convincing was the illusion, and what happened when you played it over speakers? Can a mix be prepared that works effectively for both headphones and speaker presentation?

6. As a manipulation task in your favorite Digital Audio Workstation software, take an old Beatles recording, one of the ones in the old stereo mixing style where instruments are panned hard left or right. How easy is it to separate out and isolate particular parts? Can you make creative use of EQ or use other tricks to further clean up the sources? Why is this task hard in general with more contemporary mixing styles? (We shall return to these issues in Chapter 3.)

7. Source some a cappella vocals from the Internet, perhaps from Freesound. Taking your Beatles materials from the previous exercise, create a mash-up which combines these different elements.

8. Download and explore the open-source Mixxx software (Windows, Mac and Linux all supported, www.mixxx.org). Using this software, how well can you mix electronic dance music, as compared with late-18th-century classical music?

9. Carry out your own original piece of copyright research (plagiarizing, whilst ironic in this instance, is not condoned). You might investigate how much it has cost to clear a famous sample, when permission has been sought before the event, and when permission was sought after the release of a recording.

10. Using just pen and paper, design a layout for your own sequencer. What type of musical information will your sequencer treat, and how will it be represented onscreen? Consider how screen space will relate to the passing of time; will you favor horizontal or vertical, or find alternative solutions?

2.10

FURTHER READING

Begault, D. R. (1994). *3-D Sound for Virtual Reality and Multimedia*. Academic Press, Cambridge, MA.

Blauert, J. (1997). *Spatial Hearing: The Psychophysics of Human Sound Localization*, Revised edition. MIT Press, Cambridge, MA.

Collins, M. (2004). *Choosing and Using Audio and Music Software: A Guide to the Major Software Applications for Mac and PC*. Focal Press, Oxford.

Davies, H. (1996). A history of sampling. *Organised Sound*, 1(1):3–11.

Huber, D. M. and Runstein, R. E. (2005). *Modern Recording Techniques*, 6th Edition. Focal Press/Elsevier, Burlington, MA.

Katz, B. (2007). *Mastering Audio: The Art and the Science*, 2nd Edition. Focal Press, Oxford.

Leider, C. (2004). *Digital Audio Workstation*. McGraw-Hill, New York, NY.

MIDI Manufacturers' Association site www.midi.org

Owsinski, B. (2006). *The Mixing Engineer's Handbook*, 2nd Edition. Thomson Course Technology, Boston, MA.

Pohlmann, K. C. (2005). *Principles of Digital Audio*, 5th Edition. McGraw-Hill, New York.

Rumsey, F. (2001). *Spatial Audio*. Focal Press, Oxford.

Rumsey, F. and McCormick, T. (2006). *Sound and Recording: An Introduction*, 5th Edition. Focal Press, Oxford.

Selfridge-Field, E. (ed) (1997). *Beyond MIDI: The Handbook of Musical Codes*. MIT Press, Cambridge, MA.

Watkinson, J. (2001). *The Art of Digital Audio*, 3rd Edition. Focal Press, Oxford.

White, P. (2002). *Recording and Production Techniques*, 2nd Edition. Sanctuary Publishing Limited, London.

http://www.wikirecording.org/Main_Page

Chapter 3

Analysis

'*S'il existe une machine à calcul pour calibrer la musique, nous en possédons une, prodigieuse, portative, économique: Messieurs, c'est notre oreille.* [If there exists a machine for calculating and grading music, we all possess one, prodigious, handy, economical: good people, it is our ear.]'

Pierre Schaeffer [Schaeffer, 2005, p. 27]

OBJECTIVES

This chapter covers:

- spectral analysis using the Fourier transform;
- further time-frequency analysis methods;
- auditory modeling and machine listening;
- feature extraction;
- the transcription problem.

3.1 SOUND ANALYSIS

Audio analysis is an important application domain for the computer, enabling both general insight into the structure of sound, and more specific extraction of musical features from audio data. While there is no a priori need to ground analysis procedures in models of the human auditory system, and we shall encounter more general signal models from Fourier analysis to wavelets, auditory models are a prominent strand in this field. Biological auditory systems are marvels of miniaturization and processing, and an inspiration to researchers. A substantial aim in this domain is to bring **machine listening**[1] closer to human listening, by linking audio analysis models to human auditory capabilities.

Analysis is often coupled with synthesis, to varying degrees. Some methods allow resynthesis from their analysis information, with theoretically perfect reproduction; others give useful viewpoints on the signal, which may not necessarily allow the original signal to be recovered but do provide controller information for musical processes. If two sounds have been analyzed, it is possible to consider hybrid sounds which combine their characteristics, creating sound morphs with respect to the analysis model. Analysis may lift us from one representation of a signal to another; we have already mentioned the Fourier transform as moving from the time domain to the frequency domain, and the inverse Fourier transform taking us back again to the time domain. Novel processing effects can be achieved in the frequency domain in between these transform steps, before a final resynthesis. Or frequency domain information can be directly created, and then translated back to the time domain. So this chapter is not self contained, but will inform many other parts of the book.

3.2 FOURIER ANALYSIS AND THE PHASE VOCODER

We shall only deal with discrete signals in the digital domain, and will describe the Discrete Fourier Transform (DFT). Because all interesting sounds vary in their statistics with time – changing frequencies, onsets and offsets rather than staying **stationary**[2] – we must take a series of snapshots of the signal. Each snapshot, a **window** of a certain number of samples long, is the subject of a separate DFT. When interpreting the results, the signal is assumed stationary *within each snapshot*, which is a much lighter condition than assuming no significant changes throughout the whole signal's lifetime! The windows can overlap, but are typically spaced evenly in time and each have the same size; recall the sliding window procedure detailed in Figure 1.10.

As part of the implementation of such a procedure, there is a cunning algorithm called the **Fast Fourier Transform** (FFT) that speeds up the calculation.[3] Since the FFT is so

---

[1]The term was coined by researchers at the Music, Mind and Machine lab at the Massachusetts Institute of Technology (http://sound.media.mit.edu/) and used in associated doctoral theses by notables such as Rowe [1993] and Scheirer [2000], among others.

[2]Technically, stationary signals are those whose statistics are locked; a sinusoid still varies in amplitude, but it has a stable phase, frequency and magnitude. It is always possible to apply the Fourier transform to a signal whose characteristics are rapidly changing; it is just harder to interpret the results!

[3]How it does this can be pursued by the interested reader elsewhere [Hayes, 1999; Loy, 2007b], the short answer being that it uses a divide and conquer strategy; window sizes of powers of two allow multiple binary subdivisions of the calculations. This allows a speed-up from $O(N^2)$ to $O(N \log N)$. Specialized FFT libraries are available, such as FFTW, which can even provide efficient calculation when the window length isn't a power of two.

ubiquitous in implementations, you will often see reference to 'taking an FFT' or 'FFT analysis'. Each individual FFT is said to give rise to one FFT **frame** of spectral data.

When a sequence of DFTs is carried out across a signal so that every sample appears in at least one window, the result is the **Short-Time Fourier Transform** (STFT, also called the short-term Fourier transform).

3.2.1 Short-time Fourier Transform

Any practical discrete implementation of a Fourier transform must set a basic analysis frequency. When we discussed the Fourier transform in Section 1.2.4, we already knew the answer as to which fundamental frequency to use; it was that corresponding to the period of the waveform. But what if we do not know the answer in advance?[4] What if we are analyzing a sound which is inharmonic, or a signal combining different periodic sounds?

Perhaps you cannot analyze a non-periodic sound with Fourier analysis? Actually, you can make an attempt, and a sensible thing to do is to use a large period, corresponding to a small fundamental frequency. The hope is that this period is large compared with the periods of the component frequencies of the sound you will measure. The Fourier analysis can only measure the energy at multiples of this fundamental, but by taking a low enough fundamental, the harmonic multiples can be made close enough together for practical purposes. While there will be issues with frequency components in the analysis target 'falling between the gaps', with a worst case of halfway between analysis harmonics, the signal energy will be distributed over the analysis harmonics so as to indirectly reveal the spectral presence of a sound.

Consider a sampling rate R of 44 100 Hz, and a segment of duration one second, which as a period corresponds to a frequency of 1 Hz. If this were the basis for a Fourier analysis, we would measure the energy at frequency multiples of 1 Hz, so at 1 Hz, 2 Hz, 3 Hz, ... all the way up to ... the Nyquist frequency of 22 050. Each harmonic of 1 Hz is called a frequency **bin** or **band** of the transform.

The next problem is that the input sound to your analysis may be constantly changing in its statistics – in technical terms, **non-stationary**. There are two conflicting requirements here. A small fundamental frequency (large period) means a good analysis resolution. But to interpret the results we assume that the signal is stationary during that whole period. On the other hand, a large fundamental analysis frequency will correspond to a much smaller period, within which it is more likely that a sound is not varying substantially. This is a fundamental tradeoff, where temporal resolution is set against frequency resolution, and underlies any time-frequency analysis [Loy, 2007b, pp. 131–2].

---

[4]We could employ some sort of initial periodicity detection algorithm to set up a **pitch-synchronous** analysis. Such algorithms do exist, but there are few sounds which always have a well-defined single fundamental frequency, and some pitch detection algorithms tend to use exactly the procedure about to be described as a way to find the period!

Mathematical Basis of the Discrete STFT

The Fourier transform decomposes a signal onto a basis of sinusoids. Given a frequency for a sinusoid, the analysis compares the input signal with both a pure sine and a pure cosine wave of this frequency. This determines an amplitude and a phase that indicate how well the input matches that basis element. Now, there is a convenient way to do both comparisons at once that utilizes complex numbers, and, specifically, Euler's identity ($e^{i\theta} = \cos(\theta) + i\sin(\theta)$). If you are new to complex numbers you will either have to take this on trust, or pursue the matter elsewhere [Loy, 2007b].

Let's get it out the way and just state:

$$X_t(\omega) = \sum_{n=0}^{N-1} \text{window}(n)x(t+n)e^{-i\omega n} \tag{3.1}$$

The $e^{-i\omega n}$ term is a phasor, which travels around the unit circle in the complex plane as n is incremented. Essentially, this represents the sine and cosine terms at the given angular frequency ω. Now x is the input signal to analyze; a segment of this input will be measured here which begins at sample time t and extends for $N-1$ more samples. The window function acts as an envelope on the input segment to reduce discontinuities at the window edges, which also has the effect of weighting particular times in their contribution to the analysis [Hamming, 1989]. The equation compares the windowed signal to a complex phasor (and thus, a sine and cosine) at the frequency to be probed, to measure the degree of response. The output of the sum is the complex number $X_t(\omega)$. This value can be interpreted as describing the amplitude and phase of a sinusoid which could best represent the input's spectral character at the particular frequency probed.

For a real input signal, the discrete STFT can now be written:

$$X_m(k) = \sum_{n=0}^{N-1} \text{window}(n)x(mH+n)e^{-i2\pi(k/N)n}, \quad k=0,\ldots,N/2, \quad m=0,\ldots,M-1$$

$$\tag{3.2}$$

Rather than Equation 3.1, which described an analysis for any starting sample t, and any angular frequency ω, this equation makes explicit the discrete nature of the process. We carry out a Fourier transform at each frame m within a total of M frames. Each frame tackles N samples, and we hop by H samples between frames. Thus, frame m begins at sample mH and totals N samples as indicated in the summation. The variable k refers to the **bin number**, and we speak of the kth bin. If $k = 1$ the frequency probed is the fundamental analysis frequency for the Fourier analysis; all other bins are centered at integer multiples of this fundamental, where k is the multiple in question (that is, the harmonic number).

For real input, k only goes up to the Nyquist frequency (any higher frequency components correspond to those below Nyquist, as in the sampling theorem). The angular frequency is therefore $\omega = 2\pi(k/N)$; it is written explicitly in the equation to show what would be required to compute the transform.

For each DFT on a real signal we put in N input samples, and seem to get back $N/2 + 1$ complex numbers. The output numbers $X(k)$ for $k = 0$ (DC) and $k = N/2$ (Nyquist) are both real, essentially because phase means nothing in these two cases. So there are actually N outputs for N inputs. Each remaining complex number has an amplitude and a phase. Computer FFT algorithms which calculate the DFT sometimes work in place, returning the N outputs packed in the memory where the N inputs were given; they often place the Nyquist component as the imaginary part of the dc component to achieve this.

The equations as presented here have been selected as best elucidating the process, but there are other forms which demonstrate further facets of the theory. The interested reader is referred to more detailed treatments elsewhere [Jaffe, 1987a,b; Moore, 1990; Roads, 1996; Serra, 1997a; Loy, 2007b].

We are closing in on a set of parameters for the STFT. One more concept is required before stating an algorithm for calculating it. The assumption that a signal can be neatly parceled up into segments, each of which is a recipient of the Fourier transform, has glossed over the form of windowing that is used. By default, the rectangular window is in operation; it simply selects N contiguous samples as they are. Intuitively, this may seem somewhat dangerous, for what if the segment of signal has been cut out in such a way as to leave discontinuities at the edge of the window? A menagerie of alternative windowing functions have been proposed [Harris, 1978; Nuttall, 1981] that attempt to deal more gracefully with this; these usually take the form of a symmetric hat-like function which tapers off to zero or nearly zero at the edges. The windows are often named after their inventors, so you will see popular choices such as the von Hann, Hamming or Kaiser–Bessel. Selecting a window has particular consequences for the extent to which the Fourier analysis can finely focus on the peak locations in the spectrum, and the amount of spectral spillage between bins. The worst spillage occurs with the rectangular window, even though it happens to have the most localized central lobe. The issue of spillage is an essential troublemaker for any frequency components in an analysis target that are not exactly on the analysis frequency harmonics. The rectangular window would be a good choice if we could guarantee that the input sound were purely harmonic of known period, but is a bad choice for general running analysis of any sound. The Kaiser–Bessel window has very low spillage, with a moderately focused central lobe. Choice of window can subtly affect results, but the more successful window types tend to be the defaults in software (Hann, Kaiser–Bessel).

Four windows are compared in the time and frequency domains in Figure 3.1. The four window types are shown in the left column. The second column gives each window's log magnitude spectrogram, symmetric about 0 Hz; notice how the rectangular window has high sidelobes which only slowly taper off; all other windows are better than the rectangular in this respect! For these demonstrations, the test signal consists of a full-amplitude 440 Hz sine tone, and a 900 Hz sine tone at −40 dB (not visible in the time-domain view at this resolution). The third column shows a time-domain waveform of each window multiplied by the test signal; for the top item in the third column, note the discontinuity on the right because the rectangular window does not smoothly head to zero. The final column is the magnitude spectrum showing the analysis via the different window functions; the ability to resolve the two frequency components is window-dependent. The larger main lobe of the Gaussian and Blackman–Harris windows would become a liability if the partials were closer together; in this case the Hann window would be a better choice. Note that if the frequency components to be detected were both strong, rather than one being at −40 dB, the rectangular window would have the best resolution if they were also close in frequency. The window magnitude spectrum is centered on each peak; the larger amplitude component can easily mask the smaller if the sidelobes are large.

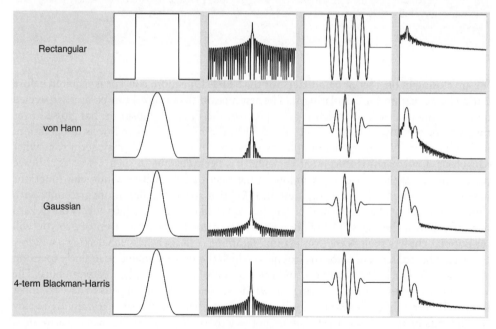

Figure 3.1 Comparison of four windowing functions. The second column gives each window's log magnitude spectrogram. The third column shows a time-domain waveform of each window multiplied by the test signal. The final column is the magnitude spectrum showing the analysis via the different window functions.

Typical STFT parameters can now be summarized:

1. window size N (usually a power of two, e.g., 512, 1024, 2048);

2. hop size H (typically half or a quarter of N; alternatively expressed as an overlap proportion or number of samples of overlap between successive windows. Often chosen to match the main lobe size of the window in the time domain);

3. frame rate $= R/H$;

4. analysis fundamental frequency $= R/N$ (bin frequency separation);

5. windowing function.

When the logarithm of power is plotted for each analysis harmonic, the graph of the Fourier analysis over time is called a **spectrogram**. It discards one part of the information gained from the analysis, namely the phase relationships in the signal. If both magnitude and phase data are preserved and treated, the **phase vocoder** is implemented. Pseudocode for the STFT is provided in Algorithm 3.1. Aside from the window multiplication and FFT steps, similar code would describe any overlapped windowing procedure, for example, for calculating other types of feature as discussed in Section 3.5. The code is therefore a demonstration of the type of bookkeeping required to create a windowed realtime processing algorithm. Since it is outside the scope of this text, the implementation of the FFT itself is given here as a call to an external function. At the expense of efficiency, this step could be carried out with a naive DFT, which would be a sample-wise multiplication between a probe sinusoid and the windowed input signal for each analysis harmonic.

3.2.2 Further Refinements to Fourier Analysis

You may be wondering whether anything could be done to improve the frequency resolution, in the case where the partials of a sound 'fall between the gaps' of the harmonics of the analysis frequency. Since not all signals are effectively modeled as a sum of sinusoids, increased frequency resolution may not necessarily improve matters. But assuming that Fourier analysis is a good working choice, and we wish to enhance the actual resolution of distinct partials, possible solutions are to increase the window size (with the possible side effect of now blurring transient information over a wider window), or to change the windowing function used if there are problems with sidebands interfering. Though it does not improve resolution per se, it is also possible to interpolate between peaks to refine a sense of the position of a peak; this can be carried out by interpolation schemes in the frequency domain, or also by the expedient of **zero padding** in the time domain. Zero padding uses the same number of source samples, maintaining the same frequency and temporal resolution. It is applied after originally windowing the source, by then adding extra zeroes and calculating the transform over a larger effective window size, and turns out to be equivalent to interpolation in the frequency domain.[5] A more refined but complicated solution uses **time-frequency reassignment**. This technique takes advantage of phase information, and requires extra FFTs to be taken (it is typically three times less efficient) but can help to focus spectrograms on the true locations of energy, rather than

---

[5]The technical reason is that there is an additional convolution with the transform of the rectangular window function, which just happens to be the ideal sinc interpolation filter.

Algorithm 3.1 Short-time Fourier transform: online algorithm pseudocode.

Input: A stream of (real) samples $x(n)$ at sampling rate R, a buffer *buf* for storing input samples, a buffer *fftbuf* for the in-place FFT, a windowing function *window* of size N

Output: A sequence of frames X_m at sampling rate R/H where H is the hop size, each frame being a complex number sampled function of frequency bin k, $X_m(k)$ where $k = 0, 1, \ldots, \frac{N}{2}$

  1: $n \leftarrow 0$ // Input sample counter
  2: $m \leftarrow 0$ // Output frame counter
  3: *bufcounter* $\leftarrow 0$ // Index into buffer *buf*
  4: **repeat**
  5:     **while** *bufcounter* $< (N - 1)$ **do**
  6:         *buf*[*bufcounter*] $\leftarrow x[n]$
  7:         *bufcounter* $\leftarrow$ *bufcounter* $+ 1$
  8:         $n \leftarrow n + 1$
  9:     **end while**
10:     Copy buffer *buf* to buffer *fftbuf*
11:     *fftbuf* = *fftbuf* $*$ *window*   // Apply windowing function by multiplying point-wise
12:     **FFT**(*fftbuf*)   // Carry out FFT in place, so output is written back to *fftbuf*
13:     $X_m \leftarrow$ *fftbuf*
14:     $m \leftarrow m + 1$
        // Prepare to fill next buffer for FFT
15:     **for** $g = 0$ to $N - H - 1$ **do**
16:         *buf*[g] $\leftarrow$ *buf*[$g + H$]
17:     **end for**   // Hop by H samples; update contents of *buf*
18:     *bufcounter* $\leftarrow N - H$
19: **until** there are fewer than H samples left in x

---

quantized to the rigid grid implicit in the FFT bins. The main algorithms are described carefully by Fulop and Fitz [2006], and are implemented in a number of sound analysis packages. Note that for some applications, sparse analysis points distributed off the grid will subtly complicate the algorithms.

Identifying the peaks in the magnitude spectrum is a step towards modeling the **spectral envelope** of sound [Rodet and Schwarz, 2007], which can give important information on dynamic timbre. For instance, different vowels in speech are recognized by particular prominences in the spectrum, of which the first five major peaks (called **formants**) are particularly critical [Gold and Morgan, 2000]. Finding local spectral peaks is also a necessary step in many models for tracking prominent sinusoids in a signal over time, the process of **peak tracking**. In a paper originally aimed at the automatic analysis of speech, but with application to any amplitude–time signal, McAulay and Quatieri [1986] outlined a sinusoidal model where strong tracks in the magnitude spectrum over time are collated.

The algorithm first finds peaks in a given spectrum, and then attempts to join up the peaks between this frame and the previous one. A **peak matching** algorithm tries to find a sensible allocation of these peaks to each other. Particularly when the signal is changing rapidly at a transient, and the assumption that it is non-stationary is weakest, it may be difficult to find smooth paths. Peaks are always still accounted for, but may be marked as births or deaths of tracks if no clear match can be found, and the changeover of tracks is maximal at unstable transient regions. Looking at the example in Figure 3.2 you should see many tracks, each with a distinct birth and death.

Psuedocode for a basic **tracking phase vocoder** following McAulay and Quatieri [1986] is provided in Algorithm 3.2. The algorithm also refers to the resynthesis parameters, as further explained in Section 3.2.3. Fuller details of the peak matching and resynthesis steps in particular can be obtained from the original paper, or pursued elsewhere [Serra and Smith, 1990; Beauchamp, 2007b].

Algorithm 3.2 Tracking phase vocoder after McAulay and Quatieri [1986].

Input: M input FFT frames X_m at sampling rate R/H where H is the hop size, each frame being a complex number sampled function of frequency bin k, $X_m(k)$, $k = 0, 1, \ldots, \frac{N}{2}$.

Output: A list of sinusoidal tracks S_m for each frame of the input apart from the last, which connect up adjacent frames. The tracks at a given frame m note start and end frequencies, start and end amplitude, and auxiliary parameters for successful oscillator resynthesis (to control a phase interpolation function)

1: Initialize data structures PV and $PEAKS$ for holding temporary phase vocoder and peaks data. The $PEAKS$ data lists peak frequency locations and amplitudes for each spectral peak
2: $m \leftarrow 0$ // Input frame counter
3: **repeat**
4:    $PV_m \leftarrow$ **CalculateMagPhase**(X_m) // Calculate magnitudes and phases for frame m
5:    $PEAKS_m \leftarrow$ **FindPeaks**(PV_m)
6:    **if** $m > 0$ **then**
7:       $S_{m-1} \leftarrow$ **MatchPeaks**$(PEAKS_{m-1}, PEAKS_m, S_{m-2})$ // Run the peak matching algorithm, storing into list S_{m-1} all tracks connecting peaks between frames, and additional tracks representing births and deaths. S_{-1} is empty
8:       **PreparePhaseInterpolation**(S_m) // For each partial track, calculate auxiliary parameters for a cubic function which will interpolate between known phases and frequencies at the previous and current frame. This 'phase unwrapping' step is necessary to avoid discontinuities of phase, which may otherwise introduce distortion
9:    **end if**
10:    $m \leftarrow m + 1$
11: **until** $m = M$

SPEAR

Illustrative of the tracking phase vocoder is Michael Klingbeil's SPEAR (Sinusoidal Partial Editing Analysis and Resynthesis), a cross-platform application where the user can individually select and manipulate partial tracks gained from analysis, through a graphical user interface [Klingbeil, 2005]. The user has access to various tools to select sinusoidal tracks through individual point and click, vertical and horizontal selection, a lasso tool for drawing out arbitrary selections, and more. Partial tracks can then be dragged in time and frequency, and the sound immediately resynthesized via either inverse FFT (IFFT) or oscillator bank resynthesis. The software is convenient yet powerful, and well worth exploring (http://www.klingbeil.com/spear). A screenshot appears in Figure 3.2.

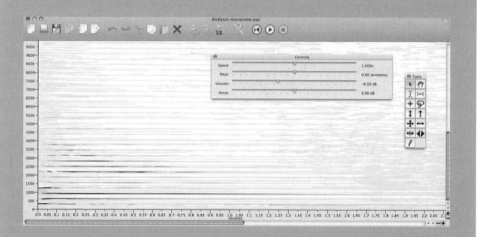

Figure 3.2   SPEAR: partial tracks for a sitar note. Reproduced by permission of © Michael Klingbeil.

3.2.3 Resynthesis after Sinusoidal Modeling

There are two standard methods for the resynthesis of sound, given sinusoidal analysis data. While this chapter is ostensibly about analysis, the potential resynthesis of sound from a spectral representation is intimately coupled to discovering the composition of a sound. This will also be required in the next section, since the error function between a resynthesized analysis and the original signal can provide useful information for further decomposition of that signal.

The principle of **additive synthesis** is simply to build up a complex sound from individual sinusoidal components. For noisy aperiodic transient sounds which aren't modeled well by sinusoids, this may require a prohibitively large number of components! For periodic sounds, a more constrained number of sinusoids is sufficient to capture the main qualities of a sound. Resynthesis can be carried out by taking the inverse Fourier transform to move back from a frequency-domain representation to the time domain, or more flexibly by direct resynthesis in the time domain using a summation of sinusoids. Phase vocoder analysis provides the requisite amplitudes and phases, and we proceed a window at a time as per the original STFT.

For an IFFT (inverse fast Fourier transform) the calculation expense is fixed; a complex spectrum of amplitudes and phases at the analysis frequencies is the starting point for the inverse transformation. An inverse discrete Fourier transform is mathematically very similar to a DFT (see sidebar), and the IFFT can be obtained using a very similar algorithm to the FFT, just acting on a complex-valued input. Both magnitude and phases are required, for otherwise there are an infinite number of possible inverse solutions. In the case where the phase and amplitude values have not been adjusted since the original analysis, in principle (give or take minor floating point errors) the procedure can recover the original signal exactly.[6] However, any spectral processing which has changed amplitudes and phases has an intimate effect on the signal obtained from the IFFT. In particular, there is no guarantee that a signal that was originally windowed to go to zero at the endpoints will now go to zero: new discontinuities can be introduced. For this reason, an **overlap-add** structure is used to crossfade consecutive resynthesized windows of samples, a procedure which reduces glitches due to discontinuities but can blur the output sound to some degree; hop sizes of $N/4$ are advised to avoid side effects.[7] The efficiency gain of the IFFT resynthesis method has meant its wide adoption, particularly for realtime resynthesis. The IFFT method can be used even where partial trails might be varying during a frame, by taking mean frequencies and amplitudes of trails over the frame, and relying on sufficient overlap-add to smooth the output [Rodet and Schwarz, 2007, pp. 217–8].

---

[6]That is, recover the original signal post windowing. The original signal itself can only be perfectly regained if the window was non-zero at all points, as for a Hamming window, or where the overlap-add structure is carefully designed to compensate.

[7]The crossfading implies further windowing of the output signal, and thereby further blurring of the spectrum. This is due to the time-domain multiplication = frequency-domain convolution relation described in Section 4.2.2. It is necessary to have a sufficient frame rate, essentially a small enough hop size, to avoid noticeable aural side effects if transforming a spectral signal prior to resynthesis; Allen and Rabiner [1977] consider this problem in more detail.

Inverse Discrete Fourier Transform

We'll just consider one frame of N samples, rather than the full STFT. The forwards discrete Fourier transform for N input samples $x(n)$ can be written as:

$$X(k) = \sum_{n=0}^{N-1} x(n)e^{-i2\pi(k/N)n}, \quad k = 0,\dots,N-1 \qquad (3.3)$$

N complex numbers $X(k)$ result; here we won't worry about the windowing (imagine it incorporated into x already) or the redundancy among the output for a real input. Each spectral coefficient $X(k)$ is a measure of how strongly the input real vector of samples projects onto a given frequency complex exponential (the transform can be interpreted as a change of basis; see Jaffe [1987a]). By summing over all samples n we end up with a value for a single frequency bin k.

Now for the other direction, we define the inverse transform:

$$x(n) = \frac{1}{N} \sum_{k=0}^{N-1} X(k)e^{i2\pi(k/N)n}, \quad n = 0,\dots,N-1 \qquad (3.4)$$

This is very similar to the previous equation, but for a scale factor and a change of sign for the exponential. The sum is now over the frequency bins, adding up the contribution of each complex exponential based on how strongly that exponential is present in the original x. Note how for a fixed time point n, the current state of each contributing complex exponential is checked and weighted by the $X(k)$.

The proof that the forwards transform followed by the inverse really does give back the original input comes from the orthogonality (but not orthonormality, hence the scale factor) of the particular complex exponentials used in the transform definition, and is provided elsewhere [Jaffe, 1987a]. It is straightforward to program a computer to calculate the forward or inverse transforms directly in $O(N^2)$ operations, summing N values for each of N coefficients, just by following the equations. But the FFT and the inverse version, the IFFT, are used in practice for a lucrative saving in time, at $O(N \log N)$.

The second method is direct re-enactment of a given spectral decomposition in the time domain, by summing up a sinusoid for each known partial trail. This **oscillator bank resynthesis** is a costly procedure whose efficiency varies with the number of sinusoids to be used. It has the advantage of fewer potential artifacts, and explicit control of all parameters of sound, though there is a lot of data to juggle! The final output of resynthesizing a given frame in this manner will normally still require some form of cross-fading with overlapping neighboring frames. The greatest challenge of the resynthesis, particularly when dealing with peak trails extracted by the tracking phase vocoder, is to calculate phase in a consistent way between frames; phase must be very carefully treated here [McAulay and Quatieri, 1986; Serra and Smith, 1990; Beauchamp, 2007b].

Given these methods of resynthesis, sound transformations are plausible, such as the changing of pitch by expanding sinusoidal frequency data. Without preserving the dominant formants in the spectral envelope, 'munchkinization' effects can become apparent here. Indeed, spectral artifacts are easy to introduce through processing, particularly via the IFFT resynthesis. Even for oscillator bank resynthesis, it is simple to create acoustically unrealistic sounds by changing inner sound relationships in a way incommensurate with the natural world. This may of course be a compositional intention, but you are warned that many aural side effects of FFT processing have become somewhat cliché.

3.2.4 Not All Sounds are Periodic: Coping with Noise

From what has been explained so far, it should be apparent that Fourier analysis does not always fit signals well, especially when the sound to be analyzed is aperiodic and highly transient in its behavior. While noise might refer to anything in a signal which interferes with what you want to seek, in this section noise essentially means a sound with a wideband power spectrum. White noise, for instance, is a statistical process that demonstrates equal energy at all frequencies over time; it's exactly the sort of thing a sinusoid-based model finds it hard to treat. Representing white noise with sinusoidal modeling requires a spectrum full of sinusoids! A number of developments of spectral analysis therefore seek to separate the noise components of sound from those periodic components more suited to sinusoidal representation.

Xavier Serra proposed a scheme often known as the **sines+noise** model, or as a **deterministic plus stochastic decomposition** [Serra and Smith, 1990]. We begin with a Fourier analysis to extract the deterministic sinusoidal components. By subtracting what has been modeled so far from what is to be modeled, the remainder – called a residual – is isolated. This error between what the sines can resynthesize and the original signal is then taken to be a noise component which can be modeled by a separate mechanism, a stochastic noise generation in this case. Pseudocode is provided in Algorithm 3.3. Once the decomposition is obtained, independent transformations and resynthesis of sinusoidal and noise components are possible.

According to a review by Risset and Wessel [1999], the sines+noise model is the best working model of timbre we have. While there are rival models, and greater insights into the

---

Algorithm 3.3 Deterministic plus Stochastic Decomposition following Serra and Smith [1990].

Input: M input FFT frames X_m at sampling rate R/H where H is the hop size, each frame being a complex number sampled function of frequency $X_m(k)$, $k = 0, 1, \ldots, \frac{N}{2}$

Output: For the deterministic output, a list of sinusoidal tracks S_m active for each frame; a series of spectral envelopes E_m which model the stochastic component for each frame

1: Initialize data structures PV and $PEAKS$ for holding temporary phase vocoder and peaks data
2: $m \leftarrow 0$ // Input frame counter
3: **repeat**
4:     $PV_m \leftarrow$ **CalculateMagPhase**(X_m) // Calculate magnitudes and phases for frame m (phase vocoder step)
5:     $PEAKS_m \leftarrow$ **FindPeaks**(PV_m)
6:     **if** $m > 0$ **then**
7:         $S_{m-1} \leftarrow$ **MatchPeaks**$(PEAKS_{m-1}, PEAKS_m, S_{m-2})$ // Run the peak matching algorithm, storing into list S_{m-1} all tracks connecting peaks between frames, and additional tracks representing births and deaths. S_{-1} is empty
8:         Resynthesize a frame f_m using the latest sinusoidal tracks S_{m-1}
9:         Calculate magnitude spectrum $|F_m|$ by another FFT after windowing f_m
10:        Calculate residual $R_m = |X_m| - |F_m|$
11:        Model the residual magnitude spectrum R_m with a spectral envelope E_m // Straightforward options are a linear segment approximation or the residual itself
12:    **end if**
13:    $m \leftarrow m + 1$
14: **until** $m = M$

---

human auditory system, the principle of dual representation of periodic and aperiodic components is a powerful one. The Spectral Modeling Synthesis software from Xavier Serra's active Music Technology Group at Universitat Pompeu Fabra in Barcelona provides a cross-platform free open-source implementation of this technique (see the SMSTools application at www.clam.iua.upf.edu). Xavier Serra's research group have taken this representation far in terms of applications, too, from voice-substitution karaoke (control Madonna's voice with your own!) to singing voice synthesis, as implemented in *Vocaloid*, a collaboration with Yamaha (www.vocaloid.com).

Some researchers have gone further, for example to the 'sines+noise+transients' model of Levine and Smith [2007], which only applies sinusoidal modeling where the harmonic modeling has a good chance of adequately describing the signal, that is, outside of fast-changing transient regions of sound (also see Verma and Meng [2000]). A variant for dealing with noise is to allow for some at each frequency bin, so modeling a sound as a combination of noisy sines, rather than pure sines. The 'Reassigned Bandwidth-Enhanced Additive Sound Model' as implemented in the Loris software utilizes this principle (http://www.cerlsoundgroup.org/Loris/). There are a variety of further sinusoidal and noise-modeling methods in the signal processing literature. Comparative evaluations of the effectiveness of different models are rarer, but Wright *et al.* [2000] provide an exception; with many possible input parameters and implementation differences, no one algorithm can be picked out as the 'best', and it is usually contended that general models always require some tweaking to fit individual cases of sounds.

3.3 ALTERNATIVE REPRESENTATIONS FOR ANALYZING SOUND

The sinusoid might be the simplest *periodic* sound in Fourier analysis, but it is not the only possibility for defining a family of basic analysis waveforms with which to decompose complex sounds. For instance, the square wave is a digitally convenient periodic waveform, since it takes on just two distinct values. In a Walsh–Hadamard transform [Roads, 1996, pp. 153–6]; [Loy, 2007b, pp. 525–6], a sound is analyzed in terms of a set of square waves at harmonics of the analysis frequency. The advantage is sheer speed of calculation by avoiding trigonometric functions; the transform domain of 'sequencies', however, is less intuitive than the Fourier domain's frequencies.

In general, a sound can be analyzed with respect to a **dictionary** of time-frequency **atoms**. Each primitive atom is restricted, depending on its form, in localizing information in the two domains simultaneously; there is a tradeoff between the atom's support in the frequency domain and its support in the time domain. An atom which is good for detecting transients (accurate time resolution) will be poor at resolving different frequencies (which necessarily take more time to reveal themselves); conversely, fine frequency sensitivity is at the expense of determining accurately the time of an event. The two extremes are exemplified by the impulse (full wideband spectral response, sample accurate position) and the sinusoid (theoretically infinite time extent, pure singular frequency). This revelation may go some way to explaining why Fourier analysis was only half the story and the sines+noise transform is a more effective combination of viewpoints for signal analysis![8] The 'best' compromise between time and frequency resolution, meaning the minima of the tradeoff, is supplied by Gaussian windowed sinusoids, so-called **Gabor atoms** after the physicist who carried out early work on such signal representations.

Many different families of analysis functions, each with their own special properties, have been identified. In one formulation, the analysis functions are called **wavelets** and are related not by being parameterized by frequency directly, but by being rescaled versions of a master waveform shape. The property of time scaling has an advantage, in that different scales support different periods; scaled small, the waveform will match high frequencies; scaled larger, low. The sinusoidal basis for Fourier analysis was applied in the STFT with

---

[8]This tradeoff of time and frequency localization in the context of quantum mechanics is the Heisenberg Uncertainty Principle, and is a general restriction on signal processing [Mallat, 1998, pp. 30–3].

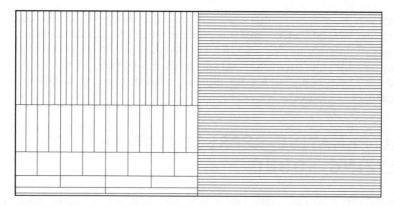

Figure 3.3   Time-frequency tilings. Two time (x) versus frequency (y) tilings are shown side by side. On the left is the tiling for an octave-spaced filter bank, as per a wavelet-scale transform. On the right is the Fourier tiling, linear and with the same time resolution at each frequency.

a fixed window size, so that smaller periods recurred multiple times across the window. With wavelets, **multi-resolution** analysis is possible, different scaled wavelets being applied simultaneously with different windows. Figure 3.3 shows one way this could be used to tile the time-frequency plane (in practice, overlaps may still be useful). This property makes time resolution frequency-dependent, as might be intuitively expected.

Fourier analysis applies a linear spacing in frequency of the bins. This is well matched to the harmonics of the analysis frequency, though harmonic sounds with another fundamental will fall between bins.[9] But the scaling does suit harmonic sounds, and will represent them linearly on a spectrogram. However, this is not necessarily commensurate with the human auditory system's more logarithmic (particularly over 1000 Hz) distribution of hair cells on the basilar membrane. There are a number of techniques, such as the constant Q transform [Brown and Puckette, 1992] or other frequency-warping techniques using psychoacoustic scales such as Mels, Barks or ERBs (equivalent rectangular bandwidths) to refine frequency data towards the sensitivities of human hearing. Such techniques bring us to the realm of auditory models, further discussed below.

The reader will possibly be wondering whether there are any better ways to analyze a sound's frequency content, without the restriction of a basic analysis frequency as assumed in the FFT. There is a brute-force way to look at a signal in any way you desire, and that is to use one filter per frequency at which you wish to measure energy. The definition given for the Fourier transform was explicitly based on harmonics, and the FFT algorithm is dependent on that, but we can drop the restriction at the price of efficiency of calculation if we are willing to accept $2N$ complex operations (multiply by phasor and sum) for each

---

[9]Consider the case of an analysis frequency of 50 Hz and a fundamental of 137 Hz; since 137 modulo 50 is prime, the harmonics of 137 will take on the 50 possible inter-bin integer positions in Hz!

frequency to be probed. The basic step for a given probe frequency is to modulate the input by a complex phasor and sum the result, a process which is equivalent to a band-pass filter. With this in mind, the Fourier transform can be considered a bank of band-pass filters which, when spaced with their center frequencies at analysis frequency harmonics, has an efficient implementation in the FFT.

There are plenty of more exotic signal processing spaces, including such alluringly named entities as the chirplet transform, the fractional Fourier transform and the Wigner–Ville distribution. These have not been extensively adopted directly in computer music, often for reasons of mathematical tractability and efficiency, or because such techniques take a while to percolate from signal processing journals to practical applications. There is a fund of experience with the Fourier transform in computer music that overwhelms that for alternatives, but interested readers could find much to occupy them here [Roads, 1996; Mallat, 1998]. It is also worth noting that many parameterized sound models can be declared – for instance, taking a signal to be a sum of an unknown number of sinusoids and a noise term, where each amplitude, phase and frequency of the tonal components is to be determined, as well as the amplitude of the noise and the 'best' number of sinusoids – bringing to center stage the assumptions of a particular analysis model, and employing various solution techniques, e.g., a Bayesian framework (see [Klapuri and Davy, 2006]).

Nevertheless, it is worth featuring one particular general view of time-frequency analysis that is proving to be an exciting option, one where the analysis model can adapt to the input signal itself. This is **dictionary-based analysis** [Daudet and Torrésani, 2006; Sturm et al., 2008], and uses an over-complete set of time-frequency atoms. By having many atoms available – the particular choice of dictionary is open, but might contain various varieties of wavelets, Gabor atoms, a Fourier basis and the like – a sparse representation (the **book** of best fitting atoms) can be built up using a clever iterative procedure called matching pursuit. The sparsity here means that the first selected atom for the book is typically that which describes the most prominent energy feature of the signal, subsequent atoms building up an increasingly accurate analysis of the signal. We only take as many atoms as there are iterations of matching pursuit that are needed to meet some condition.[10] There are various catches, including the CPU cost of running the matching-pursuit algorithm for the initial analysis, but some interesting new sound transformations are plausible once the book is identified, from signal compression to separating out transient and periodic components by selecting among the book's atoms. Figure 3.4 demonstrates the potential of this methodology.

3.4 AUDITORY MODELS

Although there are mathematical signal processing models to draw upon which do not relate to human physiology, the human activity of music is most readily supported if

---

[10]Compare Fourier analysis, where we end up with as much spectral data as input samples; a sparse representation can get by with far fewer measurements, while possibly allowing a more accurate overall signal analysis to emerge!

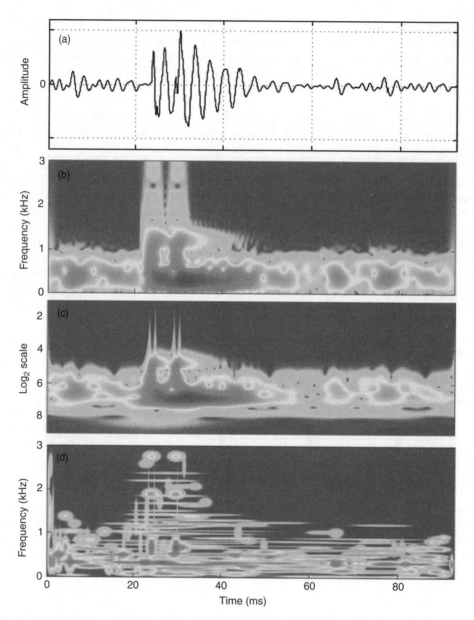

Figure 3.4   Dictionary-based analysis compared with Fourier and wavelet methods. A 100-millisecond sound is analyzed by three methods. The top graph is a spectrogram, the middle one a scalogram (squared modulus of the short-term wavelet transform), and the bottom one a wivigram, created from a dictionary-based analysis. Observe the enhanced time and frequency resolution (exhibited in the sharpness of the image) of the bottom plot compared with either of the two above. Reproduced by permission of © Bob Sturm.

we can model closely the human auditory system. Human beings are after all the basic ground truth of musical capacity! Many human abilities are incompletely understood from a neuroscientific perspective, and have not yet been convincingly modeled by machine, especially for complex stimuli consisting of many sound sources at once. The motivation may be to study human biology and specifically auditory capability in a scientific capacity, but the musical implications of any such study are wide ranging. So an important strategy in tackling certain harder problems in computer music is to imitate the way humans accomplish tasks. For such reasons, we now move onto analysis methods founded in knowledge of the human auditory system.

Higher-level processing of music involves the frontal lobes and emotional centers, and, indeed, the whole brain can potentially light up in response to the highly cognitively engaging stimuli of music [Peretz and Zatorre, 2003]. Neuroscience is furnishing an exciting degree of information on the sites and function of neural processing of audio, though the complexity of the brain still shields many secrets. Scanners do not have high enough spatial or temporal resolution, there are too many neurons at too fine a scale to be tracked; while you wouldn't put it past neuroscientists to develop all manner of wonderful devices, recording from all the individual neurons in a brain is currently a fantasy. Much useful information comes indirectly from patient histories, from much meticulous research and from ingenious experimental settings, with the brain the ultimate puzzle to crack.

3.4.1 Physiologically Inspired Models of the Auditory System

The neuroanatomy of the auditory system is an advanced topic at the forefront of research. Even if the broad outlines of the human auditory system are established, there are many gaps in our knowledge, even at relatively early stages in the processing chain. For instance, research on hair cells in the cochlea is still ongoing. Nevertheless, there is a fund of anatomical (structure description) and physiological (structure explanation) data, and a host of psychoacoustic experiments have been run which probe the parameters of basic auditory processes [Yost, 2007; Moore, 2004; Pickles, 1988]. Where these experiments treat peripheral audio processing, they have been most successfully tied to the physiology, but at a surprisingly early point in the central auditory system the frontier of understanding is reached and models become more speculative.

Auditory processing, at least at the early stage of the cochlea, can be considered as a filter bank. The cochlea does not use an FFT; it is a biological parallel processor which records thousands of simultaneous measurements pseudo-logarithmically spaced in frequency. If we could run 3500 filters[11] in parallel on a DSP chip, we would be closer to the operation of the human auditory system. The output of a filter bank provides one channel of audio for each filter band, a viewpoint known as **spectrotemporal** processing in that the set of bands gives spectral information, but each filter output signal is temporal. In practice, the restricted

---

[11]The number here approximates the number of inner hair cells (IHC). Reality is more complex, in that each IHC innervates around eight nerve fibers with different dynamic ranges. There are also more limited afferent (brainwards) connections from outer hair cells, which are likely to be involved in the active feedback mechanism, but may nevertheless carry some pertinent auditory data; it has even been speculated that at high volumes vestibular cells respond to bass.

frequency band of a given filter means that the data can be downsampled for each channel, so there is not necessarily a huge explosion of the amount of data processed.

Table 3.1 reviews stages of a typical auditory model. Note that most of the stages detailed here are in the peripheral auditory system. Models differ widely once the central auditory system (brain loci of the central nervous system) are reached, not least due to differing interpretations of the incomplete physiological evidence. A plot at an intermediate stage in an auditory model is provided by a **cochleagram**, which graphs the received energy at a basilar membrane location against time, that is, the output of the cochlear filter bank (Figure 3.5 demonstrates a cochleagram).

Table 3.1 Stages in a generic auditory model.

Stage	Anatomical locus	Processing
Early processing	Outer (pinna, auditory canal) and middle (eardrum, ossicles) ear	Filtering represents the frequency sensitivity of the ear
Frequency analysis filter bank	Inner ear (basilar membrane motion within the cochlea)	One filter represents one location on the basilar membrane; typical gammatone filter banks used in models might have 64 or 128 channels, while the human ear has around 3500! Later stages of the auditory model operate on the multiple output channels of this filter bank
Rectification	Hair cell	Half-wave rectification on each channel simulates the mechanical characteristics of the hair cell (the stereocilia only open ion channels when shearing in one direction)
Neural transduction	Vestibulocochlear (eighth cranial) nerve	Tracking change from baseline neural activity; an additional neural spike is provoked when an innervating hair cell releases enough neurotransmitter. This firing may be phase-locked to an incident waveform, that is, with a sufficient peak in a given channel. Some models explicitly encode the discrete spike timing; others maintain continuous signals representing the probability of a spike. Since the maximum firing rate of a nerve is 1000 Hz [Yost, 2007, p. 122], each channel may be low-pass filtered and downsampled. This processing speed limit (refraction period of around 1 ms) does not mean that the auditory system cannot represent higher frequencies, since each channel is a detection signal for activity at a particular frequency. Dynamic compression can also be employed; an inner hair cell innervates multiple nerve fibers with different dynamic sensitivities
Central processing	Central auditory system	Models differ substantially here; options include correlograms, interspike interval histograms, or other forms of auditory image. Various extensions tackling particular properties of sound have been proposed

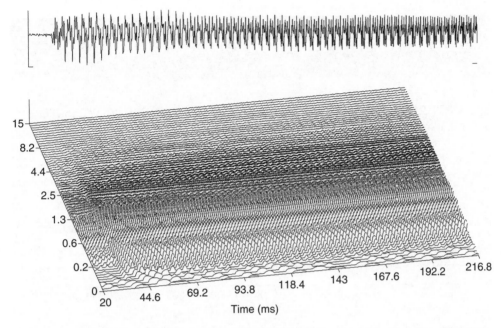

Figure 3.5 A sitar note analyzed through a filter bank which models the human cochlea, i.e. a cochleagram. The image was created using the first two stages of the Auditory Image Model.

Once sound has been transmuted into electrical action potentials, the signals from the two ears begin to cross early on in the brain stem. Models of sound localization take this into account, but the models mentioned here concentrate on the signal arriving at a single ear.

Auditory modeling can inform engineering, though the models adopted for specific applications in sound are often diluted with respect to the scientific models. This may be done for reasons of efficiency of implementation: even if the brain does not use a fast Fourier transform, it is cheaper on computer resources to use one, and there are frequency warping techniques to recover nonlinear frequency spacings. Yet there are some interesting correspondences between computational algorithms and the biological way of doing things. Various pitch and onset detection algorithms, for example, have been inspired by observed neural mechanisms [Slaney and Lyon, 1990; Smith, 1994; Klapuri, 2006].

3.4.2 Computational Auditory Scene Analysis

The brain has fantastic abilities in **auditory scene analysis** [Bregman, 1990], the understanding of complex stimuli which may contain multiple sound sources. How do we distinguish particular speakers at a noisy cocktail party, or resolve competing information in the hubbub of the urban jungle? Computers have been employed to construct models of

MATLAB and Auditory Model Toolboxes

MATLAB is a proprietary software package for mathematical modeling from The MathWorks (www.mathworks.com). It provides a useful framework for research into signal processing and audition, and is worth noting because of a number of specialized Toolboxes (extension sets) available. An open-source alternative, compatible with much existing MATLAB code, is Octave (http://www.gnu.org/software/octave/). Table 3.2 lists a selection of MATLAB Toolboxes for auditory modeling.

Table 3.2   Table of MATLAB Toolboxes.

Toolbox	Author(s)	URL
Auditory Toolbox	Malcolm Slaney	http://cobweb.ecn.purdue.edu/~malcolm/interval/1998-010/
Auditory Image Toolbox	Roy Patterson and colleagues	http://www.pdn.cam.ac.uk/groups/cnbh/research/aim.html
HUTear	Researchers at the Laboratory of Acoustics and Audio Signal Processing	http://www.acoustics.hut.fi/software/HUTear/HUTear.html
IPEM	Marc Leman, Micheline Lesaffre, Koen Tanghe	http://www.ipem.ugent.be/Toolbox/ (Windows only)
Cochleagram code and more	DeLiang Wang and colleagues	http://www.cse.ohio-state.edu/pnl/software.html – also see www.casabook.org

these processes, in the field of **computational auditory scene analysis**, often abbreviated CASA [Wang and Brown, 2006].

When this work is couched more generally as a signal processing problem, it is often referred to as **source separation**, though here the onus is not to model the human auditory system, but to find any signal model which can support separation. The ultimate algorithm would be one which could take an existing polyphonic source and perfectly extract component sounds; this allows the backwards engineering of a piece, as further discussed when we consider automatic transcription in Section 3.6. There are many technical reasons why this is a rather challenging proposition; theoretically, source separation requires as many independent channels in a complex mixture as sources to separate. For a monophonic mixdown of a recording, there is no realistic expectation that the original tracks from the master tapes could somehow be reconstructed, though this hasn't stopped some brave attempts and some speculation on how instrument models might allow such a feat [Every, 2006; Virtanen, 2006].

Making sense of an auditory scene almost certainly does not require perfect extraction of simultaneous sound streams [Scheirer, 1996; Martin *et al.*, 1998]. It is speculated that human beings use a number of tactics to focus attention on one important source among many, perhaps swapping attention rapidly between layers when tracking multiple objects, and certainly taking advantage of much prior knowledge about the expected form of sounds. Work here is of great future utility, since the auditory scene analysis problem is central to more developed musical understanding by machine, but currently remains at the forefront of research, rather than being generally available in applications.

A specific book surveying CASA research [Wang and Brown, 2006] and its associated web site are recommended here (www.casabook.org).

3.4.3 Perceptual Audio Coding

Auditory models have provided the inspiration for audio compression schemes throughout the history of telecommunications, though historically there has been a particular emphasis on models of speech in lieu of general models of human hearing. Such modeling can support low data transmission rates, necessary for the bandwidth restrictions of the many simultaneous conversations taking place on a telephone network or the Internet. Auditory models useful for speech include traditional vocoder schemes (multi-band energy envelope representations) and Linear Predictive Coding [Gold and Morgan, 2000].

Analyzing most other audio cannot depend on a monophonic speech model, but can take advantage of a more general model of human hearing. Whenever the human auditory system would not pick up on some information, that information can be discarded; those components most prominent to the ear are allocated the highest priority and bit rate.

The most famous current applications are perceptual compression schemes, as adopted in MP3, and other **perceptual audio codecs** such as ATRAC, AAC, Vorbis and WMA (also see Section 2.4) [Rumsey and McCormick, 2006, pp. 237–240]; [Pohlmann, 2005, pp. 315–413]; [Watkinson, 2001, pp. 275–326]; [Painter and Spanias, 2000]. Perceptual audio coding in this vein aggressively exploits the phenomenon of masking [Moore, 2004; Yost, 2007], whereby higher-amplitude frequency components can conceal lower-amplitude components nearby in frequency. The shape of the masking curve is amplitude dependent, higher amplitudes corresponding to greater reach of influence in the spectrum, though always biased in such a way that the masking sound masks higher frequencies more than lower (a property which can be tracked to the mechanics of the basilar membrane). The full dynamics of masking, which involves temporal as well as spectral influence and uses different masking curves for sinusoidal and for filtered noise sources, is described in the references provided here.

The upshot of the perceptual model is that a masking level can be determined throughout the spectrum. This masking level becomes a new noise floor, rather than the full-scale dynamic range. Quantization noise can be increased as long as the noise stays under the masking level, and this means that each band of the spectral data can be suitably encoded at a potentially reduced bit rate rather than full rate. Figure 3.6 demonstrates this principle of threshold adjustment in the case of an 80 dB SPL sine tone at 1000 Hz.

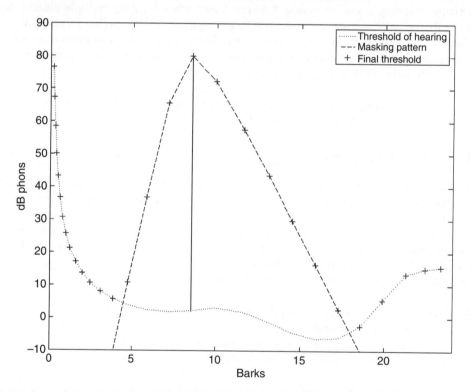

Figure 3.6   Masking by an 80 dB SPL sine tone at 1000 Hz. The plot is actually in phons, relative judged loudness compared with reference tones at 1000 Hz. The threshold of hearing is taken as a 2 phon curve from the ISO 2002 equal loudness curves dataset. The masking function and frequency to Bark scale conversion follow Painter and Spanias [2000]. The Bark scale is one of the psychoacoustially motivated scales which better approximate the frequency sensitivity of human hearing. In this case, 1000 Hz is around 8.5 Barks, and 25 Barks are more than enough to cover the full range of human hearing.

Perceptual audio codecs also employ standard lossless file compression techniques from computer science to further save space, and can comfortably achieve ten-to-one compression ratios for reasonable quality audio reproduction. Necessarily, however, they are lossy compression routines which are dependent on the accuracy of psychoacoustic data, and there is a tradeoff between quality of reproduction and file size as usually expressed in the overall bit rate selected for coding. Note that a decoder does not need to make any auditory modeling calculations; the hard work is done once only, by the encoder.

The ultimate reductionist scheme is exemplified in **object coding**, where audio events are recognized, and the many samples replaced by much terser symbolic description. Such coding is dependent on the quality of audio analysis algorithms available; as detailed in the previous subsection on CASA and in the section to come on the transcription problem, object recognition is hardly a solved problem! Nevertheless, with certain preconditions on the allowed signals, some advances are possible along these lines, and the tradition of modeling specific types of source has already been raised in the context of models of speech. The **structured audio** of MPEG-4 [Rumsey and McCormick, 2006, p. 240], where both objects and acoustic environment can be represented, is one attempt to make explicit this situation, though the technology lags behind the statement of the principle.

3.5 FEATURE EXTRACTION

Many different quantities can be obtained from an audio signal. These **features** may be related to physiological auditory models or to spectral models of sound, or simply be mathematical quirks that happen to show some sort of promise as a sound **descriptor**. In some cases, these derived signals present alternative possibilities for computer music, stepping away from traditional music making; but most features of proven worth in applications can be related in some way to human auditory abilities and real-world sound production.

To give a flavor of these signals, Table 3.3 lists examples, with a brief summary of the algorithm and motivation. Features are usually calculated at a lower rate than the sampling rate, typically by operations on blocks of samples at a time, such as summing, taking the maximum or more complicated calculations. As is the case for the short-time Fourier transform, the blocks can be described in terms of window sizes and hop sizes. Feature signals are therefore defined over a sequence of **frames**. For spectral features derived from spectral data, the features will follow the same frame boundaries as the STFT itself. Many features can be calculated using arbitrary window sizes (for example, the framewise maximum or variance of an audio signal in the time domain). Systems often use a common **frame rate** for all their features for later ease of calculation, but it is also possible to calculate features simultaneously at a number of different rates, and resample feature signals as necessary when polling values at a given time.

Table 3.3   Examples of low-level features.

Feature	Description	Calculation
ZCR	Count (positive) zero crossings within N samples	$\sum_{k=0}^{N-2} x(k+1) \geq 0 \wedge x(k) < 0$
RMS	Root mean square amplitude calculated over N samples	$\sqrt{\dfrac{\sum_{k=0}^{N-1} x(k)^2}{N}}$
Max power	Maximum power in a block of N samples; often used in sample editor waveform displays when zoomed out	$\max_{k=0}^{N-1} x(k)^2$
Spectral centroid	Statistical measure over the spectrum	$\dfrac{\sum_{k=0}^{N/2-1} k|X_m(k)|^2}{\max(\sum_{k=0}^{N/2-1} |X_m(k)|^2, 1)}$
Spectral flux	Change of spectrum between frames	$\sum_{k=0}^{N/2-1} \left| |X_{m+1}(k)|^2 - |X_m(k)|^2 \right|$
Spectral fall-off	The spectral envelope can be modeled by fitting a curve to the magnitude spectrum. Spectral fall-off fits a single line to model the typical drop in energy at higher frequencies in sound, as one helpful timbral indicator, but more complex models are available	Rodet and Schwarz [2007]
LPC coefficients	Linear predictive coding models the spectrum of the input with a source-filter model; it is a useful compression technique	Gold and Morgan [2000]; Rabiner and Juang [1993]; Makhoul [1975]
MFCCs	Mel-frequency cepstral coefficients; given a spectrum, the **cepstrum** approximates the principal components, and is a useful timbre descriptor; it also deconvolves (separates) an excitation and body response and gives some idea of pitch	Gold and Morgan [2000]; Logan [2000]; Roads [1996, pp. 514–8]

As the table indicates, these features may be gleaned from any analysis process. The table only gives a set of examples. There are a large number of ways to derive new features from old, using standard statistical methods for modeling distributions (mean, variance, kurtosis and higher-order moments) or calculus and signal processing operations (differentiation, integration). Certain processes will also calculate multiple feature values at once, so-called 'multidimensional' features. An example is the Fourier transform, which creates N output values ($N/2+1$ amplitudes, $N/2-1$ phases) for an input window of N samples. Other examples appearing in the table include the sets of mel-frequency cepstral coefficients (MFCCs) or linear predictive coding (LPC) coefficients, originally from the speech recognition literature but now frequently utilized in computer music. Any analysis algorithm can supply useful features, from FFT bin values or wavelet coefficients to further stages of refinement, such as the number of spectral peaks detected in a given frame.

Normalizing can also be an issue, in that it is helpful to applications to have a set of features within a common range, but each feature's distribution is highly dependent on the source material being analyzed. Statistical normalization (subtract the mean and divide by the standard deviation) can help to compare the distributions, while normalization by the minimum and maximum is dependent on the outliers but will restrict values precisely within the bounds 0.0 to 1.0. Questions arise as to whether normalization should be carried out with respect to the feature values in hand – for a given audio example – or treated with respect to more general limits obtained from a corpus of examples larger than the individual audio data in question.

Features are ubiquitous in the musical signal processing literature and the reader can gather ideas and code for many by looking at current systems and research. Some suggested starting points are Schwarz [2004], Klapuri and Davy [2006] and McDermott *et al.* [2006]. Features are used as a low-level starting point for data-driven machine learning (data mining) in music information retrieval, as discussed in Section 7.2. They can be used as inputs to control algorithms for interactive music systems, as discussed further in Section 6.4.3.

A hierarchy of features can also be built up, with higher-level features determined by combining lower-level ones, a **bottom–up** rather than **top–down** methodology. The higher-level features tend to be music theoretic descriptors which coincide with the language of everyday musicianship, as opposed to signal processing. Feature extraction is really a method of refining representations of a musical signal, and can be detailed at a number of timescales depending on the algorithm; some papers discuss 'mid-level' representations as way stations between more easily extracted low-level signal features and the tricky task of creating an informal high-level musical description language.

Table 3.4 details some more musically intuitive parameters, at a higher level of cognition. Note that these features themselves can be defined as neutral processes on the audio signal. But most make implicit assumptions about the sort of signal they best operate on, and a typical requirement is that the input signal is monophonic. The polyphonic case has been approached by some descriptors, 'polyphonic timbre' for example [Aucouturier, 2006], but is most intensively investigated in the CASA and transcription research programs detailed elsewhere in this chapter. Some features also make stylistic assumptions about music itself; not all music conforms to a Western notion of major and minor keys, or prioritizes harmony!

Physiological correlates for the higher-level attributes of sound are not settled, and while some neuroscientific experiments have identified plausible loci for the processing of features like pitch, the exact mechanisms remain somewhat speculative. There is controversy in some cases over the level of cognitive activity for particular tasks. Some psychoacoustic aspects, such as perceptual onset and attack time [Collins, 2006a; Wright, 2008], loudness [Glasberg and Moore, 2002; Timoney *et al.*, 2004] or sensory dissonance [Sethares, 2005; Mashinter, 2006] do not admit trivial models, and have not been listed in the feature tables here. In the case of loudness, a number of approximations are in common use, from decibels

Table 3.4 Examples of higher-level features.

Feature	Description	Review references
Onset detection	Identifying the physical beginning of sound events	Bello *et al.* [2004]; Collins [2005]; Dixon [2006]
Pitch detection (monophonic)	Finding the fundamental frequency that would be selected by the human auditory system	de Cheveigné [2006]; Gómez *et al.* [2003]
Melody extraction	Transcription of a lead melody line, for example, as a sequence of discrete notes	Gómez *et al.* [2003]
Pitch detection (polyphonic)	The more general case of multiple simultaneous voices	Klapuri [2004]; de Cheveigné [2006]; Klapuri and Davy [2006]
Key and chord recognition	Detection of harmony	Gómez [2006]
Beat tracking and rhythm extraction	Determination of tempo, of beat locations and other metrical structure, and of rhythmic patterns	Gouyon and Meudic [2003]; Gouyon and Dixon [2005]
Instrument recognition	Timbral categorization	Herrera-Boyer *et al.* [2003]; Klapuri and Davy [2006]

to the fourth power of amplitude [Puckette, 2007, p. 92], but a fully developed model must take account of excitation patterns, auditory masking, neural inhibition, temporal integration factors and other psychoacoustics. Although these features are typically seen as calculated at earlier stages of the central auditory system, auditory-model-informed processing is still required to treat them more richly, and open questions concerning the degree of top–down interpretation remain. Onset detection can be traced in part to cells in the cochlear nucleus, an early structure in the auditory path within the brain stem [Smith, 1994], but again there may be top–down factors relating to expectations engendered by particular musical settings. Beat tracking, the extraction of 'foot-tapping' pulse, is often taken as a low-level ability, but in many cases is highly contingent on cultural factors themselves related to particular timbres and patterns. There may even be both low-level energy-based periodicity tracking, and higher-level setting-dependent tracking which must identify higher-level context as a prelude to the identification of within-measure or within-pattern position [Thaut, 2005; Collins, 2006b].

A hallmark of higher-order features is a reduction of the amount of data, from higher sampling rates for lower-level features to terse, musically cogent descriptors. Summarizing by key or meter is a state far removed from simply providing audio samples. The progression is typically to the timescale of sound events, what in some musical settings can be grossly dubbed 'notes'. We have already raised the substantial compressive benefit of object coding, where a musical signal is summed up as a succession of sound events. However, this symbolic solution to music representation is in no way universally valid – for instance, it fails to capture dynamic variation within sound, such as a woodwind player's continuous changes of breath – and should be taken with a pinch of salt for now; it is further problematized in Section 3.6.

In order to further examine musical features, the following subsections will confront in turn a few important higher-level feature types, revealing basic algorithms for their determination. Each feature denotes an area of intensive investigation with a large literature, so these demonstrations are provided as an entry point rather than as a complete explication. Feature extraction modules and code are a common component of audio programming languages and libraries for audio analysis, and many of the computer music environments highlighted in this book provide pitch detectors, loudness models, onset detectors and the like.

3.5.1 Pitch Detection

Alain de Cheveigné [2006] provides a clear review of the many different monophonic and polyphonic pitch detection methods which have been proposed. We shall defer discussing polyphonic pitch detection until Section 3.6. He separates methods into temporal (time domain), spectral (frequency domain), and spectrotemporal (auditory filter bank with per-channel processing and eventual integration) schemes. Some basic pitch detection methods, such as counting zero crossings, do not cope at all well with the *phenomenon of the missing fundamental*, where there is no signal energy at the fundamental frequency f0, but energy at harmonics. The brain is able to reconstruct a clear pitch even with a missing f0! This is one of the reasons why pitch is a much more complicated psychoacoustic attribute than the acoustic property of frequency. For example, struck metal bars may appear to have a pitch, though their spectra are more properly described as inharmonic; it just happens that the human auditory system picks up on a few higher harmonically spaced components to come up with a plausible fundamental which is not actually present in the original sound.

Two main candidate pitch detection methods that *can* accomplish the feat of virtual pitch are **autocorrelation** in the time domain, and harmonic template **pattern matching** in the spectrum. Alain de Cheveigné demonstrates the deep near equivalence of these two main monophonic pitch detection methods, and also MFCC-based pitch detection to boot [de Cheveigné, 2006, p. 53].

Let's start with the mathematical definition of periodicity: simply, that at some time delay, the signal repeats itself exactly. That is, for some time delay P (the period), $x(n+P) = x(n)$ for any n. This motivates the following equation:

$$\text{autocorrelation}(\tau) = \sum_{k=0}^{N-1} x(k)x(k+\tau) \tag{3.5}$$

The autocorrelation of a signal $x(n)$ is measured within some window of N samples, and is parameterized by the delay times τ, known as lags.[12] By trying out all possible lags, and

---

[12]There is a more general equation, the cross-correlation, whereby one signal is correlated with another at some relative delay, but we do not need that here.

taking the lag with the highest-scoring autocorrelation function, we can identify the most plausible period. We are asking the question: how well does the signal match up with itself at different lags? There are two complications; first, that some signals are not periodic, so no clear winner will be found, and second, that a normalization factor is required to adjust for the different number of measurements that fit within the N-sample window for different τ.[13] Figure 3.7 plots a normalized autocorrelation function (parameterized by lag time) for an input periodic sound.

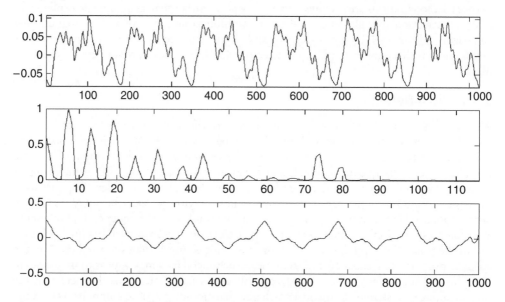

Figure 3.7   Autocorrelation method of pitch detection. The original time-domain signal, a bowed cello note, is on top and the spectrogram of the time window below, demonstrating some harmonically spaced energy in the signal. The normalized autocorrelation function is plotted on the bottom. The first peak in this plot from the left other than a lag of 0 gives the periodicity, in this case corresponding to a lag of 170 samples, or 259.4118 Hz at $R = 44\,100$.

By way of comparison, Algorithm 3.4 gives pseudocode for a basic pattern-matching procedure in the frequency domain for didactic purposes. In this instance, 12-note equal temperament is assumed, and the algorithm only checks each semitone between MIDI notes 36 and 95 as possible fundamental frequencies. The algorithm can be refined in a number of ways. To test less coarsely, you can reduce the inter-note interval ratio and increase the number of positions to test. In general, any histogramming method would have to select a resolution; it is possible to operate hierarchically, and gradually home in without testing all possibilities at the finest gradation. There are also more advanced methods that consider instantaneous frequency information from the phase vocoder [Brown and Puckette, 1993],

---

[13] It would otherwise be possible to allow different window sizes based on τ.

Algorithm 3.4 Per-frame note estimate using pattern matching.

Input: A sequence of frames X_m at sampling rate R/H where H is the hop size, each frame being a complex number sampled function of frequency bin k, $X_m(k)$ where $k = 0, 1, \ldots, \frac{N}{2}$

Output: A sequence of pitch estimates of notes p_m at sampling rate R/H where H is the hop size

  1: *lowestfreq* ← 65.4065   // MIDI note 36, two Cs below middle C

  2: *ratio* ← 1.0594630943593   // Frequency ratio increment for generating test notes; 12-note equal temperament here

  3: *notestotest* ← 60   // From MIDI note 36 to 95

  4: *harmonicweights* ← [1, 0.9, 0.8, 0.7, 0.6, 0.5, 0.4, 0.3, 0.2, 0.1]   // The pattern to match will be a harmonic comb, with different harmonics weighted by this array
        // Iterate over frames

  5: **for** $m = 0$ to $M - 1$ **do**

  6:     *maxscore* ← 0   // Initialize for finding maximum match score

  7:     *maxindex* ← 0   // State for maximum calculation
          // Iterate over note candidates

  8:     **for** $n = 0$ to *notestotest* **do**

  9:         *basefrequency* ← *lowestfreq* $* 2^{\frac{n}{12}}$ // Convert from MIDI notes to frequency domain

10:         *tempscore* ← 0   // Temporary variable for summing score over harmonics
            // Iterate over harmonics

11:         **for** $h = 0$ to 9 **do**

12:             *harmonicfrequency* ← *basefrequency* $* (h + 1)$

13:             *harmonicbin* ← *harmonicfrequency* $* (N/R)$ // Convert to FFT bin position; here we count the analysis fundamental frequency as FFT bin 1

14:             *harmonicscore* ← **GetEnergyAtBin**(*harmonicbin*)   // Get energy at this bin position, using interpolation as necessary
            tempscore ← *tempscore* + *harmonicscore* $*$ *harmonicweights*[h]   // Increment current match score by score for this harmonic

15:         **end for**

16:         **if** *tempscore* > *maxscore* **then**

17:             *maxscore* ← *tempscore*

18:             *maxindex* ← n

19:         **end if**

20:     **end for**

21:     p_m ← *maxindex*   // Store winning candidate

22: **end for**

---

estimate the confidence of pitch estimates (how clearly distinct is the top score compared with the runner-up, for instance) and otherwise take into account various psychoacoustic factors. The reader should note that a certain timbre with a fall-off in harmonic energy of one over the harmonic number is assumed in the pseudocode, and might like to consider how instrumental timbre is a much more dynamic attribute than this.

Given a pitch detector, various post processing methods might be used to smooth out the trails over time. Detectors are prey in particular to invidious octave errors, causing temporary glitches in otherwise stable estimates; use of a median filter or other smoothing technique can help to extract the final fundamental frequency trail.

Finally, pitch detection is only a well-defined task for a monophonic pitched instrument input, for otherwise we enter the even more challenging realms of predominant f0 estimation, where a lead melody line might be obtained even in the presence of background accompaniment. More challenging still is multiple f0 estimation, bringing us to full polyphonic transcription. In this case, pitch detection could be iterated, with each discovered pitch having its components extracted from the spectrum before the hunt for the next begins. However, it is a hard problem to estimate how many notes are actually present at a given time, and alternative schemes including simultaneous estimation have been proposed. Work by de Cheveigné [2006]; Klapuri [2004]; Klapuri and Davy [2006] will give the reader a start down this difficult road.

3.5.2 Onset Detection

The segmentation of a signal into discrete sections is a problem that recurs in many contexts, from the detection of musically significant events and boundaries to triggering actions in response to sensor data. It is a necessary part of the transition between a more continuous representation, and a sparse representation apprised of important moments in time.

As in the case of pitch detection, a large number of algorithms have been proposed. Most of the simplest to describe examine signal energy, looking for sudden large positive changes. Such an increase in energy is often a cue to a new event, yet there are also many situations in which false alarms occur, such as for amplitude modulation (tremolo) in a note which is already underway. It is now recognized that energy-based detection alone is appropriate for percussive sound events, but of limited use for many other cases, such as for slowly attacking sounds, or notes linked by smoother transitions like portamento pitch glides. A more general consideration of event detection views any signal change as being a possible indicator of a new event within a given context; this might be a change of pitch, or a change of vibrato characteristics, or a combination of many sound features altering at once. The more complicated algorithms reconcile multiple sources of information, utilizing more advanced mathematical techniques from machine learning and probability theory to make decisions.

This warning aside, it is nonetheless instructive to consider event detection by energy alone to build a percussive onset detector. Three possible low-level energy features that are candidate signals on which to base our onset detector are now stated. Equations are provided, using N for the window size, H for hop in samples, time-domain signal $x(n)$ at sample n and spectral bins $X_m(k)$ for bin k at frame m.

1. Time domain: Maximum power per window; difference between successive windows $\max\limits_{k=0}^{N-1} x(mH+k)^2 - \max\limits_{k=0}^{N-1} x((m-1)H+k)^2$.

2. Frequency domain: First-order difference of high frequency content $\sum_{k=1}^{N-1} |X_m(k)|k$.

3. Frequency domain: Bandwise difference of powers, acknowledging positive increments only $\sum_{k=1}^{N-1} \max(0, |X_m(k)|^2 - |X_{m-1}(k)|^2)$.

Figure 3.8 plots these functions in order below the original waveform, a hi-hat pattern. It should be clear that detection functions differ in the amount of noise present, and that any noise obstructs a clean detection of an onset.

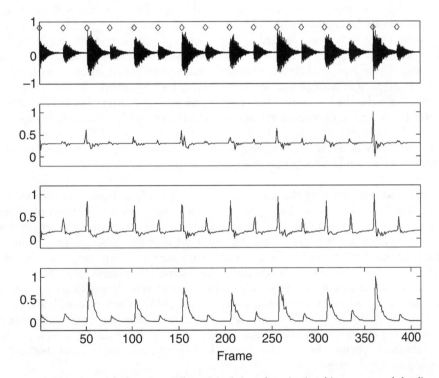

Figure 3.8   Onset detection functions. The original time-domain signal is on top, and the diamonds indicate the locations of hi-hat strikes as annotated by a human expert in a sound editor. The three detection functions described in the text are shown below it.

This is not the end of the story. The detection functions must be **peak-picked** to find the actual onset times. There are a number of tactics here, too, to cope with fluctuation around the threshold of detection, such as various forms of hysteresis after triggering (temporary shifts in the threshold of detection) [Puckette, 2007] or adaptive thresholding [Bello *et al.*, 2004], which tracks the average detection function value slowly over time.[14]

3.5.3 Beat Tracking

Synchronization between musicians requires them to have similar expectations about future events in the music, and thus to be able to commit to actions within a shared timebase. Even computers operate at latencies, and effective music making relies as critically on anticipation as on reaction. One example of a shared understanding in music is the concept of a beat; the beat does not have to physically exist in the audio signal, but is a culturally and stylistically contingent marker with respect to which other events hang. Of course, in the most literal cases (for example, a four-to-the-floor kick drum in electronic dance music) the beat is pumped out; but many more subtle possibilities are available. Further, beat as an isochronous marker is not the end of the story; consider the multiple hierarchical levels of pulsation in operation with respect to a meter in Western scores (beat subdivisions, beat, measure level, hypermeasure), or particular central patterns around which other event streams are defined in complex polyrhythmic textures (for example, the clave pattern in Latin music) [Parncutt, 1994; London, 2004]. In some ways, **beat tracking** is an insufficiently high-level term, for consideration of meter, or reference pattern, must be made to give a true sense of location in a timebase for most music. Various related tasks have been defined in the literature, from **tempo tracking** irrespective of exact beat locations, to **meter tracking** and **downbeat extraction**, which acknowledge the greater scope of the problem. But for casual purposes, if we assume certain basic types of Western music, it may be sufficient to speak of the 'foot-tapping' or 'hand-clapping' beat[15] as the most prominent pulsation level within an understood meter (such as 4/4).

Computational beat tracking then seeks to determine beat locations, and thereby to get a better handle on the music. Such procedures can inform further analysis of an audio signal, perhaps by giving a clue as to how best to segment it (providing boundaries with respect to which to extract further features), or assist interaction between a human and a machine. Establishing a timebase is also a necessary step to interpreting rhythms. While exact timings could be recorded, it is useful to get a sense of expressive timing with respect to a beat, and quantization operations rely on this separation of the metrical structure from the expressive deviations [Gabrielsson, 1999; Bilmes, 1993]. If you play with a sequencer, you often allow the sequencer to impose a metronome from the beginning. However, more advanced systems, particularly those which can analyze an existing audio file or work sensitively in live performance, do not have this option or information available, and beat tracking is a requisite step.

It should be apparent that the rich problems of metrical analysis provide a serious challenge to the algorithm designer. In general, it is a very difficult problem because of the interaction

---

[14]Real neurons have recovery periods before they can fire again (on the order of at least one millisecond) as well as threshold shifts over time when constantly stimulated. [Pickles, 1988; Smith, 1994]

[15]The relation of the beat to the human body is no accident here, and the important links from music to dance, and preferred beat timescales to human physiology, are highlighted in the literature.

with cultural convention and the difficulty of accounting for the multiple instruments and events which demarcate time cycles. Nevertheless, there are some relatively simple procedures that have been explored to extract beats in less demanding scenarios. The easiest case is that of some forms of mainstream electronic dance music where many redundant clues to the beat exist, where a steady metronome was used in the original recording sessions, and where a gross four-to-the-floor often provides an obvious clue in the energy of the audio signal itself! But if you imagine the many 1960s pop records where no click track was used during the recording, you should realize that metronomically precise beats are a luxury of modern recording technology, and even then are often dispensed with in settings favoring fluid human timing. So the challenge is increased, and the beat might have to be continually reassessed. Two procedures will now be briefly sketched, namely **cross-correlation** and **IOI histogramming**.

As Scheirer [2000] has observed, there are some similarities between the pitch and beat detection problems. We can consider a beat as a periodicity, just one taking place at a slower rate than the 16–20 Hz lower frequency threshold of the ear. 30–240 beats per minute, or 0.5–4 Hz, to take one estimate of the range of human beat perception [London, 2004], corresponds to periods from 2 seconds down to 250 milliseconds. We could therefore use autocorrelation over long time windows (typically 3–6 seconds in existing algorithms) to try to determine the most prominent pulse speed.

Actually, let's employ the more general **cross-correlation**, because in this way we can estimate simultaneously both tempo and the best fitting beat locations (in rhythm perception research these are also called period and phase, in analogy to periodic signals).

Mathematically, we now look at comparing two signals, rather than one signal with itself.

$$\text{cross-correlation}(\tau) = \sum_{k=0}^{N-1} x(k+\tau)y(k) \qquad (3.6)$$

If we imagine signal x to be an energy signature for the audio we have to analyze, y will be some form of pattern we want to match against it. Let y be the impulse train consisting of a one every P samples, and otherwise zero. Then P is the period and τ is an indicator of the phase we would be testing via the cross-correlation; we vary P and τ to try out different possibilities, and find the best match of the beat pattern y to the signal x. Because this beat pattern is only non-zero at a few discrete points, this substantially cuts down the amount of calculation we have to do to effect this. Figure 3.9 illustrates this, by applying a grid of beats (y is marked by the dashed vertical lines) to an energy signal derived from a windowed segment of sound file. In fact, this method, due to Laroche [2003], has been implemented in commercial soundcards. Laroche proposes more developed beat patterns that mark out subdivisions of the beat at reduced strength as well as the primary beat locations; it is possible to also search for matches with straight and swung sixteenth-note positions to further differentiate groove. Yet these patterns make substantial assumptions about time signature and subdivisions; Laroche varies the weights within the patterns to differentiate styles.

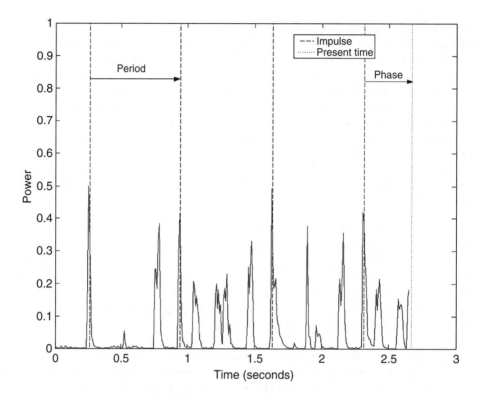

Figure 3.9   Cross-correlation method for computational beat tracking.

Inter-onset interval (IOI) histogramming [Gouyon, 2005] is a variant that acts on discrete events. It can be useful for MIDI event-based beat tracking, or for audio signals where an onset detector has first identified event locations. By forming a histogram of all the possible intervals between all events in a given time window, combining evidence from double- or half-speed layers and favoring tempos near 110 bpm or so, an estimate of tempo can be made. Once the tempo is known, the event time positions must themselves be examined to try to determine the beat locations that best explain the events.

Both these methods operate on a wide window; just as for an FFT, it is assumed that the signal is stable within the window. Larger windows give more stable estimates, and in some applications a window is taken of the size of the whole track; this assume the track keeps to one tempo throughout. Real music includes slow ups and fast downs, and other forms of abrupt and continuous tempo change, so the algorithm can easily become confused at musical transitions. Further, the size of window (and hop size) have a direct bearing on how quickly the system will be able to react after such a change. This stability–reactivity tradeoff is fundamental [Gouyon and Dixon, 2005]. Human beings can 'turn on a die' because they have all sorts of further contextual information to go on (a score, prior rehearsal, improvisation experience in a given style); so the two algorithms described here would require development to cope with this, and perhaps you realize from this discussion that computational beat tracking itself remains in many respects an open research problem.

3.6 THE TRANSCRIPTION PROBLEM

'[P]erceptual analysis does not involve a reconstitution of the score. For once a certain level of complexity is reached, perception can no longer handle all the information received in real time.' [Deliège, 1989, p. 213]

The ultimate expression of automatic analysis capabilities is sometimes claimed to be a machine which could produce a score of any music just from the audio signal alone. In the most optimistic version, a computer program is sought which is a universal transcriber of polyphonic music, capable of rendering audio into a symbolic reduction that nevertheless captures all salient psychological aspects of the events and sources from which that music was constructed. In some cases, rather than a hypothetical universal symbolic representation, the representation for the transcription is specifically a Western classical score. Either case is problematic in claims about the existence of musical universals spanning all cultures and styles, but the common practice score especially so, since such scores themselves have been criticized on so many grounds by ethnomusicologists [Brăiloiu, 1984; Stobart and Cross, 2000]. Bartok's problems with the lack of timbral and fine expressive timing detail in scores are described by Emmerson [2000a, p. 120]: 'From the detailed transcriptions made by Bartok in the villages of Hungary (and elsewhere) the clash of the prescriptive notation and the descriptive score he sought to make of a rich oral culture was obvious.'

Even in the sphere of Western classical music, consider the many ambiguous situations where multiple solutions exist. Contemporary scores in particular are a minefield of ambiguous time relationships which admit many potential transcriptions (e.g., Boulez's *Le marteau sans maître*), but uniqueness is lost even for the relation of 3/8 to 3/4. The slow movement of Grieg's piano concerto, for instance, is written in 3/8 at slow tempo when it might be more naturally notated in 3/4. Smoliar [1999, p. 102] gives the example of a cor anglais solo by Wagner, where recovering the original score from a performance would fail, since any expressivity on the part of the performer conceals the barline location; transcription relies on the score allowing an inversion. It might be asked whether recovering the parts of a complex orchestral score (say of Stravinsky's *Rite of Spring*) is even slightly realistic, given the sound mass of orchestration which masks certain instruments:[16] 'we are often limited by masking processes in hearing out inner voices' [McAdams, 1989, p. 190]. Bregman [1990, p. 489] notes the case of *ensemble timbre*, for instance, the situation

---

[16] It is an open question whether a computer could do better than a human being in this situation; is there somehow more available in the audio signal than the human ear can discern, even though human ears have been so intimately tied to the construction of the works?

in classical orchestration of a quiet flute doubling the strings at the octave. One might recognize the brightening of timbre, but be unable to recognize individual harmonic components necessary to separate the sound sources.

Even those classical pieces which are most traditionally tied to the score format admit all sorts of expressive nuances consisting of micro-timing and pitch alterations from the score in their performed interpretations. Indeed, such 'systematic deviations' are intimately tied to marking musical structure [Clarke, 1999b]. The differentiation of expressive timing deviations from notated durations inherent in the 'quantization problem' [Desain and Honing, 1992] already arose in the context of computational beat tracking above. Given a recording, the challenge is surely only exaggerated by a conductor's interpretative choices, the recording environment and individual performer errors; though perhaps a comparison of multiple interpretations might go some way to establishing the urtext! A transcription program would certainly require multiple scans performed outside of realtime causal constraints. Hainsworth [2004] provides results of a survey of human transcribers which reveal that transcription is hardly a perfect and immediate operation for human musicians, who often use iterative testing by trial and error, and in all cases multiple sweeps. One standard tactic is to target outer parts first, and then to fill in inner parts by overall harmonic rules. This concentration on important parts, and a sensible reconstruction of the rest, is the likely tactic behind Mozart's publicity-stunt transcription of Allegri's at the time unpublished *Miserere* [Sloboda, 1985].

It is straightforward to make a psychological case that the score artifact cannot adequately represent all facets of music as experienced by listeners. It is also perhaps unnecessary for music understanding; Dixon [2001], Scheirer [1998] and Goto [2001] all note that beat induction does not require full score knowledge to operate: the average listener knows little music theory, and yet taps along happily to the beat. The very idea of extracting all note events while listening is attacked by Scheirer [1996]; he does not accept the validity of the 'transcriptive metaphor', giving the example of Bregman's 'chimerae', the possible phantom interactions of sound objects: 'When cues that favor vertical integration are present, the auditory system treats the combination as a unit, and whatever properties are extracted are assigned as global descriptions of this unit. When the cues favor segregation, the combination is treated as accidental and only the individual, nondissonant tones are perceived' [Bregman, 1990, p509].[17] The machine listening work at MIT [Martin *et al.*, 1998] models the non-musician as the primary listener, rather than the specialist musician. Engineering solutions for such tasks as beat tracking or music classification operate on functions of a signal where note events are implicit, not explicitly determined as a prerequisite to useful music understanding work.

Although these critiques of automated transcription have some force, the goal of machine transcription has still motivated much cutting edge research, and intersects with the most difficult problems of musical audio analysis by computer. Investigations of the problem of

---

[17]It has been contended, however, that such low-level groupings are reassigned and resolved into larger-scale objects based on higher-level principles, guided by learned schema, as in the Blackboard model [Godsmark and Brown, 1999].

multi-part transcription date back to James A. Moorer's PhD thesis from 1975. Attempts to build working transcription systems have often concentrated on polyphonic pitch detection [de Cheveigné, 2006] and metrical induction as core tasks [Klapuri, 2004]. While some polyphonic pitch transcription schemes have shown increasing ability in recent years, we are by no means near a definite solution. In an edited volume specifically on musical transcription by machine [Klapuri and Davy, 2006], reported results are highly context dependent. For example, transcription errors increase with the number of voices in a mixture, with one advanced algorithm based on an auditory model achieving around 12% error rates for four voices and 22% for six. [Klapuri, 2006, pp. 260–262]. Perhaps the most successful attempts have concentrated on specific instruments in specific styles. Transcription of piano music has been targeted by companies, particularly for the restoration of old recordings via a new rendering on a MIDI-controlled concert grand. In one recent project, Zenph Studios reported the extraction of sufficient pitch and onset data from an old Art Tatum recording to rerecord it [Hamer, 2005]; this is the product of concentrating a lot of effort on one piece, with semi-automatic transcription under the guidance of a human engineer/musician. We do not yet have any sort of general transcription facility. In some cases, however, polyphonic pitch detection and source separation technology is coming to market in commercial products within limited cases (such as all notes from the same non-noisy timbral source, as for Direct Note Access in Melodyne http://www.celemony.com/cms/), and the area remains a productive one for new audio analysis technology.

3.7 MACHINE LISTENING AND CAUSAL REALTIME ANALYSIS

One issue that has not been sufficiently elucidated up to this point is that human hearing operates in a causal manner in real time. Not all audio analysis procedures are built for realtime use, or for causal operation. **Realtime** implies that the calculations for a segment of audio can take place at least as fast as the duration of that segment; otherwise an algorithm is **non-realtime**. **Causal** requires that only knowledge of past and current samples can be assumed. Some **non-causal** algorithms can take account of future samples when calculating their output for a given time, because they are given a whole audio file in advance. For instance, the analysis stage of a peak-tracking phase vocoder can be improved by running the algorithm on a sound in reverse, a non-causal operation. Accuracy is improved because the offsets of sounds are less rich in confounding transient noise than onsets, so tracked sinusoidal partials can be established more easily. Yet this trick could never be employed for an analysis system in a concert situation, where audio data is streamed in rather than being delivered as an existing recording. Another example is the use of a whole audio file to calculate a stable estimate of tempo (a procedure which assumes a dominant stable tempo throughout the track); in a concert setting, waiting until after a piece finishes to definitively establish tempo would make for an ineffectual musician!

In order to react, there is a necessary delay to process information. The criticality of anticipation has been raised already as a mechanism by which synchronization can be recovered; by means of expectation of future events, a human participant in music overcomes the inherent processing delay. All machine listening processes operate at some latency. Even if the latency of machine algorithms is actually less than human reaction speeds over the whole auditory and motor loop, it is still present. A good experiment is the task of singing along to a piece you've never heard before; a musician should be able to lock onto a melody line soon after it is presented, to almost give the illusion of knowing it already; but the delay will be palpable. A machine pitch tracker can potentially run at even less perceptible delay (in part because the response can be synthesized almost immediately), but since the stable detection of a frequency might require multiple periods of the fundamental to pass, it is impossible to have zero delay unless there is some form of prediction on which to risk acting.

Finally, to mention one technicality, the creator of realtime machine listening algorithms will also have to contend with the design of audio processing software. This software, for efficiency reasons, runs on a block-based processing scheme, whereby rather than calculating one sample at a time, a **block** of samples, customarily 64 at a time, are calculated. This sets up a minimal latency. Furthermore, many analysis routines require large loops over samples (for example, calculating a wavelet transform or an autocorrelation). To avoid sudden CPU spikes, deliberate extra delay may have to be built in to allow for the amortizing (spreading) of the CPU load over multiple blocks. Extra latency is traded off against smoothness of resource demands. This would require the design of a re-entrant algorithm that can store its state of processing between calls, an extra burden on the designer. The interested reader might consult open-source code for machine listening plug-ins and externals in SuperCollider and Pd, for instance, to see examples. In non-realtime work, this technicality becomes irrelevant.

3.8 SUMMARY

In this chapter we have addressed many methods of audio analysis available to the computer musician. This has led us to various technicalities of using the discrete Fourier transform and developments relating to the phase vocoder. We have also encountered alternative signal representations for sound analysis including filter banks, wavelets and more exotic transforms. One important venture is modeling the human auditory system, and we have seen how this influences work in computational auditory scene analysis and perceptual audio coding. Whether founded in auditory modeling or not, feature extraction can operate at a variety of levels from low-level signal features to more musically relevant high-level properties. This method is central in many current investigations in computer music, from music information retrieval to feature-based synthesis. We have explored some particular machine listening tasks, such as onset detection, pitch detection and computational beat tracking, all of which might be useful to building interactive music systems. The difficulty of the 'transcription problem' has been discussed, to give insight into why audio analysis is not yet an entirely solved problem. Finally, we have covered some technicalities pertaining to the practical implementation of machine listening algorithms, differentiating realtime from non-realtime and causal from non-causal work. The rich body of methods in this chapter underlie and intersect with all the other chapters in the book.

3.9 EXERCISES

This being a more technical chapter, many of these exercises require both mathematical and programming skills (for example, MATLAB allows fast programming solutions to some of these, or you may explore them in C or Java). However, it is possible to pick up some principles by using the built-in analysis features of existing software.

1. Choose one sound file with lots of noise sources (e.g., a drum loop) and one sound file with monophonic pitched sounds (e.g., an a cappella singer, or a sample of a flute or clarinet). Compare spectrogram plots for these two, bearing Figure 1.5 in mind. Change the N (window size) in the FFT analysis parameters for your spectrogram program, and observe what happens to the results.

2. Consider the grid of measurements involved in a spectrogram. For a particular window centered at one moment in time, measurements of energy are obtained for a set of harmonics of the analysis frequency. The spectrogram is a three-dimensional (3D) entity (time, frequency, amplitude squared) and typically plots log energy as color intensity for particular points in the time-frequency plane. Zoom into a spectrogram plot in an audio editor (such as Audacity). Do you see the grid? Further, investigate waterfall plots, which use 3D to represent the energy distribution, rather than color (software options here might include sndpeak from the Princeton Sound Labs, http://soundlab.cs.princeton.edu/software/sndpeek/, or Christoph Lauer's Sonogram Visible Speech http://sourceforge.net/projects/sonogram).

3. Create a program which implements the sliding window as detailed in Algorithm 3.1, but rather than using an FFT, finds the root mean square amplitude for each successive window, for $R = 44\,100$, $N = 1024$, $H = 512$ (use a rectangular window). Apply your program to a short sample to extract the RMS feature for each frame. Add to your program the extraction of the zero crossing rate, making a feature vector of two features for each frame.

4. Let's assume a sampling rate of 44 100 Hz. Calculate the energy in frequency bins one to twenty of a $N = 1024$-point Fourier transform by using an existing FFT implementation, or by brute force – you can write your own DFT by following the equation:

$$X(k) = \sum_{n=0}^{N-1} x(n) e^{-i 2\pi (k/N) n}, \quad k = 1, \ldots, 20 \tag{3.7}$$

and get around using complex numbers by applying Euler's formula to split the complex exponential into cosine and sine parts; calculate the energy as the sum of the squares of those two parts:

$$|X(k)|^2 = \left(\sum_{n=0}^{N-1} x(n) \cos(2\pi(k/N)n) \right)^2$$
$$+ \left(\sum_{n=0}^{N-1} x(n) \sin(2\pi(k/N)n) \right)^2, \quad k = 1, \ldots, 20 \tag{3.8}$$

Compare the result for two different input signals, each a sine tone, but the first at 344.53125 Hz, and the second at 350 Hz. Explain your results. This first part assumed rectangular windowing. Now repeat the question with a von Hann window (window$(n) = 0.5 - 0.5 \cos(2\pi n/N)$).

5. This question considers psychoacoustically motivated scales, such as the Mel, Bark and ERB scales, which model the frequency sensitivity of the basilar membrane. Here we follow Klapuri [2006, pp. 236–7] in using the ERB scale. The main conversion equation from ERB scale units to frequency is:

$$\text{frequency in Hz} = 229 * (10^{0.046728972*\text{erbs}} - 1) \tag{3.9}$$

and there are approximately 42 ERB rate scale units across the human hearing range. Using the equation, find the center frequencies for 100 equally spaced filters ranging from 1 to 42 ERB scale units. Create 100 linearly spaced frequencies between 26 and 20 782 Hz. Plot the two distributions on a graph (with linear and log frequency axes) to see how they compare. (If you want to go even closer to hair cells, you could take 3500 rather than 100 filters!)

6. Investigate the SPEAR software, and after making some manipulations export the peak tracking data as a text file. Examine this in a text editor; you should see the peaks listed per frame with frequencies and amplitudes. Now try exporting the data in SDIF format (SDIF is the Sound Description Interchange Format, a way of passing audio analysis data between different programs). Load the data into a second analysis program (e.g., SNDAN, SMS, Loris, or an IRCAM package such as AudioSculpt), play with it there, and then try to return it to SPEAR (see also Wright et al. [2000]).

7. To try out the effectiveness of pitch detection algorithms, you might need to do some singing. The Tartini software by Philip McLeod is one cross-platform option, and there are many other plug-in pitch detectors for computer music systems which could be used for this task. When tracking your voice, does the pitch detector make any octave errors? When does it get into trouble? Explicitly try out vowels and consonants separately. Also try passing a non-monophonic sound file through the algorithm. Can a monophonic pitch detector pick up on a lead melody line in the presence of confounding materials? Compare different pitch detection algorithms if you have them available, in different musical settings.

8. Build a simple onset detector using one of the three detection functions outlined in the text, to run on an input sound file of your choice. Once you have the detection function, consider how to proceed to a decision about onset locations. You might first try a fixed threshold and take all locations above the threshold. You will probably then want to introduce a delay (perhaps up to 50 milliseconds) after detecting an onset before the system can retrigger, to avoid double hits where the detection function fluctuates. Can you think of any more elaborate peak picking schemes, perhaps based on scoring local peaks with respect to the last N values, or the surrounding $-N$ to N for each possible onset location?

9. Investigate human beat-tracking ability and anticipation. Choose a number of pieces in divergent styles, from rigidly metronomic (such as electronic dance music) to free time (such as an opera recitative or alap). You may need to get a friend to help test you, or you might write a program to set up this experience. Tap along, after the music is started at a random position. How quickly can you achieve synchronization with the flow? Stop the music at a random point, but try to keep tapping; how well were you anticipating what would happen next in the music?

10. Implement Algorithm 3.4 in your computer music environment of choice, as a causal realtime plug-in.

3.10

FURTHER READING

Beauchamp, J. (ed) (2007). *Analysis, Synthesis and Perception of Musical Sounds*. Springer, New York, NY.

de Poli, G., Piccialli, A. and Roads, C. (eds) (1991). *Representations of Musical Signals*. MIT Press, Cambridge, MA.

Dolson, M. (1986). The phase vocoder: A tutorial. *Computer Music Journal*, 10(4):14–27.

Hayes, M. H. (1999). *Digital Signal Processing*, McGraw-Hill, New York, NY.

Gold, B. and Morgan, N. (1999). *Speech and Audio Signal Processing: Processing and Perception of Speech and Music*. John Wiley and Sons, New York, NY.

Klapuri, A. and Davy, M. (eds) (2006). *Signal Processing Methods for Music Transcription*. Springer, New York, NY.

Loy, G. (2007). *Musimathics* (Volume 2). MIT Press, Cambridge, MA (Chapters 2, 3 and 10).

Mallat, S. (1998). *A Wavelet Tour of Signal Processing*, 2nd Edition. Academic Press, San Diego, CA.

Roads, C. (1996). *The Computer Music Tutorial*. MIT Press, Cambridge, MA. (Sound Analysis, pp. 493–609; Appendix: Fourier Analysis (with Philip Greenspun), pp. 1073–1112).

Roads, C., Pope, S. T., Piccialli, A. and de Poli, G. (eds) (1997). *Musical Signal Processing*. Swets and Zeitlinger, Lisse, the Netherlands.

Smith, S. W. (1997). *The Scientist and Engineer's Guide to Digital Signal Processing*. California Technical Publishing, San Diego, CA (www.dspguide.com).

Wang, D. and Brown, G. J. (2006). *Computational Auditory Scene Analysis: Principles, Algorithms, and Applications*. John Wiley and Sons/IEEE Press, Hoboken, NJ.

Chapter 4

Processing

'Get hold of some new ears, or else you will soon no longer hear what is new but merely the records of your leaky centuries-old memory.'

Karlheinz Stockhausen [Stockhausen, 1989, p. 129]

'I feel that the processing is only there to emphasize things that are already there .... I'm never very interested in the kind of sound processing that leads me way too far away from the original sound, *unless* it really makes connections.'

Hildegard Westerkamp [Norman, 2004, p. 85]

OBJECTIVES

This chapter covers:

- more on digital signals;
- convolution and filtering;
- lots of audio effects.

The concept of processing a sound links audio analysis and sound synthesis. There is a whole field, called **digital signal processing** (often abbreviated as DSP), which denotes any treatment of digital audio signals; this extends out to analysis, and to the generation of novel signals as well. But this chapter will concentrate on manipulations of existing signals, combining and transforming them. With a proliferation of effects plug-ins in computer music software, this is the commonplace understanding of the idea of processing. This chapter provides a useful place to bring together some fundamental results for signals, including the special operation of convolution, which will help us gain a fuller understanding of digital filters. It also describes a general suite of digital audio effects. Intuitive understanding will be pursued, but there is inevitably a mathematical side to all this; for the interested reader, you'll find extra mathematics in some sidebars.

4.1 MORE ON SIGNALS

4.1.1 Signals and Sampling Rates

Aspects of signals and digital audio were introduced in Chapter 1. Signals are time-varying values which must be discrete to be processed by computational systems. Any time-domain signal in a computer has been sampled in time and quantized in amplitude. The nth sample of signal x is denoted $x(n)$.[1] So if the sampling rate R is 44 100 samples per second, the value $x(563\,713)$ occurs at a time of $\frac{563\,713}{44\,100} \approx 12.783$ seconds since the start of the signal.

Imagine we have a signal sampled at a rate R_1, but want to run it within a digital system which operates at a different rate R_2. This situation might arise for a sound file which was originally recorded at one sampling rate, but is to be sent to a sound-card DAC operating at a different sampling rate. The process of adapting a signal to a rate different from that at which it was originally sampled is **resampling** [Hayes, 1999, pp. 110–114]. Two basic resampling procedures are available, which either increase or decrease the sampling rate by an integer factor:

- To **upsample** by a factor L, make a new signal where $L-1$ zeroes are inserted between every sample of the old signal. Then low-pass filter with a cutoff of the old Nyquist frequency, and a gain of L, to reconstruct the intermediate values where there are currently zeroes (the filter is an anti-imaging filter, since images proliferate within the new sampling rate when the zeroes are inserted).

- To **downsample** by a factor M, low-pass filter first with a cutoff of the old Nyquist frequency divided by M (this is an anti-aliasing filter). Now form a new signal by taking every Mth sample.

Because standard sampling rates are integers, and their ratio L/M is therefore a rational number, we can convert between them by first upsampling by L and then downsampling by M. The filter steps can be combined into a single low-pass filter by just taking the lower

---

[1]Some signal processing texts use $x[n]$ for discrete signals; we're a little more informal here, following the precedent of other computer music textbooks.

of the cutoff frequencies, and we can also remove the greatest common divisor of L and M from the ratio before we start.

What happens for any real number, one which can only be well approximated by a complicated rational? (What if the sampling rate was 44100.314156 or worse to start with?) It is possible to cope with general sampling rate ratios as well, even time-varying rates, using appropriate interpolation filters. This is reminiscent of the problem of sample playback that we already introduced back in Section 2.7.3. A pointer position into the original signal is used, which is updated by an arbitrary amount with each output sample step. The fractional sample position is then the input to some form of interpolation scheme which combines local information in the original signal near that position.[2] In wilder playback rate manipulations, some distortion may be part of the effect sound, and gross pitch shifting may distract attention from aliasing and amplitude distortion among other side effects. Nevertheless, some schemes, such as band-limited interpolation [Loy, 2007b, pp. 480–482], are available that provide high-quality results approximating the theoretical maximum performance available.[3]

As depicted in Figure 1.1 two signals $x(n)$ and $y(n)$ can be combined by addition to form $(x+y)(n)=x(n)+y(n)$ and by multiplication to form $(xy)(n)=x(n)y(n)$. This means that at each moment in time the signals' current values are added or multiplied together. If x is varying while signal y is constant, the result of $x+y$ is a DC (direct current – from electrical engineering) offset. We get back the shape of signal x displaced on the amplitude axis by y. If x is multiplied by constant y we attain a scaled version of the signal. Why are these mathematical tricks useful? Because the range of one signal might have to be modified to make it suitable for use elsewhere. Imagine a frequency input to a sine oscillator: sensible values here might be numbers from 16–16 000, to cover the audible frequency range in Hertz of an adult human. If we wanted to plug in a sensor to control this frequency, we might have values from 0–5 (volts) or 0–127 (MIDI values), or some other range. We can use scaling and offsetting to convert between the different ranges. In general, if one value is in the range a to b and we would like it to be in the range c to d, the function for rescaling is:

$$\text{new value} = c + (d-c)\left(\frac{\text{old value} - a}{b-a}\right) \tag{4.1}$$

When the target range is from 0 to 1 ($c=0$, $d=1$) we have carried out a standard **normalization** by the maximum b and minimum a of the original range. If we start from the convenient range of 0 to 1 ($a=0$, $b=1$) it is straightforward to rescale to any other desired range. As an immediate exercise in understanding, you might try substituting 0 and

---

[2]Effective interpolation filters can be designed to tackle this problem, though the filters are 'polyphase', which means that the exact filter coefficients vary during use and track across a family of associated responses. Think of linear interpolation for different fractional positions t; the multipliers for combining adjacent samples change with the interpolation position according to $(1-t)*x(n-1)+t*x(n)$. Linear interpolation is prone to various drawbacks including amplitude and phase distortion [Dattorro, 1997, p. 769], motivating alternative schemes such as all-pass filter interpolation or higher-order polynomial fitting.

[3]A sinc filter is the theoretical best choice, corresponding to a brick-wall filter, but only if we sum over an infinite number of input samples! There are better choices for combining a finite number of samples. You'll have to delve into heavier signal processing textbooks for more details.

Why complex numbers keep turning up in signal processing

There are parts of signal processing that depend on an understanding of complex numbers. This is because they actually end up making the mathematical analysis more revealing, and sometimes operations more straightforward to express, even though for someone new to complex numbers it hardly seems like that in the short term. Complex numbers have the benefit of being a closed algebraic domain, whereas real numbers are not sufficient to describe the solution of even the simple polynomial $x^2 + 1 = 0$. I've tried to keep this 'complexity' optional in this book, but it is essential for some explanations, and the mathematically literate reader may want to pursue the insights that follow along these paths.

The mathematics of linear operations in signal processing is often based on asking what happens to a sinusoid, and then working up to more complicated signals through the Fourier transform (we know we can express a general signal by a sum of sinusoids, so if we know the effect on a sinusoid the linearity extends the result over the sum). It is convenient to carry out these mathematical operations on complex exponentials, which encapsulate sinusoidal behavior via Euler's relation $e^{i\omega} = \cos(\omega) + i\sin(\omega)$. Using the complex exponential and working within the complex domain avoids having to consider sine and cosine terms separately, a boon because trigonometric functions are more mathematically awkward to deal with [Jaffe, 1987a]; we return to the real numbers at a late stage of the process.

We can also rearrange a trigonometric function in terms of complex exponentials, so that $\sin(\omega) = \frac{i}{2}(e^{-i\omega} - e^{i\omega})$ and $\cos(\omega) = \frac{1}{2}(e^{i\omega} + e^{-i\omega})$. In doing so we obtain a new insight into the real trigonometric functions; they are actually composed of half-strength positive and negative angular frequency components in the complex domain. A real sinusoid then has a spectral representation as two (related) complex components, each of which takes half of their magnitude (in a sampled system, the two exceptions are for 0 Hz and the Nyquist frequency, where the negative and positive frequencies fall at the same place). In practice, because of the conjugate symmetrical relation between the negative and positive frequencies, we might only deal with the positive frequencies, for example, in the plot of the spectrum of a real signal obtained through a Fourier transform, but the negative frequency components are still implicitly present.

The short lesson is: it's hard to avoid the complex domain, even if only analyzing real signals.

1 for the pairs a and b or c and d in the above equation to see how the mathematics gets simplified.[4] This deals with the linear case; an exercise at the close of the chapter will take you through conversions between linear and logarithmic domains.

4.1.2 Ring and Amplitude Modulation

Modulation in signal processing refers to the control of an aspect of one signal by another.[5] The controlled (modulated) signal is the **carrier**, and the controlling signal the **modulator**. Modulation is a nonlinear process, since the functions involved typically go beyond a linear sum and scaling, meaning that new frequency components can appear in the output spectrum that weren't present in either input. When these new components fall in frequency either side of a carrier component frequency, they are termed **sidebands**. In this section we consider what happens when two time-varying signals are multiplied together. Since we need to consider the spectral consequences of this process, a good engineering approach is to investigate what happens to two sinusoids, and then go on to make more general assertions about more complex sounds. This is a principle worth keeping in mind; if we know what happens to a sinusoid we're usually in a good position to see what happens to a more complex signal, with a little help from Fourier.

A straight multiplication of two signals is called **ring modulation** (RM). Such a basic multiplication is entirely symmetric and the names modulator and carrier can be assigned to the two involved signals either way around: carrier∗modulator or modulator∗carrier, it makes no difference. Standard signals whose amplitudes can take on both negative and positive values (for instance, oscillating from positive to negative around zero amplitude) are called **bipolar**. Both the signals are bipolar in ring modulation.

Now for the multiplication of sinusoids; this is bound to involve some mathematics. There are trigonometric formulas that convert products of sines or cosines into sums, and using such a formula gives us exactly the analytical answer we need. The version for pure cosines would run:

$$\cos(C)\cos(M) = 0.5(\cos(C - M) + \cos(C + M)) \tag{4.2}$$

Thus for sinusoids[6] the spectrum ends up with two frequencies (two sidebands), at $C - M$ and $C + M$, where C is the carrier frequency and M is the modulator frequency. Note that if we labeled C and M the other way around, we'd get $M + C$ and $M - C$. Since a negative frequency is always convertible into the positive mirror-image (with a possible

---

[4]The composite transformation in the equation is actually a mapping from the interval $[a, b]$ to $[0, 1]$ and thence from $[0, 1]$ to $[c, d]$.

[5]Modulation in telecommunications is used to encode many band-limited signals within an available overall transmission bandwidth (frequency range). The signals to be transmitted are used as modulators for allocated carriers. Although we cover RM and AM here, frequency modulation (FM) and single-sideband modulation (a more tightly packed version of the ring modulation described in this section which uses complex numbers) are the standard mechanisms. At the receiver, demodulation recovers the original signal to the audible frequency range rather than playing back the modulated carrier signal, which was boosted up to very high frequencies for transmission purposes.

[6]Angular frequencies $2\pi f$ should really be used, but there is no change to the principle of the mathematics, so the simplest version is used here for demonstration. For a sinusoid, there is generally a fixed phase offset to cope with, but try plugging $C = \omega_1 + \phi_1$ and $M = \omega_2 + \phi_2$ into the formula and you'll see how the phases get taken care of as well.

phase change), this is really the same thing we already have. It is what we'd expect from the inherent symmetry of the situation, and the commutativity of multiplication in arithmetic.

For more complicated waves than sines, we get many more components to the spectrum of the multiplied signals, essentially from all the cross-modulations between sinusoidal components, all affecting each other. If the carrier were a sum of three sinusoids, and the modulator a sum of five, ring modulation would create 15 multiplications and thus 30 output frequency components. This is a cheap way of getting a more complicated spectrum out of simpler parts, and this process is taken to its logical extreme in other nonlinear manipulations such as frequency modulation (see Chapter 5).

Amplitude modulation (AM) is similar to ring modulation but with a subtle difference: the modulator is **unipolar**, that is, always positive. So now there is something which differentiates the carrier (which is usually bipolar) from the unipolar modulator. Mathematically, amplitude modulation can be shown to be ring modulation with an additional term caused by the constant offset in the unipolar signal. In the case of our favorite cosines, where the carrier goes between -1 and 1 and the unipolar modulator is rescaled to lie between 0 and 1:

$$\cos(C) * (0.5 + 0.5 * \cos(M)) = 0.5 * \cos(C) + 0.25 * (\cos(C - M) + \cos(C + M)) \quad (4.3)$$

The spectrum ends up with the sum and difference frequencies we saw in ring modulation, at $C + M$ and $C - M$, as well as the original carrier frequency C passing through.

Note that modulation of two complex sources inevitably makes very rich output spectra, often *too* rich, so some care is required. Ring modulation and amplitude modulation can easily be used for sound effects, and while radio transmission applications typically use a simple sinusoidal carrier and a rich modulator, we can proceed either way around in creative musical applications.

Consider ring modulation using a single sinusoid carrier whose frequency is within the audible range (> 20 Hz or so) and a rich input modulator signal. Sidebands will result, centered around the carrier frequency (recall $C - M$ and $C + M$), with a copy of the original signal spectrum shifted up above the carrier frequency C following from the $C + M$ part, and, more confusingly, a frequency-inverted copy (the lower sideband) below frequency C. I say below, but due to aliasing and reflection of negative frequencies around 0, the sideband information can also creep back up into the audio range, or down from Nyquist, further complicating the aural picture (see Figure 4.1). In one special case, if the carrier and the modulator are exactly the same signal, ring modulation will produce a DC (0 Hz) signal (which could be filtered out) and otherwise double all frequency components ($C - M = 0$, $C + M = 2C$). With lower-frequency oscillations (< 20 Hz) periodic rhythmic effects are produced, which we'll examine next by considering slow amplitude modulation and enveloping.

Stockhausen made extensive use of ring modulation in his electronic music such as *Telemusik* (1966) (to modulate recordings from around the world) and live electronics work such

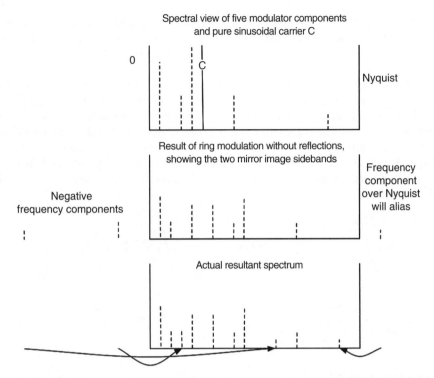

Spectral view of five modulator components
and pure sinusoidal carrier C

0   Nyquist

Result of ring modulation without reflections,
showing the two mirror image sidebands

Negative   Frequency
frequency components   component
                                                            over Nyquist
                                                            will alias

Actual resultant spectrum

Figure 4.1   Spillover of sidebands. Ring modulation between a modulator consisting of five sinusoidal components (dashed lines) and a single sinusoidal carrier at frequency C. The
diagram demonstrates how two sidebands are created around frequency C of mirror
images of the original modulator components, and how any component that falls outside
of the digital frequency range from 0 Hz to half the sampling rate is reflected back into
that region.

as *Mantra* (1970) (effecting the two pianos), though here the difficulty of creating analog
ring modulators gives some additional richness to the sound [Roads, 1996]. In the digital
domain, ring modulation is a sufficiently simple effect to implement that it would be a good
candidate if you wanted to try building your first audio processing plug-in, for instance.

4.1.3 Mixing and Splicing

The linear operations of adding signals and scaling them by constant multipliers are the
backbone of mixing multiple signals together, such as rendering tracks in an audio recorder
to a final mixdown. In DAW software there is a maximum reference amplitude allowed
in the system without distortion. Typically, a 0 dB level is the working maximum and a
little further headroom is available as leeway in case of overloads, since the distortion sound
is so absolute and usually avoided at all costs. Actually, with floating point audio we can
normalize later, perhaps when we add the signals up before final output, though individual

scaling factors for different layers will need to be set for balanced aural results. Even so, we may need some sort of **dynamic processing** to assist in keeping peak levels under control and signals balanced within a mix; we'll discuss this in Section 4.3.1.

Mixing can be highly time dependent, and it is unlikely that different tracks are always set to the same fixed levels. Layers may fade in and out, or follow arbitrary gain control signals. Time-varying gain control like this is also a way of confronting 'awkward' runs of audio; hide it if it's really bad! This time-varying control of the gain of different contributing audio parts is effectively a form of amplitude modulation, with the modulator the amplitude **envelope**. A fade in, sustain and fade out could be easily modeled using the ASR (attack–sustain–release) shape. Figure 4.2 depicts two standard and two more complicated envelope shapes.

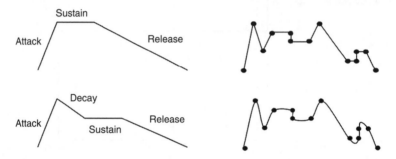

Figure 4.2   Envelopes. The left two envelopes have labeled segments depicting standard shapes, familiar from synthesizers. As well as the time duration of each segment, there would be parameters for the levels which the envelope reaches. The right-hand diagrams show arbitrary envelopes constructed from breakpoint functions. The same breakpoints appear in the top and bottom diagram, but are interpolated in two ways; by straight line segments on the top right, and a smoother curve on the bottom right.

There are various ways to store envelopes, including just keeping them as sampled functions of time, but a common representation for an arbitrary envelope is to store a list of **breakpoints** (sometimes also called control points) as time–amplitude pairs. Segments are the transitions between each pair; the number of segments will be one fewer than that of breakpoints. Rather than directly storing (x, y) positions for the breakpoints, it is also common to have separate lists of target amplitude values and the times for shifting between these values (there would be one more amplitude value than time difference, so one amplitude for each breakpoint and as many times as segments). Because not all envelopes are made up of straight line segments, there may also be further parameters, for the overall curve, or on a per-segment basis, controlling the shape of the interpolating curve. Envelopes are generally useful in sound synthesis as well; sounds vary over time, and there is great opportunity to use envelopes as control signals for synthesis parameters. To illustrate the two common methods consider depicting the top right ASR envelope in the diagram as four breakpoints in the form of (absolute time, amplitude):

$$(0.0, 0.0), \ (0.05, 1.0), \ (0.1, 1.0), \ (0.25, 0.0)$$

where linear interpolation is assumed for each segment. Alternatively, we might write the information as two separated lists, first the amplitude values and then the durations for each segment:

$$(0.0, 1.0, 1.0, 0.0),\ (0.05, 0.05, 0.15)$$

The first representation could also have been carried out with time differences rather than absolute times, so you'll encounter a number of variations here.

Mention of amplitude modulation may set you wondering about the aural consequences of any enveloping. The short answer is that the aural side effects are usually minimal, due to the slow rates of change involved. Slow rates of variation under 20 Hz or so fall outside of the bounds of our hearing system, and components need to be loud at low frequencies to hear anyway. Following AM theory, plugging in small Ms can result in beating in many critical bands of the auditory system, contributing a little roughness to the sound. The sharper (i.e., straight line rather than more smoothly curving) envelopes will have higher-frequency components which can cause audible side effects, though even here the higher-frequency terms have diminishing amplitudes.

Digital editing makes **splicing**, the connection of arbitrary segments of audio, easy. There is always a danger that the points at which you cut are not compatible between segments, because of a **discontinuity**, a sudden jump in amplitude value. Digital audio editors usually provide a facility to search for zero crossings in order to limit this, though even that basic continuity is not necessarily enough; it is also possible for signals to be discontinuous on the level of the 'smoothness' of the curve, as measured by the first and higher derivatives (see Figure 4.3).[7] In this case, zero crossings in a consistent direction can be matched up (positive or negative) though again the rate of change may differ at the join. Clicks are the familiar consequence of a less than smooth transition; they're a feature embraced in much glitch music, as celebrated in the title of the Mille Plateaux *Clicks and Cuts* compilations. In the worst case of an abrupt discontinuity, a wide-spectrum transient noise results from the sudden amplitude jump.

Let's say that there is a portion of audio we really want to grab and splice to another, but we can't find appropriate samples from both sides at which to effect the transition without introducing a noticeable artifact. To impose a controlled transition itself, a **crossfade** assists blend between the two signals during some window of overlap. If we were overlaying many segments of audio, perhaps a whole swarm of segments as in sample granulation, each segment could also be given an individual envelope (with its own fade in and fade out) without linking up one segment's fade in to another segment's fade out.

The important question now is: what makes a good fade in and fade out? Your ears will be an important guide here, for the perception of loudness can be an involved topic, and auditory models of this sound-dependent phenomenon are more complicated than

---

[7] Because we are treating discrete sampled functions of time, the meaning of continuity is within a certain tolerance rather than the analytical limit definition, since there is a maximal slew rate (change per sample) possible, determined by the sampling rate.

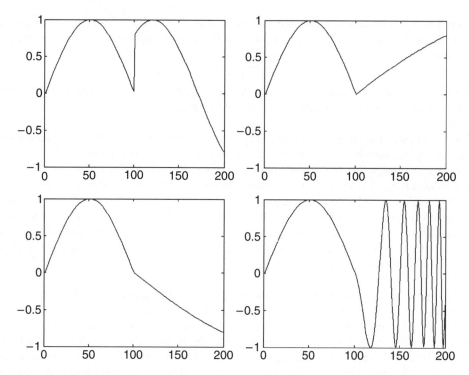

Figure 4.3   Discontinuities. In these four examples, the discontinuity always occurs at the midpoint of the function. This is clear in the case of the abrupt jump (discontinuous x values) in the top left, and the discontinuous first derivative of the top right and bottom left. In those two cases, there is no significant direct jump in amplitude, but the rate of change of the curve is clearly different on each side of the discontinuity; in the lower left, at least the change is in the same direction rather than abruptly jumping back on itself. The lower right is a subtler effect, with a discontinuity in the second derivative (the frequency of the curve in the right portion is steadily increasing).

a simple amplitude-based equation. A basic perceptual solution could use equal loudness contours to account for differential sensitivity to spectral content (this would just be a measure of instantaneous loudness without modeling temporal integration processes; see also Section 3.4). Nevertheless, there are also some common rules of thumb used in computer music. Figure 4.4 shows some of the options for shaping a fade out. In terms of how convincing the fade is – in avoiding overly arousing the suspicion of our auditory change detectors! – one critical factor is the timescale over which a fade occurs. For enveloping to avoid abrupt discontinuities, anything from 1–30 milliseconds may be required. For calm fades in or out for songs, much longer time durations come into play. Fade outs in particular can be tricky compromises in finding the right balance between the need to stop and the need to do so subtly. Often when checked at higher playback volumes, a linear fade will reveal its inadequacies here, as what seemed to be an effective fade out is revealed as being too abrupt. Puckette [2007, p. 93] recommends the quartic (fourth power) curve as a good approximation of a 40 dB change over the fade interval. Similarly, many computer music systems use a quadratic or cubic function, all of which tend to be better approximations to perception than a linear curve.

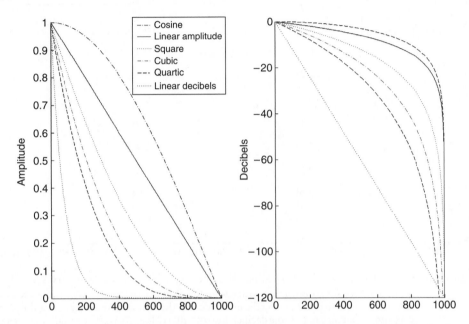

Figure 4.4   Fade-out curves. Linear amplitude and decibel-based graphs (reference amplitude of 1) are provided for a variety of shapes of fade outs. Since neither the linear nor the decibel scale is necessarily the best auditory representation of loudness for complex sounds, the curves should not be treated as an absolute depiction of the virtue of any particular curve; they do illustrate, however, the relative speeds of the drop-off for different standard shapes as amplitude and as decibels. The perceptual result is critically dependent on the timescale of the change, which is over 1000 samples here.

Figure 4.5 demonstrates interlinked fades in the crossfade. The linear crossfade is really a linear interpolation between the two signals over some transition timeframe. A drawback is that there is a loss of signal power (rather than total amplitude) at the midway point, which can be noticeable. To overcome this, the total amplitude can be allowed to go above 1 (in general, we'd have to be careful about system limits), while the total power is kept steady. Because of the trigonometric identity $\sin^2(n) + \cos^2(n) = 1$, a quarter period of a cosine and sine are frequently used for fade out and in functions for the departing and incoming signals respectively (so the individual fades in and out are less effective, but the combination with the associated masking has some good properties). Another, less symmetric option is depicted on the right in the figure, showing how a more perceptual quadratic curve fade out is traded off against a cruder asymmetrical fade in. Every DJ mixer and every digital audio workstation has a crossfade implementation based on some variation of these principles, often compromising between the equal power condition and the need for good individual fades for each signal.

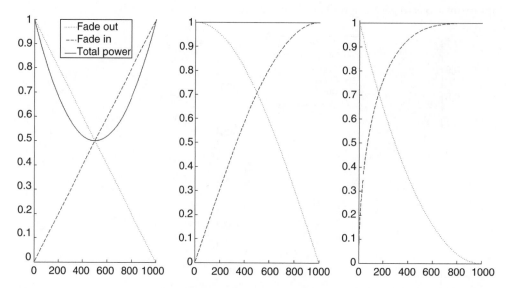

Figure 4.5   Crossfade curves and associated power. Matching fade-out and fade-in curves are illustrated for three situations, along with a solid line showing the total power (sum of square amplitudes) at each point during the crossfade. On the left, since the total power drops to 0.5 from 1, there is a noticeable decibel drop of 6 dB ($10 \log_{10}(0.5)$). The middle curves are trigonometric cos (fade out) and sin (fade in) functions whose sum of squares is always 1. Finally, on the right, the fade out is the curve $y = x^2$, and the fade in is calculated to preserve overall power at 1, causing the asymmetrical shape illustrated.

One situation where envelopes are used extensively with small fade in and out times is that of granular sample manipulation [Truax, 1988; Roads, 2001]. Lots of small segments, named **grains**, of recorded sound are fired into the musical texture, producing bubbling pockets or dense streams. Unless segments can be carefully prepared by automatic methods (extracting physical onsets in event analysis, working with zero crossings in wave sets), each grain will commonly be enveloped to avoid any clicks in playback (who knows where those grains have been sourced from and where they were cut!). One common envelope is a half cycle of a sine function, which tends to produce minimal amplitude-modulation artifacts. Another option, for optimal time–frequency resolution, is a Gaussian envelope (roughly, an e^{x^2} shape); there are various engineering tradeoffs for window shapes that were encountered in Chapter 3. The compositional applications of granulation run from stutters (tight repetitions at rhythmic or even pitched rates; think of Mantronix's *Bassline* (1985) or drill and bass), to disintegration and coalescence effects.

4.1.4 Delays

An exercise at the close of Chapter 1 asked you to draw out a signal processing graph for a filter. One step in completing that exercise was to imagine a unit generator for delay. Delays are critically important to treat the passing of time in a digital system, as might be required when modeling a sound wave propagating in space, or within the body of a musical instrument. To express a delay of D samples to a signal $x(n)$, we simply write $x(n-D)$. This forces a time of D samples to pass before we can access the original signal, since n must now be D in order to get to index $D-D=0$ in x.

So what does a delay do to a sinusoid of known angular frequency w? The equation $x(n)=\sin(\omega n/R+\phi)$ becomes $x(n-D)=\sin(\omega(n-D)/R+\phi)=\sin(\omega n/R-\omega D/R+\phi)$. Because D is fixed, $\omega D/R$ is a fixed phase offset deducted from ϕ. As we might intuitively expect, this 'holds back' the sinusoidal signal by a fixed amount of phase. Note that since ω is involved, there is a linearly increasing amount of delay with frequency, as required to keep the same overall time delay in seconds; this is known as a linear phase response.

We can always implement a delay by using a buffer of samples as a holding area, called a **delay line**. If the buffer has D samples, it can implement delays up to D samples long. The circular buffer architecture is the standard way to accomplish this, as depicted in Figure 4.6. Note the separate read and write pointers. In standard operation, both pointers increment by one sample in the buffer with each sample of output calculation, wrapping around to the start whenever they 'fall off the end' of the delay line. If an exact delay of D samples, the whole length of the line, is all we ever need, the pointers can point to the same place, reading an output sample before replacing the buffer contents at the current index with a new input sample. A variable-length delay line is implemented by letting the read pointer shift about to different separations from the write pointer. Chasing at different distances is equivalent to particular delays. This is already giving us tools for basic delay effects units; by using multiple read pointers at a set of desired delays or 'taps' you'd get a multi-tap delay line, suitable perhaps for modeling early reflections in reverberation.

There are a few technicalities to confront. What happens if you 'cross the beams'? If a read pointer overtakes a write pointer, there will be a jump from reading back data from the near past to reading back data from the distant past, with no guarantee of continuity of sample amplitudes. Similarly, the opposite jump occurs if the write pointer overtakes the read pointer. This establishes certain limits on any variation of the delay, via the update speeds for the pointers. Possible rates of change depend on the relative position; you can 'break the bank' in either direction by speeding up or slowing down, and larger leaps are always more likely to promote discontinuity. The read pointer can always be safely shifted to new offsets which correspond to new delay times up to the length of the delay line as long as the update rate of the read pointer is the same as that of the write pointer. Yet note that if the read pointer moves at a constant rate which is any slower or faster than the update rate of the write pointer, then there will eventually be overtaking (if read is slower, write overtakes read; if faster, read overtakes write). To avoid this, the read pointer must be

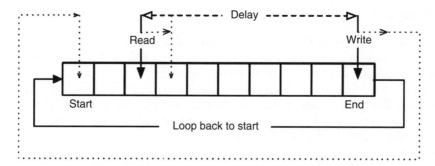

Figure 4.6   A circular buffer, also called a ring buffer. A one-second buffer at 44 100 Hz sampling rate would have 44 100 slots; for clarity, this diagram just represents a maximum possible delay of 10 samples ($\frac{1}{4410}$ of a second at that R). Memory is finite, hence the wraparound trick. In this figure, a variable-length delay line is depicted. The delay is the (fixed or dynamically varied) separation of the read and write pointers, which chase each other around the wrapping topology. Stepping off the end is equivalent to going back to the first slot in the buffer. The dotted arrows depict an update of the pointer positions by one sample, as everything shuffles right and around the loop. In general, read pointer(s) and write pointer(s) can be independent. This same construction could describe reading from a preloaded sound file in memory, with just a read pointer moving around the data array. Or a multitap delay line would use one write pointer and multiple read pointers, one for each tap.

working without the interference of a write pointer (simple playback) or be varying its rate either side of the update rate while maintaining a mean speed (a type of modulation which leads to various standard effects) [Puckette, 2007].

In the discussion of resampling above, the problem of arbitrary resampling rates was raised. Recall again Section 2.7.3 and the discussion of read pointers which move by an arbitrary amount (not just multiples of a sample). Just as for playback of buffered sample data, we can also consider fractional delay lines. This is necessary if we are modeling the real world. Imagine the delay line is being used to model the transmission delay for a traveling wave on a string. To get different pitches we can imagine stopping the string at different points, in effect shortening the delay length. There is nothing about a violin fretboard that requires you to only put your finger at positions corresponding to an exact integer number of samples! Even the 12-note equal temperament scale doesn't fall neatly on integer sample boundaries for any sampling rate. So to allow for any periodicity, we need to have the ability to 'look between the samples'. As discussed earlier, this amounts to some form of interpolation, which may introduce some distortion. Algorithm 4.1 gives pseudocode for reading and writing from a delay line with linear interpolation.[8]

---

[8]More advanced schemes include polynomial interpolation such as Lagrange interpolation [Puckette, 2007, pp. 43–47] and all-pass filtering [Dattorro, 1997]. One general scheme for delay lines by Rocchesso [2000] uses interpolation at both the write position and the read position, in 'fractionally addressed delays'.

Algorithm 4.1 Example of reading and writing from a delay line with linear interpolation on read pointer position. The code doesn't check whether the read and write pointers cross. Note how the read operation always takes place before a write, so delays of the length of the full delay line are handled (but not delays of 0, for which write has to precede read).

Input: An input signal $x(n)$ at sampling rate R, required delay line size D, starting delay for read pointer *initialdelay*, update rate for read pointer *updateread* (write pointer update rate is 1)

Output: N samples of a signal $y(n)$ at sampling rate R giving the output of the read pointer
 1: Allocate buffer *delayline* of size D for storing samples
 2: $writepos \leftarrow 0$ // Write pointer position; start at beginning of buffer
 3: $readpos \leftarrow (writepos + D - initialdelay)\%D$ // Read pointer position; modulo keeps indexing correct
 4: **for** $n = 0$ to $N - 1$ **do**
 5:   $prev \leftarrow floor(readpos)$ // Get previous integer index
 6:   $next \leftarrow (prev + 1)\%D$ // Get next integer index; because of wraparound, need modulo for safety
 7:   $t \leftarrow readpos - prev$ // Get fractional position of read pointer
 8:   $y[n] \leftarrow (1 - t) * delayline[prev] + t * delayline[next]$ // Linear interpolation for reading from delayline
 9:   $readpos \leftarrow (readpos + updateread)\%D$ // Update read pointer for next time, modulo wraps it
10:   $delayline[writepos] \leftarrow x[n]$ // Write to delay line
11:   $writepos \leftarrow (writepos + 1)\%D$ // Update write pointer for next time; modulo wraps it
12: **end for**

4.2 CONVOLUTION AND FILTERS

We can now work up towards a fuller understanding of filters. But there is a special operation called **convolution** to be introduced first.

4.2.1 Impulse Responses and the Convolution Operation

Imagine clicking your fingers in a room, to investigate the reverberant properties of that environment. Ideally, you'd be able to click your fingers so fast that the sound you create is a simple impulse; at least, let's assume you can move your fingers that fast for now![9] In digital terms it would look like this:

$$\dots, 0, 0, 1, 0, 0, 0, \dots$$

with a one denoting the click itself and zeroes either side. The response of the room is measured from the moment of the click, and the **impulse response**, that is, the reaction

---

[9]Acousticians would use an impulse generator, or pop a balloon, rather than clicking their fingers or firing a starting pistol, to get a purer impulse when studying a room's acoustics.

of the room to the stimulus, is recorded via a microphone. In passing, it should be noted that the response will vary based on the position in the room of the source sound and the microphone, but we'll sidestep such subtleties for now. A real room response might be seconds long before the reflecting energy becomes insignificant. Clearly discrete early echoes are followed by a build-up of reverberation causing a more continuous tail – ten seconds for a cathedral, two seconds for a concert hall, fifty milliseconds for a dry recording studio live room. For convenience of explanation, let's work with something shorter. Say that we get the following impulse response back:

$$0, 0, 0, 0.9, 0, 0, 0.5, 0.2, 0.1$$

where this signal is measured as starting at the sample of the impulse itself, and there are thus three samples of delay prior to any returning signal. The length of this response is nine samples long; it is simply zero afterwards (we count any initial delay as part of the response, but the response ends with the last observed reflection). Again, we're bypassing real acoustics for the moment for the sake of the exposition. Early reflections happen within the first 50 milliseconds or so, or 2205 samples at our favorite CD sampling rate. A delay of only three samples would indicate a rather strange speed of sound or room dimensions!

The impulse response has some interesting properties. Assuming linear absorption characteristics for the walls in the room, if we clicked our fingers with half the amplitude, sending out:

$$0.5, 0, 0, 0, \ldots$$

we would get back half the original response:

$$0, 0, 0, 0.45, 0, 0, 0.25, 0.1, 0.05$$

Furthermore, now imagine clicking twice in short succession, once at full amplitude and once at half:

$$1, 0, 0.5, 0, 0, \ldots$$

What would happen? Well, measuring time in samples from the first impulse, the first click would cause the first impulse response listed above. The second impulse, at reduced strength and with a two-sample delay, would also return its own response, delayed by these two samples relative to the first click. The principle of superposition, whereby the traveling waves do not interfere with each other, would then give a total response obtained by summing up these two independent responses:

0,	0,	0,	0.9,	0,	0,	0.5,	0.2,	0.1,	0,	0
					+					
0,	0,	0,	0,	0,	0.45,	0,	0,	0.25,	0.1,	0.05
					=					
0,	0,	0,	0.9,	0,	0.45,	0.5,	0.2,	0.35,	0.1,	0.05

Notice that the length of this new combined response is the length of the stimulus signal where it is non-zero (three samples) plus the length of the impulse response (nine samples) minus one; that is, 11 samples.

For a linear system, any combination of impulses will cause a corresponding combination of impulse responses. Each impulse of given delay and amplitude will cause an appropriately scaled and delayed copy of the impulse response. All the impulse responses from each respective source impulse can be safely added up in the same manner as above. Now take any arbitrary signal x of N values:

$$x(0), x(1), x(2), \ldots, x(N-1)$$

We can think of this as N impulses, at consecutive samples, scaled by $x(k)$. So each $x(k)$ will cause its own copy of the impulse response h. If h is denoted by:

$$h(0), h(1), h(2), \ldots, h(M-1)$$

then the final response for the whole input sequence will be the **convolution** of x with h, that is, the sum of the following individually scaled and delayed responses:

$x(0)h(0),$	$x(0)h(1),$	$x(0)h(2),$	$x(0)h(3),$	$x(0)h(4),$	$\ldots,$	$x(0)h(M-1),$	$0,$	0
$0,$	$x(1)h(0),$	$x(1)h(1),$	$x(1)h(2),$	$x(1)h(3),$	$\ldots,$	$\ldots, x(1)h(M-1),$		0
$0,$	$0,$	$x(2)h(0),$	$x(2)h(1),$	$x(2)h(2),$	$\ldots,$	$\ldots,$	$\ldots, x(2)h(M-1)$	
$0,$	$0,$	$0,$	$x(3)h(0),$	$x(3)h(1),$	$\ldots,$	$\ldots,$	$\ldots,$	$\ldots$
$0,$	$0,$	$0,$	$0,$	$x(4)h(0),$	$\ldots,$	$\ldots,$	$\ldots,$	$\ldots$

$$\ldots$$

where the last row would be a delay of $N-1$ zeroes and then the impulse response scaled by $x(N-1)$. The whole table has not been filled in since its size depends critically on N and M. The final array would have N rows and $N+M-1$ columns.

If you examine the indices at each time step (read across the columns left to right), you'll see that the indices for x and for h add up to the current time step n. To give one specific example, look at column two; the index pairs are $(2, 0)$, $(1, 1)$ and $(0, 2)$, which all add up to 2. Note how the indexing for x in the columns increases down the page, and for y it decreases; but the overall set of index pairs is also symmetrical, in that the assignment of indices works both ways round. Recall how carrier and modulator can be swapped symmetrically in ring modulation; convolution is also an entirely symmetrical operation, so we could equally speak of the impulse response as the source signal and the source as the response! The mathematical way to write this as a summation over the N delayed impulse responses is:

$$x * h(n) = \sum_{k=0}^{N-1} x(k)h(n-k), \quad n = 0, \ldots, N+M-1 \qquad (4.4)$$

where $*$ is the symbol for convolution. Because n can go up to $N+M-1$, and x and h are only non-zero within their lengths, any indexed value outside of 0 to $N-1$ or 0 to $M-1$ respectively will be taken as a zero. Each $n-k$ corresponds to a particular delay k, so that for later-occurring samples of x, the impulse response will not begin playing back into the output sum until that delay has passed.

A graphical depiction of this is given in Figure 4.7. The impulse response of our imaginary room is used, with a source sound of:

$$1, 0.7, 0, 0.4, 0.6, 0.2, 0, 0.9$$

which only magical fingers could snap out. For the sake of the exposition, only positive values have been used; amplitudes can be negative in general (in the room example, negative equates to lower pressure than the atmospheric baseline, for instance).[10]

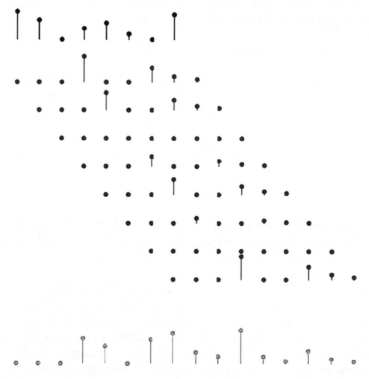

Figure 4.7 Convolution: the top line is the source signal. The next eight lines correspond to the scaled and delayed impulse response; the scale factors of successive lines correspond to the successive amplitudes of the source samples, and the delay to the sample index. The bottom line is the actual convolution output, by adding up the eight responses. You can also see copies of the original signal on the diagonals, scaled by the amplitude of the starting sample amplitude of the impulse response; reversed copies of the impulse response appear on the verticals (read up from the bottom starting in the middle of the diagram, for example).

---

[10]If you're familiar with the long multiplication algorithm, you've encountered a form of convolution before. Convolution as an operation can actually be used to multiply very big numbers together! You can also encounter convolution in image signal processing, where a 'kernel function' point of view is used; in the audio case, the kernel consists of reversing the impulse response, which is then matched to the source with different delay offsets (essentially implementing the mathematical sum in the definition).

Congratulations on making it this far! If you've followed this exposition, then you now not only understand the time domain operation of convolution, which can be calculated for any two signals, but you've also encountered a very practical processing application: the convolution reverb, created by convolving an input signal with a room's impulse response. It is possible to convolve any two sounds together, allowing some interesting transformations, along the lines of playing one sound 'through' another. We now proceed to relate convolution to the frequency domain, and a fundamental connection with filters will eventually follow to justify our attention.

4.2.2 Convolution and Multiplication

Convolution is at the heart of a spectacular relationship between the time and frequency domains. To cut a short mathematical proof short [Mallat, 1998, p. 24]:

- Multiplication of two signals in the time domain convolves them in the frequency domain.

- Convolution of two signals in the time domain multiplies them in the frequency domain.

As a corollary, ring modulation causes convolution of the carrier and modulator spectra in the frequency domain. This is what gives rise to the $C - M$ and $C + M$ frequency pattern for sinusoids, and why things quickly get messier for more complicated signals.[11] Conversely, multiplying one spectrum using another is equivalent to time-domain filtering, as will be explained below.

Because convolution in the time domain is multiplication in the frequency domain,[12] we now have the ingredients to detail a fast algorithm for convolution, which goes under the unsurprising name of **fast convolution**. The idea is to individually convert the signals to be convolved to the frequency domain, and then to simply multiply them, before returning to the time domain with the answer. The algorithm employs the fast Fourier transform to get the speed-up, and is typically faster than direct calculation in the time domain for anything greater than or equal to 32-sample-long signals [Mallat, 1998, p. 59]. A form of distortion can arise with this technique if adequate space is not allocated for the calculation. The FFT size must be exactly[13] $N + M - 1$, with appropriate zero padding. To explain this, the previous convolution equation is more conveniently expressed as the **circular convolution**:

$$x * h(n) = \sum_{k=0}^{N+M-1} x'(k)h'(n-k), \quad n = 0, \ldots, N+M-1 \qquad (4.5)$$

---

[11]If you're comfortable with the complex representation for the cosine, you can see this for cosine waves by considering their spectral convolution. The half-amplitude positive and negative frequency components to the modulator are centered by convolution at the carrier's half-amplitude positive and negative frequency components. In terms of a real output, the resulting quarter-amplitude $C - M$ and $M - C$, and $C + M$ and $-(C + M)$, pairs can be recombined, corresponding to real cosines at half strength at $C - M$ and $M + C$.

[12]There is also an inverse process called **deconvolution** which uses division in the frequency domain to try to recover an input signal from a convolved signal, given the impulse response. Deconvolution is a hard problem in general, since the impulse response is not necessarily known and must be estimated from example data of final convolutions!

[13]In practice, the FFT can be further zero padded, for example by using $N = M$ when partitioning both input signals, and thus adding another zero to each.

where x' and h' are defined as periodic functions of length $N + M - 1$, which are x and h over N and M samples, respectively padded by $M - 1$ and $N - 1$ zeroes to bring them to a common size.

Circular convolution happens to give an insight into the symmetry of the convolution operation, and the reason why size $N + M - 1$ is required. Lining x' and h' up against each other, reading one forwards from index 0 and one backwards from index n, it is impossible not to get a symmetric one-to-one correspondence which reads the same when read in reverse (both sequences have the same size of $N + M - 1$ in circular convolution, rather than different sizes). However, if there is not sufficient space, for certain n, there will be accidental overlaps which aren't in the original definition of the convolution sum. For $n = 0$, the convolution sum should only contain $x(0)h(0)$. But if we had chosen length $N + M - 2$ instead, the circular convolution would actually also contain $x(N - 1)h(-N + 1) = x(N - 1)h(N + M - 2 - N + 1) = x(N - 1)h(M - 1)$ (by the periodicity of $N + M - 2$), which is potentially a non-zero junk data term.

The reverberation examples with which convolution was introduced were unrealistic, in that the impulse responses were too short. A real room response could be of the order of seconds. Because the convolution sum is just a summation, it is possible to split either or both of the convolution input signals x and h into parts. This gives rise to a partitioned convolution algorithm (sometimes also called sectioned convolution), which can allow the calculation of convolutions in real time for a very long impulse response; this is the basic algorithm used for realtime convolution reverb plug-ins. There are further refinements to make minimal delay versions of this process [Gardner, 1995].

4.2.3 More on Filters

We temporarily deferred discussing the relation of temporal and spectral filtering, but no longer.

By introducing convolution, we have armed ourselves to tackle filters. Finite impulse response (FIR) and infinite impulse response (IIR) filters are united by the mention of an impulse response; conveniently, we have just explored this. If we know what happens when we pass a single sample impulse through a linear time-invariant system, then we can use scaling and delay just as in the convolution examples above to find out what happens to an arbitrary signal. Indeed, convolution gives us a useful definition of the working process of a linear time-invariant (LTI) filter, as the convolution of an impulse response with an input. The convolution reverb could be seen as filtering an input signal, using the room's impulse response to impose the acoustic characteristics of that environment. In the same way, we can filter a signal as if it were routed through an acoustic instrument body (if we have an impulse response for that body), to impose the character of that instrument.

For impulse response h, we can write the output as:

$$y(n) = x * h(n) = \sum_{k=0}^{N-1} x(k)h(n-k), \quad n = 0, \dots, N+M-1 \tag{4.6}$$

Recall the equation for an LTI filter from Section 1.2.6:

$$y(n) = \sum_{k=0}^{M} a(k)x(n-k) - \sum_{k=1}^{N} b(k)y(n-k) \tag{4.7}$$

Consider the FIR filter, where feedback coefficients b are all zero:

$$y(n) = \sum_{k=0}^{M} a(k)x(n-k) \tag{4.8}$$

If we pass in an impulse, the output of the filter over time can be expressed as $a(0), a(1), a(2),$ $a(3), \dots, a(M-1)$ where there are M coefficients in a. In this case, the impulse response h actually *is* the finite list of feedforward coefficients! You might also have suspected this from examining the equations.

For an IIR filter, the situation is not quite so neat, but we could still work out the impulse response in terms of the filter coefficients:

$a(0), a(1) - b(1)a(0), a(2) - b(2)a(0) - b(1)(a(1) - b(1)a(0)),$
$a(3) - b(3)a(0) - b(2)(a(1) - b(1)a(0)) - b(1)(a(2) - b(2)a(0) - b(1)(a(1) - b(1)a(0))), \dots$

which keeps accumulating forever (an *infinite* impulse response). The feedforward part will stop within a finite number of terms, but the feedback potentially keeps on recirculating. Because the multiplications of the coefficients continue over time, there is a danger of the magnitude continuing to increase. If the impulse response blows up in this way, so will anything else passed through the filter; remember that the behavior of the filter is described by the behavior of the impulse response. On the other hand, the multiplications may lead to the response's magnitude decreasing over time, which with a computer leads to a zero response after a finite time because of the limited floating point resolution of any discrete machine.

A linear filter can be analyzed in terms of its effect on spectral content. A filter will modify the gain of a signal in a frequency-dependent manner according to the **frequency response**, and selectively delay component frequencies according to the **phase response**. Only the identity transformation $y(n) = x(n)$ (give or take a constant gain factor) can succeed in a flat frequency response and zero delay at all frequencies. All other filters cause some sort of coloration to the spectrum of an input, whether in amplitude or phase of component frequencies or typically both. The sidebar says more about this, mathematically speaking. Intuitively, the spectrum of the impulse response multiplies the spectrum of the input, because of the relation between convolution and multiplication. This is the origin of the sense of a room, instrument body or general filter's character getting imposed on a sound.

Filter Mathematics Part 2

The z-transform is a generalization of a discrete-time Fourier transform which also translates from the time domain to the complex number domain. (The letter z is habitually used for complex numbers, and the complex plane is often called the z-plane.) If signal $x(n)$ is non-zero only for $n \geq 0$ then the z-transform of x is defined as:

$$X(z) = \sum_{n=0}^{\infty} x(n)z^{-n} \tag{4.9}$$

where z is any complex number to be tested 'against' discrete sequence x. The z-transform is useful because it has an interesting property when acting on a delayed signal $x(n-d)$, which will allow us to transform the filter equation. By substituting $x(n-d)$ in the z-transform equation we obtain $z^{-d}X(z)$ ($\sum_{n=0}^{\infty} x(n-d)z^{-n} = \sum_{n=d}^{\infty} x(n-d)z^{-n} = \sum_{m=0}^{\infty} x(m)z^{-(m+d)} = z^{-d}\sum_{m=0}^{\infty} x(m)z^{-m} = z^{-d}X(z)$). Taking the LTI filter equation and writing Y for the z-transform of y as well as X for that of x:

$$Y(z) = \sum_{k=0}^{M} a(k)z^{-k}X(z) - \sum_{k=1}^{N} b(k)z^{-k}Y(z) \tag{4.10}$$

This equation can be rearranged by grouping all the Y terms together, and taking a ratio of the z-transform of the output Y to that of the input X. This forms a rational function of z, a quotient of complex polynomials, the **transfer function** $H(z)$:

$$H(z) = \frac{Y(z)}{X(z)} = \frac{\sum_{k=0}^{M} a(k)z^{-k}}{1 + \sum_{k=1}^{N} b(k)z^{-k}} \tag{4.11}$$

By evaluating the transfer function on the unit circle (substitute $z = e^{i\theta}$ where with normalized angular frequency $\theta = \pi$ is the Nyquist frequency), the frequency and phase response of a filter can be ascertained from the magnitude and argument of the resulting complex number $H(e^{i\theta})$.

Recall that convolution in the time domain is multiplication in the frequency domain, and a filter is defined by the convolution of the impulse response with an input signal. The Fourier transform of the impulse response provides all the useful information about the character of the filter, and, indeed, the transfer function H evaluated on the unit circle *is* the discrete-time Fourier transform of the impulse response (the z-transform of the impulse response is the full transfer function above).

In analyzing a filter, the polynomials can be further broken down by factorization. You may have seen filter plug-ins which refer to poles and zeroes, which are the solutions of the denominator and numerator polynomials respectively. A FIR filter has only zeroes, and is always stable; an IIR filter has both poles and zeroes. If poles are not carefully handled, and whenever they stray outside the unit circle in the complex domain, the filter will be unstable and will blow up. At this point it should be realized that a knowledge of complex analysis feeds directly into filter mathematics, and the design of filters can become an optimization problem in the complex domain.

As well as the linear filters presented here, it is also possible to have nonlinear filters such as $y(n) = x(n)^2 + 0.5x(n-1)^{0.47} + 0.02x(n-4)y(n-2)^4$, containing higher powers and crossterms, but in this case the mathematics becomes less tractable. For their mathematical convenience, linear filters are a central tool of the signal processing engineer, but nonlinearities must be reintroduced at critical junctures to provide the richness of real music, from distortion to models of real instruments. One case of nonlinearity will appear later in this chapter when we come to discuss the technique of waveshaping in the context of dynamics processing and distortion.

4.2.4 Examples: Comb and All-pass Filters

Filter design is an involved topic, and relating filter coefficients to tangible effects requires some elaborate mathematics. Here we will content ourselves with studying two basic filter types of great utility in effects, the **comb** and the **all-pass** filter [Puckette, 2007, pp. 184–193]; [Roads, 1996, pp. 412–419]; [Zölzer, 2002]. These can provide basic units for effects from simulated reverberation to flanging.

A comb filter is a filter which combines the input signal with a delayed copy of itself, through either a feedforward step (the FIR comb) or a feedback step (an IIR comb). Both have spectral consequences; you can imagine that the choice of delay determines which frequencies will be pronounced and which will be attenuated by the processing, because each frequency has an associated period. If the period aligns with the delay length, then a constructive boost of twice the amplitude will always take place. But if the period were twice the delay, a sinusoid at that frequency would line up with a version of itself at a phase shift of half the period, causing total cancellation! Other cases are intermediate, and in fact this leads to a series of boosts and cuts in the spectrum that look much like a comb (Figure 4.8). An all-pass filter is a filter which has an entirely flat frequency response, while the phase response varies. This allows it to be applied as a frequency-dependent delay unit, of service in simulating diffusion (scattering) of sound waves or as potential compensation for the phase response of another filter.

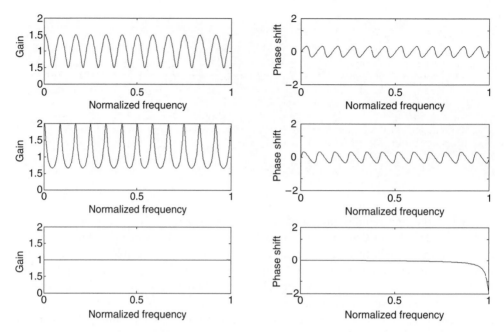

Figure 4.8   Frequency and phase responses for three filters. The FIR comb is on the top row ($g = 0.5$, $d = 1000$, sampling rate $R = 44\,100$). If g were 1, total cancellation and summation would occur; for $g = 0.5$, the signal swings between 0.5 and 1.5 in value at different frequencies. The spectral peaks are spaced by the reciprocal of the delay period with respect to the sampling rate. The middle row shows the IIR comb (same g, d), which has a much more pronounced effect for larger g due to the feedback. The lowest row is the all-pass ($g = 0.5$, $d = 1$), with a flat frequency response and a phase response which drops off at higher frequencies (so higher frequencies are more delayed than low). The normalized frequency of 1 in this case is the Nyquist frequency, and the phase shift is measured in radians.

The processing graph in Figure 4.9 shows the action of a 'universal comb filter', adapted from [Zölzer, 2002, p. 66].[14] This plan can be used to create a FIR, an IIR comb or an all-pass filter by appropriate choices of constants and delay. The time-domain equations for each are given in Table 4.1 with the appropriate settings for the universal comb. Figure 4.8 plots the magnitude and phase response for each of these three filters. The strength and width of the peaks and troughs of the comb, and the exact shape of the phase response in the all-pass, vary based on the gain parameters.

In general, filters are prepared especially for use by musicians, so as to make their perceptual effects as closely locked as possible to the controls. Although direct manipulation of filter coefficients, even poles and zeroes, is possible, it is far more intuitive to manipulate a center frequency or degree of cut and boost. The design of filters for computer music systems is

---

[14]In technical diagrams for filter designs the explicitly named 'delay d samples' would be replaced by the symbol z^{-d}, following the z-transform.

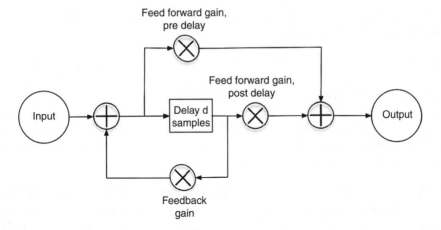

Figure 4.9 Universal comb filter.

Table 4.1 Parameters for universal comb filter.

Filter type	Feedback	Feed forward gain pre-delay	Feed forward gain post-delay	Delay	Equation
FIR comb	0	1	g	d	$y(n) = x(n) + g * x(n - d)$
IIR comb	g	1	0	d	$y(n) = x(n) + g * y(n - d)$
First-order all-pass	$-g$	g	1	1	$y(n) = g * x(n) - g * y(n - 1) + x(n - 1)$

an advanced topic, and the information gathered here is just a starting point for further investigation.

4.3 A COMPENDIUM OF MARVELOUS DIGITAL AUDIO EFFECTS

No musician has yet suffered the death of a thousand audio effects plug-ins, but the variety of digital effects available surely puts many an innocent recording at risk of being swamped in processing finery. Despite the way electric guitarists stack up long lines of hissing pedals on stage, I'm not aware of any world record for the application of effects in series, though I bet a program could be written to win such a competition automatically. But the overuse of effects leads inexorably to the loss of the original signal. The sound of the processing itself comes to dominance as the frequency and phase characteristics of the original are successively perturbed. Yet used in moderation, all sorts of marvels are available. For particularly distinctive-sounding effects, it is always worth trying out different kinds of input – periodic, glissando or chirp, noisy, speech, complex audio scene, different kinds of music – to see how much of the end result is the subject of an effect itself, and how much due to the character of the stimulus.

Table 4.2 collates many representatives of the class of digital audio effects. While some subjects are tackled in this chapter, for further implementation details Zölzer [2002] and the proceedings of the Digital Audio Effects (DAFX) conferences (available freely online, www.dafx.de) are recommended reading. Trevor Wishart [1994] also provides an engaging discussion of the many digital processing effects implemented in the Composer's Desktop Project software, a respected library of command-line tools for time-domain and spectral processing, along with compositional applications.

Although some processing routines can be specified solely in the time domain, full understanding of the processing side-effects requires an appreciation of frequency-domain analysis and digital signal processing technicalities. For example, in understanding where and how aliasing might be introduced, we know we should not introduce new frequency components above Nyquist, for once appearing in the digital domain they foldover back below Nyquist and we can't get rid of them. Precautionary low-pass filtering before a nonlinear effect, or even full sample rate conversion (upsample, process, downsample) may be required.

As well as their own natural parameters, effects commonly allow for multiple variants of a basic type, such as multi-band versions of an effect acting separately on each band output of a filter bank, with the final output summed from these multiple channels. Filter banks can be formed through analysis front ends (such as the linearly spaced filters of the discrete Fourier transform), or by brute application of time-domain filters. One useful technique to mention in this regard is **complementary filtering**. A low-pass filter can peel off a low-pass signal from the original. This is then subtracted from the original signal to get a second complementary band. The technique can be applied iteratively, as in multi-resolution filter banks and some practical implementations of the wavelet transform.

Time variation of parameters of an effect is the classic manner in which musicians have fun with signals. Varying the coefficients of a filter can have repercussions, causing transient behavior in a system in response to the sudden change of its transfer function [Puckette, 2007, p. 245]. Most audio effects are relatively smooth in changing under continuous adjustment of parameters; otherwise musicians sometimes enjoy the abrupt changes they can introduce.

All effects outputs can be mixed proportionally with the original signal to give a preferred ratio of **wet** (with effect) to **dry** (without effect, original) signal. Not all processed signals are mixed back in with the original; be forewarned that if an effect plays with the phase relationships in a signal, recombining it with the original may lead to frequency-dependent filtering due to new superpositions.

More complicated effects tend to rest on particular signal models that may favor a certain class of signals. The effects may utilize various analysis front ends with the processing

Table 4.2 A collection of digital audio effects.

Effect	Description
Tremolo	'Human rate' amplitude modulation
Phasing	Time-varying phase cancellation and reinforcement effects: signal combined with a copy which has been run through a cascade of notch or all-pass filters whose center frequencies are time varying
Wah-wah	Time-varying center frequency/resonance for band-pass filter
Vibrato	Frequency modulation, by oscillating the read pointer in a delay line: 5–10 ms average delay time, 5–14 Hz modulation rate
Chorusing	Mixing together many delayed copies (1–30 ms delay), each of whose delay times is modulated by low-pass filtered white noise
Flanging	Combining the signal with a variably delayed copy of itself (delays 0–2 ms with low-frequency oscillation)
Echoes	Slapback/doubling (10–30 ms delay – think John Lennon's voice on his solo material) or explicit echoes (over 30 ms delay)
Dynamic processing	Nonlinear remapping of amplitude
Distortion	A nonlinear effect (like dynamics processing) also often based on waveshaping functions; can be used in the modeling of analog components such as valves
Independent time stretching and pitch changing	Various time- and frequency-domain methods; see below
De-noising	Techniques to filter signals selectively to remove undesired noise components
Sample granulation, wavesets	Time-domain buffer effects for breaking down signals and building them back up again in new combinations
Spatialization	Various simulation procedures for auditory spatial cues
Vocoding	One example of resynthesis using a simple filter bank; energy envelopes are extracted in each band (the analysis), and then used to control a bandwise sound
Feature-based control	Extracting parameters for an analysis model, and then using these to determine resynthesis; the model need not allow perfect reconstruction of the original in order to give sound transformations
Sound morphing	Interpolating between different source data sets or states through the parameters of an analysis–resynthesis model

being a result of associated transformations and resynthesis, as detailed in Chapter 3. By combining models with dynamic variation of their parameters, particular **sound morphing** effects are possible which can flow between timbres.

In more intelligent signal processing, any of the analysis methods could be used to extract features which guide particular effects [Arfib *et al.*, 2002b; Verfaille and Arfib, 2001]. Musical knowledge, whether gleaned by clever automatic analysis procedures or provided by a host application for the effects unit, can guide effects to follow particular temporal structures, such as an amplitude modulation which is locked to the tempo of the material it modifies. The table does not present a well-developed taxonomy of effects, and with all the different possible signal models and overlaps of techniques which can be applied, there are innumerable possibilities.

A selection of further processing effects are detailed in the following subsections.

4.3.1 Dynamics Processing, Distortion and Waveshaping

We have noted already that the full dynamic range available in digital audio is impressive, limited only by the bit resolution in theory, and attached analog recording and playback equipment in practice. Yet many producers or broadcasters, particularly in popular styles of music, do not take advantage of this full range. Imagine listening to classical music over the radio in a car; unless you have a very swanky automobile, the background noise means that quiet sections are easily masked. One solution is to compress the dynamic range, on the understanding that the overall acoustic contrast is lost, but the perceptibility is improved for a less than ideal listening environment. Audio is also compressed in dynamic range for advertising punch, and the loudness war [Katz, 2007] sees recordings compressed in mixing, further compressed in mastering, and compressed a third or more times during radio broadcast!

Dynamics processing is a nonlinear mapping of the amplitude of a signal to a new range. If the action of the processor isn't instantaneous, it is necessary to track a signal to know when to adjust the output gain, but we'll come back to that after considering the nonlinear map itself. The remapping essentially comes down to a **transfer function** which takes input $x(n)$ and produces output $y(n)$. Unlike a filter, which we have seen as a linear function of past inputs and outputs, we will now consider a nonlinear function just of the present input. The same formulation proves useful for modeling distortion (such as a classic guitar amplifier), and is also at the heart of a method for efficient sound synthesis called **waveshaping** [Roads, 1985e].

The transfer function can be defined by a discrete table, or by an analytical description such as a polynomial. Figure 4.10 shows a few plausible input–output functions. The diagonal line (the curve $y = x$) corresponds to no change to the input, the identity operation. The 'soft clipping' and 'dynamics' curves work on the principle of shifting the gradient of the input curve at different points; both are symmetric about zero. The soft clipping curve boosts the amplitude more quickly for small amplitudes, and then tails off the increase with a quadratic curve (the soft knee of the curve) before clamping it entirely to a fixed maximum. Any input above 2/3 or below −2/3 (so of absolute value greater than 2/3) is mapped to an output of 1. Such processing might model distortion, going from a region of normal operating behavior (with gain) through soft clipping (the quadratic curve) to the final hard clipping. When the bit resolution of digital audio is reached, hard clipping is an automatic response, and this sort of transfer function is one way to restore a more gradual distortion characteristic, like that of analog equipment. You must still be careful not to exceed the ultimate limits, but a richer behavior near the limits is often used by engineers for musical effect.

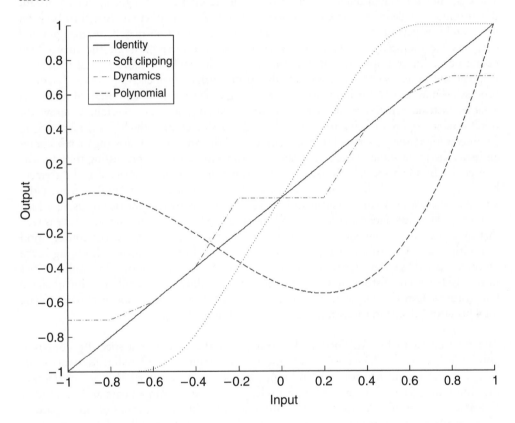

Figure 4.10   Four transfer functions.

The dynamics curve demonstrates five regimes:

- **noise gate** – low amplitude is mapped straight to zero, thus removing noise below a threshold;

- **expander** – the input is boosted faster than normal, 'expanding' the original dynamic range (curve gradient > 1);

- **linear** – the input is left alone in this zone, where the curve matches $y = x$;

- **compressor** – the input is reduced more quickly than normal, 'compressing' the original dynamic range (curve gradient < 1);

- **limiter** – an ultimate maximum is reached and the output signal cannot go beyond it (curve gradient $= 0$, infinite limiter, hard clipping).

The cases not illustrated include a curve with infinite gradient, straight up for an instant discontinuity – a definite source of distortion! The 'polynomial' curve does turn back on itself, and it is perfectly possible to define any arbitrary function map between input and output values, jumping inputs around with reverse of direction. While the curves here operate over linear amplitude for didactic purposes, it would be more typical to see the map laid out in terms of a more perceptual measure such as decibels. In practice, dynamics processing may not be so immediate as to reassign every sample amplitude directly via a table. Instead, a measure of root mean square amplitude over a certain window (or other loudness-approximating feature) is derived in a **side chain**, which sets the active gain parameter for a time duration. The responsiveness of this amplitude following then becomes an issue; the input signal would be delayed to compensate for the processing time for the side chain. In some special effects, the side chain processes not the signal to be treated, but a separate control signal; examples would be the 'ducker' effect familiar from radio where a broadcaster's voice takes priority over the music, or the practice of using a kick drum signal to modulate other layers of the texture in electronic dance music. Note as well that dynamics processing, specifically compression, can be used to allow the combination of multiple signals without such pronounced build-up of total amplitude. Limiting is the ultimate case, though all dynamics processing must be in moderation, for nonlinearities introduce harmonic distortion. Compression may also allow the overall boosting of signal level (observe how the output amplitude is limited to 0.7 in the figure above, allowing a safe total boost of 0.3 within the assumed digital audio limits of ± 1).

The final curve to be explained looks stranger to the eye; it is a specially contrived polynomial ($x^3 + x^2 - 0.5 * x - 0.5$). The most basic nonlinearity, x^2, will tend to introduce energy at the second harmonic of any input frequency. You can see this by considering the ring modulation of a sinusoid with itself, giving rise to components at 0 Hz and at $C + M = C + C = 2C$. A more complex input sound will show a more complex pattern of interactions among its own components, but the general effect will be a doubling of the overall frequency range of the signal.[15] This may lead to aliasing, so we must be careful what content we feed in to begin with. This principle can be used to remodel an input *sinusoid*'s frequency content in a controlled manner. The **Chebyshev** polynomials of the first order [Loy, 2007b, pp. 405–409] are primitive polynomials for forming transfer functions of deliberate design. The output of the nth polynomial when fed by a full amplitude sinusoid is the nth harmonic of that sinusoid.[16] Chebyshev polynomials can be combined by addition to form more complicated harmonic recipes; the polynomial in Figure 4.10 is

[15]In general, the nth power leads to an n-fold increase in bandwidth of a signal.
[16]I say sinusoid; the derivation is usually carried out with cosine waves only for simplicity. The use of a general phase offset ϕ in the input $x(t) = \cos(\omega t + \phi)$ has the consequence that each harmonic is offset in phase by $n\phi$.

the combination $0.25 * T_1 + 0.5 * T_2 + 0.25 * T_3$. When fed by a full-amplitude sinusoid, it would therefore give rise to the first three harmonics with amplitudes of 0.25, 0.5 and 0.25 respectively. This is the basis of **waveshaping** as used in sound synthesis [LeBrun, 1979; Arfib, 1979; Roads, 1985e]; plug in a sinusoid to a transfer function, and get back a more complicated harmonic recipe! While efficient, it has the drawback that the trick only works for full-amplitude sinusoids (with a nonlinear behavior of crossterms for other amplitude inputs), and there is no dynamic control of the individual phase of each component.

4.3.2 Time Stretching and Pitch Shifting

Changing the playback rate of a sound file always causes shifts in pitch. It is desirable in many circumstances to decouple these, to create independent control of changes of pitch and playback rate. Current DAW software provides engines which innately offer such facilities, such as those integrated into Pro Tools, the Time Machine in Logic or the 'warping' facilities in Ableton Live. Time stretching (without pitch shifting) effects are also familiar from many works, including Metalheads' *Terminator* (1992), the central breakdown section of Fatboy Slim's *Rockafeller Skank* (1998), or from a more experimental art angle, Leif Inge's *9 Beet Stretch* (2005), which extends a recording of Beethoven's Ninth Symphony to last 24 hours.[17]

The standard mechanism for time stretching is to use the windowing process familiar from analysis. In an **overlap add** (OLA) architecture, input windows are grabbed from the input audio stream at one rate. However, the output rate is different (see Figure 4.11). Which one of the input or output rate is varied for a given application determines the nature of the artifacts and the place where computational costs are incurred. If the input windows are more frequent, the analysis cost is incurred more frequently. If the output windows are more frequent, the rendering cost is heightened. Further, the nature of the overlap itself has an impact on artifacts in analysis (due to potentially missing information) or output rendering (due to the final summation). To really slow down the output, input windows of data may need to be repeated in some way, leading to potential repetition artifacts as the 'wheels spin'. Without safeguards, repetition of transient segments of signal can occur for some odd 'double hit' effects. Transients are vulnerable portions of the signal for processing, and should be left alone if possible by detecting their presence; this is further discussed below.

The best position at which to crossfade between overlapping output windows is refined by cross-correlation in SOLA (synchronous overlap add) [Zölzer, 2002, pp. 208–211], which looks for the peak offset at which the two signals best align. For speech and monophonic instrumental sounds, the PSOLA method (pitch-synchronous OLA) can take account of the fundamental frequency[18] in determining input window positioning. The analysis rate is thereby pitch dependent, and with input windows fitting more neatly to the period of the input, a better lock is achieved. Time stretching is accomplished by repeating (or missing out) periods, choosing the closest period to the output time position

---

[17] http://www.park.nl/park_cms/public/index.php?thisarticle=118
[18] There is no single f0 for noisy sounds or complicated polyphonic material.

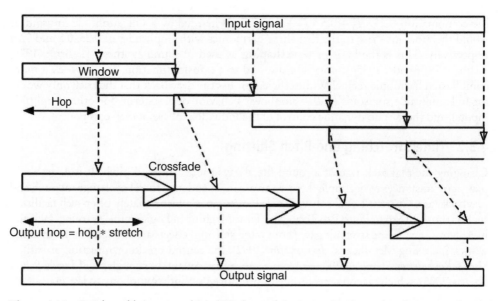

Figure 4.11 Overlap add time stretching. Windows of the input signal are placed at new points in time; the input is analyzed at a constant rate (hop size) and the output is generated with windows spaced at new intervals based on the stretch factor. In the extreme, the windows could be very small segments (grains) of sound, but standard FFT analysis window sizes would be more typical to reduce amplitude modulation artifacts ($N = 512$ or 1024 for $R = 44\,100$). Note that one window is missed out entirely; this might happen in a realtime implementation where the input buffer cannot be indefinitely large. Outside of realtime, the audio can be stretched as much as desired, and we can just source audio data however we like. For extreme stretches segments may have to be repeated or at least a very small hop size used; there must always be room for some sort of crossfade between consecutive windows of samples.

to be synthesized. The PSOLA mechanism uses relatively small 'grains' of sound, and is connected to wavetable and granular synthesis methods.

While the overlap-add mechanisms provide basic time stretching, complementary algorithms concern pitch shifting.[19] A few signal processing tricks can allow pitch shift for special cases, such as octave doubling using a comb filter [Puckette, 2007, p.184]. Pitch shifting is more commonly tackled using spectral operations, since we need to 'get at' individual frequency components. These methods are not necessarily formant-preserving. The spectral envelope of sound is a major factor in its timbre [Rodet and Schwarz, 2007], and disturbance of this shape – for example, by a uniform multiplication of component frequencies by the tritone ratio of 1.414214 – a major cause of unreal sounds, such as can be

---

[19]Pitch shifting is not frequency shifting. A number of signal processing methods allow gross frequency shifting, moving all frequency components by a fixed amount, which does not preserve harmonic relationships nor formants. These include ring modulation with a sine and high-pass filter to remove the lower band, and single-sideband modulation making use of the Hilbert transform and analytic signal.

heard in the chipmunk effect which accompanies naive playback rate alteration. Modeling and preserving spectral envelope in sound transformation is the arena of the spectral analysis models of Chapter 3.

Indeed, the most powerful independent time-stretching and pitch-shifting methods employ the more developed analysis models, and we alluded to such resynthesis possibilities there. In using oscillator-bank or inverse FFT resynthesis, the original spectral envelope can be reimposed on the sinusoidal data, even if individual partial tracks have been frequency shifted as needed. One advanced method is described by Bonada [2000] and employs a variation of spectral modeling synthesis (the sines+noise model). In order to avoid unreal disturbance of transient regions of sound, the method detects transients and passes them through the time stretching at the appropriate moment without repetition or processing.

Since the best methods for independent time stretching and pitch shifting rest on advanced signal models, they may necessitate instrument-specific variants. While it is difficult for composers to resist more overt sound-transformation parameter settings, algorithms are always most effective for subtle changes. It is worth asking yourself: do you really expect to hear a slowed-down sound as you would a normal sound? Perceptual limits are very much in play here; our auditory system has evolved to interpret real-world sounds at a standard information processing rate, and it is easy to diverge from 'reality' with audio processing tools, sometimes to interesting effect, and other times with grosser misrepresentation.

4.3.3 Implementing Spatialization

Recall Table 2.5, which listed some primary considerations in the simulation of spatial sources and environmental acoustics. Many facets of spatial perception can be modeled by gains, delays and filters, though we must be careful with the details. Not all cues are as effective, but the combination of mutually supporting cues helps to create effective virtual images, even as contradictions can harm the illusion.

We won't go over every cue mentioned in the table – for more information see Rocchesso [2002] – but we will provide extra implementation detail for a few common situations.

Panning laws

One important cue exploited in spatialization is interaural intensity difference, essentially a change in intensity between the two ears, and modeled by the relative power emitted by a set of loudspeakers. Although IID is frequency specific [Begault, 1994, p. 41], to a first approximation we can simply model gain on speaker channels rather than employ more elaborate filtering, because most sources contain energy at a range of frequencies. The allocation of gains to speakers, based on the desired virtual image position to be evoked, is called **amplitude panning** after a panorama. A particular function for panning is a **panning law** or a **pan pot law**, named after the rotary dials which embody turning a sound to a desired angular location. These laws vary in their realism, and are dependent on speaker configuration.

Stereo requires two speakers typically placed at a distance and 30° either side of the median line, or for headphones at opposite sides of the head; though the same pan law tends to be used for both situations (this is one source of the discrepancy between headphone mixing and monitor mixing). Larger speaker configurations are also seen (such as for Dolby 5.1), but the laws governing the relative gains of the different speakers become more involved. Forming a virtual image in stereo depends on the listener dependably staying at a sweet spot, which is easy with headphones, and hard for a large cinema or concert audience!

The inverse square law for sound states that the intensity (energy) is inversely proportional to distance squared. To maintain a constant distance – moving on a circular arc to keep radial distance the same – intensity would have to remain fixed, as we pan a sound between a left–right speaker pair. Whatever formula we choose must maintain the same overall intensity, while changing the gains at the two speakers. If we use gain L for the left speaker and R for the right, the total intensity arriving at the listener is $L^2 + R^2$. The intensities are summed because the ears are independent receivers.[20] We need to select a function f such that with valid pan positions expressed as angles x from 0 to $\frac{\pi}{2}$, $f(x)^2 + f(\frac{\pi}{2} - x)^2 = 1$. This is reminiscent of the crossfading problem described in Section 4.1.3, and has the same potential solutions, including the classic $f(x) = \cos(x)$. Just as for a crossfade, if we had used a linear function, the total intensity would not be preserved and the midpoint of the fade would see a drop in power of 6 dB.

More general panning laws for multiple speakers exist. A vector formulation of pan laws, **vector-based amplitude panning** (VBAP) [Pulkki, 1997], uses the closest stereo pair of speakers on the plane, or a triple of speakers for full 3D positioning; VBAP is adaptable to any speaker layout, including highly irregular set-ups. In ambisonics, signal is always emitted from all the speakers in the room, of course to varying degrees, for each virtual source to be cued [Malham and Myatt, 1995].

Evoking motion

John Chowning's compositions *Sabelithe* (1971) and *Turenas* (1972) incorporate the simulation of sound moving through space, as researched by Chowning since 1964 [Chowning and Roads, 1985]. Describing his set-up [Chowning, 1971], Chowning explores the main factors that must be synthesized for convincing motion. As well as source position cues, distance cues from frequency-dependent attenuation in air, and the relation of the reverberant signal to the direct one, he notes the increasing localization of reverb with far distance, and to achieve this separates a local and a global reverberation signal. Three components of sound motion are noted:

- angular shift in energy (change of position cues, for equidistant positions on the surface of a sphere around the observer);

---

[20]At least in initial neural transduction, though signals cross over early on in the central auditory system. The approximation used here is that intensity is equivalent to loudness, which is a simplification. We are also ignoring crosstalk from the speakers themselves, where a delayed signal from the left speaker also arrives at the right ear, and from the right speaker to the left ear; further crosstalk cancellation algorithms exist to combat that.

- radial shift in energy (change in position cues, for motion on a line directly towards and away from the observer);

- radial shift in frequency (the Doppler effect).

These can all be treated via the spatialization cues for sound source position as they change over time relative to the observer position, given an adequate model. We shall investigate Doppler shift here in particular.

There is an easy way to simulate Doppler shift, by using a delay line. The distance in air from a source to the observer is the radial distance required, and a shift in delay time corresponds to a shift in the transmission time. If we use an interpolating delay line, to cope smoothly with any fractional positions, we simply update the delay time as the source moves. Calculating Doppler shift, rather than requiring direct use of the formula in Table 2.5, means knowing the radial distance. This can be obtained directly in a polar or spherical coordinate system, or the Pythagorean formula can be used for the translation from rectangular coordinates. The discontinuity in frequency shift is due to a discontinuity of first derivative in the radial distance; as a sound passes from in front to behind, where the delay to the observer was decreasing before it returns suddenly to increasing. Figure 4.12 shows this for a source passing on a line directly to the right of the observer. We could model sound transmission to the two ears separately (and introduce frequency- and angle-dependent head shadowing effects and all the rest), but just the right ear is shown in the diagram. The distance to the source path line on the right is known, and the movement of the source on its path is created by the line generator. Use $r = \sqrt{a^2 + b^2}$ to obtain the radial distance in meters, and use this to create a time delay by r/s where s is the speed of sound. To make an effective illusion, at least the amplitude cue (inversely proportional to radial distance) should also be added in.

Humans are by no means perfect at localizing moving sounds. Transient sounds are easier to localize, particularly for moving sources [Begault, 1994, p. 51]. Our evolutionary heritage can make us more alert to planar (ground) motion than motion above. Some pragmatism is useful in working to evoke spatial sound, especially when trying to simulate continuous movement within a loudspeaker arrangement. Stockhausen's solution, of recording real movement with multiple microphones, via his famous revolving speaker tables, is one pragmatic approach, as first used for *Kontakte* (1958–60). Harrison [1998] notes that in performance the four loudspeakers appear more in a cruciform arrangement, disturbing the accuracy of the reproduction (but adapting to larger audiences). Live diffusion of sound can allow some compromise in venues, as already discussed, but there is no need to give up on the dream of flying sounds through space if some care is taken in preparing sonic illusions. As a last resort, swing the speakers themselves or have a mobile phone orchestra run around!

Room acoustics

Modeling the absorption and reflection of sound waves within a room is an involved and computationally demanding task. Although this has been attempted from first principles

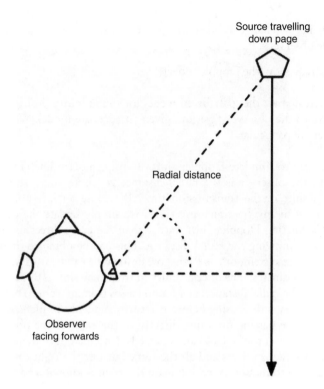

Source travelling
down page

Radial distance

Observer
facing forwards

Figure 4.12   Calculating radial distance for a Doppler effect.

in computer models of architectural acoustics, practical realtime implementation of digital reverberation units makes use of simple unit generators rather than geometric models. For the blurred reverberation tail this might mean low-pass (frequency-sensitive absorption), all-pass (diffuse reflection, phase perturbation at walls) and comb (traveling time, standing wave) filters, as well as explicit delays for early reflections within the first 50 milliseconds. The combination of these units is an art, because many choices of times and gains for the various filters could potentially lead to pronounced resonances that overly color the sound; despite sound coloration being one aspect of room acoustics, there is a balance between subtle and overt processing. Real room dimensions and impulse response recordings can help inform the decay coefficients for the tail, and the selection of tap times for the early reflections, while the main body of the reverberation in the tail is approximated by a network of filters.

We have already encountered the convolution reverb, which provides a more processor-intensive way to play any sound through a known room acoustic. A reverberator that can support many different room types would require a library of impulse responses. To some extent, particularly when early reflections and the diffuse tail are already marked up, some chopping and changing of responses is possible for special (if contradictory) effects, such as playing with the diffuse reverberation of a cathedral and the close initial reflections of a small room! But filter network reverberators tend to have more natural control parameters, explicitly for RT60 (the time to drop by 60 dB) and the frequency characteristics of the tail such as proportion of low to high frequencies ('warmth').

Though geometric modeling is intensive, it has still received attention, drawing from computer graphics and also from physical modeling sound synthesis (see Section 5.2). Ray tracing, as used to trace out the path for light waves, is only a first approximation for sound, since each reflection in a room requires scattering (diffusion) modeling [Roads, 1996, p. 485]. James Moorer [1985] gives an example of a concert hall where a diffuse tail begins even among the supposedly isolated early reflections, demonstrating the complexity of room modeling. Nevertheless, he also illustrates phantom source modeling by computer to produce the pattern of reflections over time for a given room geometry. Richard Moore has suggested a 'room within a room' model which explicitly considers the travel times for direct and reflected sound to reach particular speakers from a given virtual source [Moore, 1990; Rocchesso, 2002]. It is also possible to use waveguides (dual directional delay lines) from physical modeling synthesis to model the traveling times. Yet given the number of events which blend into a reverberation tail, some approximation is entirely appropriate for such a statistical system.

4.4 SUMMARY

This chapter has covered some important principles of digital signal processing, and some explicit audio effects. We have seen some basic operations on signals, including the consequences of multiplying two signals together. Ring modulation has provided an example of an overt effect which is easy to build in a digital system (just multiply a sound by a sine) and has noticeable spectral ramifications. We have discussed the mixing of signals, the use of fades to avoid discontinuities, and applications of crossfades from splices to later discussion of overlap-add procedures. Introduction of the operation of convolution then motivated another look at digital filters. By the end of the second section, comb and all-pass filters, as well as the convolution reverb, had been outlined. The final section has given some further insights into the creation of digital audio effects. In particular, we have covered dynamics processing and waveshaping distortion, methods to independently control pitch and playback rate for sampled material, and ended with some further implementation details for sound spatialization.

4.5 EXERCISES

1. Signals can be scaled so as to make them conform to a standard range. There are two approaches, one founded in the normal number range $[0, 1]$ and one based on a statistical notion of standardization. Each has its advantages. Numerically, the number range $[0, 1]$ is the easiest to rescale to any other range. Given the sequence

$$5, \ 7, \ 8.56, \ 9.1, \ 2.3, \ 2.4, \ 4.63$$

   in the linear range 2.2 to 9.4, rescale these values into $[0, 1]$. Standardization requires a longer sequence to establish good estimators, but let's run the small-scale example for teaching purposes anyway. Find the mean μ and standard deviation σ of the seven-number sequence above using

$$\mu = \frac{1}{N} \sum_{n=0}^{N-1} x(n) \quad \text{and} \quad \sigma = \sqrt{\frac{1}{N} \sum_{n=0}^{N-1} (x(n) - \mu)^2}$$

   Now remap the sequence by $x'(n) = (x(n) - \mu)/\sigma$. This gives a sequence with a mean of 0 and a standard deviation of 1. To see how this differs from sending numbers to $[0, 1]$, consider what happens to outliers (the extreme values). Assuming that a sequence has a normal distribution over time, we can state, for instance, that 95% of values occur within $\pm 2\sigma$. Invent a much longer sequence as input to the process (or source one from sample values or other numerical data, for instance), and again compare normalization and standardization.

2. Another standard mapping is the conversion between linear and logarithmic scales. For many psychophysical attributes, such as aspects of vision, hearing and touch, human sensitivity to stimuli can be approximated by 'Weber's law', which essentially says that a perceived attribute is proportional to the logarithm of a stimulus divided by a reference level; just like the equation for getting decibels from amplitude. When we convert between linear and logarithmic ranges, we want to be careful about taking the logarithm of zero, which is a bit difficult (this is actually the negative infinity that you see on mixers, a not very practical number). One way to convert $[0, 1]$ as linear to a logarithmic version (let's say to the natural base) would be $x'(n) = \log(x(n) + 1)/\log(2)$, and to go back again we could use $x(n) = e^{\log(2)x'(n)} - 1$. Convert the $[0, 1]$ normalized number range from the previous question to a logarithmic domain and back, plotting the numbers.

3. For ring and amplitude modulation, prove that if C and M are related by being in a harmonic series, the sidebands are also harmonics. What frequency components at what amplitudes result if $C = 0.1 * \sin(440 * 2\pi t) + 0.9 * \sin(660 * 2\pi t)$ and $M = 0.5 * \sin(110 * 2\pi t) + 0.5 * \sin(220 * 2\pi t)$ ring modulate?

4. Load two small percussive or polyphonic sound files into a sound editor or DAW software (or extract two appropriate regions from one file). Experiment with splicing these two together, by trying to find the best join point without sacrificing much audio. Can you get a good fit without using any fade and merge operations? How does crossfading help, and can you hear any noticeable artifacts of the process, particularly for different crossfade times and shapes?

5. As a compositional application, investigate using inverted envelopes in your favorite computer music system. The envelope shape should start and end at 1, but go down to lower amplitudes in between. You should experiment with triggering this envelope by pressing a key or sending some other message. Your action reduces the overall volume, so that your input energy actually temporarily reduces the power of the system, holding back the dam!

6. How would we write down an expression for the output of a multitap delay line where input $x(n)$ is delayed by 51, 317 and 400 samples?

7. Convolve 1, 0.5, 0.3, 0.1 and 1, 0, 1.

8. Calculate the first ten samples of filtered output for the filter with the following coefficients:

$$a(0) = 0.5, \ a(1) = -0.7, \ a(2) = 0.3, \ a(3) = -0.1, \ b(1) = 0, \ b(2) = 0.05$$

with input:
$$0.2, \ 1.0, \ 0.8, \ -0.3, \ 0.05$$

First do this directly. Now calculate the first ten samples of the impulse response for the filter by passing in $1, 0, 0, \ldots$. Convolve this impulse response with the input sequence, over the first ten samples. You could write a program to do this, in which case you could try plotting out many more samples of the result. Do you get the same answer via the two techniques?

9. Using a portable recording device, record clicking your fingers (or creating a more definite impulse with a spark generator or other device) at a number of source and microphone positions within a number of differently shaped and sized rooms. Obtain some dry anechoic recordings (there are various Internet sources if you don't have your own anechoic chamber, such as http://theremin.music.uiowa.edu/MIS.html) and apply the room impulse responses via convolution, comparing your results.

10. As another composition exercise, try out some outlandish plug-ins. Apply each to a number of different audio files. Which has the most all-consuming sound transformation? Is the effect still highly sensitive to the input file, or does it just cause the same audio effect whatever the input?

4.6

FURTHER READING

See the digital signal processing references in Chapter 3, and also alternative computer music textbooks as cited in Chapter 1.

Julius O. Smith has provided a wealth of online materials covering many aspects of digital signal processing and particularly musical applications (http://ccrma.stanford.edu/~jos). His various books are also available in printed editions.

DAFX conference series: www.dafx.de

Zölzer, U. (ed) (2002). *DAFX: Digital Audio Effects*. John Wiley and Sons Ltd, Chichester.

Chapter 5

Synthesis

'The generation of voltage functions from quantized samples is a practical, powerful and useful method when coupled to modern computers.'

Max Mathews [Mathews, 1969, p. 7]

OBJECTIVES

This chapter covers:

- generating sound from scratch with a computer;
- surveying sound synthesis algorithms;
- modeling real-world sounds with a computer;
- how computers can sing.

5.1 THE SPACE OF SOUND SYNTHESIS ALGORITHMS

Digital sound synthesis has been the subject of intensive research since Max Mathews's early experiments. Many powerful approaches have been cataloged, and it is fair to say that many of the good design choices in the space of sound synthesis algorithms have now been identified. It is certainly easy to come up with a poor sound synthesis algorithm that leads to rather unimpressive sounds; as Max Mathews himself warns: 'almost all timbres are uninteresting, and many timbres are feeble or ugly .... It is VERY HARD to create new timbres we hear as interesting, powerful and beautiful' [Collins and d'Escriván, 2007, pp. 85–86]. Some of the successful techniques originated from analog music studios before finding further application in the discrete domain, and others have been a specific result of computer music research. Many are inspired by existing acoustic instruments and sounds, because these provide historically proven models and ecologically valid stimuli, and therefore an important test of the quality of sound synthesis [Smith, 1996, p. 45]. Although existing sounds make good signposts, don't let that entirely dissuade you from more radical exploration, for there are also some interesting if eccentric procedures entirely in the realm of the electronic. Computer music textbooks often allocate much of their space to sound synthesis methods, and specialist books entirely on sound synthesis are available; some further reading appears at the close of the chapter.

While we may be cautious about any taxonomy, especially since methods are often combined in practice in sound design, a number of respected researchers have proposed categorizations of the different algorithms. Julius O. Smith III originally outlined a scheme in 1991 [Smith, 1991], and since this also maps well onto the system utilized by Eduardo Miranda [Miranda, 2002, p. xvi] in his book, I present it here, with Miranda's versions of the categories in italics:

- **processed recording** – time-domain manipulation of existing data (*time-based approaches*);

- **spectral model** – frequency-domain synthesis motivated by sound analysis (*spectrum modeling*);

- **physical model** – models of actual sources and sound propagation supplied by acoustics (*source modeling*);

- **abstract algorithm** – the employment of any mathematical algorithm whose output can be cast into the audio frequency range (*loose modeling*).

We already explored processed recordings simply by raising the topic of sampling in Chapter 2. Miranda has noted that all the digital sound synthesis methods have some model as their basis, even if some models are not related to real-world physics or the analysis of existing sounds. The chief model informing the processed recording category, for instance, is the theory of digital audio.

Xavier Serra identifies the two most important current trends as spectral modeling and physical modeling [Serra, 1997b, 2007], and discounts the older abstract algorithms as obsolete. Yet the proven utility and distinct sound of many earlier methods will always guarantee their status even as newer schemes become widely available; for example, the well-known and well-worn FM algorithm, which we shall soon discuss in more detail, is a common subject of new 'retro' implementations. Even bearing Mathews's warning in mind, the space of esoteric models may always have some new sounds to reveal, and where we explore computer music to reveal new sonic possibilities, we cannot discount entirely a new corner in design space opening up. It is clear, however, that spectral and physical models are those routes most respectful of the human auditory system and the acoustics of real-world interaction.

Given any sound synthesis algorithm, we can consider the method with respect to a number of salient dimensions. Serra [1997b] identifies four chief factors important in comparing different sound synthesis algorithms:

- sound quality – ability to convince the human ear of its merits;

- flexibility – expressiveness with respect to the algorithm's control parameters;

- generality – the size of the potential timbre space supported;

- compute time – efficiency of rendering.

Historically, the efficiency (CPU cost) has been an important factor; since realtime rendering is a desirable musical property, research methods have often failed the test of practicality. What may seem an efficient technique for a single voice is typically multiplied in cost by the number of voices required. So efficient abstract algorithms may retain advantages over complex new physical models when many voices must be synthesized at once.

To give an example, sampling in its raw form is very efficient for playback (simply play back stored samples), and the sound quality is as high as a digital system can manage, that is, utterly convincing reproduction given sufficient sampling rate and bit resolution to accommodate the human ear (and similarly compliant converters and loudspeakers). Since any real-world sound which can be picked up by a microphone can be recorded, most acoustic phenomena can be captured, providing a very general timbre space (recordings of any new synthesized sound are of course also open to the technique of sample playback). However, the method falls down on flexibility, since without any further analysis there are very few real control parameters to playback (playback rate and position, essentially). Spectral modeling, for instance, is one way to try to obtain more flexibility from this starting point, but raw sample playback alone is inflexible. It should also be noted that calculation time in computing is often traded off against space; so sampling takes orders of magnitude more raw memory than do some of the purer synthesis models we shall soon encounter.

The intimate relationship between analysis and synthesis is brought to the fore in spectral modeling. The analysis models surveyed in Chapter 3 become operationalized for novel synthesis effects, though there is a dependency on the source analyzed. Synthesis of sound can also exist independently of analysis. It is quite straightforward just to write signal values; but, as I warned above, this is unlikely to lead to acoustically realistic, and humanly stimulating, sounds. Despite such cautions, many experimenters have played with time-domain waveforms, with abstract sound synthesis. There is a natural human curiosity to try this out, and it provides one route into sound synthesis. It is sometimes liberating to work with an abstract algorithm's quirky parameters, to find new ways to create sounds via a loudspeaker. But we shall see by the end of this chapter that physical modeling and source-informed spectral modeling provide deeper routes to new sounds that relate well to our auditory proclivities.

5.1.1 Classic Algorithms

Huge resources of computer-generated sound are available due to a proliferation of sound synthesis methods, some seeking a close affinity to naturally occurring sound, and some exploring uncharted vistas of loudspeaker movement. Because of the evolutionary closeness of production and perception, models of acoustic and psychoacoustic phenomena tend to be the most powerful in invoking convincing dynamic sounds, but there are more abstract mathematical algorithms that have also opened up some new sound worlds. Table 5.1 summarizes a variety of classic sound synthesis methods. Though they can always be used directly for synthesis from user-provided parameter data, algorithms usually have an analytical dual, and the table makes clear the connection to audio analysis that can inform a given synthesis scheme.

The control data for these algorithms varies from a few parameters to the rich analysis data output by a particular spectral model. Even in the case of minimal parameters, time-varying control essentially creates more dynamic sounds.

We should also be careful before claiming that these are really singular algorithms standing apart in creative work, since the outputs of one method can form inputs to the next, and the whole is always amenable to enveloping, scheduling of events, further processing and other signal and musical treatments.

It must be emphasized that this is only a selection; many more techniques have been investigated. Fashions in sound synthesis may change based on compositional taste, though there is consensus that the richest simulations of existing instruments and sound sources unsurprisingly require an active engagement with specific modeling of that instrument or source, whether informed by spectral analysis or acoustics.

5.1.2 Waveforms and Wavetables

Much of the toolkit for sound synthesis has been developed already; we looked at envelopes, amplitude modulation, filters and more in Chapter 4. One rather sweet infatuation in current practice is the simulation of older generation analog synthesizers. This effort in **analog modeling** may go so far as to approximate the quirky nonlinearities of Moog ladder filters and other warmly temperamental circuitry.[1] A basic technique for periodic sounds is to grab a standard waveform shape to repeat at the fundamental frequency, and pass it through a time-varying filter and amplitude envelope.

---

[1]We might wonder how far back to go: virtual Telharmonium, anyone?

Table 5.1 Classic sound synthesis methods.

Algorithm	Description	Analysis front end	References
Sample-based synthesis	Recordings played back	Usually simple recording, but feature extraction can be introduced	See Section 2.7.3
Wavetable synthesis	Rather than complete sample playback, isolates a set of representative short periods	Fourier analysis	Bristow-Johnson [1996]; Beauchamp [2007a]
Amplitude Modulation (AM)	Most typically used as an effect or for enveloping, but has spectral consequences	Demodulation, envelope extraction [Zölzer, 2002]	See Section 4.1.2
Frequency Modulation (FM)	Actual implementations often use phase modulation, since frequency is rate of change of phase	Some attempts to use a genetic algorithm to backwards engineer parameters	Chowning [1973]
Subtractive synthesis	Source+filter model. Start with a complex signal, and selectively filter it. Very popular method for analog synthesizers and their digital simulations	Deconvolution to separate source and filter; LPC [Makhoul, 1975] or MFCC analysis [Gold and Morgan, 2000]	Gold and Morgan [2000]; Arfib et al. [2002b]
Additive synthesis	Building up complex sounds from sinusoids	Fourier analysis	See Chapter 3
Granular synthesis	Building up complex sounds from primitive atoms	Dictionary-based analysis, see Section 3.3	Roads [2001]
Non-standard synthesis	A catch-all term for a panoply of individual procedures from 1970s waveform assembler languages to Xenakis's probabilistic breakpoint synthesis method	Haphazard, usually just direct empirical synthesis methods	Roads [1996]; Collins [2008]
Spectral modeling	Resynthesis after complex analytical model, such as the sines+noise model	Various, see Chapter 3	Serra [1997b]; Amatriain et al. [2002]
Physical modeling	Inspiration from acoustical equations, close consideration of sound production in particular instruments and environments	Mathematical analysis, impulse response measurements on real instruments	Karjalainen et al. [2001]; Välimäki and Takala [1996]

The mainstay of analog synthesizers is **subtractive synthesis**: starting with a complex source, components are subtracted from the raw sound to make a more carefully sculpted sound. This is also termed a **source plus filter** model, since the spectral sculpting is carried out by a filter on the source. To maximize the possible liveliness white noise is a good starting point for sculpting inharmonic noise sounds, or a rich many-harmonic sawtooth wave or impulse train (equal amplitude harmonic source) for periodic sound.

Working in the opposite direction is already familiar, for the classic building block in computer music is the sine tone. Rather than starting with something complex and taking energy away to sculpt a sound, we can start with simple building blocks and add many of them together to create more involved sounds; this is **additive synthesis**, often informed by sinusoidal analysis.

Now, since adding up signals is a fundamental operation in providing a richer ensemble sound, subtractive synthesis might have the filter act on a sum of multiple sources, or add up multiple voices after each is individually filtered. Because the components aren't pure sinusoids (unless the filter was a particularly tight band-pass) and there tend to be fewer voices than the massed ranks of sinusoids required to regenerate complex sounds, this is not pure additive synthesis, but it employs addition all the same. This simply demonstrates that given various signal processing operations, such as summation, multiplication and filtering, we can immediately start to explore quite complicated recipes for sound synthesis and have all sorts of interesting choices about the sounds we design.

Analog modeling with a digital system is complicated by that most important restriction of digital sampling; nothing above the Nyquist frequency can be represented. If we use 'sharp-edged' waveform shapes that change faster than the digital system can represent them, we will instantly introduce aliasing distortion into a sound. One way to avoid this is to use **band-limited** waveforms, shapes that are engineered as sums of sinusoidal components all below Nyquist frequency. For periodic sounds, these will of course be harmonics of the fundamental. Depending on the output fundamental frequency, this approach would require us to take varying numbers of harmonics, because there is a varying amount of space below Nyquist (consider a 44 100 Hz sampling rate, and f0s of 440 and 1734. How many harmonics fit below 22 050 for each of these cases? The answer will be the floor of (greatest integer below) 22 050/f0). There are recipes for constructing band-limited waveforms from basic band-limited impulses [Stilson and Smith, 1996; Brandt, 2001].

Figure 5.1 depicts four standard waveforms that commonly appear in synthesizers. It is possible to work out the recipe to build up a complex waveform shape through Fourier analysis, and this is indeed how the diagram was constructed; the line spectra in the right-hand column give an idea of the breakdown of component strengths for the harmonics, used to build the band-limited waveforms in the middle column.

While it is insightful to see component harmonic recipes from the frequency-domain viewpoint, if a waveform is to be used over and over in the time domain, there is no

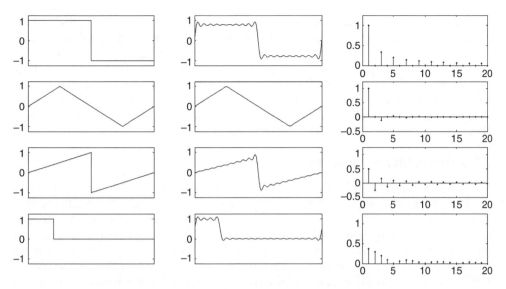

Figure 5.1 Waveforms: each row gives one standard waveform, with the mathematically perfect graph on the left, then a band-limited approximation, and finally a set of line spectra showing the component strength of sinusoids on the right. The band-limited waveforms use the first 20 harmonics. The four rows depict, from top to bottom, square, triangle, sawtooth and pulse waveforms. For the pulse, the duty cycle can be varied; in this case, the pulse is 'on' for one-fifth of the period. The sinusoidal component harmonics converge to a triangle very quickly, so the band-limited version looks very similar to the target but for a slight rounding at the direction changes (the fast convergence might be suspected from the way the harmonic strengths drop off so quickly in the line spectra). The line spectra for the first three waveforms show what amplitude multipliers to use in adding up pure sines at the harmonics. Only pure sines are needed because each of these waveforms is an odd function (like a sine). The pulse wave in the final row is a different case; the line spectrum here is a magnitude spectrum, and since the pulse is asymmetrical about zero in this case, it was formed by combining sines and cosines (i.e., general sinusoids).

point recreating it from sinusoids every time. Waveforms could be created directly from their mathematical equations, but this is also not the most efficient way to proceed. The most efficient method is to take a cue from sample playback and use table lookup. The waveform shape is sampled and stored in a **wavetable**, ready for reuse. The usual issues of interpolation now appear (compare Sections 2.7.3 and 4.1). Practically speaking, a wavetable of 256 samples or more (powers of two are typical) with at least linear interpolation is a safe bet. While band-limited waveforms may seem to require additional calculation, selection from a set of pre-calculated wavetables can take place based on the fundamental frequency. Indeed, the use of multiple wavetables in sound synthesis can also be used to impart time-varying sound rather than a static timbre (as well as such mechanisms as time-varying amplitude envelope and filter).

Wavetables are efficient in use, but there is a way to save further on storage, or provide time-domain handles on waveform shape. This is to specify a waveform shape indirectly using **breakpoints** (also called control points) [Roads, 1996]. Such a design was essentially already introduced in Figure 4.2, where an envelope was summarized by a series of line segments or curve segments. This allows what is essentially non-uniform sampling, but since ultimately uniform samples must be output, the breakpoint set either must be rendered back into a wavetable each time it is modified, or else used as a special lookup chart based on the current phase within a period. The usual dangers of aliasing are present.

5.1.3 Frequency Modulation

Musicians are already intuitively familiar with two basic forms of modulation. Tremolo is a fluctuation in volume (essentially, amplitude modulation), and vibrato a fluctuation in frequency. The former is possible, for example, by fast repetitive bowing on a stringed instrument, or beating your own chest while singing. Vibrato is evident in singing, as a singer warbles either side of a central pitch; the deviation of some opera singers' vibrato is around plus or minus a semitone of what is heard as the stable central pitch [Sundberg, 1999]! Vibrato is also evidenced from the rocking of the left finger position on a string instrument to effect subtle excitation of the sound, but here, as in most natural sound production, amplitude modulation and frequency modulation are somewhat interlinked. The human auditory system is also highly sensitive to modulation; there are specialized amplitude and frequency modulation-sensitive neurons in the brain [Pickles, 1988].

We met amplitude modulation already in Chapter 4 along with enveloping. Many of the early methods of synthesis are of note as much for their efficiency of means as for their resulting sound. **Frequency Modulation** (FM) derives from the idea of plugging one sinusoid into another, allowing complex spectra to be synthesized using only two sinusoids. Though invented for radio and explored in some analog music studios, FM was first applied to digital sound synthesis by John Chowning in 1967, though he published his results later [Chowning, 1973]. Yamaha licensed the patents as well as developing their own variations (such as feedback FM) and in 1983 released the Yamaha DX7 synthesizer, which went on to sell around 300 000 units, the most commercially successful synthesizer of all time.

Recall the idea of the modulator and the carrier from Section 4.1.2. Rather than using the modulator to control the amplitude of the carrier, we're going to plug the modulator into the carrier frequency. There are three basic parameters, the carrier frequency C, the modulation frequency M, and the modulation depth or frequency deviation D. The modulation depth is often made to work relative to the modulation frequency by defining an index of modulation I such that $I = D/M$. Figure 5.2 depicts three relevant unit generator networks, showing how the units are plugged together for variants of FM. Equations for these three as digital systems are:

$$y(n) = \sin(2\pi(n/R)C + (D * \sin(2\pi(n/R)M))) \tag{5.1}$$

$$y(n) = \sin(2\pi(n/R)C + (M * I * \sin(2\pi(n/R)M))) \tag{5.2}$$

$$y(n) = \sin(2\pi(n/R)C + Fy(n-1)) \tag{5.3}$$

where R is the sampling rate, I is the modulation index, F is a feedback parameter, and no phase terms have been added to the sinusoids, leaving them as pure sines.

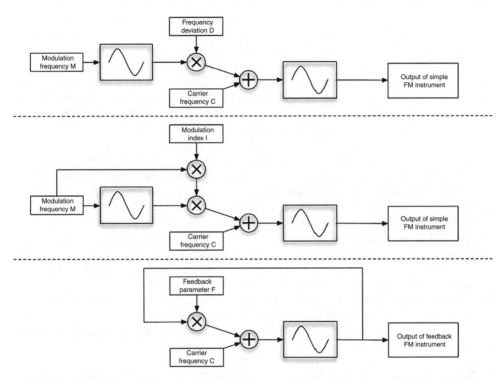

Figure 5.2   Three simple FM algorithms. The top two are actually equivalent, but the middle row rewrites the top row in terms of the modulation index I. For simplicity of exposition, further elements of a developed synthesis patch, such as the amplitude multiplier on a final signal from scaling or an amplitude envelope, or potential initial phase inputs to the sinusoids, are missed out. The oscillators are assumed simple sines with only a frequency control input.

Rather than the respective two or three output components of sinusoid-based ring or amplitude modulation, FM generates a potentially infinite number of components in the spectrum, but of varying strength. Usually only a few are significant, though the timbral power of FM is in allowing a continuum from simple to more complex spectral results based on the control parameters, especially the index of modulation I. Because FM output spectra can be very rich, it is only really necessary to work with sinusoids or at most a few harmonics; in simple FM, just plugging two sinusoids together is enough. Based on the values we choose for the parameters C, M and D (or I) we can make very dense spectral energy distributions, or only a light modulation effect. The output components turn up at $C + kM$ where k is any integer, so that as well as the original carrier frequency C, components occur symmetrically at $C + M, C - M, C + 2M, C - 2M, \ldots$.

By changing the modulation frequency and depth, the energy in the sidebands is redistributed; the actual formulas for this use Bessel functions. Because in practice musicians tend to use their ears, and because FM has been done to death in the literature, I'm going to take the liberty of missing out the Bessel equations, and leave you to look them up if you're curious [Roads, 1996; Dodge and Jerse, 1997]. The modulation index I comes in useful here, however. If I is small there is little audible FM effect. The higher I is, the stronger the energy in the sidebands (a rule of thumb is that $I+1$ rounded to the nearest integer is a measure of how many components on each side have significant energy). It is also possible to control how harmonic the resultant spectrum is by choosing the ratio $C:M$ carefully. For example, if $C=M$, then all the negative components will fall on 0 Hz or existing positive components, and a harmonic spectrum always results.

In practice, phase modulation is often employed instead of frequency modulation. To see why this might be so, consider that the rate of change of phase is frequency. To give a worked example, if there are 44 100 samples per second, and a sine wave moves in phase by $\pi * 0.02$ per sample, it is moving at $1/100$ of a cycle per sample. If it takes 100 samples to complete a cycle ($100 * 0.02 * \pi = 2 * \pi$ and each cycle of a sinusoid has 2π radians in it), the frequency is $44\,100/100 = 441$ Hz. So the rate of change of the phase (really, angular frequency) can be directly converted to a frequency in cycles per second. Instead of modulating frequency, most practical implementations of FM proceed by modulating phase instead, without any aural difference when correctly implemented. Phase modulation is useful because it is a more basic standpoint, closer to a wavetable position pointer: if you know the phase, you know exactly where you are within a cycle, and phase modulation tells you where to shift to next, whereas frequency modulation manipulates the rate of change of rate of change of phase at one further step removed.

There are also many different variants on the basic FM algorithm, introducing multiple modulation steps and asymmetrical spectra [Dodge and Jerse, 1997], and incorporating feedback. Feedback FM tends to smooth the spectral energy out, rather than giving the interference pattern of Bessel function bumps of the standard FM algorithm [Tolonen et al., 1998]. Dynamic sounds are produced by changing the FM parameters over time; an envelope for the index of modulation is a good brightness control, and linked to an amplitude envelope simulates something of the physics of real sound sources, whose spectral rolloff is correlated to volume.

Despite its ubiquity in teaching texts, and the many historical implementations and compositions which have employed it (from Jean-Claude Risset's *Mutations I* (1969) through John Chowning's own *Stria* (1977) to 1980s popular music production), FM is but one potential sound source among many nonlinear algorithms. Its virtue has always been an economy of means, and the great efforts in sound design using FM that have cataloged the many possible sounds; one wonders if equivalent efforts in some other algorithms may be similarly rewarding. One important principle to take away from FM is that any synthesis control can be modulated, that is, changed over time by some oscillator or other signal. In this sense, a lot of the fun of experimental synthesis comes down to plugging one thing into another to see what happens!

5.1.4 Granular Synthesis

In **granular synthesis** complex sounds are formed out of short grains each normally in the region of 10–100 milliseconds long [Roads, 2001, 1996; Truax, 1988]. When coupled to analysis, the grains may be motivated by particular time–frequency properties, creating an atomic decomposition of an existing sound (see Section 3.3). It is also possible to bypass the analysis–synthesis path and directly synthesize new clouds of sound. We might use grains extracted from existing sound files, or create them from scratch, for example by enveloping sine tones. When lots of these microsounds are combined into big swarms, we can make macroscopic soundscapes. Granular synthesis is often a bridge between low-level synthesis methods for individual small sounds and structure on a wider scale.

Such control depends on scheduling, using stochastic or deterministic algorithms to select the timings and parameters of grains making up the output stream. Over time the characteristics of the swarm can be changed, for example by manipulating density in grains per second. One of the headline granular effects is a granular wipe or crossfade, which can be most dramatically manifested as a dissolution of a sound into sparse particles followed by a coalescence into another sound (there is no need to have a sparse intermediary, since a probabilistic blend of grains from two signal sources could be maintained at uniform power throughout a transition). Two examples are shown here. In Figure 5.3 two streams are depicted. An exclusivity condition guarantees that only one can sound at once. A linearly changing probability effects the wipe from lower to upper stream, but the overall effect is synchronous to the grain generation rate. In Figure 5.4 there are independent rolls of the dice for each stream, but with opposite chances of sounding; as the upper stream gains in prominence, the probability of any involvement of the lower one diminishes, and vice versa. Arbitrary probability distributions could be used as controls for this process (see Section 8.3.2).

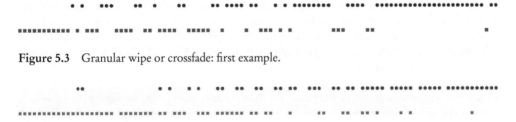

Figure 5.3 Granular wipe or crossfade: first example.

Figure 5.4 Granular wipe or crossfade: second example.

Depending on the synthesis method for individual grains, each grain may have many different parameters attached to it; some salient ones might be a fundamental frequency, the duration of the envelope, a pan position in the stereo field or the amplitude. The overall cloud can also have some sort of distribution for these parameters, which might lead to a 'tendency mask' determining the range of parameter values of the particles allowed at different points in time (see Figure 5.5).

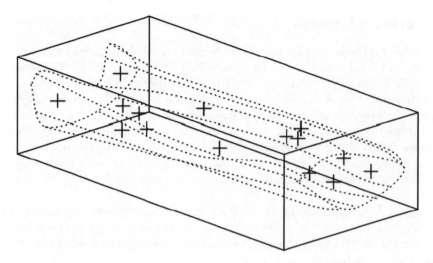

Figure 5.5   Three-dimensional tendency mask. Constraints in three feature dimensions for the choice of grains are delimited by the dotted shape outlined. You might also think of this as a succession of 2D planes, at a series of points in time along the longer axis. The plus signs depict grains selected within such an evolving feature space. Arbitrary volumes can be drawn out in higher-dimensional spaces, according to the descriptors required.

The composer's work is thus both to specify the grains, and also to control how they are used over time to make an interesting compositional structure. These techniques were first conceptualized and explored in instrumental and electronic music by Iannis Xenakis (in the 1950s), and further investigated in computer implementation, notably by Curtis Roads and Barry Truax, from the early 1970s on. Realtime systems became plausible in the 1980s; Truax's *Riverrun* (1986) intensively explores a natural river analogy: 'From the smallest rivulet to the fullest force of its mass, a river is formed from a collection of countless droplets and sources.'[2] Basic granular synthesis on existing sound materials is a well-established technique, and a sometimes overused source of inspiration. As with most methods that manipulate sound files, it is easy to make rich and varied sounds, but the nature of the processing is often obvious.

Granular synthesis can easily embrace rhythmic rates, manipulating segments of sound around the size of conventional acoustic events such as percussive hits. Curtis Roads tends to differentiate asynchronous probabilistic spray-gun effects from the more synchronous effects created under the guidance of pitched or rhythmic repetition [Roads, 1996, 2001]. I can't resist mentioning the fun that can be had with carefully placed grains inspired by electronic dance music production techniques. One example is provided by the cutting and resplicing of breakbeat loops, following the lead of hardcore and jungle producers. Generative techniques here lead us beyond manual sequencing into a world of automated cut-ups, and much engaging electronica can be provoked down such av-av-av-av-avenues.

---

[2]http://www.sfu.ca/~truax/river.html

5.1.5 Feature-based Synthesis

This section treats some interesting sound synthesis possibilities relating to features (recall Section 3.5). Musical features extracted in analysis can potentially form a guide for resynthesis. Even if the features by themselves are not enough to recreate a sound from scratch, they can serve as tags to the local window of sound from which they were obtained. With a wealth of feature types to extract, regions of sound become associated with multidimensional feature vectors. So in a substantial extension to sample granulation which might be called 'feature-based granulation', every grain is associated with its feature values, which can serve as a way to recall that particular grain. The space of grains is inherently organized by the feature dimensions, and can be read back, perhaps following the course of features extracted from a different sound.

This feature-led approach to classifying and reusing sound has been intensively explored by Diemo Schwarz as **concatenative synthesis**,[3] and the definitive statement appears in his PhD thesis [Schwarz, 2004]. The term concatenative relates to a standard speech synthesis method which connects up – concatenates – phonemes. For general audio, we can think of the successive selection of 'units' (the segments of sound), where we need to keep choosing a good link to the previous unit, and a good match to the target. The target might be directly specified feature vectors as control signals in their own right (perhaps through a graphical user interface to the database), or feature vectors derived from an independent audio stream. When run live, the target could be a live stream input of sound, whose feature values influence which units are brought out of the database.

Two costs must be balanced when determining which database segment to match to any input target segment through the feature vectors: **target cost**, a measure of proximity of the input segment and a database segment, and **concatenative cost** as a measure of how smoothly the output segments fit together. To give an example, consider two feature vectors of N features, $f(k)$ and $g(k)$, for $k = 1, \ldots, N$. We require some sort of similarity measure to compare how close these two feature vectors are; for our purposes, the Euclidean metric will do. So we write:

$$\text{similarity}(f, g) = \sqrt{\left(\sum_{k=1}^{N} (f(k) - g(k))^2 \right)} \qquad (5.4)$$

In practice the square root can be omitted, since comparing square roots of quantities and the quantities themselves will give the same answer. The target cost is the direct matching cost, essentially the value of the similarity metric for a given database entry and the input segment. If a simple target cost alone is sufficient we could carry out an exhaustive search over the entire database for the closest match to a target feature vector t:

$$\text{closest in database to } t = \min_{i \in \text{database}} \text{similarity}(t, f_i) \qquad (5.5)$$

---

[3]Some alternative names have appeared in the literature, including content-based synthesis and audio mosaicing [Zils and Pachet, 2001]. The latter refers to the visual paradigm of forming an image recursively out of other images; however, because of the timescale of auditory perception, such a recursive construction in audio is perceptually doubtful. It is still possible, though, to match segments of a guide sound to a database of other segments.

For each new window in time, the associated feature vector cues a search for the closest point in the database. Unfortunately, the closest match one window later will not necessarily be close within the database itself. This can be compensated for in synthesis by cross fading between segments, but can still lead to a lot of choppiness in the sound. We can further constrain the search by introducing a concatenation cost, which corresponds to a score for how well a new match fits to the previous match, independent of any target cost.

Figure 5.6 illustrates this process. There are many approaches here, and no final algorithm. A dynamic programming paradigm might be used to find a best-fit solution that reconciles the two constraints. There are also some ways to take advantage of modeling different stages of sounds, marking up comparable onsets, sustain portions and releases. Large transitions within the database can naturally take place where there is an abrupt transition in the guide sound, covering a jump in database read location. We may match like with like, so that an onset in the guide signal is matched by an onset from the database.

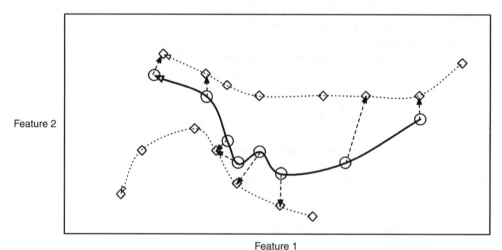

Feature 2

Feature 1

Figure 5.6 Two-dimensional feature space, target sound and two database sounds. The sounds are shown as a succession of points fitted by a curve. The central thick line and circles show the input that drives the concatenative synthesizer. The two other trails correspond to previously analyzed sounds in the database, marked out by diamonds with dotted links. The point at which to switch to another trail for resynthesis is a combination of target cost (closest in database) and concatenative cost (rewarding proximity of output units). By following the path of the target, you can see a switching between the source sounds in the database. At one point the same database unit is the best match twice in a row. The database could just be written in the space as a set of isolated points, but this diagram helps us to see how every sound involved has both momentary features and variation in time.

Efficiency of recall from the database would be an issue if an exhaustive search always had to be carried out, especially in live performance, and researchers have investigated more efficient methods to cope with this. When the database itself doesn't vary during performance, pre-calculation of an efficient representation for the feature space can be conducted, using kD-trees [Witten and Frank, 2005] or approximate nearest neighbor methods [Casey and Slaney, 2006]. Reduction of dimensionality of the feature values also assists search; Casey [2005] demonstrates a minimal example, for web computing applications, where each unit is assigned one of 26 letters, but the letter sequences still tend to encapsulate unique sounds.

Synthesis quality is typically dependent on the size and breadth of the database of units at your disposal. But many interesting compositional effects arise from less than complete databases. Bob Sturm has made some wonderful compositions using the technique. His personal response to a late-romantic-era drum crescendo in a Viennese master's second symphony, *Concatenative Variations on a Passage by Mahler* (2005), uses concatenative synthesis extensively in recasting the passage through corpora extending from saxophone to animals! One of his audio examples takes a George W. Bush speech as the driver signal, and matches it using a set of monkey noises [Sturm, 2006a].

In some ways the copyright breaching possibilities are more subtle and yet more invidious than those of old-school sampling [Sturm, 2006b]. Another artistic demonstration is provided by Sven König's *sCrAmBlEd?HaCkZ!* (2004), which is also explicitly set in opposition to old intellectual property law. This software responds to vocal beatboxing input, classifying features based on eighth-note segments according to a metronome that the player follows. The interesting twist is that each segment is matched to the audio in a database of music videos. When an audio segment is recalled, the associated video can be played back too, allowing the user to engage in an audiovisual jam with a database of pop hits. The idea can be extended further by considering visual features as well as audio, perhaps responding to both live microphone and digital camera input [Collins, 2007a].

A number of authors have also investigated matching particular feature extraction algorithms to particular synthesis algorithms [Hoffman and Cook, 2007; Park *et al.*, 2008], inspired by simultaneous work in music information retrieval where features are central to so many algorithms (see Section 7.2). We have already noted how this is a natural byproduct of any analysis model, to establish a dual to resynthesis, and thereby empower possible transformations, sound morphing included. Many interesting processing effects and radical resyntheses are allowed here [Arfib *et al.*, 2002b; Verfaille and Arfib, 2001]. Commercial products are on the rise for these techniques. One successful synthesizer based on a similar technology is Synful (http://www.synful.com/). While it is controlled by MIDI, the synthesis engine is context sensitive, and draws on a large database of samples with expressive variations. The samples can be cross-synthesized in a natural way taking care of transitions. This uses some advance knowledge of note order, thus working best with a prearranged sequence, but does not do badly even in response to live input, albeit with a slight latency. A conventional MIDI-controlled synthesizer would be stuck reacting only to individual notes.

5.2 PHYSICAL MODELING

For a sound synthesis method that truly reflects what goes on in the real world, you need to take account of physics. **Physical modeling** synthesis is the investigation of sound synthesis from principles of acoustics. The models are often involved to build, sometimes hard to control, and specifically developed for each given sound source, but probably supply the most realistic sounds of all the synthesis methods short of the inexpressive method of sampling. While any sounding object could be simulated [Cook, 2002; Rocchesso and Fontana, 2003],[4] we'll concentrate here on the virtual simulation of real musical instruments. Because models are based on real-world mechanics, the control parameters for them are familiar, though perhaps more from an engineer's point of view: lip tension, bore length, string cross-sectional area, bow velocity .... Controlling physical models in an intuitive musical way is itself a subject of active research. There is also the issue of skilled performance, where studies of expressive and virtuosic playing must be connected up to the instrument models themselves.

Computer sound synthesis is sometimes criticized for dwelling on the recreation of existing real-world sounds rather than the extended possibilities of loudspeaker music. Concerning the synthesis of surround sound, Malham [2001, p. 31] asserts that 'it is perhaps only by learning how to achieve a full simulation of the real and natural that we can appreciate the full extent of what is possible in the synthetic.' This justification also works well in support of physical modeling. Another defense is the proximity of production and perceptual mechanisms, for what we can hear is closely linked to the physical environments in which humans evolved. Sounds can be convincing because of an incorporation of physics in their dynamics, even though they still achieve new sonic results. My favorite example is David Jaffe's virtual sounding model of the Golden Gate Bridge, which appears in his physical modeling showcase work *Silicon Valley Breakdown* (1982) [Chafe, 1999].

While good physical models are more computationally expensive than classical sound synthesis algorithms, easy-to-use realtime models are within reach. Physical models appeared in hardware synthesizers such as the Yamaha VL series (the VL-1 was released in 1994), and are now readily available as commercial software, from IRCAM's Modalys, through Applied Acoustic Systems' Tassman software to the PianoTeq virtual instrument plug-in. With an increasing number of successful designs, and certainly more to come, a virtually modeled (rather than multi-sample-based) orchestra is feasible in this era. There are also practical applications in telecommunications, where object coding based on source physical properties may enable very high compression rates; Sterling *et al.* [2008] give an example of a clarinet model which can encode monophonic clarinet music at a thousandth of the usual rate. Even where a particular physical model might take up a proportion of CPU resources, it might be allocated to a single CPU on a multicore machine. Dedicated external sound synthesis hardware can also make some algorithms tractable for realtime musical use. By programming a finite programmable gate array (FPGA) as a DSP chip for a physical model,

---

[4]See also http://www.soundobject.org/

Chuchacz *et al.* [2008] have demonstrated a highly convincing drum synth playable in real time. Yamaha have even released a Virtual Acoustics Plug-in Board (as an extension board for hardware synthesizers and to an appropriate computer soundcard), at a price around 40 times less than that of the original VL-1!

The compositional possibilities are inspiring, from 'impossible' instruments which morph their physical character while being played, to making musical sequences that are too difficult for a human performer realizable through computer rendering. These ambiguities between real and unreal are a truly exciting compositional territory. Through involvement with many different algorithms, composers have been exploring these possibilities [Chafe, 2004; Kojs *et al.*, 2007], and the commercialization of the techniques makes them available to all. The live generativity, rather than pre-canned samples, of physical models make for much more dynamic sounds. Proper modeling of interactions between instrument components, such as the sounding board of a piano and feedback to individual strings, are effects not easily achieved using a multi-sampled piano.

There are a number of techniques in physical modeling. While all take inspiration from scientific work on instrument mechanics, the method used to engineer practical systems varies. Some main avenues of exploration include:

- **analytical and numerical solutions** – direct implementation by solving acoustical equations, through inspection, transform methods and other techniques (for equations without an analytical solution, numerical approximation schemes can be employed);

- **mass-spring models** – an alternative way of breaking down complex acoustical systems into finite elements, using masses for discrete points and springs for the forces acting between masses; each mass-spring pair can model a basic resonator, and complex networks are built up empirically [Florens and Cadoz, 1991];

- **modal synthesis** – study of the exact modes of vibration of acoustic systems, following Fourier analysis and experimental measurement; resonances can be implemented by second-order (two-pole) filters [Adrien, 1991; Bruyns, 2006];

- **waveguide synthesis** – building physical models out of careful combinations of simple unit generators like delays and filters, which model the propagation of sound waves and dispersion.

Any practical computer implementation requires discretization in space and time. Sometimes this may be deferred to a late stage in the process, as when analytical solutions are successfully pursued. Discretizing has consequences because of the familiar sampling theorem; we certainly can't hope to represent frequencies above Nyquist in a digital system. There is a spatial sampling issue as well, where aliasing is also possible, and which means limitations on the complexity of any represented shape and initial condition. The finer our sampling grid, the greater the computational cost, but the more accurate the approximation, so there are signal processing tradeoffs here. But practical models cannot take account of every molecule in the air or an instrument body.

While various aspects will be tackled below, it is helpful to point out one link to subtractive synthesis. Many physical systems can be presented as a source and a filter, or, in physical terms, the combination of a nonlinear **exciter** and a linear **resonator**. The excitation might be a short strike such as a percussive impact, or an ongoing energy source, such as provided by the flow of human breath or bowing on a string. The resonator models the combined resonances of a material body set into vibration, the set of strongly reactive modes stimulated based on the form of the excitation. We either imagine a pickup microphone on the body, missing out the voyage of sound in air, or we add additional propagation and reverberation models. Division into excitation and resonance serves remarkably well to describe many acoustic situations, though some care is usually taken at the point of coupling between these stages, where any feedback brings a departure from a standard subtractive synthesis model [Borin *et al.*, 1992]. It is also possible to mix and match excitation and resonance to some extent, departing from physical reality and exploring new hybrid sounds: a plectrum 'striking' a clarinet, or breathing through a drum membrane!

5.2.1 Waveguide Synthesis

We shall begin by considering an early method which can be shown to be a simple case of waveguide synthesis. The **Karplus–Strong algorithm** and its variants provide an accessible entry point into physical modeling [Karplus and Strong, 1983; Jaffe and Smith, 1983]. In its simplest form it is a bit like a comb filter responding to a burst of noise; but the recirculating delayed signal is acted upon by a further filter (Figure 5.7; compare Section 4.2.4). The physical analogies here are of the delay line to wave propagation, like a traveling wave heading down and back up a one-dimensional tube or string, and of the filter to the loss of energy during each period. One definite simplification is that rather than continuous losses due to internal friction in a string, or interactions of air and body, the losses are lumped as the effect of one filter at one point in the cycle. Nevertheless, the filter acts to dampen the sound over time. When the delay cannot be expressed as an integer number of samples, an interpolating delay line of some sort must be used; see Section 4.1.4. Alex Strong's original algorithm (dated by Karplus and Strong [1983] to 1978) used the simplest possible averaging (low-pass) filter ($y(n) = 0.5(x(n) + x(n-1))$). Because the delay line imposes a periodicity, a drum algorithm is also proposed that randomizes the sign of the signal post filter to re-impose aperiodicity (intermediate states are also possible). If we assume a once-off excitation, like a blow on a percussion instrument or pluck of a string, even the unadorned method provides a decent approximation of the character of such a sound, if not exactly the same richness.

Many extensions of the Karplus–Strong (K–S) algorithm have been unveiled, based on upgrading the filter and delay structure. By the introduction of appropriate filters for the source and around the feedback loop, Jaffe and Smith [1983] cover pick position, pick direction, attack strength and associated change in spectral brightness, fine-tuning compensation, and more realistic 'stiff' strings that become subtly more inharmonic for higher harmonic number (they can be simulated by a carefully designed all-pass filter in the feedback loop, which has frequency-dependent phase delay). They also discuss sympathetic

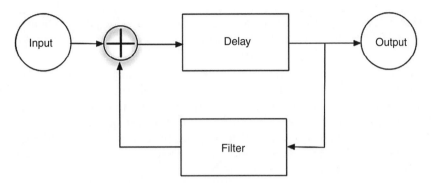

Figure 5.7   General form of the Karplus–Strong algorithm. An input excitation passes into a delay line. The delay line output provides the system output, but is also recirculated via a filter (typically a low pass, since high frequencies tend to be dampened first in real acoustic objects). The period of the output is given by the delay line length; a variable-length (interpolating) delay tap could be used for pitch changes during the course of the sound.

strings, the use of a K–S-derived structure as a general resonator, and passing the output through a further body response filter to simulate the character of a real instrument. Taking a few of their ideas, Algorithm 5.1 shows how to calculate the synthesis output on a sample-by-sample basis for a moderately complicated variation on their work. Looking over this algorithm will give you some insight into how a unit generator itself would be constructed for a computer music system, though the processing here is sample by sample and not block based. Fuller justification to support the algorithm, as well as additional refinements, are given by Jaffe and Smith [1983].

Moving on from the basic percussion and plucked string sounds of 'Karboom–String', **waveguide synthesis** is an efficient scheme for physical modeling that generalizes the Karplus–Strong approach [Smith, 1992, 1996]. Waveguides themselves are just an arrangement of delay lines, a computationally cheap way to model traveling waves. The other elements in a waveguide model are linear filters, and sometimes a nonlinear element for that real-life kick. While the delay lines deal with the aspects of the model that are distributed in space, other elements are 'lumped' or 'consolidated' at a particular point in the network of objects. This aids efficiency of calculation, and is possible because linear components can be commuted (swapped in order); some models take this so far as to employ the impulse response for the body of an instrument to the input signal, before the traveling waves of an instrument bore or string.

The traveling waves are critical because d'Alembert's general solution to the wave equation for a one-dimensional string or tube describes positive and negative traveling wave functions. Figure 5.8 shows how these are represented in practice, with the spatial position of delay lines corresponding to the hypothetical traveling waves moving within a vibrating body; the waveguide is the bidirectional delay structure. Although waveguides are paired delay lines to make opposite-direction travel explicit, there are formulations that show

---

Algorithm 5.1 Variant of the Karplus–Strong algorithm following Jaffe and Smith [1983]. This code calculates output on a sample by sample basis. For simplicity of exposition, no exact compensation for tuning is carried out.

Input: Sampling rate R, delay line of size D (period of the output will be $D + 1/2$ if $s = 0.5$, else more complicated), dynamic factor r controlling harshness of attack ($0 \leq r \leq 1$), loss factor ρ for amplitude reduction with each circulation around the feedback loop ($0 \leq \rho \leq 1$), stretching factor s which reduces loss at high frequencies ($0 \leq s \leq 1$)

Output: N samples of a signal $output(n)$ at sampling rate R as the synthesized output

1: Initialize delay line by filling it with white noise (uniformly distributed random numbers from -1 to 1)
2: Filter delay line using the one-pole filter with coefficient r, $y[n] \leftarrow (1 - r)x[n] + r y[n - 1]$. This can act to temper the harshness of the initial noise blast
3: $delaypos \leftarrow 0$ // Initialize delay line reading and writing position
4: **for** $n = 0$ to $N - 1$ **do**
5:     $x[n] \leftarrow delayline(delaypos)$ // Get delayed value
6:     $feedback[n] \leftarrow \rho * ((1 - s) * x[n] + s * x[n - 1])$ // delay stretching has a frequency-dependent effect, gain control for loss factor
7:     $delayline(delaypos) \leftarrow feedback[n]$ // Recirculation, write back into delay line
8:     $output[n] \leftarrow x[n]$ // Direct output is latest value retrieved from delay line
9:     $delaypos \leftarrow (delaypos + 1)\%D$ // Update delay line position, modulo delay line length
10: **end for**

---

comparability between the Karplus–Strong style **single delay loop** and the multi-delay-based system, explaining how the K–S algorithm fits into this paradigm [Smith, 1992; Karjalainen *et al.*, 1998].

The first waveguide models were one-dimensional models of strings and tubes, but two-dimensional plates, and three- (or higher!) dimensional meshes have been investigated [Cook, 2002]. There is an unsurprising rise in processing cost with the rise in dimensionality. Think of the change from a one-dimensional line to a two-dimensional area and the squaring required in the number of discrete points that might fit on them when uniformly spaced. Each point is attached to its local companions; while for a one-dimensional line there is but one neighbor either side of a given point, in a two-dimensional grid the tessellation leads to at least three for any point (the topology of the structure will determine the interconnections). One critical issue in all these models is how to cope with transition regions between different parts of an instrument model. This is the problem of acoustical coupling, such as might occur when pipes of different cross section are linked together, where lips meet a tube, or where string vibration is transmitted through the bridge to the resonant body of an instrument (a body that in turn is much more efficiently coupled to the air; a string on its own is a very quiet source!). A junction between sections with different properties is like a boundary between media such as air and water; energy cannot be perfectly transmitted, and some of the energy will reflect back [Loy, 2007b]. The bottom

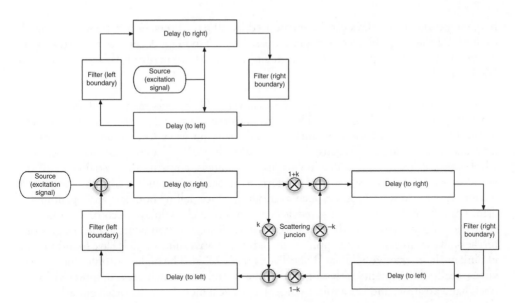

Figure 5.8   Waveguide synthesis diagrams. The top diagram shows a simple waveguide system as a pair of delay lines; trace out the circuit around the outside to see how the interconnection of the elements mirrors the spatial layout of the traveling waves. You can think of the delay length as the length of a string. The excitation is applied by writing to the delay lines at corresponding points; for a continual excitation this might be thought of as bowing near the bridge (no interaction of string and bow is assumed here). Filters represent terminations at 'bridge' and 'nut', where the waves are reflected, but may lose frequency-dependent energy. The lower diagram is more akin to a wind instrument (again without any complex interaction with the excitation itself). From the mouthpiece on the left, the length of the diagram is the length of the bore. The novelty here is that the bore changes its cross-sectional area halfway along, and the scattering junction models the way in which energy from each section is passed on and reflected within its own area. The variable k is the scattering coefficient, encapsulating the relative areas, and takes values from -1 to 1 [Cook, 2002, pp. 228–231].

part of Figure 5.8 demonstrates how this might work in practice for the case of two sections of tube, though the exact mathematical justification of the scattering junction can be pursued elsewhere [Cook, 2002; Loy, 2007b]. Things become more complex still when nonlinearities are involved. In reality, there are complex dynamics in the interaction of the excitation and the resonant structure it drives, and the combination of feedforward driving signal and feedback may send the system into different regimes; the diagrams here only show the simplest case, of a feedforward-only excitation.

Another difficulty with physical models is coping with the limit on differentiation and integration given by the sampling rate in a discrete system. Intuitively, a one-sample delay is caused by any feedback, and delay-free loops must be very carefully treated [Borin *et al.*, 1992]. Waveguides may also seem less applicable to inharmonic sounds. Nevertheless, frequency-dependent delays can be introduced by all-pass filters. When these are difficult to design, a theory of banded waveguides based on a bandwise decomposition of separate delays for different frequency modes is an alternative way to confront this modeling need [Essl *et al.*, 2004].

Because of their comparative efficiency, waveguide models have formed part of most current practical physical modeling work. There are alternative approaches, from modal synthesis to the functional transformation method, and there are ways to combine and reconcile different methodologies [Rabenstein and Petrausch, 2006]. Researchers have created a whole musical instrument collection's worth of models, covering the instruments of the world's musics, and not just standard Western orchestral fare. As indicated at the start of this section, real-world sound sources such as treading on ice, falling boulders and opening soft drinks cans have also been investigated, for applications such as Foley effects or more general electroacoustic composition than that based on traditional instruments alone. To give one further fun example of current applications, advanced waveguide models have found a home in Finland, in interactive exhibits [Mäki-Patola *et al.*, 2005]. The highest profile among these virtual-reality instruments is that of an air guitar simulator, which uses computer vision to track hand position, and lets a mime control a physical model of a distorted guitar!

5.2.2 Singing Voice Synthesis

The voice is often acknowledged as the quintessential human instrument, since it requires no external adjunct to the body for its production. Our attention is often riveted by the voice in a way not accorded to other sound sources, an artefact of the overwhelming importance of speech communication to humans in evolutionary prehistory. Many great musical teaching systems are based around the voice, such as the Hindustani and Carnatic traditions. Studies have even shown the influence of vocal patterns on compositional style as languages vary over geographical regions [Patel, 2008]. Yet one of the greatest challenges in sound synthesis is the human voice. Because of its importance to telecommunications, the spoken voice has received a great deal of attention over the years in the field of speech synthesis, including early physical modeling work. For musical purposes, we would like to give the computer a singing voice.

One of the most famous early recordings in computer music is a rendition of *Daisy Bell* (1960) by a singing voice synthesizer with Music N accompaniment, prepared by Max Mathews with the aid of the speech synthesis model of John Kelly and Carol Lochbaum at Bell Labs. Often known as 'Bicycle Built for Two' the demonstration piece was made famous in Stanley Kubrick's *2001* (1968) as the swansong of HAL. Thirty years later, Perry Cook, as part of his doctoral thesis on singing voice synthesis [Cook, 1991], added another rather more virtuosic vocal line on top. In his *Shiela and Daisy Guy Duet* (1991), Shiela shows off with melisma, yodeling, an allusion to Mozart's Queen of the Night, and ornamental vibrato and vocal swells.[5] Both the Kelly and Lochbaum and the Cook models are physical models that treat the vocal tract as an acoustic tube, and while Cook's work incorporates

---

[5]Recording available at http://www.cs.princeton.edu/~prc/SingingSynth.html

many further developments, including modeling of the nasal passages, the earlier model is exemplary as anticipating an acoustically inspired form of synthesis.

These are only two of many efforts in this field [Sundberg, 1991; Cook, 1996; Rodet, 2002], and part of an ongoing fascination by researchers and composers with this most essentially human of instruments. Like all synthesis founded in reproducing existing sonic objects, singing voice synthesis is highly informed by models of human physiology and acoustics, which for the voice means the domain of phonetics. However, many singing synthesis methods do not go so far as to model the physical production and propagation of the signal directly, even if they are driven by analyses of real voice recordings and justified by analogous properties. A form of subtractive synthesis can be used. For the excitation, vowels and voiced consonants (like 'v') have quasi-periodic sources (puffs of air let through the oscillating vocal folds) and thus a fundamental frequency, and voiceless consonants are noisy sources (impulse pops, turbulent hiss). The former might be created using an impulse train, and the latter by a noise generator. Both vowel and consonant sources are filtered by the vocal tract, where the exact constraints on air flow are provided by the current state of the system of larynx, pharynx, oral cavity (including tongue and teeth), nasal cavity and lip. Most important in the perception of speech are formant regions in the spectrum, which are major spectral peaks in the region below 5000 Hz. Five formant positions can be enough to describe at least vowel timbre effectively, and this resonance portion of the sound is naturally created with a filter.

It is worth discussing the physiology of the vocal system a little more to make the physical modeling clear. Simplifying assumptions can be taken to make the physiology tractable, if you'll pardon the pun, but the actual physiological complexity can be quite remarkable. The Praat program's in-built articulatory synthesizer has 29 distinct physiologically derived controls (representing different muscles), and the underlying physical model uses 89 tubes to model the vocal tract [Boersma, 1998]. If you've never thought to do this before, create some different vowel and consonant sounds while remaining conscious of the position of your mouth, tongue, throat; you'll find that each distinct phone has corresponding physical positions. You have a number of articulators to control speaking and singing, from muscle tension at the vocal folds, through the position of your jaw, tongue, lips, and the velum (an opening controlling the proportion of air let into the nasal passages). You're usually not aware of controlling the vocal apparatus, since once learned the physical production of speech becomes a deep-seated motor program in the brain. One way to recover some consciousness of the challenge is to begin to learn another language from a distant language family.

Returning to the formants, which are the easier route into voice synthesis, what do the spectral peaks look like in practice? Data from an ⟨æ⟩ (International Phonetic Alphabet standard English pronunciation of the a in 'cat') was analyzed to produce Figure 5.9. The plots show one-fifth of a second's worth of cycles of the waveform (an f0 of around 121 Hz), a spectral snapshot of the spectral envelope exhibiting a natural spectral dropoff and some clear peaks, and tracks of the formants over time; note the relative stability of the lower formant trails especially. The formant data was extracted by the excellent Praat software, which was also used to create the diagram (authored by Paul Boersma and David Weenink, http://www.fon.hum.uva.nl/praat/)).

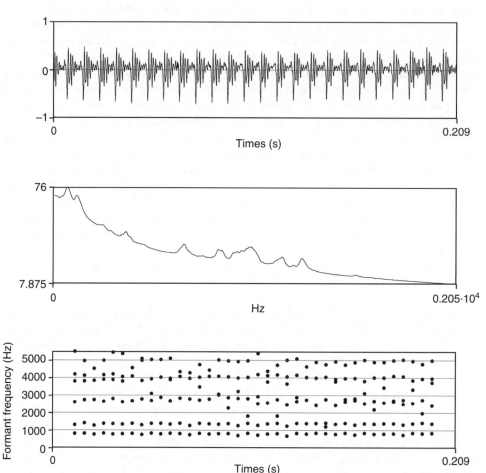

Figure 5.9   Formants in ⟨æ⟩.

If you don't want to form and analyze your own database, charts of formants can be found in the literature [Bennett and Rodet, 1989; Boulanger, 2000]; [Sundberg, 1989, p. 47]. Spectral analysis can be used to obtain the peaks [Rodet and Schwarz, 2007]. One venerable technique is Linear Predictive Coding, covered in the sidebar. Many synthesis methods can be used, given the formant data to synthesize (resynthesis duals for some analysis methods are also good candidates). A filter might be designed with resonances at the formants to impose a vowel character on a complex sound, or oscillators set to immediately provide energy at formant frequencies. The latter method tends to work best if there is some

Linear Predictive Coding (LPC)

LPC is a highly developed method drawn from speech telecommunications research, which can be approached in a number of different ways. These range from seeing it as a time domain signal prediction to capturing the spectral envelope and deconvolving a source sound from the filter, as if we could backwards engineer the vocal tract into glottal excitation and oral cavity filter. For each window of sound to model, a filter is fitted, the coefficients being chosen to minimize an error condition. The poles of a filter add resonances to a spectrum; zeroes creates notches, dampening the energy around their center frequency. By using a filter made entirely of zeroes, it is possible to flatten down peaks in a given input spectrum (within a least squares error criterion), so as to try to backwards engineer the original source. This is essentially a method of deconvolution, separating out source and filter. Once the all-zero filter is created – which comes down to the linear algebra of solving a matrix – it can be easily inverted into an all-pole filter that represents the resonances of the original sound. Because speech is the assumed target, the source is taken to be a pulse train (for the puffs of air in voiced, pitched speech) or white noise (for the basic air turbulence for unvoiced consonants).

The advantage of this analysis is knowledge about the location of formants; poles in the all-pole filter illustrate the spectral resonances. There is a choice to be made over the number of poles to utilize in fitting the spectrum; too many and too much fine detail obscures the formants, too few and we do not model a realistic vocal timbre (Lansky [1989] recommends a thousandth of the sampling rate plus a few). Cross-synthesis is also possible, by running different excitations through the filter rather than speech-like signals. This is how you might make a saucepan talk. Furthermore, the pitch is made independent of timbre, so speech could be made to sing (by imposing a desired pitch envelope), or singing to be changed in range, for example, by manipulating the rate of the pulse train for voice sounds. Windowing also allows independent time-scale modification. As if that weren't enough, the analysis also gives further insight into a voice signal, for instance, allowing the differentiation of voiced and unvoiced frames so as to enable specific transformations (such as only leaving the voiceless consonants and not resynthesizing any pitched sources at all!). Yet LPC is not a panacea, because the basic sound quality is often buzzy, and the linear analysis makes tight assumptions about the nature of the signal to be treated.

For further technical details see Makhoul [1975]. A wonderfully friendly tutorial from the composer's perspective appears in Cann [1985]. LPC is also covered to varying degrees in other computer music textbooks [Roads, 1996; Dodge and Jerse, 1997; Cook, 2002]. Paul Lansky and Charles Dodge are two composers in particular whose works have been associated with LPC analysis and resynthesis [Lansky, 1989; Dodge, 1989]. *Any Resemblance is Purely Coincidental* (1980) by Charles Dodge transforms a recording of Caruso from 1907 in wonderful ways, the tape part with the voice processing interweaving with live piano. *Six Fantasies on a Poem by Thomas Campion* (1978–9) by Paul Lansky presents six gorgeous movements founded in LPC techniques.

control over the bandwidth of a sound around the formant frequency to thicken the spectral envelope; frequency modulation with control of sidebands is one way this has been achieved [Chowning, 1989]. Specially designed techniques have also been employed, such as the FOF synthesis method, which makes use of a cunningly enveloped damped sinusoid for a single formant [Rodet *et al.*, 1984; Bennett and Rodet, 1989].

The hard part is not so much the creation of any individual formant pattern, but the continuous variation with time. A physical model can relate directly to changes in the articulators of the speech production mechanism, but other synthesis methods must interpolate between individual phones. More convincing synthesis may require tackling **diphones**,[6] phone to phone transitions. Speech synthesis based on concatenating samples of each phone is improved by working with samples of each transition. The latest singing voice synthesizers, based on large databases of spectral data, must similarly store many transitions to cope with the innumerable temporal orderings of our highly generative languages. IRCAM's Diphone software encapsulates these ideas, in a general framework supporting various sound synthesis methods, and has been used by composers since the 1980s to explore sound morphing [Rodet and Lefevre, 1996; Rodet, 1997].

Synthesis of the singing voice is also assisted by modeling vocal expressivity. Johan Sundberg has carried out extensive investigations into the singing voice. He notes that classical vibrato has an average rate of 6.6 Hz (extremes 5.9 to 7.8) and vibrato depth (frequency deviation) of 48 cents (extremes ± 31 and ± 98) [Sundberg, 1999, p. 197]. For musically acceptable vibratos, both the arithmetic and the geometric mean of the frequency trail are good estimators of the perceived pitch (we don't follow every nuance of the vibrato itself). This kind of data is invaluable to the dedicated synthesist! Vibrato is one enriching aspect that can make plain simulations of the voice more convincing and alive. John Chowning's work *Phone* (1980–1) reveals a command of vibrato in FM synthesis of singing. It also demonstrates his celebrated discovery that a common vibrato pattern helps to group formants together as a whole in a single voice even when multiple streams are being generated at once [Chowning, 1999].

Many advanced projects have now been carried out around the singing voice. These tend to be driven by a spectral modeling front end. In 1994, a team from IRCAM worked to recreate the sound of a castrato for the film *Farinelli*, synthesizing a digital blend of soprano and countertenor [Depalle *et al.*, 1995]. Commercial singing voice synthesizers have become available, based on spectral modeling and diphone (transition) database techniques, such as Yamaha's Vocaloid, which takes advantage of the work of Xavier Serra's research group at Pompeu Fabra. Current models tend to be suitable for backing singers rather than the forefront of a mix (we are so sensitive to the grain of individual voices that accurate simulation of a lead singer remains a challenge at the forefront of research). While total realism might still escape us, this is no bar to composers who wish to exploit the potential of hyper-virtuosic computer voices in their music. The output of speech synthesizers has

---

[6]Since native speakers in particular slur speech so readily – we easily compensate for poor diction from a speaker by our contextual knowledge – diphones are not always enough. There is a combinatorial explosion inherent here as longer segments are covered.

made many appearances in popular culture. One craze for repitching and stretching output of a speech synthesizer led to the creation of Cylob's *Rewind* and 386DX's cover of *Smells like Teen Spirit*. The voice also provides a powerful control source. Dan Stowell has created a style of 'cyber-beat boxing' based on realtime vocal analysis and feature-led synthesis [Stowell and Plumbley, 2008]. We also encountered vocal control already under the mantle of concatenative synthesis, and one further example here is Eric Bünger's *Let Them Sing It for You* (2003),[7] which takes any text input lyric and finds each word in a large database of pre-segmented song examples. Computers have a lot of singing to do yet.

5.3 SUMMARY

Sound synthesis was one of the first tasks to which the computer was put, and the field has received substantial investment of attention since Max Mathews's early experiments. We are now faced with a huge choice of different synthesis methods, which vary in efficiency and timbral flexibility. The most powerful of these are acknowledged to be spectral modeling, intimately connected to the audio analysis models of Chapter 3, and physical modeling, the enaction of virtual acoustics. We have also seen some other classic methods that have proved their worth to composers and synth builders, from the highly efficient nonlinear method of frequency modulation to the scheduling processes of granular synthesis. Feature-based synthesis has demonstrated a bridge between granular methods and feature extraction in audio analysis. Finally, we have examined a truly exciting challenge for computer music, the simulation of singing voices, an area where some convincing attempts have been made but a full solution remains an exciting target.

5.4 EXERCISES

1. Survey the dense swarms of freeware synthesizers (such as VST instruments), noting for each one the types of sound synthesis it offers. What are the most popular synthesis methods? By considering the interface, achievable timbres, output sound quality and CPU costs you can evaluate these synthesizers with respect to the four criteria of Xavier Serra introduced in this chapter [Serra, 1997b]. Be careful, since additional effects units built into each synthesizer will also influence the sounds you judge, and there are many hybrid methods. Informed by this investigation, create your own taxonomy of sound synthesis algorithms.

---

[7] http://www.sr.se/p1/src/sing/

2. Although the harmonic series is based on an equal spacing of harmonics, real strings are stiff, and tend to increasingly stretch the frequency of upper partials [Rossing and Fletcher, 1998; Cook, 2002; Klapuri and Davy, 2006]. A basic recipe for this effect is $f_n = n f_0 (1 + \beta + \beta^2 (1 + \frac{n^2 \pi^2}{8}))$ where f_n is the nth partial (stretched harmonic frequency). The constant β can be related back to the physical properties of a string, but you can freely experiment with the value for our purposes. Synthesize a series of sounds using additive synthesis, based on variations of this formula, comparing it with conventional linearly spaced harmonics.

3. John Chowning's *Stria* is based on a 1.618:1 'octave' rather than 2:1. If the $C:M$ ratio is 1:1.618 and C is 1000 Hz, where do the side components fall? Using the rule of thumb of index $+1$ significant side components in each sideband, for what modulation index I will noticeable aliasing occur caused by reflection at the Nyquist frequency for a 44 100 Hz sampling rate? The charm of the 'golden section' number $\phi = 1.618$ in FM is that some powers (psuedo-octaves) can be related to additions (in the $C + kM$ formula). For example, the second psuedo-octave from a base carrier frequency C is equivalent to the first positive component in FM synthesis, since $\phi^2 = 1 + \phi$. This makes for a nicely self-contained system for composition, an alternative pitch and timbre space using the FM sound synthesis method. You may want to explore this empirically, or to pursue Chowning's original scheme in more detail [Meneghini, 2007].

4. Consider the different timescales at which to approach granular synthesis. Using your favorite general computer music environment (or by exploring third-party granulation software), create grain clouds first of isolated single grains and then dense asynchronous swarms, and also synchronous 'rhythmic' grain streams. Can you create a granular gesture that combines all three states over time? How might you tackle two granular streams at once that are first independent, then merge and interfere with each other, and then move to independence again?

5. In order to investigate feature-based synthesis, you will need a computer music environment that supports feature extraction (you may also want to look at Sections 3.5 and 7.2). Some options for concatenative synthesis are Michael Casey's SoundSpotter for Pd and Max/MSP (http://soundspotter.org/), Diemo Schwarz's CataRT for Max/MSP (http://imtr.ircam.fr/index.php/CataRT) and Bob Sturm's MATConcat for MATLAB (http://www.mat.ucsb.edu/~b.sturm/researchACSS.html). Explore the feature-driven nature of such methods by trying them out on various input sound files. Change between different databases of sound as synthesis corpuses, and as control input targets.

6. Take the equation:

$$\frac{\mathrm{d}x}{\mathrm{d}t} = \frac{\cos(2\pi 440 t)}{2\pi 440}$$

Use a naive Euler ordinary differential equation solver to synthesize an output solution on a sample by sample basis, say over two seconds, starting at $x = 0$, $t = 0$. (The basic Euler method is simply to update a variable $x(n)$ by the most straightforward approximation to the derivative, a first-order difference

$$x(n+1) = x(n) + \alpha \frac{dx}{dt}(n/R)$$

α controls how quickly you update, and one over the sampling rate R might be a good first choice for the steps in time. dx/dt is evaluated at the discrete time $t = n/R$). If that went well, now try and tackle

$$\frac{d^2x}{dt^2} - \alpha x^3 + \beta x = 0 \tag{5.6}$$

where α and β are free constants to experiment with (this equation is the Duffing equation – see Strogatz [1994, p. 215]). You might just use the naive Euler method again, but if you're brave, compare the fourth-order Runge–Kutta numerical solution scheme. You can compare different initial conditions (e.g., $x = 0.1$) and boundary conditions ($-1 < x < 1$ is a natural choice for floating point audio, but what will you do if x diverges outside these bounds? Clamp and get stuck, reset or wrap and get a discontinuity, fold and get a discontinuity in the derivative ...).

7. Take a long monophonic recording and look at the overall spectral profile (you might do this by taking many short-time DFTs and creating a histogram of the spectral data, or by a large single spectral analysis frame). Transient data may skew this analysis, so you might refine this by averaging spectral shape over a large number of steady state portions of marked-up notes. You will need some methodology to explore the overall spectral envelope shape independent of pitches, perhaps by making sure your recording contains a good variety of notes from a given instrument (there is a simplifying assumption here that the main resonances of the instrument body are not register dependent). Having extracted the main formants of the instrument body, see whether this knowledge improves your ability to synthesize the instrument (you might investigate an FFT-based filter that employs the spectral envelope).

8. Create a computer program that instantiates the bottom part of Figure 5.8. Although you might also attempt this by plugging together unit generators in standard computer music software, you could get into trouble with the feedback loops and block-based calculation. You may find it easier to implement by working one sample at a time (it is also possible to set many computer music environments to a block size of 1 to facilitate experimentation).

9. Record yourself singing. Study the vocal waveform in a sound editor, zooming in in the time domain on periodic repetitions, viewing a spectrogram to see transients and harmonics. Isolate a single period of a vowel during a steady state oscillation. By spectral analysis, extract major formant positions. Try a number of methods of sound synthesis to recreate this spectral envelope, and compare your result with the originating sound.

10. Record some speech into an audio editor or DAW software. Segment the phonemes, and repitch and stretch them to impose an interesting melody. Seek out existing examples of this technique, such as that used by 386DX (http://www.easylife.org/386dx/).

5.5

FURTHER READING

Popular computer music magazines have some very friendly tutorials on sound synthesis, including recreations of famous sounds.

The main computer music texts all have their own takes on sound synthesis. Further recommended resources include:

Boulanger, R. (ed) (2000). *The Csound Book*. MIT Press, Cambridge, MA.

Chowning, J. and Bristow, D. (1986). *FM Theory and Applications: By Musicians for Musicians*. Yamaha Music Foundation, Tokyo.

Cook, P. (2002). *Real Sound Synthesis for Interactive Applications*. A.K. Peters, Natick, MA.

Miranda, E. (2002). *Computer Sound Design: Synthesis Techniques and Programming*. Focal Press, Oxford. (Older edition was Miranda, E. (1998). *Computer Sound Synthesis for the Electronic Musician*. Focal Press, Oxford.)

Rossing, T. D. and Fletcher, N. H. (1998). *The Physics of Musical Instruments*, 2nd Edition. Springer Science+Business Media, Inc, New York, NY.

Russ, M. (2004). *Sound Synthesis and Sampling*, 2nd Edition. Focal Press, Oxford.

Serafin, S. (2007). Computer generation and manipulation of sounds, in *The Cambridge Companion to Electronic Music* (eds N. Collins and J. d'Escriván). Cambridge University Press, Cambridge, pp. 203–217.

Smith, J. O. (2008). *Physical Audio Signal Processing for Virtual Musical Instruments and Audio Effects*. Available online at http://ccrma-www.stanford.edu/~jos/waveguide

Tolonen, T., Välimäki, V. and Karjalainen, M. (1998). *Evaluation of Modern Sound Synthesis Methods*. Technical Report 48, Helsinki University of Technology. Available online at http://www.acoustics.hut.fi/publications/reports/sound_synth_report.pdf

Chapter 6

Interaction

'Often, I will find myself looking at an object and thinking, "How can this be made into a musical instrument?" This has led me to create the Sonic Banana, a two foot long rubber tube played by bending and twisting; the Slime-o-tron, in which a player manipulates conductive slime (a version of the gooey kids' stuff) to control musical parameters; and the Slink-o-tron, which translates the *boing* of a suspended spring toy into a sonically useful chaotic function.'

Eric Singer [Singer, 2008, p. 207]

OBJECTIVES

This chapter covers:

- the nature of interaction;
- interfacing, and input devices in particular;
- interactive music systems in various settings;
- virtual musical agents;
- evaluating interaction.

6.1 INTRODUCTION TO INTERACTION

This chapter covers both the interfacing technology that supports communication between humans and computers, and the different settings within which such interaction takes place.

With computers now so thoroughly intertwined in society, they are certainly not restricted to vaults and offices, but can feature in concerts, art galleries, home entertainment systems; anywhere a microchip can be placed. The notion of **ubiquitous computing** (ubi-comp) sees a multiplicity of small computing devices threaded throughout our environments. Most electronic devices in the home carry a microprocessor, and most of us carry a mobile; we interact with all manner of computers on a daily basis. For the purposes of this book, we are particularly interested when the computers are employed in musical tasks. But, thanks to 'everyware', musical interaction could be taking place on a train or, as already suggested in the introduction, in the shower!

Interfacing between biological human beings and digital computers requires ways to transduce between different types of energy. For example, how can kinetic human movement be translated into a form the computer can process? We have already met this problem in the case of sound waves, and have described moving between analog and digital signals by sampling. For pressure waves in air, a microphone allowed an intermediate conversion into an analog electrical signal, and thence by an ADC into samples. By using some form of **sensor**, human motion can similarly be turned into an electrical signal, and again digital sampling will provide us with information the computer can treat. We could use a digital camera, an array of sonars or capacitive field effect devices, a motion-tracking body suit full of accelerometers and bend sensors, and force sensors on the floor among many other possibilities. This chapter will survey many sensors, calling on various principles in physics, all of which have musical potential. Just to give one application for the case of human movement, imagine having dancers able to control the music to which they dance, due to a computer that interprets their motion and synthesizes appropriate responses.

An interface between human and computer consists of both input and output devices, however. By covering sound and music analysis and synthesis, the rest of this book provides much material relevant to processing and output. In computer music, the most common modality of information returned to a human user is audio, via speakers of some description. But there are other possibilities, including tactile and visual feedback, whether through the physical feel of an input device, deliberate force-feedback (vibration sent to a joystick, for example) or on-screen or projected visual data. In musical robotics, commands from a computer may drive motors, to physically enact musical gesture. You might even have the grand opportunity for computer control of a fireworks display or laser light show.

The role of computers, their duties in a particular setting, vary enormously with the interaction designer's wishes, so that there is no one central practice to highlight. As we are concerned with musical interaction, we shall be biased to seek examples with substantial auditory feedback and musical control. A wide range of scenarios can be acknowledged, including installations, computer games, and various forms of musical performance. These may involve any number of human participants and computers in a complex network of interaction. There is the case of the multi-participant gallery installation as well as the concert with participating audience to consider, even if much research in new digital instruments concentrates on extensions for the solo performer. Robert Rowe has popularized the term **interactive music systems** [Rowe, 1993] to describe computer-mediated musical interactions, and we will adopt this here, while recognizing that the systems could be rather complex networks of both human and machine agents. In most cases, individual components involving computation can be isolated, such as a single hyper-instrument, or an autonomous musical robot.[1] Multi-agent interactive set-ups will also naturally feature in Chapter 7 when discussing networks.

It is also worth noting further relevant currents in computer science. The discipline of **human–computer interaction** (HCI) [Preece *et al.*, 1994; Sears and Jacko, 2008] formally treats those zones of accommodation between human action and computer facilities. There are evaluative tools within HCI that can be of benefit to interaction designers in gaining feedback on the success of their designs in practice. Further, with constant investment in technological development, a flurry of new devices and techniques are emerging all the time to impact on musical practice. Many new devices do not fall into the desktop computing paradigm, and the graphical user interfaces (GUIs) of conventional office computing are in some cases being replaced by tangible user interfaces (TUIs) which physically rather than virtually represent computational state. Any and all developments in computing can interact radically with music.

New input devices and interaction techniques don't have to be just for concert use, but may simply provide new ways of working, supporting a variety of offline computer music tasks. Much of the material here is applicable to studio, classroom and laboratory away from any concert venue or gallery, even if the challenges of realtime music making drive fantastical innovation in this field. The aim of this chapter is to provide starting points for your own interactive investigations.

6.1.1 Defining Interaction

Interaction is a much-used term, and much debated as well. Adopted as a useful umbrella descriptor for this chapter, it allows for many forms of interactive system and interfacing technology. In its stricter sense, interaction is a concept of two-way influence; '*Interaction is a two-way street*', as Winkler [1998, p. 3] chooses to begin his book on interactive music. Yet in order to treat a divergent set of examples, we shall not require that all parties in a multi-agent exchange have the same control over or gain the same feedback from an encounter. More one-sided models will be explored, where a computer system is closer to a tool or traditional musical instrument under direct human control, as well as situations where the computer shows much more independent agency.

As a thought experiment, imagine a large red button, which when pressed schedules the output of an entire symphony of noise – in 13 days' time! Because the instigator probably wouldn't be there, or recognize their contribution to the event if they did, this is not a

---

[1]There are some computer systems which are internally composed of many different agents with varying responsibilities, but may present a unified interface to the external world. There are also multi-agent teams of software programs and robots! This distributed hive intelligence has been hypothesized to be present in an individual human mind, as in Marvin Minsky's society of mind. We shall sidestep such matters for now.

site for interaction. Indeed, any delay longer than a second is typically enough to convince a human that their action has no effective consequence; conversational pauses as turn-taking cues are on the order of 200–300 milliseconds [Dix, 2008]. We've all experienced the annoyance of other humans when we've not been fast on the uptake (caused by a lack of familiarity with a ticket vending machine on our first visit to a new country, for example). Social interactions such as conversation or music making are highly time-critical, and extremely fluid in their circumstances, providing a great engineering challenge when designing technology which can naturally support such activities. In order to effectively engage with human beings as musical participants our computer technology must be able to navigate the same timescales, and to respect human expectations of interaction.

In order to further analyze interactive systems, it is convenient to partition interactive systems into inputs, processing and outputs [Bongers, 2000]. Figure 6.1 illustrates this, making the potential feedback loops clear. We must be careful, however, to realize that this separation is a theoretical convenience, which may not necessarily represent the integrated end-user experience (it is notoriously difficult to separate perception cleanly from cognition in the human brain, for instance). Sergi Jordà's thesis on 'digital lutherie' [Jordà, 2005] looks at a complete system containing any hardware interface, along with any software computational component, as the instrument. This is in accord with the views of human–computer interaction specialists, who recognize the indivisibility of input device and output feedback in user experience [Hinckley, 2008, p. 162].[2]

To give an example of how processing considerations might inform the design of systems, consider using various sensors to control a parameterized sound synthesis model. Hunt and Wanderley [2002] differentiate one-to-one, one-to-many and many-to-one mappings based on how the interconnections are established between the two stages; in general this is a many-to-many mapping between n input dimensions and m output dimensions. Any choice of the mapping has consequences for the complexity of using a given system. Too simple a mapping and the system may prove to lack depth as you master it too quickly; too obscure a set-up, and you may never find a way in. Making a manageable relationship between input data and output result is a real challenge for the designer. A human may only be able to consciously control a small number of degrees of freedom at once, but still seek a rich musical experience, perhaps necessitating the use of special interpolation algorithms which optimize the control power of a few-to-many mapping [Goudeseune, 2002]. Unsurprisingly, perceptually informed and meaningful models prove very important in studying effective mappings from a human perspective [Hunt and Wanderley, 2002; Arfib et al., 2002a].

Systems vary substantially, however, in their model of interaction. Some follow a more traditional instrument role, closely tracking input gesture with sounding output, while others exhibit greater independence, potentially similar to human agents. So not all control

---

[2]Though see Magnusson [2009] for an opposing viewpoint. It is argued there that the heavy knowledge engineering in computer music software makes digital instruments sufficiently different from acoustic instruments that the processing system is highly separable from the input interface.

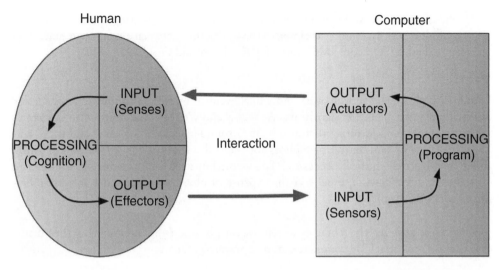

Figure 6.1   Feedback loops in interaction. The human and the computer are differentiated in this figure in the nature of their inputs, processing and outputs. The feedback loops could be effected in a number of modalities (stimulating different senses or sensors) such as touch, sound or visuals. Adapted from Bongers [2000] by permission of Bert Bongers.

has to be considered as a direct single-stage mapping, when in between input and output devices the full power of the computer can be employed. To follow one dimension of Robert Rowe's taxonomy of interactive music systems [Rowe, 1993], we can move on a continuum between **instruments** and **players**. For the players, there is potential for any artificial intelligence (AI) technique to contribute to musical discourse, a topic of virtual musicianship we shall return to later in this chapter. This also highlights the full complexity of the causal loop in Figure 6.1, if two independent agents in an environment are coupled through their senses and actions. Let us take a moment to discuss further the different levels of control the participants in interaction may have over the systems they interact with.

6.1.2 Directness of Control and the Physicality of Gesture

In traditional gestural acoustic musicianship, there is a tight coupling between the instrument as extension of the human body, bodily motion, and the ensuing music. Computers allow much more abstract relations between input and resultant. Indeed, the mappings that can be established are arbitrary, and entirely at the behest of the designer of a given system. Commentators have theorized on the more abstract control possibilities enabled by computer technology:

> Perhaps the most obvious metaphor of interaction in music is the manipulation of a musical instrument by a performer .... Viewing a computer as a musical instrument provides access to a large range of resources of musical literature and

> traditions for the evaluation of controllers, even if many existing applications reproduce a situation that is closer to the interaction between a conductor and an orchestra (i.e., score-level control). [Wanderley and Orio, 2002, p. 70]

Rather than personally setting every individual event in motion, a conductor in the latter case manipulates higher-level algorithms. As Wessel and Wright [2002] outline, in discussing various metaphors for control that also include sound-file scrubbing, drag and drop, and 'dipping', 'One of our central metaphors for musical control is that of *driving* or *flying* about in a space of musical processes.' The algorithm itself can therefore become more central than direct gesture, usually at the expense of physical action and a corresponding increase in virtualization.

Joel Ryan has criticized the tendency to remove the physical from interfacing in the pursuit of the 'effortless', attacking commercial music products that are

> ... emphasizing rather than narrowing the separation of the musician from the sound. Too often controllers are selected to minimize the physical, selected because they are effortless .... In designing a new musical instrument it might be just as interesting to make control as difficult as possible .... Effort is closely related to expression in the playing of traditional instruments. [Ryan, 1991, pp. 6–7]

Many other authors have addressed the role of the physical, considering the loss of traditional grounds of musical appreciation. Smalley [1986, p. 83] writes that 'many a listener's problem can be related either to the loss of tangibility created by the severance of direct gestural ties, or to the difficulties in comprehending the remoteness of new surrogacy.' He outlines three levels of *surrogacy*, from the instrumental context (*first-order surrogacy*), through the abstracted gesture (*second-order surrogacy*), to the case with no links to causality (*remote surrogacy*) where 'physical cause cannot be deduced and we thus enter the realms of psychological interpretation alone' [Smalley, 1986, p. 83]. Yet the charms of computers still tempt many artists, and trends to aphysical music are acknowledged by Emmerson [2000b, p. 212]: 'The assertion of human presence within music produced by and through technology will take many different forms as humans become increasingly alienated from purely physical sound production.'

There is no right or wrong answer here, but an extension of the possibilities for musical control, by taking in different orders of abstraction. It is important to be aware of this issue, as many authors have highlighted the importance of embodiment in human cognition. Individual projects may lead one to either extreme on a continuum from direct to indirect gesture, accompanied by different levels of interrogation of the physical.

6.2 INTERFACING

In order to achieve interaction in the first place, a computer must interface to the real world. This section will concentrate in particular on input devices, the great variety of sensors that are available to transduce physical quantities into analog signals and from thence via ADCs into digital information fit for computer processing. Manual human action, from finger movements through speech to whole body movement, can be translated into a computer, so as to direct the course of processing. If computers are to supply new musical possibilities, it is particularly critical to consider various roles for the human body in new digital instruments, and to allow computers to gain data from the environment. While complete description can intimately depend on more holistic treatment of a system and its users [Jordà, 2005], especially when system response is closely coupled to sensor observations, it is helpful to review sensors semi-independently of the larger uses to which they can be put. As the reader no doubt appreciates, it is difficult to provide general rules for interactive systems, when their artistic and technical aims can vary so much, but examples will be sprinkled throughout the text to provide a flavor of the possibilities.

While we focus on input devices most intensively in this section, computers also have to have the capacity to return information to the environment, since otherwise they are pretty useless interactors. This chapter will not treat output so extensively, leaving that duty to the rest of the book. For the processing of input that a computer enables, other chapters also provide more information. Yet it is important at least to raise the prospect of further output modalities beyond audio, such as:

- control information – e.g., MIDI sent to hardware synthesizers, or data around a network of computers;

- visuals – GUI, screen projection, computer-controlled LEDs, lasers, fireworks and lighting rigs;

- kinetic output – driving motors, and hence motion;

- haptic feedback (e.g., force feedback from a joystick).

Just as various input devices will be cataloged below, there are many output possibilities that can extend the computer's environmental role.

6.2.1 A Survey of Input Devices

A complete survey is impossible, given the constant developments in this arena, but there are many commonly found input devices that will be covered here. As a rule, whenever a new device becomes available, it is likely to be applied in a computer music application before long; witness the number of 'Wiimote' (Wii Remote) drumming videos that appeared on YouTube soon after the Nintendo Wii games console went on sale! There is a dedicated conference series, NIME (New Interfaces for Musical Expression), in which inventors describe a panoply of new devices specifically designed for music each year. While there are many controller possibilities, fewer make it to market, and fewer still gain mainstream support – the Wiimote and other gamepads provide examples of those sufficiently mass-produced to have become widely adopted de facto – and there are many cases of devices being discontinued even after reaching a consumer stage (for example, the P5 Glove from CyberWorld, Inc., a glove controller originally released in 2002). The alternative to relying on commercial products, of course, is to build your own!

That there is a spellbinding choice of different input devices for gathering control data is a testament to the ingenuity of humans in exploiting sometimes esoteric principles of physics. As well as mechanical affordances, the roll-call summons properties and states of electromagnetic waves (infrared, visible light, polarized light, laser light, optoelectronics, the piezoelectric effect) and pressure waves (sound, ultrasound) in particular. Devices can be passive detectors, or actively sense the environment by transmitting probe signals (with radio waves, for example, for radar, or sound waves for sonar).

Since this book is concerned with computer music, it is assumed that a computer will be involved somewhere in the signal processing chain. However, computational devices of differing specification can be involved as processors of sensor data, including **microcontrollers** (less powerful but of much smaller size and cost than the internals of laptop and desktop computers). Such chips may be programmed from a standard computer, but then become autonomous for deployment in standalone circuits. These are exactly what is required to make lightweight wearable computing devices; you wouldn't fix a laptop to the underside of a viola, but you might get away with a smaller bundle of electronics. Microcontrollers contain ADCs and DACs, and are able to convert analog electrical inputs from sensors (typically dealing with a 5-volt range). They often act as the first stage of sensor data collection, passing on information to more powerful computers downstream. Many input devices also handily carry out the analog to digital conversion themselves, ready to pass information directly on to a computer.

There are a mass of conventions for interfacing digital devices together. Historic and contemporary computer connection standards include Universal Serial Bus, FireWire, RS-232 serial port and others [Pohlmann, 2005, pp. 550–551]. Microcontrollers may be the first stage in obtaining analog sensor data, passing on information via one of these connectors, perhaps using a network protocol like Open Sound Control, or another industry standard; some interface options even use MIDI directly. Alternatively, sensor data may also be transferred via audio streams, as used with the TeaBox interface marketed by Electrotap. To give an example of interfacing to an existing sensor device, John Eacott's *Floodtide* (2008) creates a live algorithmically generated score for musicians following the tide, by using a water flow speed sensor. The data is eventually received into the computer by polling a USB connection; the National Marine Electronics Association (NMEA) standard defines the protocol in this seaworthy case.

There are plenty of references to follow to find out more about sensors: Sears and Jacko [2008, Part II – Computers in HCI]; Preece *et al.* [1994, Chapter 11]; Roads [1996,

Chapter 14]; Bongers [2000]; O'Sullivan and Igoe [2004]; Miranda and Wanderley [2006]; Mataric [2007] (www.sensorwiki.org). The survey collected in Table 6.1 draws from resources in the *The Human–Computer Interaction Handbook* [Sears and Jacko, 2008] and particularly the chapter on sensors [Wilson, 2008, pp. 178–183]. Aside from the table's coverage, it is worth mentioning conventional computing input devices such as pointing devices (mice, trackballs, joysticks, tablets, touchpads, touchscreens) and text entry keyboards, for GUI-based windowing systems [Hinckley, 2008]. Such office computing will be specifically investigated below. Subsequent subsections will treat the readily available and high quality data sources from audio and video, the practicalities of interfacing to sensors via microcontrollers, and the potential of biosignals.

Table 6.1   An overview of sensor possibilities, following Wilson [2008, pp. 178–83].

Sensing mode	Notes	Examples
Occupancy and motion	Detecting human presence and motion (many security applications)	Pressure mat, passive infrared detector
Range sensing	Calculating distance to an object	Infrared beam, sonar, stereo computer vision
Position	Determining 3D position in some reference frame (body, room, world)	Global Positioning Satellite (GPS), Wi-Fi, wearable motion capture system, visual or audio tracking
Movement and orientation	Detecting change of position	Mercury tilt switch, accelerometer, gyroscope, magnetometer
Touch	Close contact or near proximity required	Button, pressure sensor, strain gauge, capacitive sensing
Gaze and eye tracking		Saccade detector
Speech	Automatic speech recognition front end	Microphone(s), then computer audition
Identity	Object and person recognition	Computer vision, voice recognition, biometrics (e.g., fingerprint or iris), radio-frequency identification (RFID) tags
Context	Environmental sensors	Meteorological sensors (air temperature, humidity)
Affect	Tracking subjective emotion/ mood/feeling, physiological sensors	Galvanic skin response (GSR), electrocardiogram (ECG, EKG)
Brain interfaces	Correlates of neural information processing via electrical signals or blood flow	Electroencephalograph (EEG)

There are multiple digital artworks that have incorporated any one of these sensors [Miranda and Wanderley, 2006]. The specific pluses and minuses of input devices with regard to resolution, accuracy, expense and the like are highly individual to application and sensor. Sensors also differ in their post-processing load, in that some require more extensive computational treatment (computer vision is a case in point, highlighted below). All sensors are potentially noisy, and it is unrealistic to expect them to provide perfect knowledge, particularly in all possible environmental conditions [Matarić, 2007, p. 70]! Just as for extracting meaningful discrete events out of an audio signal (see Chapter 3), sensor data may be parsed with a view to isolating spatial and temporal positions of objects in the environment, the same signal-to-symbol problem. Computation may be easier once such objects are identified, but extracting locations from more continuous sensor data streams requires some effort (similar signal processing techniques such as onset detection can be applied, as per Section 3.5.2) [O'Sullivan and Igoe, 2004, pp. 195–216]. Alternative formulations employ such sub-symbolic computing techniques as neural nets, perhaps to associate states with combinations of data from multiple sensors. The mapping and refining of input data is part of the computer's workload in considering any response, though many commercially available sensors may also do some preprocessing internally (for example, Hall effect sensors often include an amplifier to bring the signal to a reasonable normal sensor range, say 0–5 volts).

6.2.2 Office Computing for Music

The office control interface for computers has been standardized for some time, and is ingrained in much workflow at the computer. The WIMP paradigm for software (window, icon, menu and pointers), with mouse and keyboard interface controlling a graphical user interface, has been a stable part of computing since home computer operating systems first appeared in the 1980s (research prototypes such as the 1960s work of Doug Engelbert or the Xerox Alto from 1973 had laid the groundwork [Preece *et al.*, 1994, p. 287], but most early computing was text based). It is doubtful whether the keyboard will ever be replaced as a text manipulation tool; while voice recognition software is available, it is by no means universally effective and natural language processing remains a challenging area of research; a lot of computer code is quite far from natural language, and touch typing surpasses speaking rate. Hinckley [2008, p. 168] estimates handwriting speeds at 15 words per minute (wpm), automatic speech recognition at 30 wpm, and touch-typing at 60 wpm.

The WIMP paradigm is the standard one for the control of much music software, some of which is designed for live performance, but subsists in live use via the same interface that would be employed in the office or bedroom. Without even an attached MIDI controller, the operator of a computer could be reduced to tapping the keys to obtain gestural data![3] We shouldn't underestimate the cunning use of keyboard cueing and mousing in some live computer music, but much laptop control is not gestural at all, in the sense of any one-to-one

---

[3] This is not quite true of modern multimedia laptops, however, since many interesting sensors – such as the sudden motion detector that protects the hard drive in the event of a laptop falling – are actually within the chassis and accessible via the operating system. Built-in digital cameras and microphones are important sources to which we shall return.

direct correlation of physical action to musical event. Although pressing a button within a graphical user interface could set a process in motion, many of the musical processes are not singular events but whole sequences or algorithms committed wholesale, the parameters of which provide an indirect tweaking of resultant musical events. This surpasses the 'one gesture to one acoustic event paradigm' [Wessel and Wright, 2002] in computer music, and is the route of various live algorithmic systems, as well as more mundane sound mixing applications.

A classic interactive system following the GUI template is Laurie Spiegel's *Music Mouse* (originally written 1986, http://retiary.org/ls/programs.html) where qwerty and mouse control sets in motion music sequences from single- to multi-note patterns. Since the mouse is a good match to real-world hand movement, the program allows for overt gestural control, even within the office computing paradigm!

In passing, it is healthy to raise one reaction against the gestural heritage of musicianship, lest it appear that the ideal for computer music should always be the most active transduction from human movement. To go to one extreme might be to rest on the keyboard alone, and to glorify the computer on its own terms. In **live coding**[4] computer musicians admit that a great deal of their practice time is spent programming, so why not elevate coding to be the central performance [Collins *et al.*, 2003; Wang and Cook, 2004; Nilson, 2007]? While interpreted programming environments nourish code development, they also enable text-centered live performance. The challenge is to type and juggle your ideas fast enough to keep an audience with you! Placing the computer programming environment at the heart of performance, and the human programmer at the heart of that environment, a human presence is maintained even among the algorithms, and live coding may even be a natural way to explore algorithmic music in a live setting. A central focus on algorithm – particularly modifying algorithms during performance – makes this a definite case of 'composer-pilots' exploring more abstract spaces. Live coders often project their screens, to avoid the situation where any observers are entirely cut off from meaning, though performances vary in how much they concede to the knowledge of a general audience! Live coding provides an interesting thought experiment, and a real performance scene, from which to get a fresh view on musical gesture and computer music practice (http://toplap.org).

6.2.3 Audio and Video Tracking

With microphone and digital camera now built into new laptops, and processing speeds well accommodated to processing in real time, audio and video are extremely useful sources of performance data. Both types of stream are non-invasive sources of information, in that air molecules or photons can transmit useful gestural information from a musician or dancer without the attachment of auxiliary sensors. While there are other ways to gather data

---

[4]The origin of this term is a little mysterious, but my best guess is that it was coined by the French composer Fabrice Mogini around 2002; as Julian Rohrhuber has noted, before the term live coding stuck, 'ASCII music' or 'interpreted music' were in use. A number of alternatives such as 'interactive programming' or 'on-the-fly programming' have been suggested, and live coding actually encompasses a suite of practices from high stress solo performance to more gentle offline collaborative work.

on human action with sensors at a distance (e.g., infrared, ultrasound), audio and video provide two immediate data-collection mediums with cognitive relevance as primary human sensory modalities.

Audio processing has already been covered in Chapters 3 and 4; it is sufficient to note here that it is a primary source of data for many interactive music systems, which can analyze features of incoming sound, as well as transforming that sound. As Ryan [1991, p. 10] notes,

> ... the issue of physical instrument design is bypassed in order to enable collaboration with virtuoso performers on conventional instruments. The composer/programmer then has the corresponding virtuoso task of musical pattern recognition.

A MIDI input would provide information already within a symbolic format, but an audio signal has a higher density of potential gestural information, and is readily accessible to timbral transformation and resynthesis. It is worth mentioning that speech input is also a possibility, aside from the tracking of singing, instruments, environmental sound and the like. Automatic speech recognition [Lai *et al.*, 2008; Rabiner and Juang, 1993] has the potential to provide one of the most human of interaction modes. The fact that it is not the default standard for human–computer interaction at present may indicate to you that the task is rather harder to achieve than to state. Robust speech recognition, comfortable in noisy environments and with a variety of speakers, is the ultimate goal of large-scale research programs. Nevertheless, systems trained on a specific interlocutor may be useful for some interaction purposes. Tracking of the human voice in most interaction work at present tends to concentrate on more general timbral features than the meaning of exact utterances.

Video tracking is worth a few paragraphs. As machine listening grants the computer sound analysis capabilities, so **machine vision** techniques [Forsyth and Ponce, 2003; Morris, 2004; Levin, 2007; Wilson, 2008]; [O'Sullivan and Igoe, 2004, pp. 234–247]; [Matarić, 2007, pp. 107–119] break down a sequence of images captured by digital camera into more meaningful attributes. Just as for machine listening, an attempt is made to identify higher-level objects moving within a scene from lower-level features. By looking at pixelwise differences within a single frame, or at changes between frames, it is possible to track motion or to attempt to isolate objects from their edges. It is off topic for this book to go into the full details of computer vision algorithms, but the reader may follow up the references given here. Computer vision modules are available for many of the standard arts computing packages (e.g., Processing, Max/MSP, Pd), and information gleaned using one package can often be passed on to another by a protocol like Open Sound Control (see Section 7.1.1).

It is a challenge to make machine vision as robust to changing lighting conditions as human eyes. As with many other forms of sensor, prolonged use may require environmental calibration at intervals [Wilson, 2008, p. 190]. It is simplest in many situations to give a helping hand to the algorithms themselves. For example, by artificially applying regions of bright color (or other fiduciary markers designed to assist tracking) on the limbs of a dancer, the tracking of their movement can be turned into an easier computational problem. Jason Freeman has produced a number of works which use computer vision and realtime notation to influence the course of musical performance. In *Glimmer* (2004) a large audience is segmented into several groups; waving light sticks, each group's activity level, as tracked by camera, affects the scored material for an orchestra in real time (see Figure 6.2). Audience and musicians all move around in *Flock* (2007) for saxophone quartet, the four players being individually tracked by colored light hats, and 100 audience members wearing a white light hat. A ceiling-mounted computer vision system with fish-eye lens tracks all the positions, with a number of recipes to transform this input into the realtime score [Freeman, 2008].

Figure 6.2 Jason Freeman's *Glimmer*. From a performance at the Hamabada Art Center in Jerusalem, Israel, 25 March 2006. Reproduced by permission of © Jason Freeman.

The tracking of movement is a classic application area for machine vision; if 'dance music' is a category of music meant for dancing, video tracking supports 'music dance', the creation of music in response to the tracking of a dancer. Of course, a number of other techniques are available for tracking dancers within a space, from full body sensor suits to measuring the occupancy within a room by a grid of sensors; Léon Theremin's *terpistone* (1936) utilized the same capacitance field effect as his eponymous instrument, to allow a dancer to control oscillators via a floor plate.[5] Nevertheless, computer vision techniques are a good source of

---

[5]http://www.thereminvox.com/article/articleview/17/1/1/

complex information on dance, without the need for any intrusive electronics on the bodies of the dancers themselves [Ng, 2002]. Multiple cameras can be used to establish a sense of depth (two cameras can approximate our own stereo vision). Aside from dancers, it is also interesting to track the movement of musicians, including conductors. Again, there are multiple ways to employ sensor systems to achieve this; for the case of tracking conductor gestures, see Miranda and Wanderley [2006, pp. 67–9]. Computer vision has also been used for face recognition and facial control of music, and object tracking (locating the brightly colored balls being juggled, for instance). The long-standing multimedia project EyesWeb (http://www.infomus.org/EywMain.html) has investigated human expressive gesture, with a substantial contribution from machine vision software [Camurri *et al.*, 2005].

Both audio and visual modalities provide prime cues for musical expression, and are readily available streams for analysis in multimedia computing systems. The combination of audio and visual information, of machine vision and listening, is also becoming a staple of live audiovisual acts.

6.2.4 Physical Computing

In the world of ubiquitous computing, computers are thoroughly integrated into human social environments, from cell phones to smart houses to wearable computing. Rather than concentrate on the traditional office-locked desktop computer, we must acknowledge the great variety of computational devices now available, varying in both their power and their size. Computer music as a field expands to accommodate new technologies, and we shall return to consider networked devices and mobiles in particular in Chapter 7.

Here, we touch on elements of physical computing [O'Sullivan and Igoe, 2004], a realization that the interface between physical and virtual is of extreme importance in human–computer interaction, and that the office computing scenario unnecessarily restricts the environmental remit of computing. As Hinckley [2008, p. 172] notes concerning the centrality of physicality:

> We will continue to interact with computers using our hands and physical intermediaries, not necessarily because our technology requires us to do so, but because touching, holding, and moving physical objects is the foundation of the long evolution of tool use in the human species.

This tool use includes musical instruments. Computer music can be a part of active physical music making and sound art.

The practical side of bridging the physical–virtual divide must now be confronted. If a laptop is too valuable or too bulky to sew into your interactive cushions, your cloak of sound or your augmented accordion, there are other computers that can be installed. The cheapest and smallest are microcontrollers, simple computers on a chip, which can be directly integrated into electronic circuit designs as information processors for sensors [O'Sullivan and Igoe, 2004; Barragán and Reas, 2007]. A microcontroller could be intended to stand alone, or be part of a wired or wireless distributed network of computers. Many different microcontrollers are available, varying in cost, ease of integration (number of and form of inputs and outputs to the processor) and ease of programming. Two popular options are Parallax's BASIC Stamp and Microchip's PIC (Programmable Intelligent Computer); the PIC is cheaper, but harder to set up [O'Sullivan and Igoe, 2004]. As is typical for micro-controllers, a conventional computer can be used to initialize the program that will run on the chip, which once debugged can run autonomously. While hardcore microcontrollers have traditionally been programmed via a serial port, USB is available[6] for some friendly platforms such as Arduino, Wiring and Phidgets.

Figure 6.3 shows a Wiring board interfacing to some sensors. The board is programmed via the freely available Wiring software on a standard computer, with the program being downloaded over to the board via USB [Barragán and Reas, 2007]. It is possible to get sensor data easily into a desktop computer via the board, if more extensive processing power is required (perhaps the sensors are controlling a complex interactive music system with synthesized responses).

While some electronics knowledge is required in using the cheaper microcontrollers, there are readymade sensor packages. A particular sensor might simply have a USB connector to plug straight into a computer, with accompanying software, or general-purpose interfaces for sensors to MIDI, OSC or audio are available [Miranda and Wanderley, 2006, pp. 161–5]. New systems are released all the time, with new developments including wireless transmitting devices.

It should be emphasized that interfaces also support output, which could be used to change the physical state of a system; from turning a light on or off, giving tactile feedback, to driving a motor or solenoid [O'Sullivan and Igoe, 2004]. Physical motion tends to cost larger amounts of energy than are available directly from a microcontroller, so integrating motors can require some electronics work. There are USB-based solutions such as Phidgets (physical widgets, see www.phidgets.com), which provide the necessary externally powered circuits for motors.

This section will now be rounded off with some examples of inspiring physical interfaces.

Tangible interfaces bring to centre stage physical elements representing computational operations [Ishii, 2008]. A number of groups have been promoting tabletop interfaces for electronic music, which enable collaborative performance at a shared and embodied interface. Tabletop systems usually combine manipulable markers with camera tracking of their movement, and may project additional graphics onto the surface to give additional feedback. Ishii [2008, pp. 478–479] gives the example of Audiopad (http://www.

---

[6]Under the surface, the RS-232 standard is often utilized, so USB serial drivers may have to be installed.

Figure 6.3 Wiring board and sensors. USB power comes from the laptop seen at the edge of the shot; three sensors are attached (dial, switch and accelerometer concealed in Lego brick).

jamespatten.com/audiopad/), where by moving tokens around the surface users manipulate sample playback and processing. Recent high profile coverage has been accorded to another augmented table, the Reactable, a project based at Universitat Pompeu Fabra [Jordà, 2007] (http://reactable.iua.upf.edu/). The Reactable is a tangible version of a graph-based modular synthesizer, which can be shared by multiple participants leaning over the table. A computer vision system (Reactivision) is employed which can track fiducials, markers which are deliberately designed to be easy to track, and which represent the oscillators, filters and other unit generators in a sound synthesis network.

Maintaining the theme of 'music-dance' from the previous section, now explicitly for 'dance-music', Ulyate and Bianciardi [2002] describe an interactive dance club that was run at SIGGRAPH98. Visitors to the club could control music playback in multiple zones by dance-mats, large levers and wheels, with both solo and shared interfaces.

Physical computing has overtones of real sweat and effort. In one of his long-standing performance works, *The Hands*, the much admired performer and artist Michel Waisvisz (in collaboration with interface experts at the Dutch institute STEIM) made a highly explicit physical controller. Multiple sensors mounted in a pair of graspable gloves, reminiscent of a partial exoskeleton, tracked the movement of the fingers, hands and arms. *The Hands* has been through at least three distinct versions, but its long existence since 1984 helped Waisvisz to demonstrate mastery of the instrument commensurate with intensive years of practice. As a controller, The Hands sent MIDI information which was plugged into a wide variety of MIDI synthesizers, but has also been used as a front end to the LiSa live sampling software. As Waisvisz noted on his website, 'I would be able to walk, move and even dance while making electronic music' (http://www.crackle.org/TheHands.htm).

6.2.5 Physiological State

With human participants necessarily central to music the tracking of the human body has already featured substantially in this chapter, but here we will focus on some particular techniques that can directly probe physiological state, and provide tantalizing glimpses into our interior worlds. Although we have already surveyed many sensors which can externally track human physiology, through measurement of the human body in motion through space and acting on external objects, we shall introduce **biosignals** [Miranda and Wanderley, 2006, Chapter Four] here as a view into the interior medical, emotional and cognitive state of human beings. As Mandryk *et al.* [2006] have observed, there is potential to provide objective measurement of an individual's subjective feeling through monitoring of human physiology. However, the reliability of such techniques in real practice is an open research area; biosignals are 'relatively easy to qualify but rather difficult to quantify' [Miranda and Wanderley, 2006, p. 180].

Medical sensing technology provides the equipment for measuring physiological state, with application in health, security (biometrics) and, of course, art. Bio-electricity-based sensor options include the electrocardiogram (ECG) for heartbeat, electromyograms (EMG) for muscle activation, and the electroencephelogram (EEG) for surface cortical activity in the brain measured from many electrodes placed in contact with the head. Although access to such state seems attractive for use in interactive systems, medical sensors can be costly, and vary in their diagnostic consistency.

In bio-feedback, participants can become more aware of their own bodily processes when given the data from bio-sensors.

> The term 'biofeedback' ... [refers] to the presentation to an organism, through
> sensory input channels, of information about the state and/or course of change
> of a biological process in that organism, for the purpose of achieving some

measure of regulation or performance control over that process, or simply for the purpose of internal exploration and enhanced self-awareness. [Rosenboom, 1997].

Controlled performance via biosensors requires a great deal of practice. Biofeedback can also have runaway effects. Imagine if your heart rate controlled the tempo of club music to which you were dancing; increased engagement with the music might drive heart rate faster, further ramping up the tempo! Such a feedback is not sustainable in this case, but identifies how the tight coupling of body and music implies some delicate balances.

If music is an emotional regulator par excellence [Juslin and Sloboda, 2001], the tracking of the emotions of participants in musical activity is of great relevance. **Affective computing** is the subfield of computing attuned to the emotional states of users. We reveal emotion in a number of ways. From a distance, camera tracking of facial expression and postural cues can potentially record body language. Biosensors also provide data, but the interpretation of this data is problematic and hardly free of ambiguity. As an example, galvanic skin response (GSR) measures the conductivity of the skin, which varies with sweat gland activity. GSR is an indicator of arousal or stress, but the exact emotional correlates are diffuse, and this would only be part of measuring a subject's emotional state; Mandryk *et al.* [2006] use GSR as one element of a system to detect emotional state for gaming, but multiple sensors are combined through machine learning algorithms to attempt finer estimates.

By suggesting sensors for mental processes, the prospect of mind reading is raised, neuroscience not having been shy in promoting research agendas in this sphere. Although fundamental tracking of human thought in real time remains science fiction, a number of indicators of cognitive activity can be gained from EEG and other brain scanning techniques. We have already pinched the salt of this endeavor; even granting how marvellous the technology is, current scanners are far lower on spatial and temporal resolution than would be needed to give an exact moment-by-moment reading of the neurons in the brain! fMRI (functional magnetic resonance imaging) measures mental activity via blood flow in the brain over a window of seconds. While empowering many insights into the mind in current research [Peretz and Zatorre, 2003], practical fMRI use in music making is somewhat restricted by the large noisy scanner, the restricted movement of those in the scanner, the large magnetic field which prevents use of metals in the scanning room, and the slightly large price tag. But writing here is speculative, since developments in scanner technology will no doubt change the playing field. There have been studies on musicians within scanners; I'm not currently aware of any network music performance carried out using plastic instruments by musicians within two fMRI scanners at different sites, but there is no stopping some neuroscientists.

Electronic musicians have a history of employing brain scanning techniques in their work, though focusing on the rather more practical EEG, with its excellent temporal resolution. We can trace works from Alvin Lucier's *Music for Solo Performer* (1965), through the investigations of pioneers such as Richard Teitelbaum and David Rosenboom, to the present day. Eduardo Miranda describes his group's work on the *BCMI-piano* (Brain Computer Music Interface piano), an instrument whose algorithmic music controller is influenced by mental choice as interpreted from EEG rhythm [Miranda and Wanderley, 2006]. Low-cost EEG interfaces for gaming are coming onto the market, so much more brain–computer music is no doubt in store.

6.3 INTERACTION SCENARIOS

Our attention now turns more to the role of the computer in different interactive settings. The complete systems which introduce computation to musical interaction have been called by many names, but perhaps the most general common term is **interactive music systems** [Rowe, 1993]. This term may cover a whole range of possibilities, with systems especially varying in the amount of 'cognition' they achieve. Many systems are very tightly coupled to their inputs, highly reactive but not convincingly interactive in the strict sense. They function like augmented instruments, but not especially intelligent ones. Fewer systems really engage with the domain of artificial intelligence, but a number of designers have built advanced systems which can exhibit more autonomous behavior.

It is worth pausing to consider the justifications for the existence of such systems. Why bring computers into the music making loop? Here, there is overlap with general justifications for computer music; new technology always raises new musical avenues, and sheer human curiosity drives new aesthetics a long way. Computers may offer the scope for entirely new forms of interaction; an example is given by Jonathan Impett's exploration of emergence, his system for trumpeter and computer implementing a hierarchy of hive-like intelligence from which new musical behaviors emerge in the course of improvisation [Impett, 2001]. Nevertheless, many systems operate within the grand tradition of instrument building (Sergi Jordà's 'digital lutherie' [Jordà, 2005]), and the instrument model is particularly strong where a system closely follows human input. The computer in this case can offer expanded sound transformation and generation in alliance with physical instrumental control. Since traditional acoustic instrument interfaces have proven themselves over centuries, they provide strong starting points for new lines of investigation. Yet, though they may be well adjusted to their existing niche, they are not necessarily the only starting points available in design space, and a designer may wish to go back to the drawing board of human physiology and mentality, or even alien physique, depending on their aesthetics!

The continuum of autonomy, from instrument to independent virtual performer, is one part of Robert Rowe's taxonomy of interactive music systems (the instrument–player dimension) [Rowe, 1993], but one especially worth emphasizing here. Rowe goes on to consider the form of material generation and processing, and to differentiate scenarios locked to a known score from those which are more freely performative. Suffice it to say that any developments in computer science, particularly artificial intelligence and robot control, are available to the musical luthier who wants to expand the cognitive side of their system. Enhanced cognitive components in the system can expand the scope of interaction between human and machine, but may also establish potential musical autonomy with greater artificial personality. Virtual players are not exclusively meant for concert settings, and may take part in rehearsal and even daily practice for educational and therapeutic settings. Authors have variously characterized their potential for interactive companionship [Thom, 2003], self-reflexive music making [Pachet, 2003] or for setting up novel improvisatory situations [Lewis, 1999].

The following sections break down systems into a number of different interactive settings. We'll aim for rounded coverage, but the reader is encouraged to pursue the further reading to discover many more interesting projects than there is space for here. However, it should be acknowledged that many hybrids are possible, from online multi-user computer games to installations in a conservatoire intended for expert musicians.

6.3.1 Installations

Music does not have to fixate on concert venues, and one of the healthiest arenas of new sound-based interaction is the installation. Art gallery settings aside, sound art has been located in many public venues, from parks and carparks to the sides of buildings. The principle of public engagement drives many works, so that interactivity becomes an important locus. Yet, just as for concert systems, many installations have been criticized on the grounds of the profundity of interaction they offer. As Garth Paine has noted, they often do not support mutual influence but only reaction. In terms of the sort of experience installations might ideally engender, he notes: 'We must seek to develop experiences that are not predetermined, and that reflect each individual's nuance of input in a unique and fulfilling manner.' [Paine, 2002, p. 303]

The attention given by participants to installations is usually entirely under their own control, and the artists cannot guarantee attendance throughout the unraveling of a scenario. Many visitors only ever see a snapshot of the work in action, and the contributions of one participant may impact on future interactions for other visitors. Artists set up an exploration of a process or concept, an aesthetic adventure space; the model is often far from linear concert presentation.

Computers can certainly be part of installations, and sound artists especially grapple with the physical computing angle. But a great many artworks (particularly historic works) use analog electronics rather than digital, for often a great deal can be done just with transducers like microphones and speakers. In Edwin van der Heide's *Wavescape* (1998), 24 underwater microphones (hydrophones) are reproduced over 24 loudspeakers at the waterfront (http://www.evdh.net/). In such works, themes of acoustics and psychoacoustics tend to be more prevalent than any traditional musical form, often bypassing any need for complex programming logic. Nevertheless, computers necessarily crop up in networked installations, or more complicated audiovisual processing engines, and form the backbone of so much modern technology that it's often hard to avoid them!

Figure 6.4   Spatial Sounds (100 dB at 100 km/h). Installation by Marnix de Nijs and Edwin van der Heide. Reproduced by permission of © Edwin van der Heide.

Installations also support multi-user scenarios, and many interactive instruments have appeared in gallery settings for public exploration, such as the ReacTable. Mobile phone-based installations are a recurring theme, picked up again elsewhere in this book. Indeed, installation artists tend to be fascinated by the potential of telecommunications and telepresence in general, often setting up encounters between disparate locales; Maryanne Amacher's *City Links* series (1967–) might be a standard-bearer for such ideas of transmission and connecting disparate spaces and sound worlds, but the Internet is the current communications craze. We shall return to network music projects in Chapter 7. Many installations are highly multimodal, featuring large-scale sculpture, robotics, architecture and projection. Jon McCormack has created interactive audiovisual installations where visitors can explore and influence an artificial life world, such as the sonic ecosystem *Eden* [McCormack, 2003]. As shown in Figure 6.4, *Spatial Sounds (100 dB at 100 km/h)* (2000), by Marnix de Nijs and Edwin van der Heide, is a loudspeaker on a robotic arm which maps out its surroundings by sonar, and can rush after visitors, swinging fast! Trimpin's oeuvre is robotics incarnate, a powerful demonstration of computer-controlled instruments, almost always 'acoustic synthesis' rather than mediated by loudspeaker. His works reach enormous scales, from percussive clogs on a duck pond (*Floating Klompen*, 1989), incredible control of water droplets (*Liquid Percussion* 1991), aluminum balls on large ringed tracks tuned to a 3:4:5 ratio (*Der Ring*, 2006) to the tower of automated self-tuning electric guitars permanently installed at the Seattle Experience Music Project (*IF VI WAS IX: Roots and Branches* (2000)).

While some of the concerns of sound art can certainly be differentiated from those of traditional musical performance, this book does not draw too hard a line between fine art and music, believing instead that there are many intersections in practice and materials, and that continua exist along multiple dimensions between the idiomatic examples in either supposed camp. See Landy [2007] for more on these issues, and there are a number of good sources on sound art and digital art to consult [Kahn, 1999; Wilson, 2002; LaBelle, 2007; Licht, 2007].

6.3.2 Computer Games

In terms of mass audience, video games win out over the other sites of interaction here. Games are a massive entertainment industry with a greater revenue stream than movies. Admittedly, music is not a central concern of most games as multimodal experiences, either from a technical point of view or from an aesthetic one. CPU allocation in games prioritizes graphics, and even game AI, above audio; a standard method of music playback is simply to stream pre-made audio, and sound effects are typically triggered samples. Innovation is usually restricted to spatialization effects for atmosphere. Further, many a gamer has been known to turn off the in-game music, generative or not! Sound effects are more likely to be retained, since their assistance to audiovisual integration may provide reaction-time advantages, and they can carry off-screen action through all-round localization cues where front-biased sight fails.

Having cautioned about this pro-visual bias, I note also that recent years have seen an influx of musical games, which necessarily bring aspects of music to center stage. Some games have even begun to employ machine listening technology; for example, Codemasters' *Dance Factory* uses a beat-tracking algorithm in order to allow users to generate game levels from their own CDs, rather than pre-annotated tracks. Microphones naturally appear in karaoke-style games, which offer private pop-star experiences to the humble home user, and may employ pitch tracking to rate quality of singing.

Although singing is an essential musical skill, the representations utilized in some 'rhythm games' can seem a little primitive to experienced musicians, with scrolling piano-roll-like editors, position equating to pitch and events strung out over time as the screen scrolls. The interfaces, however, are part of the charm, from dance mats to psuedo-guitars. Strong timing skills (with some latency to cope with) are required in progressing through levels; the games are often reminiscent of a shoot-em-up inside a basic MIDI sequencer. Even if these rhythm games offer a compromised sense of musical instrumentation, this has not stopped some game obsessives from putting in as much practice time as a dedicated musician would. As there are world championships in air guitar, there are also competitions for *Guitar Hero*. It is certainly easier to get to conduct an orchestra through *Wii Music* than to gain time with a real orchestra!

Game platforms are also frequently used with music authoring software. The 8-bit scene's connections to handheld computers, via the Nanoloop tracker for example, is well established. The interfaces tend to be similar to those of conventional music software for desktops and laptops, even though used via a game controller, and may focus on certain easy-to-achieve modifications suitable to the screen space and interface device. Yet, because they get the user standing up and dancing about rather than sitting down, handheld computers are compatible with extra human movement in performance!

6.3.3 Concert Performance

Some of the most central and sociable musical experiences take place in a concert setting. These vary in the degree of participation allotted to all parties, from a communal sing-song to a mass audience witnessing a solo performer. When there are audiences, different occasions may merit different levels of attention, and social conventions have changed over time.[7] Even in an age of respectful quiet for masterworks, classical musicians are talked over at receptions, while some bar-based performances can rivet attention so much as to bring a noisy venue to a standstill. Various extra-musical factors can impact on performance, and the incorporation of technology into performance provides yet another way in which the music is at the mercy of outside forces, from power companies to those who might accidentally spill beer on a laptop ....

The array of input devices discussed so far in this chapter provides plenty of opportunity for the construction of novel musical controllers, typically on the instrument model. There is sometimes reluctance on the part of musicians to grant the status of an instrument to a new interface that is not as fluid and immediate as a traditional instrument proven over the centuries. Those new electrical instruments in the 20th century which gained classic status are amplified traditional instruments (such as the electric guitar), or the theremin and the turntable, all of which are direct in their action, though the turntable is a particularly interesting case in its flexibility of timbre through analog sampling. The present era is replete with competitors for the status of new classic, but most of these are promoted by a single developer. Fewer ideas make it to commercial mass production, many of those that do just being further flexible components to assist with custom systems, rather than complete instruments. Often, the enjoyment of building new personal devices is the most important facet of all, and the opportunity to create your own unique system is a wonderful temptation aside from any worries about the longevity of design. The most important background issue is one of practice; it is wise to reflect on how much effort musicians put into learning traditional instruments, and consider how this intimate training regime might translate to new interfaces.

We have already covered many facets of the control problem, mapping strategy being directly connected with the physical interface in terms of the perceived control loop. Piggy-backing existing instruments (such as sensor extensions to a trombone) is the realm of

---

[7]In Baroque times, some members of the 'audience' were more interested in an opportunity for philandering than the musical event!

augmented instruments. In commanding large-scale synthesis and processing resources, the instrument can itself take on an increased complement of artificial intelligence, the territory of **intelligent instruments.** The succeeding sections will treat the case where the emphasis on intelligence is scaled up to promote autonomous players, as potentially independent musical agents.

6.4 LIVE MUSICAL AGENTS

The notion of an **agent** in artificial intelligence characterizes computer programs as active modules, and potentially autonomous participants in transactions of information [Russell and Norvig, 2003]. There are different taxonomies of agency, and all sorts of variations in the schemes by which levels of autonomy can be measured [Collins, 2006c]. One holy grail of computer music is the creation of a live musical agent whose behaviors are fully commensurate with human music making, but whose architecture is not of flesh and blood [Rowe, 2001; Collins, 2007b].

The production of artificial musicians is really an enormous challenge in the modeling of human musicianship. Any effective combination of person and machine on an equivalent footing must take full notice of human traits and proclivities; Robert Rowe has termed the modeling of human musical abilities as the invention of **machine musicianship** [Rowe, 2001]. Though the live musical agent may be aware of human productive, perceptual and cognitive limits as a prerequisite of effective integration into machine–human interaction, it is not bound by these itself. Generative strategies that challenge accepted musical wisdom and capability may be deliberately implemented, as a way of striking out on new musical paths. Indeed, although the modeling of human musicianship is a scientific object of study on its own terms, we have plenty of irreplaceable human musicians already, so unless the virtual players take advantage of some unique ability of computer processing, the aesthetic of employing them is doubtful. It would be unkind to claim that the dream was only to engineer replacements for ourselves! Instead, these systems imply new opportunities for musical interaction, and have many potential side benefits in musical education, music therapy or pushing the forefront of research.

The exact algorithms employed are entirely open. A few systems and their strategies will be described below, but the AI literature is replete with further techniques that can be explored. In particular, in seeking high-level agency, goal-directed behavior and learning ability are key aspects of cognition to confront. In building improvising systems, conversational metaphors have often been introduced [Preece *et al.*, 1994, pp. 174–8]; [Walker, 1997; Murray-Rust *et al.*, 2006].

In order to exhibit interaction, live musical agents must have some capacity for independent contribution, effecting real mutual influence. Some musical settings, such as those locked to scores, may seem to provide minimal room for extemporization, though scores still allow some leeway of interpretation and expressive detail. Much may be settled in rehearsal, and the efficacy of machine musicians' ability to learn in human social settings is itself in question here. The social roles of musicians are an important part of different musical settings, from full democratic participation to particular lead and subsidiary roles (as per soloist and accompanist, conductor and orchestra). This full social participation, as an equal human participant, shows exactly how the musical AI problem turns into the full AI challenge.

6.4.1 Automatic Accompaniment

There are systems that are not really autonomous at all, in that they are not meant to change the musical plan, but whose technical achievements are related to capabilities often desired in interactive music systems. These systems have been devised to tackle the problem of an automatic accompanist.

For fixed score pieces, one simple approach is playback of a tape with the onus on the human performer to sync up, a case still seen at many current electroacoustic music festivals.[8] A pragmatic improvement is a cue system where an operator triggers sound events manually to match critical points in the score [Madden *et al.*, 2001]. The automation of accompaniment is a natural yet tricky further step. For monophonic instruments (like the flute), this has been achieved by pitch-tracking algorithms and pattern matching against a score. Barry Vercoe's Synthetic Performer was an early system (1984) developed at IRCAM, used for tracking flute and violin; it took advantage of fingering information from sensors as well as the audio stream. Dannenberg [1989] reviews early attempts at automatic accompaniment, including his own equally early 1984 system and its subsequent developments.

Current state-of-the-art systems use statistical pattern matching to position the accompaniment at the most likely score location given an audio signal from the soloist [Orio and Déchelle, 2001; Pardo and Birmingham, 2002; Raphael, 2001]. These systems improve results by rehearsal with the musician they will accompany, exactly as a human accompanist would. Polyphonic instrument tracking is extremely difficult, but some success is possible simply by using features of the audio stream (like spectral density), rather than attempting a complete ongoing transcription solution [Jehan *et al.*, 2002]. Raphael [2004] has demonstrated some success in the tracking of a pianist by using spectral templates for each expected chord, constructed by mixing a harmonic model for each note.

For robustness in the face of expressive timing and performer error, Chris Raphael's Bayesian system Music Plus One [Raphael, 2001, 2004] is impressive. I have first-hand experience of working with the system; I composed a *Concerto for Accompaniment* (2002) for Chris Raphael on oboe with his realtime computer accompanist on piano. The Concerto

---

[8]Certainly in much historical practice, the inability to render certain gestures in real time and the perfectionist craft of electroacoustic tape composition has been a factor here.

is so called because it involves various challenges to the accompaniment system; entries that are difficult to synchronize with the soloist, and virtuosic (not humanly performable) material (Figure 6.5). That the accompaniment system can play robustly under these conditions shows the potential of such technology for new music. Chris has further explored this in recording two works by the Swiss composer Jan Beran written for Music Plus One, *Winter711* (2004) and *Mist Covered Mountains* (2005).[9]

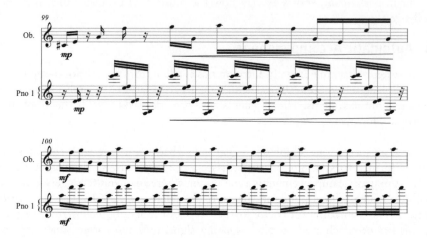

Figure 6.5   The difficulty of automatic accompaniment – an extract from the first movement of the Concerto for Accompaniment, for human oboist and computer pianist, showing virtuosic material that must be synchronized.

6.4.2 Robot Musicians

The advantage of robots is that they are embodied and exhibit real presence. They confront the pressing problem of existence in the world, the ultimate challenge in AI. Above puny silicon-locked virtual players, the robot musician may seem to be the ultimate manifestation of an artificial musical agent.

Mechanical music anticipated the glib virtuoso musical possibilities of the computer by centuries, wherever machines could play streams of events so accurately at speed as to surpass human physical abilities. The great French engineer Jacques Vaucanson created three celebrated automata, the first a flute-player (1738) and the third playing both pipe and drum; as he noted in a letter concerning the latter, 'the Figure out-does all our Performers on the Tabor-pipe, who cannot move their Tongue fast enough to go thro' a whole Bar of Semiquavers, and strike them all.' [Ord-Hume, 1973, p. 37]. Automata themselves can be traced back many centuries, with some surprisingly early precedents. For example, the great Mesopotamian engineer Ibn al-Razzaz al-Jazari constructed a robot quartet on a boat which reputedly floated at royal drinking parties, as described in his book of 1206. It has been

---

[9]http://xavier.informatics.indiana.edu/~craphael/music_plus_one/

contended that the automata were programmable in a more modern sense of the term, and therefore truly marvelous anticipations of electrical robot musicians. Yet al-Jazari's work is itself preceded by Chinese mechanical engineering, including seventh-century hydraulic singing girls and a mechanical puppet orchestra from 206 BC consisting of twelve three-foot-high bronze instrumentalists powered by air and pulleys [Neecham and Ling, 1965]. Arthur Ord-Hume's book *Clockwork Music* reveals many more examples of early robots and musical automata, from the Kaufmann family's Orchestrion, exhibited as a 'self-acting musical instrument' in 1851, to Professor Wauters' player violin of 1907 [Ord-Hume, 1973]. The latter used independent circular disk bows and finger stops for each string, anticipating a more recent GuitarBot (www.lemurbots.org).

The history of such machines is deeply fascinating and many more recent examples are also covered by Kapur [2005]. If this theme may distract a little from computer music per se, it is still important to raise the issues, with robotics set to become such a growth technology area in the 21st century. In this computer era, the computers are being employed as electronic brains for robot musicians, even though a substantial engineering component remains a major part of any robotics work. Therefore, we shall not pursue further knowledge of mechanics, hydraulics, pneumatics and electronics, but caution the reader that a little bit of arc-wielding may await the brave robot builder; or at least, the purchase of a Lego Mindstorms kit, or some Phidgets.

It would be a pity to miss the chance to show an example of a musical robot, so Figure 6.6 portrays an interaction between Ajay Kapur on augmented sitar and his percussive robot MahaDeviBot; in respect of the Hindu goddess, the number of arms is set to increase beyond four [Kapur *et al.*, 2007] . . . .

In a splendid workshop on musical robotics at NIME2007, some prominent explorers in this field – Trimpin, Jacques Rémus, Godfried-Willem Raes, Gordon Monahan and Eric Singer – presented and demonstrated their wares, which had underlined a startling array of concerts, theatrical performances and gallery sound art. Their various marvelous machines revealed the continuum between robots as slaves and as more autonomous agents in the musical world. The connection back to Vaucanson is clear from modern updates, such as the Waseda Flutist Robot, one of a large number of musical robots produced since the 1980s at Waseda University, Japan [Solis *et al.*, 2006].

As an example of a robot that incorporates more artificial intelligence rather than being a slave to sequencer control, it is worth mentioning Haile the Robotic Drummer [Weinberg and Driscoll, 2006], an ongoing project where a barely humanoid robot (really a couple of arms and a brain with a stylized frame) shares a pow-wow drum with human percussionists. Machine listening technology is used to analyze the input of other players, with the robot's electronic brain (the good-natured computer) formulating appropriate responses in a number of different playing modes.

Figure 6.6   Ajay Kapur on E-Sitar, and MahaDeviBot. Reproduced by permission of © Ajay Kapur.

6.4.3 Programming the 'Brain' of a Virtual Musician

We now turn to the practical matter of ways to import musical intelligence into our systems. There is overlap here with the material on algorithmic composition in Section 8.3.1, though the demand for interaction brings its own criteria to the mix. Systems can subsist on relatively basic heuristics (rules), and the incorporation of more complicated artificial intelligence techniques is often tempered by musical need. Surveying interactive music systems, Camurri and Leman [1997, p. 353] write that 'few of them contain some sort of "intelligence" – knowledge by which actions are guided and adapt themselves to the environment in a way that resembles human information processing'.

Reviews of the conflux of artificial intelligence research and music have been carried out by a number of authors [Roads, 1985d; Ames, 1990; Camurri, 1993; Camurri and Leman, 1997; Miranda, 2000]. Trends in AI technologies applied to music have followed the general progression in the AI literature, from symbolic systems like rule-based expert systems and other forms of explicit knowledge engineering [Roads, 1985d; Ames, 1990; Camurri, 1993] to subsymbolic connectionism using the implicit learning capabilities of neural nets and other statistical machine learning techniques [Todd and Loy, 1991; Leman, 1993; Griffith and Todd, 1999; Toiviainen, 2000]. While subsymbolic approaches have proved useful for 'investigation of the inarticulate aspects of musical activity' [Toiviainen, 2000], Camurri and Leman [1997] advocate the combination of the strengths of the two in hybrid systems. These might typically combine low-level subsymbolic systems operating on audio signals with higher-level symbolic processes operating on extracted objects over larger timescales. MIDI representation and similar starting points give the luxury of beginning with symbols rather than signals, avoiding the signal-to-symbol problem. Thus, some systems (particularly those built before the start of the new millennium) treat only MIDI to get around the additional headache of audio analysis; many audio-based systems employ AI techniques even at early stages of signal processing. The systems designer gets a choice of what levels of description to treat, depending on the sensor data available, including the pursuit of multiple simultaneous viewpoints.

Getting anywhere near to human musicianship is one of the truly difficult and interesting problems in computer music. It is likely to require intensive machine learning, in order to match the rigorous training and practice regimes human musicians undergo [Deliège and Sloboda, 1996]. The best representation(s) of music to support such learning is itself an open question. The intrepid reader will find plenty of ideas about how to implement musical capacity, but should be warned that there are some deep issues lurking here. Specific musical situations pose intensive demands on realtime decision making, and general algorithms from AI often need careful adaptation to cope with particular musical scenarios.

However, there are redeeming points, for any musical system can *stimulate* musicians, even if its own mechanisms do not closely *simulate* their cognitive processes. Novel musical scenarios can be designed, and there are many inspiring techniques in AI ready to be applied in computer music, from evolutionary algorithms to Bayesian belief networks. We shall now investigate a few ways to form the brain of interactive music systems, hopefully to inspire you to experiment in this field!

Improvisation and symbolic feature extraction

George Lewis's Voyager system was introduced in the first chapter as an interesting exemplar of computer music. The system is built for a free improvisation setting, and is highly independent, far from the traditional notion of instrument – a paradigmatic virtual player. Lewis has been a great advocate and defender of improvisation in musical culture. Explaining how his computer program models extemporization, he explains: 'Improvisers often work in terms of rather loosely defined "shapes," which can be defined in terms of characteristics such as volume direction, pitch direction, duration, rhythm regularity, pitch or duration transposition, time between major changes in output or input, pattern-finding, and frequency of silence. You don't need or want an exhaustive transcription, but instead a fast, general analysis of what's happening at any given moment and what's been happening. This requires massive, but musically important, data reductions.' [Roads, 1985c, p. 84]. The principle of using musical features to find the important 'shapes' – or, in AI speak, **states** – will now be outlined.

Voyager collects MIDI data via a pitch-to-MIDI convertor, allowing acoustic instruments (such as George Lewis's trombone, but also the instruments of other performers) to be easily translated into a form the system can treat.[10] Lewis has programmed Voyager to translate MIDI note inputs into summary statistics that define particular states for the system. Just as when using a sliding window with audio sample data to gain frame-based features (see Section 3.5), the same idea can work with MIDI data. Our treatment here will be restricted to symbolic (MIDI-like) representations, but these notions are extensible to audio-based systems.

For realtime music making, a number of pertinent timescales might be used to determine the time of windows themselves. Notes from a single performer are typically played no faster than ten per second[11] so the window should be large enough to accommodate multiple notes. The sense of the perceptual present – those notes impacting directly on the sense of musical 'now' – is around two to three seconds. Short-term memory (STM) extends out to ten seconds or so; definite absolute time limits cannot be given, since there is an interaction with the amount of information conveyed (STM covers perhaps thirty to forty notes).

If we assume MIDI information, for each MIDI note we might have a start time, a duration, a pitch in MIDI note numbers (12-note equal tempered), and a velocity. There is also the sequence information in terms of temporal ordering, which gives rise to inter-onset intervals (IOIs), pitch intervals and other differences between successive notes. There are many possible statistics across a given window, which may or may not take into account the actual ordering of notes, some examples being:

- density: the number of notes in a given window (indicating both activity and silence);

- pitch coverage: how many distinct pitches are in the window;

- pitch class coverage: how many distinct pitches modulo 12 are in the window – all 12 different tones could indicate an atonal aggregate, a fast key change during the window, or a highly chromatic line (which one is the case would require further processing to determine);

- mean velocity (one measure of the energy of playing);

- mean start time (center of note onsets within the window), mean IOI, measures of evenness and uniformity of IOIs based on matching patterns of evenly spaced notes in the window, or the relative data in terms of an IOI histogram;

- information on the contour of note input, simplified in some way from the sequence of pitch intervals by defining only a few interval types (e.g., most crudely: same, up, down), making a histogram of intervals (which loses their temporal order), trying to fit a simple envelope shape to the complex contour and more.

---

[10]Lewis has actually spoken of the inaccuracies the conversion process brings as useful noise to stimulate the improvisational process, rather than as a limiting factor.
[11]This can be exceeded for the over-rehearsed chunking of notes together, as in two-handed piano playing or rolled finger patterns, or special techniques like glissandi.

Some more ideas for features to track appear in the Lewis quotation earlier in this section, and there are innumerable ways to bring in statistical moments and temporal sequence modeling to further summarize the observed data. Symbolic algorithms for key extraction, beat tracking and other machine listening tasks are perfectly applicable [Rowe, 2001]. More ideas will be found in the discussion of audio features and musical modeling in this book.

Similar problems to audio feature extraction occur, such as for the larger time windows of beat tracking where a change of tempo during the window cannot be recognized (see Section 3.5.3). Similarly, a key change during the window, or a sudden change in the rate of notes, will not be picked up. The tradeoff of stability of estimate (larger windows mean better averages) against speed of reaction to change (smaller windows mean more local behavior is tracked) is in play. There are also normalization issues, in that we may have adaptive normalization that uses a larger window to set the current behavioral limits for small-scale measurements, or we may set a constant normalizing factor for all time.

Now, in order to get a good balance of local and global data, these summary statistics might be taken for different window sizes. Some features might work better at different timescales, and we may even want to have windows based on the number of notes (an information processing constraint) and windows strictly determined by time. We will combine features extracted into a single feature vector representing the observations 'now' – even though 'now' might extend over varying time windows into the past for different features – and which is the definitive observation to be acted upon.

Given the observed musical features, some action must be selected for the system. Figure 6.7 gives an abstract depiction of this process (see also Russell and Norvig [2003] and Matarić [2007], for example). Imitation is a nice starting point. Try synthesizing outputs that have a similar feature structure to the incident data. Because the summary statistics are not the original data, there is an inherent abstraction here that may keep the productions of the computer fresh. Strict imitation, however, never goes beyond what François Pachet has called 'reflexive' music making. Perhaps a contrary interactive system would always aim to do the opposite of the human performer? Perhaps now is the time to launch your own ideas on musical behavior and instill your system with your own creative ideas?

Musical machines that learn

It has already been noted that learning is an important facet of musicianship that more complicated virtual musical brains must confront. It is worth pointing out a few further techniques, and trying to show the potentially strong links to the AI and machine learning literature.

Lewis spoke earlier of 'reduction' and there are many circumstances where it may be useful to try to recognize certain classes of behavior in the observations. Perhaps the interactive music system should never play during silence or low-density, low-volume situations, but join in as activities become more tumultuous. Perhaps there are a few different playing styles that the system can pick up on.

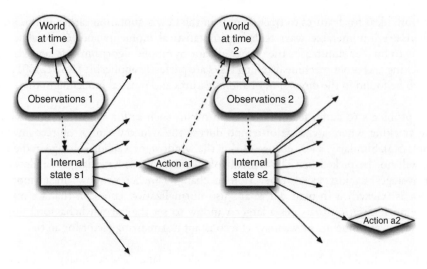

Figure 6.7   States and actions. An agent acts in the world; at a particular time, taking some observations of (extracting some features from) the environment. The feature vector is a list of processed observation data that influences the internal state of the agent (other influences might be previous system state, various forms of memory store, programmed goal and the like). The agent then has a choice of actions, selecting one to perform based on its programmed criteria. This influences the world in turn, and the sense–state–act cycle begins anew . . . .

We're reducing from lots of incoming notes to classifying a particular sort of musical behavior in the external world, to help navigate to an appropriate musical action. We could write production rules directly (if the feature values are in a certain range, do this), but a higher technology alternative is to employ some form of machine learning algorithm to cluster feature vector data. This categorization of distinct states could take place online in real time, or in rehearsal, with and without supervision, and could be placed in a more rigorous framework of machine learning theory. The interested reader might like to investigate further, using the following systems, which are only summarized here, for inspiration:

- Dannenberg *et al.* [1997] use 13 MIDI features to recognize whether the playing is in one of eight 'styles' (frantic, lyrical, pointillistic, syncopated, high, low, quote or blues), changing system output accordingly;

- Thom [2003] classifies a database of melodies, and can therefore determine an appropriate line to output when cued by a human performer, in a 'call and response' framework;

- Hsu [2008] recognizes particular gestures using two interacting timescales. His audio-based system extracts many timbral parameters in order to interface well with free improvisation (in particular, collaborating with saxophonist John Butcher, who has an arsenal of extended instrumental techniques).

Computer systems can take advantage of prodigious memories to store every piece of data thrown at them. A database of states and possible actions might be constructed by analyzing large numbers of MIDI files offline, or from live instruction by a human player, even during a concert itself. Rote learning might simply record every available fact, but more advanced inductive tools would seek to model the data and allow for generalizations, thereby increasing the generative potential. In real life, exact replications do not always readily occur, so there is often some form of approximation in finding a close match, and it is necessary to define a 'similarity' function. Probability theory can be incorporated in various ways, perhaps by looking at the frequency of certain transitions within a corpus so as to set up probabilities of each possible action from a given state.

One example of such a formulation is a Markov chain (of a certain order), where, for example, the last N pitches determine the context (state) from which the next action (next note) is chosen. JamFactory (written by David Zicarelli and released by Intelligent Music in 1987) has four virtual players that can be 'taught' by forming Markov chains from incoming MIDI data [Yavelow, 1989, p. 222]. Markov systems are mentioned at various other points in this book in tackling algorithmic composition or musical modeling. There are more recent efficient algorithms for the online construction of graphs of note sequences[12] that have been used in interactive music systems, such as the Continuator [Pachet, 2003] and OMax [Assayag et al., 2006].

Human memory is seemingly more limited in brute strength, and yet takes advantage of many as yet unknown representational simplifications to cut to the heart of musical material. Human long-term memory access can exploit parallel processing rather than linear search, making human reaction time competitive, alongside unmatched human abilities in contextual anticipation. Reading into the interlinked psychology of memory and learning [Anderson, 2000] alongside the AI and machine learning literature may provide many more ideas for machine musicianship.

6.5 EVALUATION

For some artists, all that is required of any new robot or music system is gallery space, a YouTube video, a live gig, or a release date. And indeed, such public outlets are an essential part of raising awareness about work, and also very useful for the feedback of peers. The cycle of design and testing can subsist on a relatively informal basis, and those who are least formal in analysis of their own work may still be responsible for great leaps forward in artistic practice. However, it is important at this stage to at least raise the prospect of more rigorous examination of interactive music systems, for the benefit of comparative analysis and well considered design. Such analysis may help the designer to clearly identify successful

---

[12]Such as suffix trees; the literature on pattern matching in strings becomes relevant here [Dubnov et al., 2003].

and not-so-successful points in a system, and to drive forward research from a stronger over-arching framework. These points on evaluation can apply to general studio software too, though new musical instruments are a particularly challenging domain.

Evaluation criteria for interactive music systems vary with the intentions of the designer and the setting for the work. In the case of concert systems, three main forms of evaluation would be:

- direct participant experience (those having influence in the interaction itself);

- indirect participant experience (observers, such as a general audience member or professional critic);

- technical evaluation of component algorithms of a work.

The timescale of feedback can vary from immediate and part of the system – for example, a variant of Al Biles' GenJam software was influenced by audience voting [Biles, 2002] – to delayed cultural impact over time. Different target groups provide interesting perspectives; Addessi *et al.* [2004] evaluated the Continuator with children as opposed to the usual adult musicians, demonstrating how a system can still appeal when users have short attention spans!

A new and vibrant arena for computer music research interweaves the computer science, sociology and psychology of human–computer interaction with electronic music [Wanderley and Orio, 2002]. HCI research is a useful resource for investigating why musicians might prefer the affordances of one interface over another, or why direct action[13] can appeal above abstraction. In an extensive survey of 200 participants, Magnusson and Hurtado [2007] solicited detailed feedback on users' experiences of digital musical instruments, particularly compared with traditional acoustic instruments. They found virtues and failures for both, and artists tended to employ both as needed in their works. While digital systems were judged as supporting experimentalism, introducing artificial intelligence and new sound transformations, acoustic instruments tended to be the most ergonomic as direct extensions of the human body, paying careful homage to traditional musical assumptions.

Aside from surveys, other HCI methods cover both qualitative and quantitative bases, including structured interview techniques, group exploration sessions and task performance testing, all of which might examine musical systems in or immediately after a context of use. In my doctoral thesis, I evaluated five interactive music systems using a methodology of Contextual Inquiry, where musicians performed with the machines and then reflected on each rehearsal run [Collins, 2006c]. In assessing the automatic accompaniment chord generation of the MySong system (later commercially released as Songsmith), Simon *et al.* [2008] compared computer-generated chords to those created by expert musicians, and also tracked use of the system by 13 inexperienced non-musicians. Kiefer *et al.* [2008a] compared

---

[13] In HCI, this has been studied as 'direct manipulation' [Preece *et al.*, 1994, pp. 270–2].

the affordances of the Wiimote as a musical controller to a MIDI drum pad and controller dials, through constrained quantitatively assessed tasks (with software logging of control data) and qualitative reporting. Stowell *et al.* [2009] assessed an interactive system that tracks beatboxing input, using Discourse Analysis as a formal method of transcribing interview sessions. They also examined whether human drummers could differentiate beat tracking software from another human participant or a steady metronome. Though they called this a musical Turing test, as Christopher Ariza [2009] has cogently argued, we must be extremely careful in invoking Turing, whose test of artificial intelligence is really only applicable to the full social case of language use rather than music making. Nevertheless, 'spot the difference' testing may be a useful part of evaluating how well virtual musicians blend into human musical activities.

It is extremely difficult to solicit linguistic feedback while musicians are in the flow (talk-aloud protocols do not work well during music making!). How can we then gain access to the realtime affective experience of a musician? This topic was already raised when discussing physiological sensors. The **third paradigm** in HCI seeks access to subjective response through objective sensor readings [Mandryk *et al.*, 2006; Kiefer *et al.*, 2008b]. Any advances here may also be extremely useful in simulating the rich emotional experience of music making, finding further ways to bring machines closer to human musicianship. While we must be careful not to claim too much, some measurements of affect may prove to be of worth both in evaluation and incorporated into live systems. For instance, there is no discounting the fun factor in assessing interfaces. Lazzaro [2008] gives many examples of evaluations carried out for gaming, a domain with affinity to much musical experience.

For further information, the interested reader is directed to the HCI textbooks in this chapter's bibliography. Techniques are applicable at many stages of the iterative design cycle, and while there will always be idiosyncratic and personal artistic works, interactive systems that are intended for more public use can particularly benefit from HCI methodologies. In practice, the willingness to consider evaluation is itself of great worth, and there are many benefits just to actively soliciting the feedback of other people, even on a relatively informal footing.[14]

6.6 SUMMARY

This chapter has traversed the landscape of interaction and covered interfacing the world with computers, and making computers part of effective interactions in a number of artistic domains. We have surveyed various types of input device and their connection to computers, from standard office computing interfaces to more exotic physical and physiological sensors. We have seen how interactive systems could be

---

[14]Running more formal experiments introduces definite ethical dimensions into consideration, which can be pursued in the references, but informal evaluation can still be beneficial and will not typically invoke the specter of ethics committee approval.

built for different settings from sonic art to concert pieces. The design aims of musical work that incorporates the computer stretch from new digital instruments under close human control to independent artificial intelligences. For the latter we have met the challenges of building autonomous musical agents, from more highly constrained score-based systems to free improvisation machines. Finally, we have covered some issues in the evaluation of interactive music systems that may help to inform the design cycle for future work in this field.

6.7 EXERCISES

1. How many different ways can you find to control a sine tone using the input peripherals at your disposal, from within your favorite computer music system? You might try keyboard, MIDI keyboard, mouse, tablet, joystick, audio input and more . . . .

2. Investigating alternative controllers depends on your gaining access to components, from sensors to microcontrollers, that help with interfacing. Visit your local hardware, second-hand and electronics shops or online retailers for cheap equipment, from contact mics to game controllers that can be cannibalized for components.

3. Research a recently released interface device and its musical potential. Are there any YouTube or other videos already available? Now investigate a discontinued input peripheral, such as the Nintendo Entertainment System PowerGlove, comparing availability and projects. Finally, consider the case of the theremin, an electronic instrument invented in 1920. What sort of longevity do interface devices typically achieve?

4. Write a program in your favorite computer music environment that can extract the following features from an input stream of MIDI notes: (1) the number of notes in the last three seconds; (2) the average IOI in the last two seconds (consider what value to give if there are fewer than two notes in the window?); (3) the median MIDI note pitch in the last ten seconds (sort all the pitches into an ordered list and take the middle value(s)). Using these three features as inputs, create a simple response function that plays MIDI notes back. Experiment with your program, changing its behavior and perhaps trying new variations of the features until you are happy.

5. Remember that we don't necessarily have to model the psychology of human music making with our artificial systems (even though the stimulation of human ears is

a likely goal). Create an interactive music system using an abstract mapping, such as a cellular automata, a multiple-generation genetic algorithm, or a fractal. These algorithms might be controlled by quite abstract feature data as well! How hard is it for users to feel they are having an influence on the system? Are they still inspired by some of the system's output and the music made in the experiment?

6. Build an audio-based interactive music system, using a pitch detector, an onset detector and a beat tracker as feature extractors (see Section 3.5; these components should be available in current realtime computer music systems such as SuperCollider, Pd or Max/MSP, or if you're a hardcore coder, within C libraries such as Paul Brossier's aubio). Try using this information in two ways; first in an audio signal processing graph (such as a set of filters whose parameters are based on the measured features) and secondly in a symbolic-level system that responds by spawning new musical events. (Optional extra: you can follow the same task through as a comparison with a MIDI-based system, though here pitch and onset detection is trivial and you might need to write your own symbolic beat tracker or investigate work by Winkler [1998] or Rowe [2001].)

7. Plan a gallery installation for the massive Turbine Hall of London's Tate Modern, or another large-scale art venue. Your artwork should involve some advantage gained from computation, but may involve all manner of other media and physical interfaces, though audio should be the primary modality. How are factors of space, participation and throughput of visitors involved in your design? What interaction can an individual participant recognize in the system given a five-minute visit?

8. Brainstorm a new audio-based computer game. Audio will form the primary feedback, and there should be little to no visual feedback, but the game may utilize a standard games controller as input.

9. Having built an alternative controller or interactive music system, try to solicit feedback. This could be as simple as talking a friend through your system and getting them to perform with it, or working with a larger group of participants. You might want to consider how the feedback you get from someone who simply observes a performance is different from the feedback from someone who directly performs with the system.

10. You can read more about HCI evaluation techniques in the further reading for this chapter. Here is one suggestion for guiding a try-out session on a system. In evaluation by successive revelation, you gradually tell the participants more about the system as they perform with it multiple times. The first time, they will use the system without any background information. This can provide very pertinent information about your own assumptions, how well they translated to other possible users and the immediacy of your device! The second time, you might explain a little more about the system before they play. Prior to the third time

could see you revealing everything you wanted them to know in the session, and even guiding them in training if there is an aspect that is still proving difficult. In-between the try-outs, you can ask questions, and get their reactions. It is a fine line between guiding their responses too closely (perhaps by suggesting things you want to hear because you are eager for feedback on a specific aspect) and giving them some space for wider reflection.

6.8

FURTHER READING

Collins, K. (2008). *Game Sound*. MIT Press, Cambridge, MA.

Collins, K. (ed) (2008). *From Pac-Man to Pop Music: Interactive Audio in Games and New Media*. Ashgate, Aldershot, Hampshire.

Dean, R. (2003). *Hyper-improvisation: Computer-Interactive Sound Improvisation*. A-R Editions, Inc., Middleton, WI.

LaBelle, B. (2007). *Background Noise: Perspectives on Sound Art*. Continuum, New York, NY.

Licht, A. (2007). *Sound Art: Beyond Music, Between Categories*. Rizzoli International Publications, Inc., New York, NY.

Matarić, M. J. (2007). *The Robotics Primer*. MIT Press, Cambridge, MA.

Miranda, E. R. and Wanderley, M. M. (2006). *New Digital Musical Instruments: Control and Interaction Beyond the Keyboard*. A-R Editions, Inc., Middleton, WI.

NIME (New Interfaces for Musical Expression) Conference Proceedings available online via www.nime.org

Ord-Hume, A. W. J. G. (1973). *Clockwork Music: An Illustrated History of Mechanical Musical Instruments*. George Allen and Unwin Ltd., London.

O'Sullivan, D. and Igoe, T. (2004). *Physical Computing*. Thomson Course Technology PTR, Boston, MA.

Preece, J. *et al.* (1994). *Human–Computer Interaction*. Addison-Wesley, Wokingham, UK.

Rowe, R. (1993). *Interactive Music Systems*. MIT Press, Cambridge, MA.

Rowe, R. (2001). *Machine Musicianship*. MIT Press, Cambridge, MA.

Sears, A. and Jacko, J. A. (eds) (2008). *The Human-Computer Interaction Handbook*, 2nd Edition. Lawrence Erlbaum Associates, New York, NY.

Wanderley, M. M. and Battier, M. (eds) (2000). *Trends in Gestural Control of Music*. IRCAM, Paris. Available at http://www.music.mcgill.ca/~mwanderley/Trends/

Winkler, T. (1998) *Composing Interactive Music: Techniques and Ideas Using Max*, MIT Press, Cambridge, MA.

Chapter 7

Networks

'[I]f our social lives take place within data networks, we need music to be part of it.'

Chris Brown [Traub, 2005, p. 469]

OBJECTIVES

This chapter covers:

- the fundamentals of networks;
- network music and networked ensembles;
- mobile music;
- online music distribution;
- music information retrieval (MIR).

7.1 INTRODUCTION TO NETWORKS

The idea of a network is not new, as the history of telecommunications, transport and computer science can demonstrate [Rohrhuber, 2007]. The nodes and links in abstract mathematical models of networks are in real life our telephones and wires, or our cities and roads. A relevant example from this book is the unit generator network, with the units as nodes, and the virtual wires as links. What gets passed around a network varies with these examples, from analog signals, people and goods, to digital audio and control data.

The formatting of the message itself, the protocol, is an important practical matter; MIDI and Open Sound Control provide two musical models here. Networks also naturally evoke the distribution of processing work among multiple interacting sites. Here, collaborative music motivates a possible analogy, where the nodes are the musicians and the links a number of channels of social and musical information. Musical ensembles that make the exploitation of network technology a central part of their discourse will be encountered in this chapter.

Because digital networks have become ubiquitous in our culture, it is hard to write about computer music without spending a little time in their hubs and spokes. The prime exemplar of a big interconnected system is the Internet with a capital I. Historically preceded by early networks such as ARPAnet (first inter-site connection established in 1969), the Internet arose in the 1980s as a unification of all existing networks through standard communication protocols (the TCP/IP Internet Protocol Suite). The most popular manifestation of the Internet is the World Wide Web, which provides additional infrastructure, especially the web page engine familiar through browser software. The Web and the Internet are so synonymous in most popular usage that I shall proceed in an informal way without worrying further about the niceties of their distinction, and hope that more obsessive technologists don't hunt me down for it. While this chapter will not restrict itself to web-based music, the Internet is a prime site for new musical activity and discovery.

Netcraft's August 2008 survey estimated that there were around 176 million websites.[1] Using some other statistics obtained online, the average number of web pages per website is around 300, and the average number of links per page is 40 (with 10 external and 30 internal). This works out to around 50 billion web pages, and two trillion links. To use an analogy that has recurred in various science fiction novels and online theories, one human brain by comparison has around one hundred billion neurons, and 150 trillion synapses.[2] Of course, the World Wide Web has a very different structure and architecture from the biological brain; each computer is a far more powerful individual information processor than a single neuron, and the modules of the Internet are rather different in kind from those of the central nervous system.

Flowery language might be excused at this point, since it's easy to get enthusiastic about such a hubbub of human knowledge. There may be a myriad human flaws in its implementation (particularly rival browsers' compliance to specifications) and a host of strange abbreviations to suffer, but the Internet has made a very real impact on learning (think Wikipedia), communication (think Skype), commerce (think entering your credit card details into Amazon) and more. Naturally, digital music has systematically exploited the Internet as a distribution medium for products and tools, as a collaborative and social network, and in net art, as a subject or carrier of digital art itself [Galloway, 2007; Hugill, 2005].

---

[1] There are four billion IP v4 addresses, and, because of the total numbers of processors embedded in mobiles and new ubi-comp embedded devices combined, there is currently danger of these running out! Fortunately, the computer industry always has another abbreviation in wait – IP v6 in this case …

[2] http://faculty.washington.edu/chudler/facts.html

However, just as computer music has many precursors, there are many anticipations of Internetwork music in telecommunications. These include the Théâtrophone concert transmission service (commercialized 1890), the piped music for restaurants of Cahill's great early synthesizer, the Telharmonium (1906), mail art and mail order albums (such as Frank Zappa's guitar exhibitionism), Max Neuhaus's *Public Supply* (1966) broadcast, which mixed incoming telephone calls to a radio station, and Richard Teitelbaum's *Alpha Bean Lima Bean* (1971), which saw the remote manipulation of some jumping beans in a New York gallery by brain waves transmitted via telephone from San Francisco [Rohrhuber, 2007]. To quote David Rosenboom's description of another fantastical project:

> Biotelemetry has been used in theater environments. One notable experiment, organized by Richard Lowenberg and associates in California, involved brainwave, muscle and accelerometer signal measurements from two groups of dancers, one located on the West Coast and one on the East Coast of the U.S.A. The signals were translated into sound and video displays and transmitted between the two groups by means of satellite communications provided courtesy of NASA. [Rosenboom, 1997]

Digital telecommunications offers ease and perfect fidelity of transmission. Nevertheless, the sheer computing power on offer via the Internet is a step change. Computers as service providers are tireless automatons, ready for you to shop at whatever odd hour of the morning takes your fancy, providing videos and MP3s and new audio plug-ins on demand, giving the opportunity to exploit far greater computer resources and services than you would otherwise access on your own machine. Some office work is now tied to web applications running on computer farms under deserts . . . . From a musician's perspective, it is not inconceivable that web browsers will come to support musical applications as services loaned out by audio software companies. Although time-critical applications may have to run locally, time might be hired rather than purchasing a copy. There are already many remote processing services that are available as required, such as cepstral.com's online speech synthesis interface, or the online audio plug-in compiler for Faust (http://faust.grame.fr/compiler.php).

As history has proved, new telecommunications media always provide interesting chances to connect with other human beings. In the case of the Internet, distribution models have been challenged, especially for digital products, but more abstractly for information itself, and old social structures overturned or undermined. We must, however, temper claims with the realization that only a minority of the human population is wired. According to Chapman and Chapman [2006], 16% of homes have computers with Internet access, and the proportions vary greatly between different regions of the world (many regions do not have electricity to start with, let alone regular power). As will be discussed later on, the increased CPU power of mobile phones is one way in which more of these communities are being brought online. Although many vested interests lurk here, from corporations to freedom activists, the growth of the Web to become the humane monster it is today has been so propulsive a force with so much economic and social impact that it could not help but form a major topic for computer music, and one likely to dominate many proceedings in the coming years. This is not the sole motivation for this chapter, but it is a strong background force.

7.1.1 Network Technology

You're surely already familiar with the Internet, from daily use, as spanning computers around the world, and the concept of a unit generator graph has already introduced network architectures as information flow graphs, within a single program on a single computer. You may be familiar with concepts of graphs (nodes and links) as data structures, as used in computer science, or with neuroscience or artificial neural nets. Networks are just a way of distributing information processing, potentially between every connected computational device in the world. For a general image of a network, think of lots of black boxes, each with multiple inputs and outputs, connected up together in a huge tangle. Perhaps this reminds you of your own brain? The sort of data passed around this network becomes increasingly abstract as the boxes themselves become more powerful computers. While neurons in a brain subsist on changes in electrical potential and unit generators might only be expecting audio and control rate inputs, a general box could take a whole uploaded file, or a stream of information based on an arbitrary protocol.

There are various standard architectures [Weinberg, 2005; Rohrhuber, 2007], and Figure 7.1 shows some examples. The idea of a central server to which many clients can attach themselves is one (think of multiple users connecting to a website, or games server); peer-to-peer communication without any centralized hub is another. For the World Wide Web, each accessible computational device has a unique Internet Protocol (IP) address and is accessed via a specific port number. The IP addresses are linked in a dictionary to domain names, being looked up by the computer automatically (cached, or via a Domain Name Server) when you type in humanly readable web addresses.

For the 32-bit IP v4, the IP addresses take the form xxx.xxx.xxx.xxx where xxx is from 0 to 255, and a few of the addresses are reserved; for instance, 127.0.0.1 is a loopback address, which allows a computer to send messages to itself, and, therefore, connect up different applications on the same computer as an *intranet*. Port numbers differentiate different services or programs; while 80 is a standard port number for accessing web pages from a remote server, inter-application network messaging might take advantage of any numbers from 0 to 65 535 (a 16-bit range). For instance, the SuperCollider 3 software [McCartney, 2002], an inherently network-based computer music client language and synthesis server, uses ports 57 120 for the control language and 57 110 for the synthesizer. It is possible to send messages to either one from further applications, so Pd might control the synthesis server without even using the language at all.

The Internet is just the most famous example of an internet, and network protocols can be used to set up your own messaging between applications on single or distinct computers.

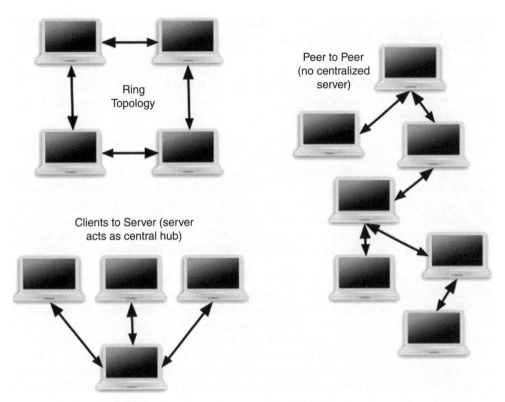

Figure 7.1 Some standard network architectures. While this diagram depicts computers, the networked entities could also be mobile phones or software programs running on a single computer, or the diagram could even model the diffusion of news through social encounters!

An example of this might be synchronizing two laptops to a common clock, or passing data between an audio and a video program when creating live audiovisuals. Two standard protocols here are **TCP (Transmission Control Protocol)**[3] and **UDP (User Datagram Protocol)**. UDP is less reliable in terms of transmission (there are no checks on whether packets of data actually arrive at their destination) but hence the padding of the data and the communication overhead is much less. In practice, UDP is fine as long as there are no major consequences to losing the odd packet. For a continuous stream of controller data, losing the occasional value is not typically a big issue. Still, lost packets can be a bigger deal when passing audio data around by UDP; as an amusing demonstration of this, the NEST (Network Examination of Serendipitous Transfer) project makes a virtue out of the gradual corruption of an audio file passed between participating computers (http://c6.org/nest/).

---

[3]You may also see this written TCP/IP where the additional IP means Internet Protocol again. IP is actually a further underlying layer common to TCP and UDP. Because these are the most important protocols for the Internet as a whole, TCP/IP is also used in a general sense – as in the TCP/IP Internet Protocol Suite.

Open Sound Control (often referred to as OSC) provides a readily customizable network protocol for computer music [Wright, 2005]. While some system designers prefer to simply send TCP or UDP messages to their own specification, OSC has many convenient existing implementations, is highly efficient, and can be customized sufficiently for most needs. Learning lessons from the assumptions built into MIDI (see Chapter 2), OSC is much less rigid in what music is actually declared to be, simply providing a way to wrap up data in messages with user-defined address tags.

OSC has been adopted by many software synthesizers and computer music languages, and is sufficiently established to actually form the basis of communication between some sensor interfaces and computers. The aforementioned SuperCollider 3 audio environment actually uses OSC as an essential part of the system, in order to communicate between a language application and a separate sound synthesis server. This makes SuperCollider an inherently network-music-ready environment, as well as supporting alternative clients within different languages. In the same way, OSC makes it straightforward to communicate between applications, allowing the combination of different software.

The World Would Work Wonderfully if we could send as much data as we liked at infinitesimal delay. However, telecommunications is still, more's the pity, restricted by the ultimate limit of the speed of light, with additional overheads from the computers themselves. Live jams combining musicians on opposite sides of the world are therefore hampered by **latency**, though a number of ways to get around this limitation through free improvisation, shared rhythmic structures or even exploiting the delay itself for musical purposes will be discussed below. An exercise at the end of this chapter will have you calculate the actual delays involved for typical international jams; you may be familiar with the ping time, as the round-trip delay to get a message to and from a remote computer. For practical purposes, same-room networks (local area networks, or LANs) have delays on the order of milliseconds, which is perceptually – well, imperceptible in most circumstances.

Musicians can accommodate a small fixed delay. Traditionally this occurs when performers are distributed widely enough that acoustic traveling time becomes a factor, as when organists play from a different position from the choir in a church.[4] Conductors, bass drum players, and those with slow soundcards often have to commence an action substantially ahead of the sounding time, and it is possible to learn to play while compensating for fixed latency, even if it is not always ideal. A ballpark acceptable ping (round-trip) time in network musical performance is around 20 milliseconds [Álvaro Barbosa, 2003; Wright, 2005]. A duo clapping experiment by Chafe and Gurevich [2004] saw the most steady performance at 11.5 milliseconds of one-way transmission delay; over 20 milliseconds caused deceleration as both parties found themselves waiting for one another. Slower Internet connections over larger distances often surpass 100 milliseconds of latency, severely compromising coordination except when certain contrivances are applied, such as playing to a measure while you hear all players' contributions from the previous measure (for example, try www.ninjam.com).

---

[4]The case of the orchestra is interesting. An orchestra spread in a semicircle of 10 meters radius would have a delay of around 60 milliseconds between players at opposite reaches of the orchestra. But a conductor coordinates players through visual signals, and light is effectively instantaneous.

Network messaging can also suffer from jitter on the arrival time of any information packet so that an evenly emitted stream arrives with random fluctuations in timing. It is possible to trade off additional delay to overcome timing jitter. For the case of evenly spaced packets, such as an audio sample stream, buffering can accommodate as much jitter as the delay line length. For unevenly sent messages, all messages can be timestamped with future times, so that they can be scheduled on arrival, as long as the delivery time is less than the introduced minimum scheduling delay. This does require the receiver's clock to be known or estimated, and is most effective when networked computers are running on the same clock (one of the exercises will have you investigate how to achieve that).

Network connections not only introduce delay but have limited bandwidth, only being able to transport so much data. In most current circumstances, it is far more practical to send multiple channels of control data than audio data, and sending (particularly uncompressed) audio data is a recipe for swamping networks. Although Internet2 links have allowed live transmission of multichannel audio streams over great distances, and speeds increase all the time to thwart authors,[5] historically network music has had to confront the issue of bandwidth intimately. Note as well that while audio codecs help with reducing the weight of data, they imply a cost in terms of encoding and decoding time, which introduces further delay. Certainly for local networks, audio data is most readily passed around by standard cables.

With a few provisos, networks provide many exciting opportunities; otherwise we wouldn't be bothering to connect our devices or go online at all.[6] Distributed processing pools computing resources, and the Internet provides access to all sorts of information, and information processing services, that no single computer could ever house.

7.1.2 Network Music and Installations

We now turn to further examples of the use of networks for music. Some related issues concerning multi-user instruments and ensemble performance will be covered in subsequent subsections.

If there is an archetypal network ensemble in computer music, it is **The Hub**, also known through their predecessor group, the **League of Automatic Music Composers** [Bischoff *et al.*, 1985; Brown and Bischoff, 2002]. Here, data is passed directly between local computers – in early concerts in a circular ring formation, later via a central hub – rather than solely via acoustic and visual cues. Although human performers are still intimately involved in the feedback loops, and the repertoire of the group consists of many different works with varied structure and network architecture, it would fair to say that the communication between the programs running on the different machines (one computer per performer) is an essential part of the aesthetic of the group. A typical set-up in The Hub is for each performer to allow

---

[5]If Moore's Law hasn't now been officially repealed, you're probably streaming 48 384 KHz 64-bit audio channels over wireless in real time as you read this.

[6]It is highly therapeutic, however, to take the odd day off from network connectivity; email addiction is a surefire way to soak up your time, and you'd be amazed at the things you can also learn from real books in libraries.

three input control data streams from other ensemble members and also to send out three streams, the interconnections being mediated by the network hub. These network computer music pioneers began to employ the Kim-1 computer kit in the mid 1970s, in California's Bay Area (they later adopted MIDI and OSC as these became available). Befitting their open and democratic politics, the group membership has fluctuated in personnel, and all members have been active in composing for the ensemble. Writing on their philosophy, Bischoff *et al.* [1985, pp. 596–599] note: 'Very high technology is *about* working together in large-scale teams, e.g. the space program. It should be no different for modern music .... Though synthesizers always offered the potential of multisynthesizer group music, and there are some nice examples, micro-computers seem to fit the group-music situation even better. One can show up at a rehearsal or a performance with little more than computer in hand .... When the elements of the network are not connected the music sounds like ... completely independent processes, but when they are interconnected the music seems to present a "mindlike" aspect'.

Following the League and The Hub's sterling example, networking has naturally been explored in much laptop music. Perhaps the idea of interconnecting computers is now so commonplace that it is less often remarked upon as a significant feature of works; the laptop ensembles and orchestras to be mentioned below employ various forms of data sharing and message passing for individual works and settings. Synchronization for rhythmic jams is one common application, as well as inter-performer chat servers (for noisy venues, displaced performers and text obsessives). The most significant networked interactions remain the exchange of digital data, for instance between audio and visual programs running on separate computers. One example here is the 'audiovisual feedback' set up by the Swedish duo klipp av [Collins and Olofsson, 2006], where audio input is analyzed in audio software and feature data then sent to visual software on a second computer to transform captured video that is itself analyzed for features to send back to the first computer, which then ....

Local area networks keep latency low enough to be imperceptible. Many projects make a virtue of network performance between much more remote locations. These projects tend to center-stage the telepresence to a much greater degree, since they must admit the latencies involved. Video links as well as audio and data transmission are employed to keep audiences apprised of remote participants in concert situations, or to abet extra-musical communication of gesture, intent and emotion between performers. Some more recent projects have attempted to use new fast high-bandwidth links, such as Internet2, to minimize latency and maximize data sharing for high quality audio.[7] In one recent performance at the 2008 International Computer Conference, groups on stage in Belfast (The Roots Ensemble), in New York (Tintinabulate) and at Stanford (SoundWire) performed Pauline Oliveros's structured improvisation *Tele-morphosis*. 'Co-located' musicians were joined by high-speed video and audio links. OSC-controlled haptic actuator devices (Curtis Bahn and Dane Kouttron's vibrobytes) provided further stimulus to guide the resulting ensemble

---

[7]The speed of light will remain a likely barrier to intercontinental and certainly to intergalactic jams free of latency in the near to end-of-time future.

improvisation; in practice, musicians responded to LEDs, except for Pauline Oliveros herself who wore three pancake motors!

Internet music provides new paradigms for remote surrogacy, with many online music systems and collaborative domains for musicians. Sergi Jorda's FMOL (Faust Music OnLine) involves a manipulable graphical world representing the different signals flowing during performance, and the system is usable both in online collaborative composition and in concert as a performance instrument [Jordà, 2005]. Auracle is a collaborative synthesizer, where each user's voice is analyzed locally for features; the data is transferred to a server for sharing and co-control, allowing multi-user jams [Freeman *et al.*, 2005]. Online gaming and online virtual worlds such as Second Life provide further sites for networked musical interaction.

Net art explores network technology, typically with the Internet as its medium. As well as enabling certain artistic ventures through the technological infrastructure, some net art also engages with the issues of telepresence and social transformation that virtual communities and remote connections bring. Three installations with a musical twist will be briefly sketched. Drawing on both acoustics and networks, [The User]'s *Silophone* project (since 2001, www.silophone.net) allows remote users to utilize a grain silo in Montreal as a reverberator, submitting their samples to be processed. Atau Tanaka and Kaspar Toeplitz's *Global String* (2000, http://www.sensorband.com/atau/globalstring/index2.html) is a multi-site gallery installation where physical strings threaded with sensors translate human action into collaborative action at a distance via virtual string models. Finally, Masayuki Akamatsu's *Incubator* (1999, http://www.iamas.ac.jp/~aka/incubator/) used a local area network in a gallery to network 50 iMacs. An updated version (*snowflake*) produced in 2008 uses gallery visitors' iPhones instead.

Distinguishing the variety of work in this area, Hugill [2005] proposes a provisional taxonomy, which takes in:

- connecting musicians in live performance through computer networks (e.g. internet jamming software, tele-music making);

- virtual worlds (musical avatars in online environments);

- network data translated into sound (sonification of data traffic);

- online collaboration (co-composition through a shared interface);

- online musical interaction, from click and play to more elaborate web interfaces (Internet radio, sound toys).

Many of the projects mentioned here and more besides, as well as further taxonomies of such work, are discussed in other articles [Álvaro Barbosa, 2003; Traub, 2005; Föllmer, 2005; Rohrhuber, 2007].

7.1.3 Further Network Music Ensembles and the Laptop Orchestra

Because one computer can be programmed with all the elements required for the playback of complete works, there is an inclination for live computer music performances to require few to no human beings. This situation includes the playback of pre-rendered sequences as well as autonomous virtual musicians and more direct interactions. However, if a sound synthesis patch has many control parameters, it can be difficult for a single human operator to tweak all of these simultaneously, even with the best MIDI control box in the world. Rather than automating less important parameters and focusing on a few manageable ones fit for a single user, multi-user instruments can be designed, and ensembles formed, which distribute the cognitive load. This has to be a deliberate design and sensitively handled; while multi-computer ensembles have appeared in the context of laptop jams, for example, players often find that they do not have an adequate sense of contributing, when it only takes one performer to fill up the whole spectrum with white noise.[8]

Perhaps multi-user concerts are the most natural domain of (often aphysical) computer music; the conflicting cognitive load of algorithmic thinking and the need for human intervention can be more fairly spread under cover of multiple performers. Live coders find it much easier to perform when they can provide cover for each other, so that they are not always exposed solo. In a 2005 panel on interactive computer music at the International Computer Music Conference[9] Sergi Jordà declared that 'it is within this *multi-threaded+shared* paradigm that new digital instruments can offer their best ... whether they are called *interactive music systems*, *extended instruments*, *composed instruments*, *intelligent instruments* ... makes no difference in the end'. This viewpoint is an interesting claim for the primacy of human beings in interactions with electronic music technology. Rather than necessarily deferring all activity to artificial intelligences, there is great interest in the points at which humans retain control. We already met a great example of a sharable instrument in Jordà and colleagues' Reactable in Chapter 6: multiple performers can lean over the same augmented tabletop, manipulating a common representation.

There is a sense in which traditional acoustic ensembles are networked, akin to a local area network, within line of sight or the limits of audition. Performing as one, perhaps synchronized from the gesture of a leader within the ranks or explicit conductor, perhaps working to a communally sanctioned structure, perhaps setting up temporary alliances and oppositions in improvisation, through acoustic and visual communication. The notion of 'distributed musicianship' is regimented on almost military lines for some large ensembles and orchestras, but also apparent in shared instruments (such as a shared piano for a four-hands duet, or the four-player reyong, a horizontal gong set in Balinese Gamelan). The sociability we have noted before as a central part of music making necessarily calls for

---

[8] This fault is partially due to the lack of experience of some performers in considerate group improvisation and performance, but is an especial danger with computer music when such extremes of acoustic power can be achieved by any single player.

[9] The other panelists were Joel Chadabe with his 'sailing the stormy seas' control metaphor, David Wessel with an argument for physicality and human agency that began with the assertion that 'the first thing I learn to do in an interactive system is work out how to turn the sound off', Robert Rowe revealing his work converting from MIDI-based machine listening to audio, and myself presenting the live coding organization TOPLAP (www.toplap.org).

distributed, participative works (solo recitals in this view are rather aberrant). Electronic music also has its ensembles: from theremin groups, through Musica Elettronica Viva[10] to Kraftwerk, Mother Mallard and beyond. Computer music seeks further ways to distribute human cognitive resources essential to the exciting, effective and disciplined live performance of a work.

The idea of placing human performers throughout a network of computers was met already with the central example of The Hub, who form an important locus in any network music discussion. The rise of the laptop has naturally also led to laptop music ensembles. Examples include multi-laptop electronica ensembles (e.g., Farmers Manual, 1995) or mixed acoustic and computer improvisation ensembles such as MIMEO (Music in Motion Electronic Orchestra, 1997). I'll continue to sprinkle in the dates of first performances of ensembles mentioned in this section to give a sense of the field.

An original chamber ensemble along these lines is **PowerBooks_UnPlugged** (PB_UP, see http://pbup.goto10.org/) who claim to be the first wireless acoustic computer folk band (their first performances date back to 2004). Drawing on up to six performers, PB_UP eschew speaker stacks, and simply play via their individual laptop speakers,[11] distributing themselves around a venue so that sounds naturally spatialize over the laptop locations (see Figure 7.2). They merge among the audience, intensifying their sense of communal listening. Each player can create processes that utilize every other player's laptop, with all the computers connected via a wireless network. They code live, sharing ideas by sharing code. As their website states:

> Another beneficial implication of the networked band architecture is the gradual vanishing of one's musical and artistic ego, along with rock star volume [as it persisted for centuries]. Since instruments and control algorithms are shared, there's no real owner anymore; the creators are discrete musical entities only if they choose to be, ideas belong to everyone. This aspect places the band's work in the context of a new tradition of multi-client, multi-user artistic practice. Even the number of band members is not a fixed one anymore: it varies from three to six or more players, like clouds coalescing and evaporating depending on local circumstances.

The laptop orchestra makes an explicit parallel to the classical orchestra. The credit for the first avowed performance might go to the eponymous **laptop orchestra** (http://laptoporchestra.net/) whose first session involved 20 participants performing at Ryogoku House, Tokyo on 18 August 2002. In terms of accumulating publicity, the most famous recent laptop orchestra is **PLOrk**, the Princeton Laptop Orchestra [Trueman, 2007; Smallwood *et al.*, 2008] (http://plork.cs.princeton.edu/), whose debut concert was

---

[10] http://www.alvincurran.com/writings/mev.html
[11] This sacrifices bass frequencies, and the ensemble retain for themselves the option of an additional networked computer controlling a subwoofer as an adjunct resource.

Figure 7.2   PB_UP: live outside and inside. Reproduced by permission of © Hannes Hoelzl.

on 22 January 2006. The orchestra scales up to 15 performers, each having an identical kit of laptop, interface devices and a hemispherical speaker at their station. Works are specifically written for the ensemble, which can exploit various computer music software environments, employ wireless networking to pass data between players, and cue musical action both electronically and via more traditional conducting channels. PLOrk has by now completed a number of seasons, establishing itself as an institution that should have the staying power to create a performance tradition and repertoire in this vein.

Both PB_UP and PLOrk show the importance of space as an element in these ensembles; things become muddy when multiple computer musicians share a PA system with fewer channels than performers, but the localization of each player's contribution at their own station (whether via hemispherical speaker or built-in laptop speakers) benefits the performer's own feedback as to their local contribution, and distinguishes multiple acoustic streams. While networking allows remote control, which again muddies the sense of precise origin, the inherent spatialization is a wonderful resource for sequences that cause events to trigger in patterns over the ensemble. Furthermore, precise control of timing through timestamped messaging allows for perfect unisons, or appropriately built-in delays, even compensating for the speed of sound travel (since the electromagnetic waves of the wireless connection outpace sound and travel at the speed of light).

The laptop orchestra's time seems to have come, with a number of other ensembles springing up, and sizes being reported from 50 performers (Worldscape Laptop Orchestra, late 2007), to 200. A list of ensembles (some of which have accumulated for single events, and are far more heterogeneous than the homogeneous Princeton model) could include the Helsinki Computer Orchestra (March 2003), Seattle Laptop Orchestra (Dec. 2005, http://www.laptoporchestra.com/about.html), CybOrk (Moscow, May 2006, http://cyberorchestra.com/), Unknown Devices from the London College of Communications (Feb. 2007) and the Stanford Laptop Orchestra (Spring 2008). Some of these ensembles allow glorified laptop jams, but others take the notions of control structure very seriously, with conductors and scores, differentiating sections of the orchestra and player roles. The power relationships in ensembles can become difficult. The Hub, for example, favor equality above hierarchy: 'An orchestra especially should have a structure that exhibits the best types of sociopolitical arrangements imaginable.' Bischoff *et al.* [1985, p. 598]. However, the enhanced flexibility of computer music in the first place makes it straightforward to rework the idea of the ensemble with every piece. The extent to which any permanent repertoire will be established will only be found in time.

7.1.4 Mobile Music

As of June 2008, 32% of the population of the world had access to their own mobile phones,[12] with more than three and a half billion handsets in existence. This compares with one billion home computers. Convergence of digital media across telecommunications platforms, bringing together television, telephone and Internet in computational devices, is most generally accessible in mobiles rather than home PCs.

With the inevitable ramping up of processing power, mobiles provide an attractive new platform for computer music making, both as controllers and as stand-alone instruments. They are, after all, built for portability and durability and have relatively long battery lives, and audio input and output is a standard part of their armory! Although development on small screens is reminiscent of the difficult programming of old hardware sequencers and synths via liquid crystal display screens, the graphics capabilities of mobiles are expanding. It may soon just be a matter of carrying around a lightweight additional monitor to plug in, just as foldout keyboards for qwerty typing are available! Even if the mobile is not the chief development hub at the moment, software can be prepared on a desktop or laptop for downloading to the phone (similarly to writing code for microcontrollers), with a number of development environments supporting phone operating system simulations. These operating systems themselves are becoming increasingly open to the general coder, from much existing support for Java including the Mobile Processing environment [Li, 2007], to newer open-source operating systems like Google's Android.[13] Smart phones such as the iPhone also provide co-optable interface technology such as touch screens, and have been hooked up by many artists to control interactive systems, or for stand-alone phone software (e.g., *RjDj* and their attempt to popularize generative music http://www.rjdj.me/what/).

Bluetooth, Wi-Fi and other wireless protocols are often used to enable remote control of computers from handheld sets and other forms of local inter-device communication. At heart, wireless employs radio transmission. One practical caution should be mentioned if utilizing such a facility in concert performance; it is wise to name devices distinctively, especially if setting up connections when many such devices might be being carried by the audience in a venue and your source is only one of hundreds available.[14]

---

[12]http://en.wikipedia.org/wiki/List_of_countries_by_number_of_mobile_phones_in_use

[13]The developer should be warned, however, that security implications in particular cause all sorts of headaches in preparing software for phones, and that processing limits are inevitably much tighter than for their larger computer brethren.

[14]Bluetooth can also fail in such circumstances, regardless of namespace (Jason Freeman, personal communication, December 2008).

Just as for laptop orchestras, mobiles are inherently spatialized en masse, and tinier yet due to their smaller size. And also, like laptop speakers, they can still be sufficiently loud to make themselves clearly heard, as anyone who has suffered overhearing a bad ringtone on a train or in an office could report. The mobile promises additional action during performance, even to the extent of performers running around a venue!

Given the ubiquity of mobiles, many digital artists have come to feature them in their work. Golan Levin and collaborators' *Dialtones (A Telesymphony)* (2001) is often cited. The audience's mobile numbers are compiled; they download specially prepared ringtones, and are assigned particular seats; the performance proceeds with the audience acting as a mass speaker array.

Greg Schiemer has been investigating multi-performer mobile music for some years, exploring various facets of microtonality in a series of pieces called *Mandala* created for the 'Pocket Gamelan' [Schiemer and Havryliv, 2006]. Each participant has a specially designed pouch for the mobile, which on a long cord can be swung around the performer's body, creating additional moving sound source effects (see Figure 7.3). In one work from this set, *Mandala 7* (2008), each performer contributes a successive chord to a polychord complex, across multiple iterations, each with its own leader. The performers get a choice of chord based on their number keypads, with varying durations for each selected chord. Having taken part in a performance of this piece, I can admit that it's pretty tiring on the arms, and it's hard to keep your concentration and not clatter the mobile against the ground ... but it can establish a wonderfully concentrated and otherworldly atmosphere for the audience. Each work in the Mandala series explores a different alternative tuning system, some also using peer-to-peer networking via Bluetooth for Java-capable phones.

Just as the laptop orchestra has arisen, so the mobile phone orchestra is being investigated. MoPhO, based at Stanford, California (http://ccrma.stanford.edu/groups/mopho/) gave their first performance on 11 January 2008. With 12 phones obtained from Nokia, the ensemble instruments are smartphones each with two digital cameras, stereo speakers, buttons, two accelerometers and of course a microphone. These first orchestral instruments have sufficient CPU power to allow four Karplus–Strong synthesis algorithm voices at once to be rendered in real time. MoPhO are working on their repertoire, exploring pieces written for phone that incorporate both musical and dramatic gestural detail. This can be seen as another direction for computer music ensemble work, with the potential to use network communication to share data, and for performers to run around a venue at the same time!

Aside from functioning as live controllers, mobiles have much potential as on-the-move audio software platforms, recording and playback devices, with inherent telepresence capabilities going far beyond those of the standard personal digital assistant. The audio capabilities of phones are an important resource, even if they have sometimes been squandered in less than salubrious ringtones. At least these are now becoming sufficiently customizable, allowing easy use of MP3s and the like, to have ruptured the market for embarrassing

Figure 7.3   Performance of Pocket Gamelan. Reproduced by permission of © Greg Schiemer.

monophonic and polyphonic ringtones (though audio snippets can still be purchased). Mobile games are now more popular, and one would expect a growth in generative audio software for mobiles, including generative ringtones that are subtly different with each incoming call. But it is the potential for all sorts of spontaneous musical participation in everyday environments that may provide the most obvious impact of the mobile in computer music.

7.1.5 Online Music Distribution

Following on from Section 2.7.2, we cannot help but treat some political hot potatoes: none of the following is intended (a) to discredit the universal joy of music making or (b) as legal advice that has any guarantee of validity for your country.

Digital distribution offers new models for musicians, with the potential to release their own material straight from home via a web server, without the need for any record label. '[I]t is hard to make the case that the music industry is anything other than middlemen' [Alderman, 2001, p.131]. A question mark hangs over whether they can ever really be cut out, though, as commercial interests have increasingly dominated certain thoroughfares of the Web. Lone musicians may get lucky in promoting their music and find interest snowballing, perhaps through word of mouth in chat rooms, a successful viral campaign or an amusing promotional YouTube video. But they cannot match the advertising budgets of major companies, nor easily gain the ear of the main media portals, which so many web surfers rely on to guide them to information. It may be straightforward to set up a MySpace page, release a CD via CDbaby and look busy from your own web page; but there are so many other artists now doing the same that headroom is extremely limited in practice. It is to be hoped, of course, that for those artists who don't wish to play the games of commerce, alternative communities (with their own forums, blogs, free download websites and more) still provide a valuable outlet without commercial connotations.

With the grand development of the Internet there have been conflicting voices to be heard, between on one side the advocates of full freedom of information and on the other the defenders of intellectual property rights. As an inherently international network of networks, the Web straddles the legal systems of many countries, making it difficult to give an exact summary of liabilities to cover all locations. Legal judgements often lag behind technologies, and it is hard for legislators to find the balance between encouraging new developments and assuaging existing vested commercial interests. The cautionary tale of the original Napster program [Alderman, 2001] is well worth reading, as eventually demonstrating the legal muscle of the Recording Industry Association of America after a period of rampant MP3 file sharing, but also its members' desire to leverage new markets, which saw Napster taken over by one of the big five[15] record companies in the midst of the lawsuit!

A suite of technologies have been developed for the diffusion of audio online, many dating back to the era of slower dial-up connections [Pohlmann, 2005, pp. 589–627]. MP3's wild popularity peaked because it was the first media format suitable to mass online distribution, preceding the larger movie downloads. MP3 (MPEG 1 Layer 3), AAC (Advanced Audio Coding), WMA (Windows Media Audio) and their ilk leverage psychoacoustic compression schemes, trading off quality against ratio of compression. Files are often streamed rather than transported en masse, supporting Internet broadcasting, for example with the proprietary Real Audio, or via more open alternatives such as Shoutcast and Icecast.[16] Mainstream recording industry interests have been pursued by many web systems since the 1990s, through various schemes for **digital rights management** (DRM). These extend from software tools such as proprietary container formats and playback engines (e.g., Liquid Audio, FairPlay, Windows Media DRM) utilizing encryption and watermarks, to hardware modification of physical media or machines. In one failed experiment in Germany in 2001, BMG released CDs that had been engineered to prevent home ripping. Unfortunately for them, they received so many returns (whether for technical incompatibility or ideological reasons) that they had to release an unprotected version of the CD! Because consumers'

---

[15]Since 2004 it is just the Big Four, if the companies haven't merged even more by now.
[16]To be fair, there is also the open source Helix DNA project initiated by RealNetworks with differentiated research and commercial licenses (https://helixcommunity.org/).

rights to make personal copies of media they own are enshrined in various laws (for instance, in the US, the 1992 Home Recording Act), DRM has remained a touchy subject.[17] At the time of writing, all major record companies are now experimenting with DRM-free music downloads across their catalogs, through a number of online retailers. Companies are also promoting subscription services (such as Emusic, Rhapsody or Spotify), which may allow a certain number of DRM-free downloads per month for a monthly fee, or a pure streaming broadcast service, potentially free with advertising, and reminiscent of a more personalized radio.

While the increased institutionalization of online music explores subscription, broadcast and advertising, it is too early to tell what business models and creative models will win out. Given the history of free music via file sharing, a process of constant negotiation is more likely between continued technical developments and legal challenges. To encapsulate the view that music could be free, and economic models are not necessarily healthy,[18] I quote one of Miller Puckette's contributions to a panel discussion on computer music:

> If composers started making music available in such a way that you could absolutely use it for anything, it would be amazing how fast the musical culture would then develop. The problem is that we're stuck on this outdated notion that the only way a composer or instrumentalist can survive is by forcing people to pay them for airtime. [Lyon, 2002, p. 28]

Alternative economic models, then, might deny copyright for recordings, or even for publishing; musicians might make money solely through live performance and merchandizing, or even not be expected to gain any profit from art. Perhaps love of music is sufficient to encourage the true musicians, and anyone who requires payment is a fraud? While some have argued that salaries must be paid to, for example, skilled orchestral musicians, there are enough dedicated high-quality players around with further jobs to undermine this notion somewhat.[19]

Even in models where musicians get paid, it is important to distinguish the deal for the artist from the interests of both record companies and consumers. The record companies are certainly no saints when it comes to fair deals for artists, and their claims to be acting in defense of artists' rights often shelter their real ambition to impose old business models behind the popularity of their more recognizable figureheads. As Robert Fripp noted in 2001, neither side in Napster versus the RIAA was really representing the artists

---

[17] One nasty complexity in the United States is the existence of clauses in the Digital Millennium Copyright Act that forbid tampering with DRM protection, even if one is only doing so for research or to make the copies supposedly allowed by the 1992 Act! It is possible to apply for exemptions in specific cases, but only on an infrequent cycle of application that can hardly keep up with technology development.

[18] A view which echoes that of Oswald [2004] on plunderphonics, and other voices of dissent from the current status quo so warped by the history of recording; see Section 2.7.2.

[19] Too many musicians are dismissed as 'amateur'. It is far healthier to regard all human beings as potentially great musicians, and acknowledge the continua of economic circumstance and opportunity for participation.

[Alderman, 2001, p. 153]! Nevertheless, the push and pull of new and old is an ongoing process. Harrower [2005] provides the interesting perspective of the UK's Performing Rights Society and Mechanical Copyright Protection Society in their efforts to come to administrate artist rights across the massive and international scale of Internet music databases. Sturm [2006b] has investigated the possible legal implications under US law for the sound synthesis technique of concatenative synthesis, which unleashes similar controversies to those provoked by digital sampling. Certainly, the wild west mentality of emerging technologies has often provided an edge some experimental artists can thrive upon, not necessarily to the satisfaction of existing rights holders!

To end on a note of hope, the Internet era has definitely opened up new distribution models, and at least you don't need a pressing factory and a fleet of trucks for mass distribution any more. Whether you want to conduct your own publicity, or try to gain access to a record company's cachet (and associated promotion and development budgets) may depend on the form your ambitions take. There is nothing wrong with smaller communities, and there are many technologies out there to help an individual establish a musical presence, and potentially get paid (most likely a small amount) through legal channels in doing so. The entry cost is owning a computer and an Internet connection.

7.2 MUSIC INFORMATION RETRIEVAL

The 2008 Digital Music Report of the IFPI [International Federation of the Phonographic Industry, 2008] announces the existence of more than 500 legitimate digital music providers online, with a combined total of over six million available tracks for purchase. The year 2007 saw 1.7 billion downloads, and increases across the sector in mobile music downloads, online store use and portable digital music player sales (online music accounted for around 15% of the market). To listen to six million tracks, assuming an average playing time of three minutes and only 16 hours available for listening every day, would take around 51 years of your life. And, of course, these statistics fail to take into account the vast array of non-commercial, experimental and independent recordings particularly empowered by new digital music tools. There were estimated to be 25 million songs on MySpace alone as of April 2007 [Fields *et al.*, 2008]; at a similar date, last.fm held 65 million songs from over 10 million artists.[20]

How can average users possibly find what they require amongst the vast number of digital music recordings available online? Once they build up a large library of digital audio files on their hard drive, how can they best organize it? This is a record collection organization problem for the digital age.[21] What of the information needs of a variety of system

---

[20]http://blog.wired.com/music/2007/04/lastfm_subscrip.html
[21]Nick Hornby's *High Fidelity* has the characters in a record store discussing alphabetical, chronological and autobiographical methods for ordering records; suffice it to say that computer science can confront many more possibilities!

users, who may have very different viewpoints on the importance of particular musical descriptors? Can we support 'personalized ways to hear and learn about music' [Casey *et al.*, 2008, p. 668]?

Music information retrieval (MIR) [Downie, 2003; Ellis, 2006; Orio, 2006; Slaney *et al.*, 2008; Casey *et al.*, 2008] is a broad church of computational approaches to the problems of cataloging and processing large databases of music, and the automatic analysis of music content supporting the many needs of digital music users. Application domains stretch from the large-scale information retrieval concerns of digital archives including libraries and search engines, to individual music consumers and producers managing their own digital content.[22] MIR has been especially developed under the potential and pressures of the Semantic Web, whose ultimate aspiration is no less than computers which appreciate the human significance of any online information. In the case of often ambiguous music, this can pose a great challenge with a sometimes moving target! Nevertheless, there are many situations where the musical problem can be sufficiently well defined to enable computational progress, and MIR provides further angles on simulating human musicking that contribute to the overall computer music field. Overt links to industry, through issues including digital rights, record sales prediction and online commerce, mean that MIR is well grounded in society at large. The discussion here will concentrate on digital audio files, but there are also large reservoirs of MIDI files, score encodings, lyrics and libretti and other musically pertinent representations that can be handled by search engines and digital libraries.

One approach to summarizing audio data to make it searchable is textual **metadata**. As 'meta' suggests, this is additional description beyond audio or music data itself, extending from any title, year of release, artist, lyricist and composer, to keywords describing the content, often including subjective descriptors of supposed emotional affect and other culturally and even individually specific descriptors. The ID3 tags that can accompany MP3 files and the genre tags on music websites are examples of this additional contextual information. All content must be tagged in some way in order to effect efficient searches (or else we'd have to start anew with analysis of audio files every time), but the important question to ask about tags is how they arise. Were they set by one user? Do they reflect a particular online community's current consensus, but a consensus that changes over time? Have any expert musicologists or even the artists themselves been consulted? There are many cases where audio files on a website are mislabeled, even deliberately so to promote one artist under another's mantle, and the trustworthiness of metadata is often doubtful.

In order to attempt to reduce bias in this process, **content-based** systems use automated analysis to establish descriptors. Indeed, such an approach often allows alternative non-verbal entry points to the searching of material, perhaps based on singing a melody or asking a search engine to find 'similar' content according to some musical property. This does

---

[22]The term MIR originates from library science and early work in computerized cataloging of music data. Kassler [1966] published an early paper describing a musical content parsing language called MIR (Musical Information Retrieval).

not entirely remove any prospect of bias, since there will be assumptions[23] in any analysis model, but at least it establishes a setting where tagging is more highly controlled and formalized. The systems are usually trained in some way on high-quality vetted metadata, and then through machine learning can generalize to help in classification tasks for new content. MIR research has investigated useful musical ontologies (descriptions) which can be automatically extracted from audio signals to empower particular searching tasks.

Table 7.1 draws from review papers and the MIREX evaluation competitions (explained below) to give a selection of the tasks that MIR has confronted. The tasks have potential impact on various groups, including consumers and other end-users, commercial and legal interests, and musicologists and artists. There is some (unsurprising) bias towards mainstream commercial music in Western economies, though authors are increasingly engaging with a wider representation of music from around the world [Geekie, 2002; Lee *et al.*, 2005; Doraisamy *et al.*, 2006; van Kranenburg *et al.*, 2007]. Most of the tasks rely on defining some form of audio similarity measure. The degree to which this takes account of important perceptual criteria in music is an open problem; many existing measures simply turn out to be coarse timbral descriptors. The tasks are often easy to state informally, but turn out to be much harder to engineer, sometimes substantially interacting with human musical subjectivity. Indeed, on some tasks, humans are hardly consistent in their criteria of success, and it is questionable whether the task itself is well defined. In many cases for music (especially more ambiguous absolute music without lyrical content), the very potential for multiple interpretations can be a strength rather than a weakness, allowing different participants to take away those aspects of value to them, varying in time and context. We should not assume that any music has one communicable meaning for all [Juslin and Sloboda, 2001; Cross, 2003].[24]

The problems are especially profound when hard categories are sometimes imposed, such as for genre recognition – ask yourself, do you always agree with the categories under which music is placed in a record store? For example, can you always tell the difference between rock and pop for every track in each decade? How many categories should there be to describe all music across all world cultures? Can an artist develop in style over time, explore pastiche, follow different models in different works and yet still retain an essential core that can be recognized? Musicologists have systematically engaged with these issues of style and genre, and MIR researchers are increasingly aware of the difficulties inherent in such material [Aucouturier and Pachet, 2003]. Nevertheless, there are definite benefits to engagement with such questions, as interfacing with common usage patterns in culture; genre classification is a widely adopted method just to get some sort of handle on the wealth of information available. A number of alternatives have also been proposed, including allowing users to gradually build up personal taxonomies or community folksonomies, and allowing for degrees of membership rather than mutually exclusive categories.

---

[23] In many cases a research publication and open-source software makes the assumptions public, but there are question marks over some commercial systems.

[24] To give two examples: a putative love song could instill varying levels of hatred as a listener starts to hear it too often; and the fact that many participants in one culture agree that a descriptor for a piece is 'sad' does not prove a universal affect across cultures.

Table 7.1 Selected tasks in MIR.

Task	Description
Audio watermarking	Digital rights management, copyright monitoring
Fingerprinting	Find exact or near exact matches, detect plagiarism, spot remixes that sample an original track
Cover song identification, composition recognition	Find different versions of the same underlying song or work, which may not match perfectly in all aspects of musical structure. Assess consistency of musicological style. Might also spot the difference between live and studio versions
Artist recognition and production style categorization	Does a particular performer or producer have a trademark sound?
Genre/style recognition	Categorize or find similar music, with respect to a predefined taxonomy
Playlist generation	Automatically produce a party mix to fit a certain mood, a transition between two songs via intermediates, or other structuring principle for a playlist
Recommendation	Based on the user's existing collection or declared preferences, recommend new works they might like, perhaps guided by certain very high-level user-defined search parameters such as music to fit a particular mood
Name that tune	Given a musical extract provided by a user (which might be as little as a person humming the melody line or tapping out a rhythm), find candidates for the actual work
Performance alignment	Given multiple versions of the same work (perhaps different pianists playing the same Beethoven sonata), automatically line them up to assist comparison
Automatic summarization	Make an audio thumbnail for fast preview of a work, presenting the most representative segments

7.2.1 Content Analysis

A significant effort in the MIR community is invested in automatic content analysis methods. The attention given to MIR in recent years has meant a great deal of extra work on variants of the Transcription Problem, with techniques developed in MIR widely applicable in many areas of computer music including interactive music systems and computational music analysis. Content analysis has close links with the audio analysis chapter in this book (Chapter 3). The attempt to automatically extract musical properties from audio signals for the purposes of tagging content engages with segmentation (onset detection), monophonic, predominant f0 and polyphonic pitch detection, key and chord recognition, beat tracking and more (consult Table 3.4).

The use of feature vectors (see Section 3.5) is typical in MIR, building up from low-level feature data to higher-level information. Figure 7.4 plots feature vectors across a three-minute song. Bundling multiple frames of vectors together without regard to order has been called the 'bag of frames' approach; when the temporal order of the vectors is preserved it is 'shingling' [Casey *et al.*, 2008]. If beat or meter tracking is employed, beat- or measure-synchronous features can also be extracted; chord- or note-synchronous feature detection is also possible if the appropriate chord or note detection algorithms are to be trusted. Investigation of appropriate features for musical characterization feeds directly into the more semantically challenging MIR tasks.

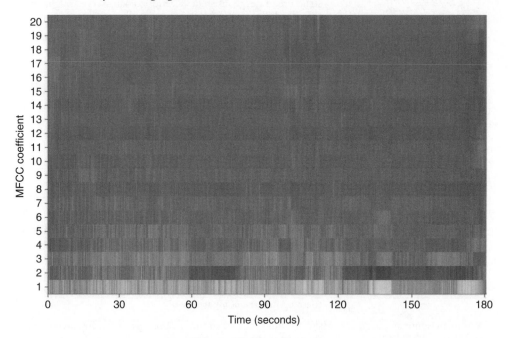

Figure 7.4 MFCC feature vectors for the just over three minutes of *I've Been Tired* by The Pixies. Feature vectors consisting of the first twenty Mel-frequency cepstral coefficients were extracted for each frame, and normalized by the global minimum and maximum. Frames are spaced out by one-fifth of a second, giving around 900 frames. The brightness of each component in the vertical strip at each time indicates one coefficient value. The second coefficient is particularly indicative in locating the chorus material (darker areas).

Because the goal of much MIR is to consider and compare whole tracks, algorithms are usually offline non-causal analyzers rather than live causal parsers. For example, assuming musical repertoire that is relatively stable, it is possible to take a chromagram or tempo histogram over a whole track to get a dominant tempo or key. The eventual unit of description is often at the work or song level; such a viewpoint necessarily overlooks aspects of temporal evolution in music within tracks, which are often an important aspect of the musical listening experience. The best way (or ways) to encapsulate such experience is an open question in musicology in general, let alone in MIR.

Anyway, feature vectors, once formed from within-frame and multi-frame features, represent points in a high-dimensional space. It is advantageous to reduce this to the most important dimensions to ease the challenge for machine learning (perhaps using principal component analysis). In many tasks, feature vectors form inputs to some classification or detection algorithm such as a support vector machine or multilayer perceptron.

It is also possible to define a **similarity measure** on the vector space between feature vectors. Such a function is critical for discussing the similarity of different parts of a work, or between works. Using a similarity measure, different feature vectors at different stages of a piece can be compared. It is possible to do this exhaustively, that is, to compare each frame's feature vector with that at every other frame, forming a **similarity matrix** (see Figure 7.5). The rationale is to try to discover important structural boundaries in a piece, though calculating the similarity matrix may only be a first step in exploring this. Distinct sections may have consistent feature vectors; taking a pop song example, feature vectors within the verse could be more similar to each other than to those in a chorus [Foote and Uchihashi, 2001]. Section discovery has applications in automatic musical analysis, or in automatic summarization of pieces by their most representative parts.

To sound a note of caution on features, it is often assumed that higher-level and longer-term features easily arise by processing lots of frames of lower-level features of smaller temporal extent. Some form of mid-level segmentational process, whether through chord boundaries, beats or other metrical structure, distinct sound events or more complicated multilayered representations of simultaneous streams, is often necessary to work up to high-level descriptors. Yet it is a hard computational problem to find the best subsets of features to work with across levels, and research is ongoing as to the best algorithms for extracting higher-level representations (and the relation of these in turn to human cognition). Aucouturier and Defreville [2007] found that while soundscape material is successfully classified by bag-of-frames approaches, music is a harder case, in that much musical identity is associated with comparatively rare feature vectors. This suggests that more work is required on the algorithms used to capture what is distinctive about music, and make prominent those components of greatest value to human auditors.

Audio analysis and machine learning are the chief technical areas of expertise required in working on MIR, and the treatment of large databases makes the computer science element pronounced.[25] The design of audio similarity measures, pattern matching schemes and classification algorithms tends to be a big part of most MIR tasks, with the adoption of such rich entities as hidden Markov models, transportation distances, string matching and Gaussian mixture models. The vocabulary of data mining [Witten and Frank, 2005] is also often used, as we will discuss further in terms of evaluation below.

Table 7.2 details a set of existing MIR research frameworks that may prove valuable. Many existing computer music systems can also be adapted for MIR research, from SuperCollider

---

[25]Yet, as with computer music in general, the inputs of music psychologists, musicologists, sociologists, mathematicians and more are welcomed!

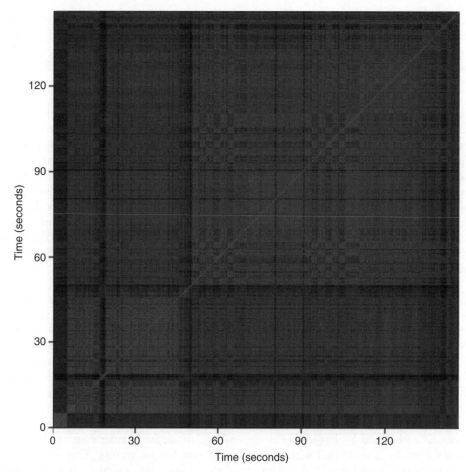

Figure 7.5   Similarity matrix for MFCC-based feature vectors in Squarepusher's *Full Rinse*. Possible segmentations of larger-scale structure are evidenced by the blocking around the diagonal, or by following a row or column. If you look at a particular time on the *x*-axis you will see the comparison of the frame at that point to all other frames in the piece on the vertical. The matrix is symmetric since every frame is compared with every other, and the similarity of frames *a* and *b* is the same as that of *b* and *a*. Maximal similarity will always appear on the diagonal. Frames are usually most similar to those in their local region, where this follows the breakdown of sections in the piece. Those further away are more differentiated, except where similar types of section recur (e.g., separated choruses may still be similar to each other). Note that it would be possible to create a segmentation function without having to go through the step of an exhaustive similarity matrix, by identifying large changes in feature vectors on a local to near-local scale only; however, recurrences of similar sections within a piece require segment comparison, and it is much more computationally efficient to carry this out on discovered segments than on original low-level feature vectors [Cooper and Foote, 2003].

to Csound. MIR systems may already incorporate useful machine learning components, or further machine learning libraries (such as Weka, libsvm or MATLAB toolboxes) can be installed. In practice, once past the audio analysis stage data tends to enter a generic form (lists of feature vectors, for example), often amenable to generic machine learning algorithms.

Table 7.2 Some developer technologies for content-based MIR.

Software	Description	Reference/Link	
MIRToolbox	MATLAB extension library including support for many standard MIR tasks	Lartillot and Toiviainen [2007]	http://www.jyu.fi/hum/laitokset/musiikki/en/research/coe/materials/mirtoolbox
Marsyas	Efficient cross-platform open source C++ library (with additional Java and Python bindings) used by many MIR researchers	Tzanetakis and Cook [2000]	http://sourceforge.net/projects/marsyas
M2K	Java framework, also used in the MIREX evaluation competitions	Downie [2008]	http://www.music-ir.org/evaluation/m2k/
jMIR	Java libraries for MIR	McEnnis et al. [2006]	http://sourceforge.net/projects/jmir
CLAM	C Library for Audio and Music; as well as general computer music tasks, this library has specific MIR support, particularly for annotation and feature extraction	Amatriain [2007]	http://www.clam.iua.upf.edu/
OMRAS2	Open-source tools released as part of a large-scale research project	Casey et al. [2008]	http://www.omras2.org

7.2.2 Annotation and Evaluation

Given a MIR system, how can we evaluate it? How do we know if an automatic genre classification system is really doing its job, or how can we possibly train up a system to make it robust enough to trust with future decisions? Evaluation for specific MIR tasks typically depends on identifying the answer a human (or poll or quorum of humans) would have given, and then testing to see whether the machine recovers this. The answer the machine is ideally supposed to give is the **ground truth**. In machine learning, such data is necessary in order to train a system up on known examples, before testing on a further data set held back for the purposes of generalization performance [Witten and Frank, 2005; Mitchell, 1997].

n-fold validation and other schemes of assessing the effectiveness of algorithms are often employed.

A laborious but necessary slog is the manual placement of musically relevant information alongside audio files, so as to provide a human ground truth for their analysis. The process of marking up this information is called **annotation**. For many tasks we might like to explore, it is often difficult to obtain plentiful high-quality annotation data, depending as this does on many person-hours of preparation by experts. The quality of annotation itself directly bears on any resulting work in machine learning. With a human activity like music, where there is always a potential issue of subjective assessment, even experts can differ wildly in their viewpoints.[26] Low-level aspects of sound are more likely to see agreement, but even here, as any psychologist would tell you, people differ, and statistical measures may be necessary to summarize trends in the data.

Researchers have often built their own annotation tools, and some open-source projects supply perfectly usable systems, such as Sonic Visualiser (www.sonicvisualiser.org), the CLAM_Annotator (http://www.clam.iua.upf.edu/), Praat or various MATLAB tools (see also Table 7.2). Some data sets of ground truth are shared amongst researchers, either publicly (i.e., through the web pages of the annual MIREX competition http://www.music-ir.org/mirex/2008/index.php/Main_Page) or for a nominal fee (e.g., the Real World Computing Music Database, http://staff.aist.go.jp/m.goto/RWC-MDB/). There are copyright issues on distributing uncleared materials, which is why there are no large ready-prepared databases waiting online, though annotation data can be shared independently. This is also the basis for some MIR web services, which hold licensed audio on their own servers and run MIR software on demand from the outside world without distributing recordings themselves at any point. Though bearing provisos in mind concerning the quality of metadata from general users, the web services of search engines and music networking sites such as Google, Yahoo, MySpace, last.fm and their peers can supply reams of data. It is also possible to adapt sample CDROMs (for example, exploiting a file format with sound file mark-up of events, such as REX2), and even to use generative music systems to produce large amounts of ground truth data. Aside from these options, running new projects with original research questions may require you to produce your own annotations without appeal to any existing data.[27]

Evaluating MIR systems has been a central concern of MIREX [Downie, 2008], the **Music Information Retrieval Evaluation eXchange**, where interested parties with algorithms for particular tasks can submit programs for comparative assessment. A neutral central authority, currently based at the University of Illinois at Urbana-Champaign, runs batches of the programs using their computing horsepower. Individual tasks and their evaluation criteria are agreed by participants ahead of the rendering stage of the competition. All those who submit programs also publish short technical papers to promote the sharing of the ideas encapsulated in each entry, and hopefully refine the state of the art for MIR systems.

---

[26]The more high-level and open to interpretation the feature in question is, the more likely this is to happen.
[27]A good survey of existing MIR databases appears at http://grh.mur.at/misc/mir_datasets.html

Though the exact criteria vary between tasks, data mining measures are often adopted, particularly for information retrieval or classification tasks where there is a well-defined notion of matching the ground truth within a set of discrete options. For binary classification, **recall** and **precision**, and their summary combination in the **F-measure** [Witten and Frank, 2005, pp. 171–2] are often used. For multiple classes, confusion matrices can be employed, and some more customized evaluation functions have been defined. When many different rival algorithms are compared, there are also statistical questions about whether the performance of an algorithm is significantly different from that of another, which can be investigated by using more advanced statistical tests [Casey *et al.*, 2008]. These issues of evaluation are also encountered in the assessment of new machine listening algorithms.

7.2.3 MIR Deployments

Table 7.3 gives a selection of real-world MIR projects, some of which you may even have used! Not all these systems are founded in audio content analysis – some primarily treat metadata – but there are working examples here of audio analysis machinery. The commercial side of MIR is in full swing, and has been for some time, even if you might suspect that the cool idea outweighs the actual quality of implementation in many offerings.[28] The table only gives a selection; the large search engines and online music dealers are all getting in on the act, and MIR is a definite growth area in computer music technology. With an increasingly packed field of players with different degrees of head start, user bases and financing, and some difficult intellectual property and licensing issues to overcome, the commercial side is highly competitive.

Many MIR systems are not only available as stand-alone applications, plug-ins and websites, but also as web services [Zadel and Fujinaga, 2004]. In this case, they can be remotely called by programmers wanting to build applications on top of them (examples include last.fm, which actively encourages third-party software based on its social data, and the EchoNest API for remote analysis of submitted audio). Search engine web services can be useful ways to source metadata, and many projects utilize web-crawling to collect audio databases. As one example, the Python code used by Fields *et al.* [2008] to scrape audio tracks from MySpace pages is available.[29] MIR applications can also include more creative tasks, and automated searches of the Internet for audio content have also featured prominently as components of many a generative art installation. Indeed, the playful side to MIR should not be overlooked; Jason Freeman's iTunes Signature Maker[30] is as much art project as summarization tool.

Such activities only go to show the riches proffered by an Internet of music projects around the world.

---

[28]Indeed, research is ongoing into all of the MIR tasks that companies are claiming to have solved. The difficulties of high-level audio analysis, discussed above and in Chapter 3, might make you suspicious of the marketing blurb.
[29]http://sourceforge.net/projects/mypyspace/
[30]http://www.jasonfreeman.net/itsm/

Table 7.3 Some examples of available MIR systems.

System	Description	Link
Shazam	Mobile phone service (since 2001) allowing the recognition of tracks, even in a noisy club environment, and further music recommendation and mapping services	www.shazam.com
last.fm	Metadata-based social networking site incorporates various technologies to track user preferences and make recommendations	www.last.fm
Midomi	Query by singing	www.midomi.com
Hit Song Science	Chart success predictor for recordings (dependent on previous trends within their audio database of previous hits, and metadata concerning a band)	http://uplaya.com/
EchoNest	Company offering MIR audio analysis technology using developments of Tristan Jehan's PhD work [Jehan, 2005]	the.echonest.com
Pandora	Primarily metadata-based engine, using data generated by the Music Genome Project, where 'experts' mark up a selection of music features claimed by the company to summarize all music (please don't take that claim too seriously). Web radio services are US-only at the time of writing due to licensing issues	www.pandora.com
Genius	Over-enthusiastically named recommender and playlist generation system built into iTunes Store (from iTunes 8); depends on comparing user profiles	http://www.apple.com/itunes
Mufin	Entirely content-based MIR system based on the AudioID analysis system developed by an originator of MP3, with colleagues	http://mufin.com
SyncPlayer	Open-source (Java) academic project at the University of Bonn, which demonstrates an architecture for a full MIR system with central server and multiple clients	http://audentify.iai.uni-bonn.de/ synchome/index.php?pid=01
Musipedia	Open Music Encyclopedia with various methods to search a directory of scored music, including pitch and rhythm entry by singing or keyboard GUI	www.musipedia.org

7.3 SUMMARY

This chapter has given us a chance to consider the importance of networked computer systems in modern life. Such technology has had a substantial impact on music distribution and the promotion of online music. We have encountered many examples of novel music making empowered by networks, and associated developments in laptop orchestras and mobile phone music. With an accumulation of resources across the world's computers, we have explored the application of data-mining methods to musical data. This has brought us into contact with multiple aspects of music information retrieval, and we have covered the aims of the research, the technology, the evaluation of systems and real-world deployments.

7.4 EXERCISES

1. I am in London and my friend is in Tokyo; we want to take part in a collaborative network jam. The distance as the cable lies is around 9550 kilometers (we'll ignore the size of the two cities, and transmission routes not lying on the Earth's surface). Assuming that transmission times achieve 70% of the speed of light ($c = 299\,792.458$ kilometers per second) and that (unrealistically) junction times can be ignored, what is the latency in our hearing each other play? How might this impact our playing? How can jitter effects, causing variable transmission delays, be overcome? Will the anti-jitter solution improve latency? You might follow up this technical discussion by seeking out some collaborative music making environments on the Web, for practical tests with large ping times.

2. You can consider this exercise as a thought experiment, or as a real challenge. Spend an hour setting up a MySpace page (or similar social networking identity) for a band that doesn't exist. Quickly create some music for them, and perhaps a dodgy video. Spend a small amount of time initially promoting the site. Track use statistics over the next week, month, year. Note down any questions this raises for you with respect to promotion budgets and strategies, instead of purely musical attributes.

3. Go to http://www.myspace.com/burakasomsistema. Research the ensemble's history, including thorough supplementary web searches (bear in mind that not all information sources on the Web can be said to have the same level of authority). Can you trace how interest may have snowballed in their case? Try to analyze this group's connections via a web service (such as third-party statistical extensions for last.fm, available via that website, or other services as discussed in the text).

4. OSC (or an alternative custom network protocol) allows the time-stamping of messages to guarantee that they occur at a certain point in the future, potentially overcoming network jitter and achieving synchronous performance across computers. This only works if the computers' clocks agree. Consider the problem of 'synchronizing the computers' watches'. Various solutions, from MIDI Time Code to audio sync signals, could be followed, but this question asks you to explore a

symbolic statistical solution for time syncing two networked computers. Consider the round-trip passing of a message from computer 1 to computer 2, and then back to computer 1. The first message is a request for computer 2 to divulge its absolute clock time; the second message is computer 2 sending back this clock time to computer 1. An expression for the observed data from one round of this messaging is:

$$\text{difference of clocks} = \text{time at clock 1 when message 1 sent} + \text{round trip time}$$
$$- (\text{time at clock 2 when message 2 sent}$$
$$+ \text{transmission time for message 2})$$

How will this expression alter if, rather than following the procedure only once, we repeat it N times and take the averages over the N instances of the various measured quantities? How does this allow us to eventually send out a message from the first computer to the second, instructing it by how much to shift its clock so as to bring them closer into sync? (Hint: in the average only, we can assume that half the round-trip time tends to the transmission time one way. Note also that, in the average, time at clock 2 when message 2 sent = time at clock 2 when message 1 sent + transmission time for message 1.)

5. Prepare a basic tool to help participants in an online jam, or LAN network music session. If you're stuck for ideas, you might look into some existing tools such as NRCI for Pd (http://ccrma-www.stanford.edu/~cburns/NRCI/) or the JITLib and NetLib extensions for SuperCollider.

6. Gather together some friends for a laptop jam. Try putting everybody through one pair of speakers via a mixer. Now try with all of the players using their own built-in laptop speakers. Which set-up promoted a greater sense of contribution for all parties? How can consideration for others be guaranteed in laptop performance, and, most generally, in any ensemble music making?

7. In an ensemble situation, now try using your mobile phones and any sound-producing software for them to which you have access. This could be as simple as manipulating ringtones. How does the extra freedom of movement change your musical experience?

8. You can take this one as far as you like. Investigate building a tuner application for musicians, on a mobile phone (perhaps an iPhone, or a phone using Android). Aside from any interface, two potential components would be tone generation at a given pitch, and some sort of pitch-tracking audio analysis to compare user input with a reference. You might start by considering a simple EADGBE guitar tuner, but then go on to support temperaments other than 12-tone equal temperament.

9. Using an online interface or audio content analysis API (such as the EchoNest 'Musical Brain'), submit two audio tracks for analysis. Compare the results; did you use rather different audio examples to begin with?

10. As a follow-up to the previous question, or as a separate task, download and explore one or more of the open MIR research systems. Try to extract audio features from your tracks, obtaining frame-based feature vectors. You might go as far as to consider a simple classification task; for instance, could you differentiate speech from music, or three different types of percussive drum sound (e.g., kick, snare, hihat)? You will need to work out how best to reduce potentially large lists of feature vectors to a small set of features for a simple classifier (Hint: perhaps consider a mean or other statistical moment across frames).

7.5

FURTHER READING

Alderman, J. (2001). *Sonic Boom: Napster, P2P and the Future of Music*. Fourth Estate, London.

Casey, M., Veltkamp, R., Goto, M., Leman, M., Rhodes, C. and Slaney, M. (2008). Content-based music information retrieval: Current directions and future challenges. *Proceedings of the IEEE*, 96(4):668–696.

Chapman, N. and Chapman, J. (2006). *Web Design: A Complete Introduction*. John Wiley and Sons, Ltd, Chichester.

Downie, J. S. (2003). Music Information Retrieval. *Annual Review of Information Science and Technology*, 37, 295–340.

Electronic Frontier Foundation, www.eff.org

Gordon, S. (2005). *The Future of the Music Business*. Backbeat Books, San Francisco, CA.

International Federation of the Phonographic Industry, www.ifpi.org

International Mobile Music Workshops, www.mobilemusicworkshop.org

ISMIR Conference Proceedings, www.ismir.net

Leman, M. (2008). *Embodied Music Cognition and Mediation Technology*. MIT Press, Cambridge, MA.

Kusek, D. and Leonhard, G. (2005). *The Future of Music: Manifesto for the Digital Music Revolution*. Berklee Press, Boston, MA.

Networked: a (networked_book) about (networked_art), http://networkedbook.org/

Orio, N. (2006). Music retrieval: A tutorial and review. *Foundations and Trends in Information Retrieval*, 1(1):1–90.

Perry, M. (2008). *How to be a Record Producer in the Digital Era*. Billboard, New York, NY.

Rohrhuber, J. (2007). Network music, in *The Cambridge Companion to Electronic Music* (eds N. Collins and J. d'Escriván). Cambridge University Press, Cambridge, pp. 140–155.

Chapter 8

Composition

'[A] new kind of musician is necessary, that of the *artist-conceiver* of free and abstract new forms, tending towards complications and generalizations on several levels of sound organization.'

Iannis Xenakis [1985, p. 173]

'In electronic music, neither the musicians' facility nor instruments need be regarded, not their synchronisability nor habitual behaviour. However, limits are set by audibility and studio technique.'

Gottfried Michael Koenig [1971, p. 65]

'The prospect for modern music is a little more favourable; now that electronic computers have been taught to compose it, we may confidently expect that before long some of them will learn to enjoy it, thus saving us the trouble.'

Arthur C. Clarke [1999a]

OBJECTIVES

This chapter covers:

- reflections on the act of composition;
- computer applications in composition;
- properties of music, across various timescales;
- formalized music and algorithmic composition.

8.1 COMPOSERS AND COMPUTERS

This chapter holds a delicate balance of materials relating to a topic that can be rather personal. We shall consider the act of composition, and explore some musical possibilities enabled by the computer. There is not enough room to present extensive coverage of compositional strategies across diverse domains, nor to adequately survey the many human lifetimes dedicated to this art. The concert music composer in the Western tradition remains a central stereotype, however fractured by the innumerable practices within which musicians now work. Hopefully, much of the material should still prove of use to installation artists, film music composers, improvisers and beyond. We shall focus on some issues supporting composition work, without seeking to solve its ultimate subjectivities. The central section of the chapter surveys various properties of musical sound and form that may prove useful starting points for ideas, and which provide an opportunity to highlight some further contributions of the computer. The third section explores algorithmic composition in particular, where the computer is (almost) indispensable in contemporary practice. We begin with some comments pertaining to the role of the composer, and the history of the computer's involvement in their craft.

8.1.1 Musical Decisions: The Act of Composition

Musical composition is a difficult activity to summarize, because of the continua between composition and performance, between design and realization. The final version of music as experienced at a unique moment in time may be the product of the decisions of many human beings, including luthiers, theorists, curators, promoters, artistic collaborators, interpreting musicians and more. Composers, in the common sense of the term, are those whom we might credit with the chief responsibility for the musical materials on offer, even if they do not control every aspect of a production, installation or performance (they are often not around to oversee it, even though they left instructions). Although talk of 'great' composers tends to focus on singular historical personages (usually in the Western concert tradition) from J.S. Bach to Webern, it is also worth contemplating the many collaborative projects where musicians work. Think of co-writing ensembles, a team working on an installation, or a film or game music composer negotiating a contribution within an existing narrative. There are just as many circumstances where the term 'composer' becomes a little awkward, and terms such as 'artist' or 'musician' might be preferred.

Compositions include fixed media products, as well as flexible frameworks for live performance and interaction. In Chapter 6 we already encountered a (rough) tripartite split of sites of interaction into art installations, computer games and concert performance. Chapter 7 provided many further examples from the perspective of distributed processing and the Internet. Indeed, at each stage of this book, artworks have appeared as illustrations, and this very adaptability of focus and means makes composition as exciting as it is varied. If the ease of recording, and the necessarily non-realtime nature of much early computer music work, have sometimes seemed to suggest that computer music is particularly specialized to the production of fixed works, this is no longer a technical restriction. A renaissance of live

12

Figure 8.1 Short score extract from *Noronquí* (2004), by Julio d'Escriván. Note the combination of flowing graphics for the electronics part and the traditional notation for the acoustic instruments. The composer writes: 'the first bar is a complex pitch cluster which glissandos from low to high in several layers at once, the following bars are granulated pitches whose tonal center can be heard clearly, thus the notated pitches, yet they breakdown throughout the bar into less pitch specific granules ... the performers can hear the pitch and then follow the 'breakdown' until the next pitch becomes audible ...' (personal communication, 16 March 2009). Reproduced by permission of © Julio d'Escriván.

and interactive computer music is in progress, and just as musicians once embraced analog synthesizers for their potential in live performance and immediate studio feedback, so the computer can be a current base for realtime electronic music.

Tension between pre-recording and live performance is a good example of how different compositions more or less rigidly create a template for later action.[1] There are different ways for composers to specify a 'work', choosing the level of indeterminacy they wish to grant – the openness of the work they create to later decisions. Some creators seek to specify their compositions in as much detail as possible, to minimize reproduction errors and interpretation differences. Other composers are happy to cede many decisions to performer planning of a particular concert, or to performance. Some people build their preferences into computer programs, which delay selecting particular configurations until run-time, as in the interactive music systems encountered in Section 6.4 and the generative music to be discussed below.

When intermediary musicians are involved in bringing a composition to fruition, there may be orally transmitted guidelines, or some form of notated score. A score does not have to be written in Western common practice notation, which may not stretch well to notate computer mediated electronic parts. Figure 8.1 demonstrates a combination of

---

[1]Interesting cases are provided by the use of recordings in a live setting, where miming or the sequencing and diffusion of recordings over a playback system may maintain a human presence.

Improvisation

Improvisation is a prominent musical activity in performance, a vital energy, which can be an entire way of musical life in itself [Bailey, 1980; Nettl and Russell, 1998; Lewis, 1999]. As a cross-cultural aspect of music making it is a core component of such highly developed musics as Indian classical music, secular Arabic music, Cantonese Opera, Flamenco and the tradition of the church organ. It has not been disregarded in computer music. Ikue Mori, for example, is an experienced laptop improviser, a regular in the New York downtown scene. Improvisation may fulfill needs for the communion of performers and environment, for a vitality and spontaneity of living music directly expressed without intermediate artifacts. Some improvisers place themselves in opposition to the cult of recording, avoiding any transfer of music outside the moment of its creation.

The extent of improvisation may vary from small embellishments and expressive details tied to set structure, through the live construction of idiomatic works within rich musical heritages, to the wholesale creation of entire formal structures and their musical contents based fundamentally on the musical–social interaction of a free improvisation group. Improvisation is not an easy route, and is as intensively studied as any other musical art [Lewis, 2000]. Even if certain generative procedures are in play in live performance [Pressing, 1988], traced to training and cultural convention, the reaction of the musician in response to immediate circumstances remains paramount. Musicians have often sought to build computer systems to support improvisational settings; George Lewis's *Voyager*, as featured in Section 6.4.3 is an important example in this regard.

traditional Western acoustic score and graphics that evocatively represent the spiraling lines and grain streams of the tape part. The exact nature of the notation also varies with the level of indeterminacy, and is inclusive of many alternative graphical representations even for acoustic works alone [Nyman, 1999].

Furthermore, creation takes place under different time constraints. You may have days, weeks or months to pore over the task, allowing for an intricate iterative design cycle that utilizes feedback from multiple trials and experiences. On the other hand, you might be under the exciting pressure to 'compose' in one take, with no opportunity to go back. In this case, the notion of improvisation comes to the fore (see sidebar). Indeterminacy is a transfer of responsibility between the composer of a work and the performers; somebody has to decide on the details of the final sounding result whenever a composer is less than explicit. Even so, the composer's drawing board can lead to highly prepared works of great worth that otherwise wouldn't have a chance to exist, for fixed works or other structures. Some music requires in its construction more human attention than can be summoned in real time.[2] Consider the many gestation months that John Zorn put into refining his game piece *Cobra* (1984), a framework for improvisation.

It still takes a certain state of mind to stand up and claim to be a composer, and some people hold back, either through fear of the overwhelming tradition that it sometimes implies, through a lack of sufficient practice, or through an ideological stance (they might be more comfortable with other terms, including artist, musician, producer, improviser, performer). But, of course, anyone can compose, and to say less is to deny you your essential human creativity. As with any human activity, variable elements of training, personality and cultural interaction influence your path, but you should never let an unhealthy awe of Beethoven or Parmegiani hold you back from taking part in the adventure.

8.1.2 Roles for Computers in Composition

Computers have inevitably impacted on composers and the act of composition. This is not always because computers are the only way to pursue an idea, nor because computers were the original inspiration for a method. Often, the boon of computers has been the ease and reliability with which particular concepts can be explored, as for microtonal tunings or rule-based music. For other concerns computers are such a natural fit that it is hard to conceive of effective work being done without them, as in any digital signal processing operations, from editing and processing to analysis and synthesis.

Simply in terms of human effort, computers have been beneficial to composers in their original sense of being fast and tireless calculating machines. At any time when composers find themselves engaged in lengthy numerical calculations or repetitive tasks, it is likely that a computational solution might help – in Chapter 1 the example was given of John Cage's manual dice rolls being taken over by a computer program. The story of Iannis Xenakis is in a sidebar, which recounts how he turned to the convenience of computers to utilize the probability distributions of his stochastic music.

Sometimes rather unsettled by its rigid demands, composers have not always taken up the computer eagerly, or, at least, have avoided the legwork of programming even though they might take advantage of DAW software. Clarence Barlow has written of being reluctantly driven to a computer only when his compositional needs finally became so complicated, in a certain numerical direction, that a computer just became the inherent way to cope with this. He has spoken of hating the act of programming, but requiring the computer in order to achieve his formal aims [Roads, 1989, pp. 26–27]. At least he wasn't forced to program

---

[2]Interestingly, perhaps computers are one way of guaranteeing certain difficult calculations within realtime constraints, though their programming can become a new locus of intensive composer efforts.

Xenakis's computational trajectory

Iannis Xenakis (1922–2001) is a complex but central figure in 20th-century musical exploration of mathematics and music, a significant influence in computer music, and the author of a much-cited book explicitly titled *Formalized Music* [Xenakis, 1992; Matossian, 1986; Harley, 2004]. His work anticipates many of the themes in this chapter. A practicing architect in the 1950s under Le Corbusier, Xenakis eventually turned full time to musical composition. As the author of an important critique of serial music on the grounds of listener perception of the mass of information ('*La crise de la musique sérielle* [The Crisis of Serial Music]', 1955, reprinted as Xenakis [1994]) Xenakis's practical response was to turn to mathematical probability theory for the generation of music. His 'stochastic music' has the fine detail emerge as a consequence of large-scale probability distributions (we shall investigate the mechanics later in the chapter). His fascination with dense clouds of sounds provides examples of the first granular composition [Roads, 2001]. While his earlier experiments in stochastic music in the 1950s saw him run the mathematics by hand, by 1962 he had adopted the use of a computer to speed up the calculating process, as in the 'ST'-prefixed series of works [Ames, 1987]. He was not bound to his theories, however, and not averse to altering the output of computer programs if he saw a good aesthetic reason to do so, showing that formalism for its own sake was always tempered by a dose of perceptual reality. Although he later returned to a more intuitive flow of compositional work free of computers, having internalized many of the shapes and structures, he found further roles for computers in other projects, such as the visual to spectral sound transforms of the UPIC (Unité Polyagogique Informatique du CEMAMu) interface, or the multi-timescale integration enabled by the General Dynamic Stochastic Synthesis paradigm, which took stochastic music to the sample level.

the early RCA synthesizer, a nightmare according to Charles Wuorinen [Boulanger, 1989, pp. 53–4]. Fortunately, programming is a much friendlier and more accessible activity in the present day, and it is rarer to find composers who are unwilling to engage with the real potential of the computer. There is also a wide variety of music software to support different entry levels; experienced computer musicians often progress to become programmers themselves, and may end up the creators of new accessible composition tools in turn.

Computers are also notable for the inhuman precision they offer, enabling exploration of territory beyond human production, but still within human perception. Metronomical electronic dance music is one obvious manifestation of this capacity, when excising expressive inflections.[3] Precision has a flip side: the need to specify in exact detail what is required from the computer, especially when rendering whole works within a computational mould. 'There is no hiding from what you are doing ... in computer music, what you play is what you get' [Lansky and Roads, 1989, p. 41]. In Section 9.4 some of the more advanced efforts to build expression back into computer performance are covered. Fast solutions include manual corrections to sequence data, or the addition of a little random jitter into performance timings.

Realtime computer editing has dramatically increased the level of feedback and flexibility available for many tasks. Score and sequence editors have some exciting affordances, and you can make full use of cut and paste, step entry and other facilitative commands. It becomes straightforward to produce music that no human being could play, but that the excellent mechanical marvel, the computer, can elegantly churn out on demand. One danger is that the ease of editing distracts from the deep consideration of the best compositional avenue, and more likely leads to imperfect or provisional solutions: 'Often, systems which are too easy to use encourage thoughtlessness' [Lansky and Roads, 1989, p. 42]. Although composers who worked with non-realtime systems before the 1980s wouldn't wish for a return to the long delay associated with each program run, they appreciated the benefit of extra thinking time. The need to really settle plans in advance of rendering was a situation that encouraged careful consideration. Writing in 1969, Max Mathews noted: 'at a scale of 1000, 20 minutes of computer time are needed for each second of sound. It must be a remarkable second to make this effort seem worthwhile' [Mathews, 1969, p. 35]. On the other hand, our present-day ability to go back and change things so readily, to cover much more of the search space, is surely a great advantage if wise use is made of the feedback.

There are more radical uses for computers in composition that center-stage the unique qualitative changes in control allowed by computation. Computer programs can embody particular theories of music, and are wonderful experimental tools for the composer to investigate the consequences of their models. This arena, of **algorithmic composition**, forms one of the main avenues in this chapter, because it is not only a central example of the possibilities of computer music, but also a powerful reflective tool for the composer to ponder the act of composition. Rather than create work directly, a composer can create a recipe for works in a particular vein, a factory for generating works. So, if appropriately programmed, the computer can produce a different variation each time it is invoked! It is also possible to interact with a running algorithm; Figure 8.2 shows an example of a generative computer program that responds to user guidance as to which procedures to use at any moment in time. There are hybrids here, as everywhere. Laske [1989, p. 120] has noted a continuum of forms of human involvement in composing a computer music work. His two outer poles are 'manual composition', where the human authors every decision

---

[3] Influence can run in two directions: human drummers have attempted to emulate machine-like drum and bass beats, making even snugger the gap between production and perception.

directly, and an 'autonomous composing machine', programmed to generate a work without human intervention at run-time. An intermediate case is provided by computer-assisted composition, where a composer might run various programs to help generate material for a work, under their close supervision.

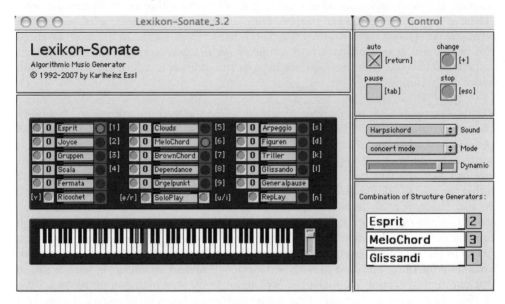

Figure 8.2 *Lexikon-Sonate* (1992–2007), by Karlheinz Essl. Different algorithms are available, derived from the composer's analysis of the Western piano repertoire, including Beethoven as well as serialism. The current output is a mixture of the three algorithmic characters listed on the bottom right. The program is freely available under a Creative Commons Attribution–NonCommercial–NoDerivs 2.0 Austria License from http://www.essl.at/works/Lexikon-Sonate.html. Reproduced with permission of Karlheinz Essl (www.essl.at).

8.1.3 Computer Music and Musical Style

The computer places no a priori restrictions on musical style.[4] It is possible to compose four-part chorales at a computer, but also to compose programs that create four-part chorales for you. Nevertheless, such a flexible tool cannot help but have had an influence on the course of musical history. The musical territory usually surveyed is a subset of electronic music, but, as argued at a number of points in this book, computers are now so pervasive a part of the entertainment industry and of the arts that they have become involved at many stages within the life cycle of sonic products. We'll try not to claim too much music for the sake of it, however, just because studio production or score preparation might incorporate a computer.

---

[4]Short of lullabies for Luddites?

Table 8.1 provides a few categories that are closely associated with computer work.[5] There are different grounds for claiming a consistent style exists, whether categorizing by chronology (18th-century music), function (dance music), technological basis (technology does not always fully determine music, even though the ready adoption of new equipment by musicians plays a big part in onwards motion), aesthetic (e.g., digital glitches) and more [Landy, 2007]. The table does not attempt to create a full cultural history, and has been kept relatively short. Scenes with massive and sprawling family trees are encapsulated in snapshots, for otherwise we'd find ourselves in the rampant genres of electronic dance music, electronica and their many children from acid house to dubstep to darkmattercore to …. Equally well, electroacoustic music is defined by some to encompass all electronic music, and, even if we restrict its remit to experimental art music for intensive listening, contains within it many schools and fashions. Because of the transition from analog to digital equipment ongoing in the 1970s to 1980s, whole waves of synth pop have also been sidestepped. Yet the gradual dominance of digital synthesizers is a notable trend in 1980s production, i.e., the Fairlight on Kate Bush's *The Dreaming* (1982) or the Emulator sampler on Depeche Mode's *Construction Time Again* (1983). These 'popular music' references are deliberate; it is best to avoid too much false differentiation of art and popular music when popularity can be independent of technical sophistication.

Besides, definitive taxonomies are treacherous, because of the wildfire nature of cultural evolution, and the complex way terminology is settled upon and revisited over time. Subgenres are deliberately created on a weekly basis by marketers, musicians and journalists, and themselves subject to the survival of the fittest term (techno was coined in 1987 to differentiate Detroit musicians from the Chicago house scene; but the Belleville Three often visited Chicago, and were working well before 1987). For analysts, it is extremely difficult to designate musical 'species' until well after a speciation event, and there are always fuzzier edges to undermine any ostensible hard taxonomy. In music, unlike real genetics, it is usually possible to cross elements from any styles, no matter how far apart in geography, equipment or time. In 'The Counterpoint of Species', Johnson [2000] eulogizes the strength gained through cross-pollination and hybridization, and the stagnation caused by being locked into a self-justifying clique closed to outside influence. He is careful to emphasize the temporary nature of any designations, describing vividly the 'lateral cultural forces which push and prod musical lineages into the shapes which they temporarily assume' (p. 26). Conservative tendencies are analogous to an immune system, to memes with built-in protectionism – don't learn about synth pop, it can't possibly have anything of value in it, stick with serious high electroacoustic art. He claims that it is always healthy to avoid seeing 'genre definitions as essential and eternal, when in fact they are only convenient ways of dividing the world into teachable and discussible sized chunks' (p. 35). More fluid models of cultural innovation like this can impact helpfully on practical composing; categories do not have to be taken too seriously, or seen as too static.

The compositional attributes of any of these styles could fill whole books in themselves, and any one might admit live interaction in many different ways, alongside fixed recordings.

---

[5]They may have evolved from work with analog equipment before the digital era, and there are always pockets of work that deny the digital and build analog circuits regardless; we know we can't entirely avoid analog when we consider sensors and speakers.

Table 8.1   Some music in which computers play an important part.

Genre	Description	A few representative works
N Music Studies	Early computer music as an artistic test of the new technology	Newman Guttman's *The Silver Scale* (1957); Jean-Claude Risset's *Computer Suite From Little Boy* (1968)
Computer stochastics	Advanced stochastic and serialist works created through computer programs	Xenakis's ST series (1962); Gottfried Michael Koenig's *Project I* (1964)
Spectralism	Audio analysis informs scores for live musicians, or electroacoustic manipulation of spectral data [Harvey, 2000]	Gérard Grisey's *Partiels* (1975); Jonathan Harvey's *Mortuos Plango, Vivos Voco* (1980)
Electroacoustic music	Computers are now the predominant production methodology in this long tradition. Many associated styles (as many or more than composers), but perhaps succinctly summarized as demanding concentrated listening, with especial focus on timbre and space [Landy, 2007]	Trevor Wishart's *Vox 5* (1986); Katharine Norman's *In the stream* (1989–90)
Sampling	Digital audio cut and paste makes copyright breach the easiest it has ever been (see Section 2.7)	John Oswald's *Plexure* (1993); Negativland's *U2* (1991)
8-bit	Original 1970s and 1980s video game music, and a modern revival movement which enjoys the nostalgia and the compositional constraint [Carlsson, 2008]	Rob Hubbard's *Thalamusik* (1987); YMCK's *kira*kira* (2005)
Dance pop production	Lots of electronic dance music (EDM) [Brewster and Broughton, 2006] and other computer-suffused popular music	Cher's *Believe* (1998); Dizzee Rascal's *I Luv U* (2003)
Hardcore to Jungle	The real potential of the digital sequencer in EDM becomes apparent as inhumanly fast breakbeat manipulations and frenetic mentasm riffs descend [Reynolds, 2008]	Prodigy's *Out of Space* (1992); Metalheads' *Terminator* (1992)
Ambient music by machine	From airports to club chillout rooms and after parties [Prendegast, 2003]	Aphex Twin's *Selected Ambient Works* (1985–92); Brian Eno's *Generative Music 1* (1996)
Glitch	Overloading error-correction circuits in digital audio hardware, intensive editing of maligned audio and deliberate synthesis of discontinuity [Cascone, 2000]	Yasunao Tone's *Solo for Wounded CD* (1985); Oval's *Systemisch* (1994)
Digital noise music and other 'others'	The manic overload of industrial, digital hardcore, breakcore and more; also, oppositional stances such as lowercase which make deliberate use of silence and quiet	Atari Teenage Riot's *Destroy 2000 Years of Culture* (1997); Sachiko M improvising with sampler

Each varies in emphasis within their musical materials. For example, stereotypical electronic dance music has an overt sense of beat to make dancing unambiguous, whereas rhythmic structure in electroacoustic works tends to be more experimental, sometimes free to the point of being ametric (as also in much ambient work). Choice of pitch materials extends from diatonic scales in 12-note equal temperament for much mainstream pop, through alternative tunings (as already explored in *The Silver Scale*), to sweeping glissandi and other more exotic configurations in frequency space that evoke timbre more than stable pitch. Timbral resources also vary from fixed instrumentations of pitched virtual synths and sampled percussion sounds, through the polystylistic appropriation of sampling, the deliberate adoption of digital audio characteristics such as lower bit rates and digital overload, to complex sound transformations in time and space as a central tenet of the music. In order to confront this variety, the next section explores different aspects of musical sound and structure.

8.2 ORGANIZING SOUND

Edgard Varèse famously described music as organized sound [Hugill, 2007]. This section investigates ways in which composers have approached the materials and structure of music, with a particular ear to computational examples. Important descriptors such as pitch and timbre will provide useful backdrops to our discussion, as well as higher level concepts such as musical form. Not all music focuses on the same aspects; otherwise musical life would be a lot duller. In composing music we decide which aspects of sound to treat, which attributes to prioritize, and therefore the appropriate structures and transformations for our materials. We adopt an operating theory of music, from an immense set of possibilities, and proceed as if the theory is 'true'; but we can always change our principles as soon as we move to the next project, or even change our mind midway through a piece.

In planning a work, the designer can engage with many timescales simultaneously. We often speak of **top–down** and **bottom–up** approaches, where in the hierarchy of timescales the 'top' is the **global** view over the longest scale, and the 'bottom' evokes the musical primitives at a **local** point in time. Between this ceiling and floor, intermediate levels run from **high level** to **low level** respectively.[6] In composing at the top level, the composer might establish an over-arching structure, a canvas to be filled; the bottom is the point of fine detail, where everything must finally be made specific (perhaps down to the small print of individual audio samples).[7] Our strategy of description in this section will essentially be bottom–up, as we work from low-level properties and sound events, to metrical structures, vertical and horizontal combinations, and global structuring templates.

---

[6]The number of stages in any hierarchy varies here, with Stockhausen noting 21 octaves' worth of time levels in his pitch–rhythm-form progression in *Kontakte* (1958–60) [Stockhausen and Barkin, 1962] whereas Curtis Roads has proposed nine major time regions, only six of which are practical; see Section 8.2.5.
[7]If it is not stretching the analogy too much, you might like to think of the progression of programming languages from high-level natural-language-like interfaces in adventure games to low-level assembler machine instructions.

8.2.1 Sound Objects and Parameters

> Each single sound has its own internal morphology. Much of this can be heard
> by the ear when listening is carefully educated. For the ultimate morphological
> study of sound objects we must go to the laboratory .... But you may also,
> accepting the work of acousticians, still continue to believe in the poetry of
> sound. [Schafer, 1986, p. 148]

In previous discussion of representation (Section 1.2.12) the **sound object** was introduced
as a generalized building block of music.[8] In theories of electronic music, a sound object
presents a much extended notion of a musical event, which embraces the dynamic time-
varying nature of sound [Landy, 2007; Wishart, 1996]. Our working definition for a sound
object might follow Curtis Roads: 'A basic unit of musical structure, generalizing the
traditional concept of note to include complex and mutating sound events on a time scale
ranging from a fraction of a second to several seconds' [Roads, 2001, p. 3].

There are various ways to treat sound objects by computer. We may stay close to the audio
signal, perhaps using audio analysis models to handle their rich time-varying properties;
multiple control functions of time could describe changing features of the sound. On the
other hand, first-order approximations are often encountered in symbolic representations
which simply use single values for each property of an event. Some Western scores and MIDI
sequences describe music as the combination of discrete 'notes' where a few clear and one-
dimensional attributes differentiate each event (i.e., start time, duration, pitch, dynamic and
assigned instrument). Since this is not a full description of the time-varying spectral content
of a sound – the minutiae of wobbling pitch with vibrato, or the attack times and levels of
different partials – work is left to a performer or synthesizer to make up the fine detail. The
work to be done is unambiguous enough in many circumstances to make the approximation
effective.[9] When speaking of 'properties' or 'attributes' of sound, and especially where
these descriptors are numeric or at least enumerable, the standard term is **parameter**. To
cope with a complex sound object, many values may be needed, whether attempting to
summarize statistics of the sound, or track a feature over time. Some properties of music
are inherently multidimensional; General MIDI notwithstanding, it is impossible to find a
single value that summarizes the aural timbre of a sound.

Even before computers became widely available as a natural tool to handle parameterized
events, parametrical thinking was established as an important current in musical thought.
An archetype is provided by Olivier Messiaen's *Mode de valeurs et d'intensités* (1949),[10]

---

[8]R. Murray Schafer [1994] further differentiates a contextualized sound event (a bell heard in an urban soundscape) from a sound object as laboratory atom for intensive listening (just listening to a bell sound for its inherent spectrotemporal qualities, escaping source bonding), in the tradition of Pierre Schaeffer's studio work. We proceed with a looser definition of a sound object in this book and use event and object interchangeably.

[9]Which is just as well for whole repertoires of Western concert music. There are parallel oral traditions of interpretation which help to resolve the differences between information in a score and in performance; reimplementing these performance traditions by computer can be an arduous task (however, see Section 9.4).

[10]Milton Babbitt's *Three Compositions for Piano* (1947) are an earlier but less historically influential example.

a highly influential study for piano which extended Schoenberg's method of ordering pitches to multiple parameters at once. The parameters here are rhythmic note spacings, scale pitches, dynamics, and different attack articulations, each of which can only take on values from a finite set of possibilities. Such a note-locked parameterization is far more straightforward for piano than for more continuously controlled instruments (such as wind instruments modulated by human breath). Nevertheless, the piece had a huge influence on a new generation of composers at the start of the 1950s in the integral serialism movement, which in turn impacted on electronic and computer music.

Through the influence of parameterization, composers have often treated as 'real' the independence of pitch, timbre, loudness and more. This reductionism does not always work in music, because even low-level attributes can show interdependencies. Rhythm and pitch in a note sequence are interlinked in melodic effect. Loudness and pitch, pitch and timbre, timbre and loudness are all psychoacoustically interrelated (a more energetic sine tone travels slightly further on the basilar membrane and can be heard as a slightly lower pitch; for more complex tones, more energetic sounds tend to be brighter; pitch perception depends on interpreting the available partial information). As Barry Truax [1998, p. 141] notes, 'technology has often allowed audio parameters to be controlled independently, something that cannot occur naturally, the most common example being a change in intensity level independent of spectrum, as practised in studio mixing'. The frequency dependence of intensity is familiar from the equal loudness contours. Nevertheless, if this proviso is born in mind, we often take low-level qualities as independent properties for convenience.

The following subsections treat various aspects of music. Proceeding from bottom to top scales, sometimes the musical attributes are easily parameterized and modeled numerically, and at other times we encounter more involved concepts, with which it can take much effort to work by computer. Though the upcoming materials often refer themselves most strongly to extended Western musical traditions, we shall discuss many basic auditory factors of usefulness to sound artists or perhaps even as jumping-off points to found new traditions. Sound art often engages with basic psychoacoustic postulates (the work of Alvin Lucier is a clever take on many principles of acoustics and audition), but can also traverse many interesting territories overlapping with music, even if sometimes driven by different conceptual narratives. Furthermore, not all aspects of sound are equal in ordinary perception, and particular aesthetics will concentrate on certain aspects to the exclusion or at least downgrading of others. In electroacoustic music, space and timbre tend to be central attributes for compositional treatment, and the notion of a sound object much more highly theorized and cherished than 'notes'. Depending on the context, authors have proposed pecking orders for parameters. For example, in discussing musical memory Snyder [2000] separates primary (pitch, harmony, rhythm) and secondary (loudness, tempo) parameters, with the former supporting recognition of patterns.

Before we commence the individual discussions, Table 8.2 summarizes some of the numerical limits on perception of auditory and musical parameters, drawing from the

Table 8.2 Some basic auditory properties.

Attribute	Description
Time extent	Perceptual present around three seconds [Pöppel and Wittman, 1999; Pöppel, 2004]; short-term memory extends up to 10–15 seconds or around 30–36 events [Snyder, 2000]
Motor production	With one hand a human can tap out no more than 10 events per second [London, 2004] (faster actions are possible through muscular chunking such as a spread chord and hand alteration; piano trills run at 12–14 Hz, for example); haptic (action) or rhythmic rates are usually quoted below 16 Hz, before the onset of pitch perception
Frequency and pitch perception limits	16–16 000 Hz for an adult hearing general frequency content; rare golden ears and younger children might hear wider still, even above 20 kHz [Moore, 2004]. For fundamental frequencies for melody, 20–5000 Hz [van Dinther and Patterson, 2005], but with some individual variability [Deutsch, 1999, pp. 236–7]
Pitch discrimination	A rule of thumb for spotting a pitch difference between consecutive tones is 6–10 cents (say, a 24th of a tone), but this is somewhat context dependent. Roederer [1995] puts the just noticeable difference for frequency for sine tones at 3% around 100 Hz (51 cents) and 0.5% around 2000 Hz (8 cents). You can use higher harmonics to help for more complex tones, giving finer resolution. For simultaneous tones, hearing out beating allows closer precision still
Spatial discrimination	See Section 2.5.1
Loudness perception	One decibel is a good guide to the just noticeable difference. But loudness perception is a complex phenomenon (like pitch perception); for instance, dependent on spectral and temporal masking. Instantaneous loudness can be approximated using the equal loudness contours
Masking	Another complex phenomenon where the presence of energy at one frequency can disturb accurate reception of energy at a nearby frequency. Masking curves are asymmetric, with lower frequencies masked less than higher by energy at a given masker frequency [Moore, 2004]
Primary timbral cues	Attack envelope, changing spectral content (both partials and noise) [Risset and Wessel, 1999]
Sensory dissonance	For simultaneous frequencies, interference occurs within a critical band of around one-third of an octave, with beating up to around 20 Hz and then a general sense of 'roughness'. Sensory dissonance is the summation of overall roughness effects from the interaction of composite sounds [Sethares, 2005]
Primary segmentation cues	Large sudden simultaneous change in frequency content (spectral energies), fundamental frequency change, recognition of representative event shapes (attack followed by onset of vibrato) and more

psychoacoustic and psychological literature (see also the further reading in Chapter 1). Many will be expanded in the subsequent sections, but there is not enough room to cover everything here.

8.2.2 Pitch

Pitch is a psychoacoustic phenomenon, a perceived fundamental frequency of a complex tone. We are sensitive to any potential periodicities present in sound, and can extract multiple simultaneous stable pitch percepts from a polyphonic sound. Pitch is a chief carrying parameter of much of the world's music, and control of pitch a valuable attribute for a musical instrument. This is not to say that all music depends on pitch, just as many interesting noise sounds do not have a clear singular pitch, but pitch tends to be a strong feature and cue when present. When we fail to hear out the fused harmonic components that lead to the assignment of a clear pitch, it is irresistible. Beyond music, our perception of pitch is coupled to tracking intonation in speech, particularly in tonal languages such as Mandarin, but also in recognizing questions in English.

The strength of pitch perception makes it an important compositional parameter, but there are many different aspects of pitch that can be exploited for musical purposes, and much overlap with timbral properties. The following list breaks down some psychological and compositional factors in pitch perception, with reference to their potential in music making. The list is meant to convey the extent of theorizing and compositional activity around this important parameter, but cannot describe everything in detail.

- Differential sensitivity in hearing over the frequency range, following equal loudness contours, with 1–4 kHz particularly sensitive (widest dynamic range), and 250 Hz to 4 kHz particularly important for recognizing speech from the formants. The ability to pick up on frequency changes also varies, with models such as the Mel scale for sine tones noting the weaker resolution for low frequencies. However, psychoacoustic data for sine tones may not extend smoothly to richer harmonic spectra where pitch determination involves reconciling more information.

- Relative versus absolute pitch. The majority work with relative pitch, and true absolute pitch (AP) is comparatively rare in the general populace, though there is greater incidence among musicians (one estimate puts it at 15% for professional musicians) and those with a first language that is tonal. Due to a prevalence of relative pitch, differences may be more important than absolute values in pitch representations. Unstable reference pitch can be observed in the beautiful repetition calls with descending center of some pygmy vocalizations, or, indeed, the beautiful gradual drift of reference pitch of some a capella choral singing. Drones are often used to provide an unchanging reference, such as that provided by tanpura in Hindustani music, or as the core of a genre of drone music. Computers are highly reliable as reference instruments, so you have to program them to deviate . . . .

- Continuous (glissandi, portamento, pitch envelopes) versus discrete (fixed scales, stable 'notes', categories). Electronic music has seen a lot of glissandi, from the theremin and ondes martinot, to Ligeti's study *Glissandi* (1957) and Saariaho's long, long glissandi between two chords in *Vers le Blanc* (1982).

- Linear versus logarithmic. Pitch is normally apprehended as an attribute of logarithmic frequency, not linear. Frequency ratios in frequency space and corresponding additive pitch intervals in logarithmic frequency space are the standard representation. Nevertheless, there is some evidence that a musical culture can form directly around a linear frequency space, as in some Aboriginal music [Will and Ellis, 1996], or from using the harmonic series for pitch materials (which is, after all, formed out of equal steps in frequency).

- Octave equivalence. The octave is a privileged interval, and allows separation of chroma and height information in helical representations [Deutsch, 1999]. This also enables psychoacoustic illusions based on a clever crossfade of chroma, allowing ever-increasing progressions, as per Roger Shepard's tones and Jean-Claude Risset's glissandi [Risset, 1989].[11] Octave equivalence can also be dropped, as in the non-octave scales of Xenakis's sieves, Chowning's *Stria* (1977) based on the psuedo-octave golden ratio 1.618:1 rather than 2:1 [Meneghini, 2007], and the Bohlen–Pierce scale [Mathews and Pierce, 1989a]. Slightly stretched octaves occur in piano tuning, and can be deliberately employed in constructing tuning systems to match particular timbres.

- Combinatorics of a set of discrete pitches. Pitch classes as representatives of particular groups of pitches under octave equivalence (a set of discrete chroma) – for example, 'all the Cs'. Pitch class mathematics underlies both analysis and composition in Schoenbergian serialism.

- Tuning systems, with equal temperament only as a special case (the ocean of alternative tunings in the world's music, Harry Partch, Wendy Carlos and more) [Carlos, 1987; Sethares, 2005; Loy, 2007a].

- Pitch inflections and expressive character. Microtonal embellishments, as in Arabic monody.

- Interactions with timbre: harmonic amplitudes change even as pitch stays stable in sound color melodies (*klangfarbenmelodie*); timbre varies with register in acoustic instruments; just intonation as minimizing beats; sensory dissonance (beats and roughness due to proximate spectral information in overlapping tones) as determining fit of timbre to pitch resources [Sethares, 2005]. A fused pitch percept can be broken down and heard out as harmonics, and by individual manipulation of partial frequencies transition further to inharmonic tones [Smalley, 1986, p. 65]. We can play with the phenomenon of the missing fundamental. Chowning [1999] groups harmonics within a mass of partials based on shared vibrato to allow pitches to appear out of previously uncorrelated sound.

---

[11] Kenneth Knowlton and Laurie Spiegel also constructed a perpetual accelerando by the crossfading of metrical layers.

- Harmony as juxtaposition of multiple pitches; cultural dissonance as societal judgments on the purest intervals, and changing musical taste for discord.[12] Elaborate systems of tension and release in harmony over time have been developed in Western tonal music, for example. New pitch resources inevitably lead to new harmonies.

- Melody as the sequencing of pitches over time, combining pitch and rhythm over longer timescales. Note however that the discrete pitched events of a Western common practice score melody are more generally a long and complicated musical line with many operating factors, one of which might be described by a pitch envelope, showing many expressive deviations and continuous inflections.

Many of these aspects, such as absolute reference, continuous versus discrete, equivalence classes and combinatorial operations, extend directly to other musical parameters.

It is worth learning various numerical systems for describing pitch, which will allow you both to cope with the well-worn 12-note equal temperament, and to deviate or slide into richer territories of alternative tunings. The sheer convenience of the computer in exploring this territory cannot be underestimated. Consider working with frequency and ratios (a compositional example is shown in Figure 8.3). Wonderful systems can be built, particularly when the tuning reference is allowed to degrade (use lots of 7/5 and 11/17 ratios over and over from a starting frequency to go up and down, and see how the octave disappears).

The fundamental equation of tuning provides the means to move between a linear and a logarithmic frequency space, by moving from ratios of frequencies to steps in log frequency. We must set up some number n of equal steps dividing a base interval ratio r, so we end up considering the nth root of r, $r^{1/n}$. If we then want to access individual equally spaced points in log frequency, the kth step is the kth power of the basic ratio, so from any starting position has frequency ratio:

$$r^{k/n} \tag{8.1}$$

The variable k can also go outside of the range 0 to $n-1$, since $k=n$ gives back the ratio r, $k=2n$ gives r^2 which is two applications of the ratio, $k=-n$ gives r^{-1} which is the inverse ratio, changing frequency in the opposite direction, and so forth. An octave is expressed via the ratio $r=2$. A non-octave system could use another base, such as the 13 notes in a tritave (ratio of 3) for the Bohlen–Pierce scale $3^{k/13}$ [Mathews and Pierce, 1989a]. Standard 12-tone equal temperament (12TET) is $2^{k/12}$; you should see that you can choose n to immediately obtain any nTET, packed into any base ratio. Unequal scales are important, and can be formed by selection of a subset of allowable indices k (such as the diatonic scale within the chromatic in 12TET, which uses $k=0, 2, 4, 5, 7, 9, 11$). Really unequal scales can be formed by very large n and selective k to closely approximate any desired intervals. One famous system is to take $r=2$, $n=1200$ to form **cents** (because there are 100 per semitone). The cents system is useful because it allows easier comparison of different scales away from the

---

[12] The chromatic aggregate at the start of Jean-Féry Rebel's *Les elemens* (1737) depicting chaos is absolutely shocking in the context of its time; in another sense, it is a brilliant anticipation of Alfred Schnittke!

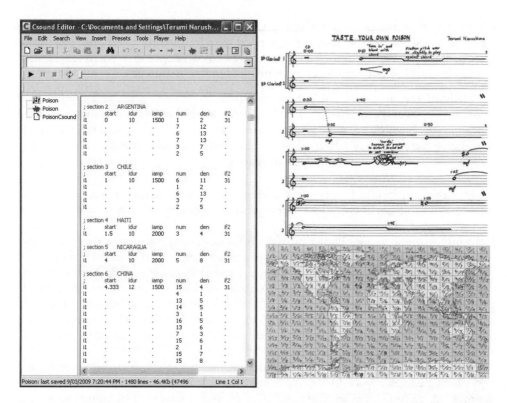

Figure 8.3 *Taste Your Own Poison* (2007), by Terumi Narushima, which is 'a microtonal work for two clarinets and pre-recorded electronics. The computer part was constructed using a map of the world, which was divided into an 18 × 18 grid (bottom right of image). This grid was treated as a Lambdoma, a way of arranging a set of ratios in a two-dimensional matrix. Each box in the grid is assigned a fraction (e.g., 1/1, 3/2, 4/5, etc.), which is then used as a tuning ratio in just intonation to generate pitch. The numerators and denominators of these ratios are represented in the Csound score (left of image) under the columns "num" and "den". Throughout the piece various countries are represented in sound as a conglomeration of pitches taken from the world map grid (e.g., "Argentina" is represented as a chord consisting of 1/2, 7/12, 6/13, 7/13, 3/7 and 2/5). Two clarinets interact with the resulting harmonies to produce beating effects and difference tones (top right of image), sometimes playing with the electronic part, sometimes playing against it' (personal communication from the composer, 11 March 2009). Reproduced by permission of Terumi Narushima, using a map by Takumi Nomura (http://www4.plala.or.jp/nomrax/GL/index.html).

mentally confusing pure frequency intervals. So it is musically convenient to be working in a linear space; this is what the piano keys, guitar frets, notes on staves and other standard representations provide for pitch.

The one thing we have missed out here is the reference pitch. The ratio obtained from the tuning equation above must be multiplied by a standard reference frequency (such as concert A at 440 Hz or middle C, 261.626 Hz, or another standard such as a baroque A at 415 Hz). The steps k will then be relative to that reference, so for concert A, $k = 0$ would return the A. With quirky Western musical alphabets, it is more typical to work relative to C, since the musical scales already 'start' at C.

There are a few systems of numerical tags for particular notes. The piano's famous 'middle C' might be written C4 (for chroma C and octave 4), or as MIDI Note 60. One octave above could be c″, MIDI Note 72, C5 .... Note that the choice of octave 4 for middle C is a generally widespread convention, but not an absolute one, since C3 has sometimes been used, or as is implicit in the name of MIDI Note 60, C5 ($5 * 12 = 60$) could be invoked. MIDI Notes can be used for fractional tones, even though the MIDI standard doesn't easily accommodate them without extensions to the specification. So 60.5 is a quartertone above middle C. In general, we use cents as a measure of pitch sensitivity (since the cent scale, at 1200 per octave, has greater resolution than our ears in all normal circumstances).

Particular discrete scales can be given as cents, or as ratios. The basic step in the all-too-familiar 12TET is one semitone, 100 cents, or the ratio $2^{1/12} \approx 1.05946$. Low integer rational ratios correspond to steps early up the harmonic series, such as the perfect fifth, 3/2, which shows how far the third harmonic is above the second; these give rise to lesser beating, for 'pure' interval sounds. Wendy Carlos's α scale is constructed from steps of 78 cents at a time; it doesn't repeat exactly at a pure octave, but provides close approximations to some other just intervals such as 6/5, 5/4 and 3/2, while maintaining an additional identity [Carlos, 1987]. It can be written as $2^{k/15.385}$ using our equation above, where the non-octave nature should be clear.

Particular scales can be analyzed for the quality of each interval between component notes. There are some intricate games of compromise here, such as minimizing beats by approximating just intonation and maximizing modulatory flexibility (self-similar transpositions and how uniform those sets are). This leads to all sorts of interesting mathematics, as theorists have sought particular collections of pitches which achieve some desirable qualities, often at the cost of others [Balzano, 1980; Loy, 2007a]. Tuning systems are further complicated by timbral factors, due to sensory dissonance. Beating or roughness from the interaction of partials can occur, especially when playing more than one note at once, but also higher up the harmonic series of a single note where the partials cluster closer and closer together. Computers can be used to search for optimal solutions to the harmonic recipe for a given tuning, and the best tuning for a given harmonic timbre, given a model of sensory dissonance [Sethares, 2005]. This is yet another way in which musical parameters interact, but also another site of the computer's great facility in investigation of pitch.

8.2.3 Timbre

Timbre usually ends up as the catch-all category for the many interesting qualities that differentiate sounds, and composers can draw on innumerable resources here. As we have seen from the powerful analysis, processing and synthesis models available, timbre is highly governable by the computer, and is one of the primary areas of investigation in computer music. It is also a multidimensional space of great potential complexity; we can end up trying to describe all possible sounds in all their richness, operating anywhere within the full bounds of acoustic or electrical production and auditory perception.

As discussed in Section 1.2.7, perceptual studies have attempted to isolate primary dimensions, especially for the timbre of periodic instrumental tones. Three recurring features are the temporal amplitude envelope (particularly the attack portion), the spectral energy distribution (as measured for example by spectral centroid) and the spectrotemporal content (amount of fluctuation in partials, spectral flux) [Hajda, 2007, p. 260]. Yet these three features may not be adequate to describe noisy sounds, only as principal components for classifying orchestral instruments. The sines+noise model has been held up as an advanced analysis tool that more generally summarizes the dynamic variation of sounds [Risset and Wessel, 1999], though even here we might want to model transients separately. Physical modeling or other specificity of acoustic model in the analysis may be required to relate timbral variation to physical variation in articulation.

It is still natural to seek ways to reduce the large data sets of analysis models to identify principal perceptual components. Aside from automated machine learning strategies, there is a role here for 'semantic' verbal models, which directly engage with the sorts of high-level descriptors familiar to musicians ('a dull cracking followed by a bright squeal'). There are more intuitive theories, usually motivated by intensive listening, extending out from 'basic' timbre to multiple aspects of electroacoustic musical experience. In the Schaefferian taxonomic tradition, Denis Smalley [1997] offers one such model in **spectromorphology**, whose very name evokes the tricky but alluring change of sound shapes in time that a theory of timbre has to contend with (spectromorphology goes on to consider some longer timescales we shall treat later). In alliance with studies of listening, composers have engaged with the psychoacoustic literature in many ways. For instance, Fred Lerdahl [1987, pp. 141–142] offers a list of five timbral qualities for timbral consonance and dissonance – brightness, vibrato, attack and release envelope, sensory dissonance and harmonicity (presence of pitch) – which makes clear the overlap with pitch perception implicit in spectral models.

It is possible to imagine flying through a timbre space [Wessel, 1979], once a set of clear features are identified to form the dimensions of that space. Families of sounds can be placed within the space according to their features, and the current position can act to select the nearest sound, as per feature-based synthesis (see Section 5.1.5). Alternatively, coordinates might directly control the parameters of some perceptually motivated synthesis model. The technical machinery of machine learning may be employed to assist in deriving such spaces using clustering tools, or to access a high-dimensional space from a lower number of control parameters. Yet these timbre spaces are not so straightforward as to make this technically effortless; sound transformations can rarely be as smooth as might be dreamed. All sounds vary in time, and the time envelopes of the spectral content of a sound are intimately tied to describing a given timbre, so as we traverse a timbre space in time we may need to access different sounds at different points in their evolution. The compatibility of the stages of different sounds is a factor in the success of the resulting hybrid sounds, and requires additional sound modeling to compensate well. Many analysis models allow the exploration of sound morphing, through interpolating model parameters, and spectral morphing algorithms are an explicit feature of Symbolic Sound's Kyma, or the CERL Sound Group's Loris. Such timbral transformations are a natural interest of electroacoustic composers seeking to reconcile diverse sound materials. Trevor Wishart's *Vox 5* (1986) or Alejandro Viñao's *Masago's Confession* (1996) provide examples that transform the human voice; there are many other works that provide successful morphs that go far beyond a basic crossfade.

Finding the extent of timbral resources is a large-scale research program. The rich range of disciplines and ideas involved in this quest includes:

- organology as the traditional study of musical instrument classification (such as the oft-criticized Hornbostel–Sachs scheme of idiophone, membranophone, chordophone, aerophone and electrophone);

- materials science and acoustics, with sound models following physical modeling – excitation and resonance, coupled acoustic systems;

- psychological studies into timbre [Risset and Wessel, 1999; Beauchamp, 2007a];

- music information retrieval engineering (see Section 7.2), and the application of machine learning in automatic sound source classification (soundscapes and music [Aucouturier and Defreville, 2007], or music and speech [Scheirer and Slaney, 1997], have been differentiated quite readily on their signal characteristics);

- ensemble timbre as the combination of sounds, as in instrumentation or orchestration [Bregman, 1990] (Snyder [2000, p. 199] calls this 'sonority', and Aucouturier [2006] discusses 'polyphonic timbre' as the composite sound of complicated mixes in audio recordings);

- novel electronic timbres in sound synthesis only possible via a loudspeaker, from probabilistically updated breakpoints to granular synthesis;

- composers' intuitive classifications, for example John Cage's six source sound categories for *Williams Mix* (1952–3): urban, rural, electronic, handmade, wind powered and 'small' sounds (quiet sounds amplified);

- theories of the sound object and sound morphology [Landy, 2007] – writings of Pierre Schaeffer, Trevor Wishart and Denis Smalley, to name three.

What about timbre as a carrying parameter of musical argument? We can easily point to the compositional import of certain associations, such as the evocation of coarse llama calls in Andean music [Stobart and Cross, 2000], or the choice of sound materials in electroacoustic music from dentists' drills to slamming doors. Distinct voices in a complex texture (auditory streams) can be separated out by a listener on the basis of their timbre, with part of the art of orchestration (with or without Western orchestra) being control of the blend of different layers, and focusing of an observer's attention on particular detail. Particular sub-attributes of catch-all timbre may be the object of attention, such as the role of beating in Gamelan, the control of sensory dissonance in the design of a progression, the manipulation of brightness in sweeping the center frequency of a filter, and many more. Tension and release can depend in this way on timbral roles. It is less clear whether timbre can be extended to form the basis for a hierarchical compositional grammar: 'What is not yet known is the extent to which variation along the dimensions of timbre can maintain perceptual invariance in the face of changes along the pitch and duration dimensions, or the extent to which listeners can acquire stable abstract representations of an ordered system of timbre relations' [McAdams, 1989, p. 190]. Fred Lerdahl [1987] carried out preliminary investigation into hierarchies of timbre analogous to discrete scales in pitch, considering tension and release based on two-dimensional planes of vibrato and harmonicity, and vowel type and brightness. While he claimed some success in his experiments, which used the IRCAM software Chant to synthesize systems of vowel sounds, the wide adoption of any such timbre model remains speculative, and composers have pursued individual systems, often on a work-by-work basis.

Despite a question mark over timbral hierarchy, timbre remains a central concern in computer music composition, sometimes for the wow factor of sound transformation, sometimes for the importance of specific sounds as materials and the dissection of their makeup in the course of composition. Timbre is also central to practices in free improvisation; in his *Hsustem* Bill Hsu's interactive computer music system performs with the saxophonist John Butcher, specifically tracking timbral parameters such as the brightness, sensory dissonance and harmonicity [Hsu, 2005], and synthesizing responses driven by these features. Part of the joy of extended models of music, and computer music implementations, is that so many jumping-off points are available for interesting compositional investigation, and timbre is a worthy adversary.

8.2.4 Space

In electronic music in particular, controlling the placement of sounds in space has become an important compositional avenue. This is most evident in the great electroacoustic music tradition and sound installations, but is also now a factor for film music and popular music mixing for cinema standards, or in electronic dance music production for some custom sound systems. Many composers have become besotted with thoughts of flying sounds through space, or evoking alternative spatial scenes despite local acoustics. There are practical obstacles to overcome, including the less than perfect ability of human observers to track moving objects and the lack of a perfect spatialization technology [Malham, 2001]. Sections 2.5 and 4.3.3 have discussed a relevant backdrop of psychoacoustics and implementation details.

Spatialization strategies reflect two considerations, based on the division between live performance and intensive studio preparation:

- pre-rendering for a specific playback technology, perhaps written in an adaptable format such as Ambisonics, or in multiple versions for different spatial set-ups;

- live **diffusion** or projection of sound under the control of a performer, usually based on some sort of diffusion score or rehearsed plan, but also potentially improvised.

These two overlap in practice. It is not that the latter category doesn't involve a great deal of careful preparation ahead of the concert itself, but that every spatial scene and movement is not irredeemably hard-coded into the source. For the former category, Malham [2001, p. 37] writes of 'a more abstract, less "performance space-centred" spatial music'. Because of the interaction between a spatialization system and local room acoustics,[13] some element of adaptation to a local performance space is the pragmatic option. The diffuser can 'work the room', matching gestures in the work with appropriate mixing in the room. Acknowledging this, some composers 'compose for diffusion', perhaps only creating stereo mixes [Otondo and Barrett, 2007], but with involved diffusion scores [Austin and Smalley, 2000; Austin and Field, 2001]. Indeed, many live performances involve just this careful balance of live mixing, even if not officially placed under the banner of 'diffusion performance'; keeping runaway bass levels under control in a club performance, or seeking to add sparkle to a scene by a judicious sprinkling of surround sound panning. Some form of live monitoring, and at least rehearsal time set-up, is usually required even for pre-prepared works.

Combining live acoustic musicians and computer processing brings its own set of problems, and the precedence effect is very prevalent here. One strategy is just to amplify the performers through the same system as the electronics. Another more subtle integration is to delay the electronic signal to the speakers so that the first wavefront comes from the acoustic source, even if there is an amplified sound afterwards; this assists the audience in assigning the location of the sound source to the performer. Even so, live spatial processing of a performer will inevitably leave the realms of normal reality, as the violin gesture you saw performed on stage rushes around the room behind you. Again, careful use of delays to match acoustic travel times can make the effect more subtle, and careful balance between electronics and acoustic parts will be required [Austin and Smalley, 2000; Otondo and Barrett, 2007].

The loudspeaker orchestra is one practical instrument for the effective diffusion of works [Harrison, 1998]. Figure 8.4 is one view of the Birmingham ElectroAcoustic Sound Theatre (BEAST) system (www.beast.bham.ac.uk). The positioning of the many speakers allows direct use of the speakers themselves as sources at a range of distances. This is a natural way to work with the precedence effect, which can otherwise destroy virtual images where members of an audience are at different distances from speakers. Adaptability to varying concert locations is a bonus; the particularities of different venues are embraced rather than seeking an ideal of playback that will only be distorted by local room conditions. Conducting the loudspeaker orchestra is a practiced diffusion artist, employing virtuosic

---

[13] Even where technology has sought to minimize such problems; think of the very different dimensions of different cinemas or concert halls, and the difficulty of holding concerts in artificially damped anechoic chambers.

fader manipulation guided by hearing. Computer automation is less prevalent, because setting up room-specific mixes takes longer than the rehearsal time available for the concert, and the arrival of an audience inevitably perturbs the acoustic.

Figure 8.4   Spatial panoply: BEAST in a test session. Reproduced by permission of © Scott Wilson.

Having considered these practicalities, please don't be dissuaded from experimenting with careful spatial movements in your works! A single sound projectionist, even with a finger on each of ten sliders, is limited in their capacity for simultaneous action, so highly active passages may only be realized by studio preparation and automation [Truax, 1998]. The specter of eventual room acoustics is no bar to headphone-based pieces, even if audience members might need to carry their own personalized HRTFs around for ideal listening [Cheng and Wakefield, 2001]. Composing for a wavefield synthesis rig, which is usually set up in a dedicated space, there is a good chance of getting back what you put in (you might need to compose a work directly on the system that will be used for a concert, but there are some instances of virtual mock-ups). Cinema dimensions may vary widely, but surround sound formats like 5.1 are rather pragmatic to begin with.

Ideas for the use of spatial cues in composition include:

- **differentiation of multiple sources** – spatial position can be an important aid to distinguishing auditory streams (distinct layers and voices) and may allow involved counterpoint; computer aid can assist tight synchronization over large distances by appropriate built-in delays to speakers, or by networking technology to guide human performers;

- **moving sound sources** – the classic whizzing effects. For most spatialization systems, imaging is less stable if trying to place sounds 'within the audience' – physically mingling audience and speakers is one pragmatic way around that – so flying paths are most effective when heard as moving outside the loudspeakers. Implementation may exploit additional cues for changing distance or motion Doppler effects. Wishart [1996] draws some rather elaborate patterns – think of bees dancing and the infinity symbol – few of which are practically realizable as perfect geometric shapes on a given spatialization system, but all of which are potentially stimulating visions of the spatialized world;

- **spatial layers** – spatial qualities and distributions for sound objects and strata, close foreground and distant background, evoking complex soundscapes;

- **spatial illusions and transformation** – playing with reality through contradictory or extreme cues, rooms within rooms, transitioning scene geometry and other manipulations of the spatial models themselves.

While space can be used as part of instrumentation, as in the first example of hearing out auditory streams, the other ideas bring space to the fore (pardon the pun) as a primary compositional gesture. The particularities of hearing out that effect on a given spatialization system at a particular concert are intricate, which is why human diffusers can stay involved with the sound right up to the moment of playback. Yet the compositional idea can be solid enough to be preserved across renditions, particularly if the composer's notes make this clear to future performers, or the composer practically provides multiple mixes for different situations. Using gains alone to mix sounds in space is unlikely to provide the most convincing results; we have seen the more involved spectral and time cues required to go beyond the IID modeling of amplitude panning, but more powerful spatial models are available to composers in computer music systems. It is also worth experimenting with filters and delays for each layer in establishing a scene; the close illusion of reality, even if not founded in a full perceptually derived synthesis model, may make an interesting compositional construction. To provide true spatial motion, it is also worth recording materials using more spatially aware microphones, such as the soundfield microphone of Ambisonics.

Electroacoustic composers in particular have written a lot on the potential and demands of spatial composition, and their writings are worth examining for further ideas [Wishart, 1996; Barrett, 2002; Smalley, 2007].

8.2.5 Time

The closest music gets to stasis is probably La Monte Young's Manhattan apartment installation *The Base 9:7:4 Symmetry* ... (the actual title is quite a lot longer), which has been running continuously, give or take a power cut, since 1993. It consists, unceasingly, of collected sinusoidal components from high up the harmonic series, featuring prime number harmonics. Even here, your conscious attention scans or slips between partials, interactions with acoustic room modes change the relative amplitudes in the pattern if you move your head, and close harmonics beat. Time is irresistible, and we now review the perception of time, and rhythmic structures, with respect to which music subsists.

Human perception of time is influenced by information content, in that the bounds of short-term memory can be overloaded more quickly by a high density of events. But the window of the perceptual present, as the sum of events forming the extended sense of 'now', is around three seconds [Pöppel, 2004]. Various integration constants operate in our perceptual systems to smooth the fine detail of variation. We can consider a number of timescales with respect to musical information, from microsound, through the perceptual present, to the overall form of a composition. Table 8.3 encapsulates aspects of time perception from the literature in order of increasing scale; the nine named timescales of Roads [2001] are also incorporated into the diagram, appearing at the smallest time at which they become relevant.

As we hear events in time, we are always constructing expectations on a number of timescales about future events [Huron, 2006]. In some circumstances, these expectancies form a particular template, a sense of meter, though we should be careful before too quickly jumping to invoke conventional Western time signatures.

So the patterning of events in time gives rise to the interlinked phenomena of rhythm and meter. Rhythm is the actual placing of events (usually up to about 10–15 per second), which in some cases may be free of any steady metrical implication, as in free time. Aside from such glorious free examples as Indian alap, much contemporary classical and electroacoustic music has deliberately avoided invoking stable repetition, sometimes a little perversely, to the loss of listeners whose expectations are not invigorated. Yet the usual state of rhythm is to be accompanied by, to work within, a sense of clear expectancy, engendered by a sensation of cyclic repetition at one or more levels. It can all seem a bit chicken and egg, but rhythm can establish a certain metrical framework, with respect to which future events are expected and interpreted. There is always the option of changing metrical field again in turn if the evidence points that way.

Different forms of metrical framework exist, and may involve some sort of hierarchy of time levels [Lerdahl and Jackendoff, 1983; Parncutt, 1994]. A Western time signature provides a set number of repetitions (the numerator) of a basic division (the denominator). There may be a level at which the divisions are grouped in non-equal portions, such as additive structures like $2+2+3$ or $3+3+2$: this is what Justin London designates NI-meter [London, 2004], the NI standing for 'Non-Isochronous'. Beyond this lie more

Table 8.3 Musical timescales.

Time (seconds)	Description	Roads [2001, pp. 3–4]
0.0	Idealized sense of now in mathematics	Infinitesimal
0.000002	Resolution of auditory system for sound localization	Subsample
0.0000226757	One sample at 44 100 Hz sampling rate	Sample
0.001	Minimal fast amplitude attack or release time for enveloping without click; Pierce's estimate of the temporal accuracy of the ear for click sounds [Pierce, 1999, p. 5]	Micro
0.01	Time to auditory cortex from eardrum [Leman, 1993, p.133]	
0.0116	Spacing of windows at hop size of 512 samples ($R = 44\,100$)	
0.02	It's hard to hear the order of individual events whose separation is under this time – window of simultaneity for tones rather than clicks	
0.03	Time to hear a sound 10 m away; horizon of simultaneity for vision and audition (vision system is slower to process, but light is effectively instantaneous)	
0.01–0.05	Chord onset asynchrony; spread over notes of supposedly simultaneous chord	
0.03–0.05	After this point, distinct echoes start to be heard	
0.001–0.1	Grains of granular synthesis	
0.075	Average inter-note timing interval in a fast piano trill	
0.1	Limit of motor production for individual events (not including motor chunking such as strumming over five fingers)	Sound object
0.18	Reaction time (sensory and command delay) [Gillespie, 1999, p. 255]	
0.2	One phoneme or short musical event	
0.25	Shortest appreciable beat	
0.5–0.6	Preferred tempo for beats	
2	Maximal beat duration	Meso
2–3	Limits of perceptual present	
3	Duration of a line of a poem, or short musical phrase	
10–15	Limits of short-term memory (also expressed as 30–36 events); limits of phrase perceived as one segment	
180	Three-minute pop song	Macro
1 800	A long tape piece of 30 minutes	
10 800	Three-hour opera	
1 471 228 928	Jem Finer's *Longplayer* (2000–3000) installation for the current millennium	Supra
∞	Idealized duration of a sine tone in Fourier analysis: not very practical	Infinite

expressive patterns still, which don't easily allow a common divisor: consider a master cycle containing irregular markers, as in a clave pattern in Afro-Cuban music, or the dance steps of Hardanger fiddle music. There must, however, be some sort of cyclic return within the bounds of mortal memory, even if marked by a particular complex pattern rather than an isochronous beat present in the music.

The metrical structure summarizes the full expectancies at various scales, and hierarchically we can build up complex sets of subdivisions of any span of time. The appreciation of multiple levels is often aided by certain clear interrelations between them, such as simple divisions by 2 or 3, or culturally well-known timbral patterns as markers. We can be aware of multiple related levels of pulsation at once [Parncutt, 1994],[14] but tend to select a preferred reference level. For conventional beats, this is often chosen close to 500–600 milliseconds (100–120 bpm) [Clarke, 1988; van Noorden and Moelants, 1999]. We are highly familiar with very explicit beat patterns, not least from the hard tread of electronic dance music. But beats can be mentally rather than physically present; Autechre's generative rhythms for the *Anti-EP* (1994) always manage to imply an underlying beat, despite changing continually with each bar, undermining their own stance on contravening a UK law meant to rein in the repetitive music of outdoor raves.[15] Where isochronous beats are present, there are tighter bounds on the appreciable pulsation rate than on a general rate of rhythmic events; the intuitive 'tapping' or 'clapping' tempo is usually selected as a central metrical level, at most 4 beats per second, and not less than 0.5 beats per second [London, 2004].

Nevertheless, faster metrical levels may be deliberately chosen from a performer's perspective: in some music in the vein of Messiaen's rhythmic theories, it is convenient to count using a small temporal quantum, in order to enable accurate creation of additive rhythms [Weisberg, 1993]. Hierarchy should perhaps not be taken too far from the perceptual present (indeed, we cannot perceive beats outside of this). It is easy to overestimate the complexity that can be tracked by listeners, particularly in novel mathematically derived time structures, but a link to physicality often assists us in gaining familiarity with even highly non-isochronous patterns, as in the culturally embedded meters relating to dance.

Figure 8.5 illustrates these ideas, providing a number of possible representations.[16] In a computer, different metrical levels might appear in an array of arrays, or a single pattern as a set of normalized time points designating events in a cycle of known length:

$$0.0, 0.3, 0.56, 0.67, 0.87$$

perhaps accompanied by a set of weights for each point. The hierarchical breakdowns in the figure are only speculative, to illustrate the presence of multiple levels of observing repetition, and to show how patterns of 'strong and weak' points in a cycle might emerge.

---

[14] It is nearly impossible to work in two fully distinct metrical systems at the same time, because it is too difficult to consciously run two fully independent timing clocks. Still, there are motor patterns that allow access to certain linked patterns, such as tuplet cross-rhythms, appreciation of the intersection of multiple parts or metrical modulation.

[15] The Criminal Justice and Public Order Act, 1994.

[16] The mathematics may be reminiscent of scale patterns, but be careful: different psychological phenomena are involved.

Of course, there is no need for any point in the meter to be physically present in the music, as long as the timbral and rhythmic cues can point to the underlying abstract meter; in practice, certain instrumental accompaniment parts, or dance steps, mark out important time points. It is worth remembering the case of a silent (yet strong) return within some Indian talas [Clayton, 2000]. The fastest pulsation is not necessarily the comfortable counting speed, and on the right springar meter example the hierarchy is not extensive. These ideas of metrical structure have found their way into many interesting works. Dan Trueman's *Lasso and Corral: Variations on an Ill-Formed Meter* (2007) is for 'violin, hardanger fiddle, bass clarinet, piano and audiovisual click-track' (http://www. music.princeton.edu/~dan/Cyclotron/index.html). Each performer has a laptop running Trueman's Cyclotron software, which uses a circular representation of time akin to the lower row of Figure 8.5.

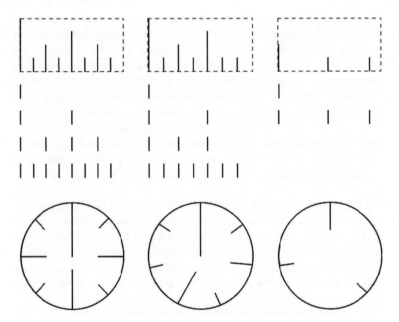

Figure 8.5 Three types of meter, shown both as linear and as cyclic time. The top and bottom depictions show the combined strength of a point within a cycle, based on the hierarchical breakdown of metrical levels in the central portion. The left shows a four to the floor, straight 4/4 beat. The middle depicts a non-isochronous meter, essentially 7/8 with a 2 + 2 + 3 grouping. The right is a springar meter from Hardanger fiddle music based on the proportions 33:38:28 (i.e., positions 0, 0.39 and 0.72 within a cycle of length 1.0).

As well as neat notated rhythms and idealized metrical structures, computer models must cope with the expressive timing manipulations of performers [Clarke, 1999b; Gabrielsson, 1999]. This requires accommodation between idealized 'quantized' beat-based representations and the absolute timings that really occur in performance. Some of this tension is already evident from the springar meter example above. Since human performers naturally play with expression built in, a computational beat tracker meant for score transcription has the awkward task of trying to separate expressive timing from the original structure – the 'quantization problem' [Desain and Honing, 1992].

There is nothing wrong in exploring the precision of machines, but noise in the motor system of human beings, and the deliberate nuances of timing introduced for expressive purposes, provide a further challenge, both in simulating human performance and in analyzing and tracking it. More developed models of rhythm attempt to take this into account, and representations of time are an important topic in computer music composition. We can measure time's progress in beats (within some metrical model at some privileged level) or in seconds. Transformations in beats are easily accomplished by changing tempo, the conversion factor between beats and seconds. But certain manipulations only really make sense in terms of absolute time because they refer to absolute physiological constraints. To further complicate matters, expressive deviation is actually a function of tempo, rather than a fixed amount, because performers learn to modify their behaviors in relation to the time they have available to carry out certain motor sequences [Desain and Honing, 1993]. Thus, in transforming between scales by augmentations and diminutions, easily possible in software when manipulating strings of numbers, the timescales themselves can have a profound impact on the interpretation of rhythm; our motor behaviors are locked to one physiological timescale, and our cognition to the perceptual present. Richer models therefore might separate an ideal quantized rhythm measured in beats (the score representation, a desired pattern for playback) and the individual expressive deviations in seconds in performance due to motor noise and deliberate articulation, and allow for different forms of transformation on this data [Bilmes, 1993; Honing, 2001].

The best tools for exploring rhythm can therefore be programming languages, which allow direct specification of the rhythmic structures themselves. Gross assumptions are often built into existing software, such as the 4/4 time signature and 120 bpm defaults of sequencers, for example. Under the hood, there are various ways of getting at wider rhythmic ideas even in these packages, such as groove templates, or master tempo curves. But the sequencers do not often embody, nor have highly developed models of, expressive performance.

As an example of a special representation in computer music, let us consider the time map [Jaffe, 1985]. This is a mapping between score or planning time with respect to some metrical framework (measured typically in beats) and performance time (in seconds). It shows the consequences of any fluctuation in tempo and any expressive deviation at every point; the function that translates from score to eventual position may take account of tempo-dependent expressive deviations, so it is possible to retain a model separating expressive and quantized components. The time map is not in itself just a tempo map, showing a tempo at every point in time, but only the evidence of translation from a quantized or ideal representation of the music's temporal structure to a final performance. This is useful because tempo maps are not in themselves adequate to depict exactly what goes on in expressive performance, or at least we should not seek to present every nuance as if it derived from changing the tempo (tempo could be stable but variation around that fixed reference applied for expressive purposes) [Desain and Honing, 1993].

Figure 8.6 shows a sinusoidal tempo canon, drawn for three simultaneous voices. This kind of structure was used by David Jaffe in the classic physical modeling-based experimental bluegrass work *Silicon Valley Breakdown* (1982), in order to allow individual voices to follow their own tempo patterns, before meeting again (dramatically) at a known moment in time. The same processes of integration are built into these maps that are used in scheduling systems for computer music; a measure of instantaneous tempo can be extracted as the gradient of the curve (the associated tempo map is integrated to get the final time map, though note again that tempo on its own may not be sufficient to fully model expressive timing variations).

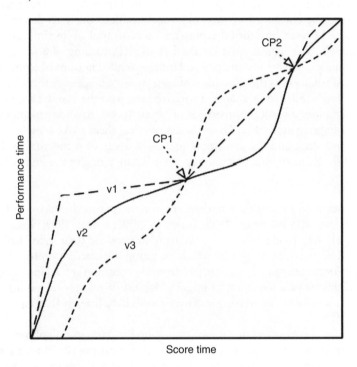

Figure 8.6   Time map for a sinusoidal tempo canon. Three voices (v1, v2, v3) wind through time. Following Conlon Nancarrow (and Johannes Ockeghem!), we can identify points of convergence (CP1, CP2) where the independent voices reach the same point in the source score at the same performance time, and then diverge anew. Note how v3 finishes the score early compared with the others, and skips the beginning of the score, while v1 runs out of time before reaching the very end. We could even have the voices go backwards in the score if the curves went to a negative gradient, but all the voices here have monotonically increasing relationships between score time and performance time.

The timescales we have been dealing with here have tended to fit within short-term memory. It is no accident that typical musical phrases (like typical spoken sentences and lines of poems) fit within such time bounds, aiding human information processing. We shall encounter longer-term structure below in a consideration of musical form. Just as for other aspects of music, events in time interact with timbre, with pitch information, and among different timescales and layers. So the full funkiness of 1980s Latin American electroacoustic music coming out of City University in London, to pick one example, is not just a simple metrical ploy, but a myriad of allusions combining various musical cultures (hear, for example, Javier Alvarez's *Temazcal* for pre-recorded computer part on tape and maracas player (1984)).

8.2.6 Local Structures

We now discuss some organizational principles for building up musical structure. Multiple sound objects can be combined in succession and simultaneously to determine the local flow of a piece. The term **horizontal** represents onwards motion in time, and arises from the convention of the x-axis as time (or the left to right reading of a score). Horizontal phenomena include conventional melody and more extended notions of sequences of sound objects, or transformation as the exhibition of continuous change over time. In contrast, the **vertical** might indicate a spectral snapshot with frequency on the y-axis, a slice at one instant in time. An example of a vertical property is an instantaneous harmony (simultaneous pitch materials), or an aggregate timbre. Nevertheless, vertical slices make sense only in relation to the before and after, and the perceptual present is a site of reconciliation between the progression of time and an understanding of what is happening in the immediate temporal vicinity.

Listener perception of a complex sounding environment is mediated by auditory stream analysis [McAdams and Bregman, 1985; Bregman, 1990; Cook, 1999; Wang and Brown, 2006]; we actively seek to identify any co-occuring sources and their individual movements through time. The gestalt principles by which we group sonic activity into the same stream include co-variation in time and proximity of features; common spatial location and timbre help to link elements of a sequence, as might closeness of register or loudness. Perhaps a composer's task is to create interesting auditory scenes for a listener to decipher!

Notions of stream are prevalent in composition, whether parts in polyphony or layers of a soundscape. The tracks of our sequencer software, and the staves of scores, are mechanisms by which more complicated ensembles are built up. It is not always the case that all the construction layers are heard out in the final sounding result. Textures are built up from closely coupled agglomerates or patterns of sound objects and may be heard as singular complex layers. In homophony, certain parts may be designed to blend into one super-instrument or synchronized backdrop. Interactions between streams can also give rise to certain aggregate musical constructions, such as the criss-crossing timbral elements of polyrhythmic patterns (kick and snare patterns, or the intermeshing of parts in West African percussion). In many electroacoustic works, as in Barry Truax's studio preparations for *The Shaman Ascending* (2004–05), many subtly processed layers are required to create a single intermediate sound object; these joys of multitracking were explored early on by pioneers like Les Paul. So layers may or may not correspond well to the auditory streams extracted by a listener, but they are always of some considerable conceptual as well as practical importance in building up a work.

When the number of voices is multiplied to extremes – as when Xenakis took inspiration from the armies of sound in warfare, or as cicadas chirp 1000-voice fugues – the quality of overall density becomes predominant. In contemporary classical music, these complex textures, such as the swarm of individual string glissandi at the start of Xenakis's *Metastaseis* (1953–4), have sometimes been termed micropolyphony. Sound masses of any desired scope can be explored via computer, and non-realtime rendering can be used where otherwise quality and quantity might be sacrificed in realtime generation.[17] The potential of sound synthesis to provide thick textures is an essential feature of such methods as granular synthesis (see Section 5.1.4). Density of texture can also change over time; a granular texture could break down and simplify, until only individual particles are left like lonely quanta. Roads [2001] reviews many ways in which masses and clouds of sound have been used, evoking analogies and examples from meteorology and interstellar gas clouds for dense note clusters and statistical distributions of microevents.

Consideration of the active layers, their relative prominence and interaction, their trajectory in time as they are born and die, is an important viewpoint from which to analyze and produce work. Continuously evolving sound layers might begin together as one agglomeration, grow apart into independent streams, and later reform [Wishart, 1994]. In an alternative setting, block-based decisions on the active parts appear frequently in electronic dance music; parts of a multitrack sequence might be switched on or off on four- or eight-measure boundaries. Whenever treating multiple layers, the lore of mixing has its own part to play; combinations of timbral layers must take account of spectral room and possible inter-voice masking. Consider also the surreality of a collage. Electronic music allows the combination of acoustic opposites in unreal, and sometimes disquieting, juxtapositions; a close-miked sound can combine with a very distant view of the same sound at the same time, with the distant sound mixed loud and the close sound subtly quiet .... Trevor Wishart [1996] has convincingly argued that true counterpoint, or counterstreaming as he calls it [Wishart, 1994, p. 109] when generalized to streams, should treat interactions between voices. Also of note here are the extended flights of Denis Smalley's theory of spectromorphology [Smalley, 1986, 1997]; he invokes biological phenomena such as flocking behaviors. The relative prominence of foreground, middleground and background, the use of accompaniment and lead line or other figure/ground relationships, transition over time, consideration of ensemble co-ordination and internal tug and pull pervade composition.

As music is presented in time, listeners scan the auditory goods on offer, hopefully focusing where the composer has cleverly guided them. Thematic materials might offer connections within a work, though the notion of a theme may be far removed from melodic motives or phrases, and the term **gesture** is often preferred to describe a short musical action of significance for a particular work. We now start to confront the demands of longer-term form in the listening experience, as gestures recur, are transformed, and interact with observer memory.

---

[17]When realtime checking is carried out with simplified versions of the synthesis, this is analogous to the 3D animation studios' use of wireframes for testing, followed by a long offline high-quality rendering process.

8.2.7 Musical Form

Our journey through various aspects of music now reaches the grandest stage, and perhaps also the most controversial. There are many cautionary tales concerning musical form, and its perception. A real danger is that the structure, which seems clear to analysts or composers working out of time, does not translate to an effective 'in-time' dramatic experience for a listener, with control of musical tension and release on a wider scale. Large-scale structure necessarily involves longer-term memory [Snyder, 2000]. It is easier to concentrate on short-term and immediate experience; indeed, this is the basis for a musical miniature or purer moment form. Various dramaturgical strategies sidestep the challenges of musical form that plague absolute music. Narrative controls drive music through film scripts, opera libretti or theatre play texts, or appear through song lyrics and spoken word. We can deny some musical experiences altogether and pursue fine art's installation forms, and the network and interactive music forms discussed in other chapters are of no small importance in offering new models of overall structure.

Remaining with absolute music for now, some musicologists and psychologists have been rather skeptical about whether there is much or any long-term appreciation of music at all [Cook, 1987; Tillmann and Bigand, 2004]. Perhaps everything of significance occurs within short-term memory bounds? In tonal music, a number of infamous demonstrations have exhibited the difficulty of defining an absolutely resolved finishing point for a work (movements were cut short and participants found it rather difficult to say if they actually continued further or not in the original). The underlying home keys in tonal sonata forms are not discernible by the majority who lack absolute pitch, except perhaps indirectly within a tolerance through some timbral qualities. It's hard to deny the locally exciting build-ups and trance breakdowns of global electronic dance music, but the DJs still chop and change records at whim, and muck up the original pitches with subtle tempo shifts. Again, though, we shouldn't overstate this case, and differentiating different figures and sections in a dance track is perfectly possible, even outside of minimalist repetitions. Section bounds in music often extend out beyond short-term memory, even if in some cases a 'verse' or other structure is formed out of smaller-scale repetitions of a core idea.

Historical musical form has bad connotations to some electroacousticians, Denis Smalley preferring to talk of 'structure' or 'structuring process' [Smalley, 1986]. But, of course, new model forms are constantly being trialed in culture; some get so widely adopted that they become treated as rigid templates (particularly as they slide into the past and become candidates for species), as in over-learned popular music song forms or sonata forms. There is no reason to reject these out of hand, not only because they provide ready-made access points for listeners, but because their combination with other forms, or their interaction with novel sound materials at various timescales, may still be productive in opening new avenues. Nevertheless, unconventional forms aplenty are possible by inspiration from outside of musical academies that are fixated on 19th-century Europe! We only have to look as one example at urban and rural environments themselves, as handled in soundscape composition, to find a clear source of access to other sound materials and timescales, still highly appreciable by our evolved auditory sensibilities [Schafer, 1994].

Earlier in this chapter we discussed where choices occur. Many interesting musical forms are predicated on letting performers or observers choose the course of events, including open form works, interactive works starring virtual musical partners or computer games. The generative landscape of a computer game can be highly nonlinear, providing a complex networked game world to explore. Participants' choice of direction is a central determinant of the journey in a gallery environment (also, in performances of Hiller and Cage's *HPSCHD* (1968–9) where the visitors are encouraged to make their own path), or on a sound walk. Rather than fixed musics, these more interactive options offer an important part of new musical practice in alliance with advances across many media.

8.3 FORMALIZING MUSIC

In exploring parameterization, we have already encountered many ways in which music can be formalized. Where music has a formal bent and can be manipulated on the level of explicit numerical operations, computers are a natural aide; they are calculating workhorses, and can be more reliable than carrying out many calculations by hand. In this section we take a moment to consider the aesthetic consequences of this.

The title of this section paraphrases Xenakis's wonderful if sometimes mathematically abstruse book, *Formalized Music* [Xenakis, 1992]. Xenakis is a prime example of a composer who has deeply engaged with the potential of mathematics in music, from probability theory to group theory and game theory. Acknowledging the intellectual appeal, the voyage of discovery for the composer through such territory, a question mark remains over how readily the mathematics translates to musically perceptible structure. The ground can shift with the algorithm: Xenakis's avowed criticisms of serialism on perceptual grounds resulted in his introduction of stochastic music. Yet whatever its out-of-time importance to the composer, the group theory underlying his solo cello work *Nomos Alpha* (1965) is of more doubtful perceptibility. In his survey of the many forms of music making in contemporary sonic culture, Leigh Landy has challenged formalists to justify their work [Landy, 2007], so we must at least make some defense to soften the process and product debate.

The benefits of formalization rest most solidly on the potential to model and explore new musical worlds. Not all worlds, or all models, are of equal success, particularly in terms of an end musical product. A basic creative tactic, however, is to analogize and transfer material between domains. In seeking new means of expression, why not look to overcome our standard habits? To quote Joji Yuasa, 'In order to counterbalance stereotypical behavior, I employ strict systematic procedures' [Boulanger, 1989, p. 58]. Formalism becomes a stimulant, a source of surprise and serendipity. Model making is also a powerful method of reflection on the act of composition, and may assist in more quickly identifying new compositional territory as assumptions are laid bare: 'Writing compositional algorithms forces me to scrutinize composition as process. I have to be aware of how compositional logic really works and how compositional priorities arrange themselves. In working with computers, musical ideas come to me that I probably would not otherwise have imagined' [Hiller, 1989, p. 75]. The higher-level viewpoint of this work can provide a refreshing vantage point for the composer, who may manipulate relatively few parameters of a model but be able to hear complex variation in results, traversing a wider musical territory. Further, it is unsurprising to be influenced by a current environment replete with calculating machines. In this vein, formalization becomes an engagement with mathematical knowledge and the computer age, and one only has to look at live coders crawling within the guts of algorithms to see some novel developments in music here.

Nevertheless, tensions between the primacy of ear and the pursuit of system have kept bubbling up in the process–product debate, and it is worth hearing a little more from the two sides, because these are salient warnings for the composer and artist. Many cautions abound, warning against 'an obsession with the machine rather than with what it produces' [Lansky and Roads, 1989, p. 42]. Denis Smalley [1986, p. 93] writes: 'Unless aural judgement is permitted to triumph over technology, electroacoustic music will attract deserved condemnation'. Integral serialism in the early 1950s probably invested too much in the system, at least for mainstream audiences, and sparked Xenakis's product-biased critique. The attitude of 'music above system' is well encapsulated in this quotation from Berlioz:

> [T]he expressive character of a piece of music is no more valid or cogent because the piece is written in strict canon; it has no bearing on the truth and beauty of the result that the composer has solved some quite extraneous problems, any more than it would if he had been handicapped by physical pain or by some material obstacle while writing it. [Berlioz, 1970, p. 219]

If this pronouncement were applied to modern art, the performance artist Matthew Barney's 'hypertrophy' work (where he draws encumbered by some physical restraint) couldn't exist without contravening it. A drawing room full of other conceptual artists, and their supporting community of buyers and critics, would argue that the main critical dimension in art since Marcel Duchamp is the process itself above the product. In process music [Nyman, 1999; Reich, 2002], such as György Ligeti's unwinding metronomes (*Poeme Symphonique*, 1962) or Reich's swinging feedback machine (*Pendulum Music*, 1968), the playing out of a process can take center stage, though arguably only effective sounding circumstances are worth a second performance. And so the debate swings to and fro.

What process–product wrangling conceals sometimes is all the loci of human decision making. It is perfectly possible that models devised by humans can capture something important about human music. Human beings write music making computer programs, and tweak their code based on a sampling of aural feedback (they can also tweak the final output of any one run of the program, and Xenakis himself was not shy of this). Systems may form only part of the composition work; Schoenberg left the fine detail of orchestration to hand craft, rather than serializing that as well. We may recover expressive detail from human interpreters by creating an intermediate score or framework rather than a fixed recording. There is a push and pull in the aesthetic of new and old, and composers (and audiences) can learn to accommodate the output of particular processes.

It is too easy to view the computer as an unforgiving device, a perfectly rational machine awaiting instructions. As Charles Wuorinen has stated, 'One is obliged to be specific whether one wants to be specific or not' [Boulanger, 1989, p. 52]. This viewpoint is a little naive with respect to more abstract interfaces empowered by natural language processing, computer vision, machine learning and the like. There are always further ways to recover 'blurry edges'. We can rest on subjectively created data, such as machine learning over a corpus of humanly composed work.[18] Ultimately, convincing automation of the compositional process may rely on effective auditory models, if we are to overcome reluctance to defer critical decisions pertaining to final output to a calculating machine rather than a human brain. Pierce [1968] anticipated this whole thread by playing down the influence of mathematics on music, but promoting the importance of psychology, and points to a reconciliation of process and product. We shall now proceed, having touched on this debate and hopefully the healthier for it.

8.3.1 Algorithmic Composition

> I specify a compositional system in which a particular composition is but one example from a class of essentially similar compositions. If certain elements are changed in the matrix of elements making up the system, its details will be new but its gross properties will remain the same. It is interesting to speculate how much must be changed to create a new work. [Hiller, 1989, p. 79]

Formally speaking, algorithmic composition is the creation of algorithms whose output has clear musical consequences of use to the composer, from the production and exploration of musical materials to the generation of complete works [Hiller, 1970; Ames, 1987; Roads, 1996; Loy, 2007a]. Taube [2004] calls this meta-composition, and we can view the composer as taking a step back, and while floating at a higher level above the exact details of a work, define processes which lead to the instantiation of new materials when they are followed. Think 'rule system to create a set of compositions', rather than just creating a single composition directly, and then look again at the quotation that heads this subsection. This indirection can be continued indefinitely to meta-meta-music and beyond until your head spins: 'composing algorithmic compositions!' [Taube, 2004, p. 65].

If we insist on a computer science definition of an algorithm, we can set aside the looser and highly subjective rule sets of 1960s text pieces or conceptual art, though the rather beautiful exhortation of Sol LeWitt that 'the idea becomes a machine that makes the art' [LeWitt, 1967] is inspiring in these contexts. We still might pursue a formal rule system

---

[18] The jury is still out on whether human beings are themselves somehow just massively parallel computers!

without a computer, though the majority of works, and, indeed, all the practical examples here, lend themselves to computational implementation. In its purest form, (computer-based) algorithmic music is the output of a stand-alone program, without user controls, with musical content determined by the seeding of the random number generator (usually by the start time, though other seeds could be passed in to recall previous runs). Most systems allow for some sort of control, however, through inputs to the algorithm, or live controls to a running process. Interactive music systems take advantage of algorithmic routines to produce output influenced by their environments, while live coders burrow around inside running algorithms, modifying them from within like programmer wasp larvae eating alive a generative caterpillar. Table 8.4 presents a collection of precedents in rule-based composition (many other precedents, from mathematical treatises on music and mechanical automata to interactive music systems, are detailed at other points in this book or can be found via the citations).

Table 8.4 Some precedents in algorithmic composition.

Date	Description
1026	Guido d'Arezzo's procedures for automatic word setting, translating from vowels to melody notes through an assigned mapping
1650	Athanasius Kircher's tract *Musurgia Universalis* describes a music generating machine for non-musicians, the *arca musarythmica*, somewhere between Guido's method and the musical dice games mentioned below
1719	Use of divination to aid composer choice; Vogt's method of casting hobnails to provide melodic contours [Loy, 2007a, p. 294]
1757	Kirnberger's *The Always Ready Polonaise and Minuet Composer* published, where a choice of bar at each step is determined by dice rolls through a lookup table. Hedges [1978] catalogs more then twenty musical dice games over the next fifty years as part of an '*ars combinatoria*' fad for mathematics and music
1843	Ada Lovelace's prescient prediction that 'the engine might compose elaborate and scientific pieces of music of any degree of complexity' [Hugill, 2007]
1931	Joseph Schillinger begins to teach his mathematical theory of music composition from Theremin's studio in New York
1950	John R. Pierce anticipates stochastic music from an information theory perspective (and anticipates its generation by computer), writing in *Astounding Science Fiction*, November 1950 [Pierce, 1968]
1952	Earle Brown experiments with statistical generation of graphical scores such as *December 1952* (1952) and pioneers open form in 1953 [Grella-Mozejko, 2007]
1956	Work on the *Illiac Suite* project begins [Hiller and Isaacson, 1959]
1962	Iannis Xenakis's ST project; Pierre Barbaud already working on computer composition in Paris
1967	Theoretical formulations of conceptual art [LeWitt, 1967]
1968	Steve Reich explicitly writes on process music [Reich, 2002]
1971	First publication of *Formalized Music* [Xenakis, 1992]

Algorithmic music has had some publicity since the *Illiac Suite* [Hiller and Isaacson, 1959], often of the 'machines will replace our composers and steal musicians' jobs!' type. Under the radar, the outputs of algorithmic composition have sneaked into many media; examples are Barbaud's film soundtracks [Hiller, 1970] or Autechre's *Confield* (2001) album. It is arguable whether many algorithms of extensive musical variability have been used in musical production in the last few decades, but there are certainly many instances of plug-ins with certain probabilistic facilities, from parameter set randomization to more significant modeling of musical structure (in algorithmic break beat cutting, BrightonART's Coldcutter or my own BBCut and its LiveCut VST version by Remy Muller might be mentioned). The center staging of the program itself has probably been less remarked upon, but the 1980s demo scene and the rise of games culture have made the algorithm play a rather more central role in many media. Old-school algorithmic composition techniques have found themselves plied under a number of rebrandings, such as **adaptive music** in games to describe the control of in-game music by scene. **Generative music** is another renaming, just meaning realtime algorithmic composition, and has gained increased public awareness through a number of routes: software and Internet plugins such as *Koan* (1994), streaming Internet radio stations such as *rand()%* (2003–5), portable generative music within novelty MP3 players such as the MadWaves' *MadPlayer* (2002), and the popularity of mobile phone-based music software. Since interaction brings us to participatory musicianship and gaming, there tends to be much more marketing impetus in these cases. But the pure paradigm of stand-alone non-interactive programs still has much to offer the composer.

It is worth distinguishing two main currents in algorithmic composition corresponding to the tug between artistic freedom and the scientific investigation of music. Ames and Domino [1992] distinguish:

- **active style synthesis** as exploring novel compositional structures through algorithms;

- **empirical style modeling** for musicological investigation of historical styles.

If we push too hard towards the scientific angle, we will leave more aesthetic territory and enter scientific modeling of the act of musical composition, where the evaluation criteria can be very different [Pearce *et al.*, 2002]; this will be tackled further in Chapter 9. The work of David Cope, most famously on his **experiments in musical intelligence** (EMI) [Cope, 2001], has often been inspiring as well as courting controversy, because he has often found himself on the borderline between these two currents. EMI works upon a database of materials; when these are sourced from historical material, the project engages with historical styles and pastiche composition, and David Cope himself sometimes seems unable to attribute it clearly to either the composition or the musicological camp.

That's enough history and review. Let's explore methods of automatically generating music with computers.

8.3.2 Implementing Algorithmic Composition

The practical (discrete) mathematics of computer science provides many techniques that can be applied in machine composition. Perhaps the most prevalent methodology is to draw from probability theory, so we shall concentrate most on probabilistic methods, essentially from a discrete point of view. We will then go on to survey some further options that utilize artificial intelligence methods.

Probability Theory

Ideally, when rolling a single dice, drawing one card from a pack, or tossing a coin, we have a situation where each outcome is equally likely. Such cases can be described with a (discrete) uniform probability distribution, formally called a **probability density function**. For a fair six-sided dice there are six possible results, and each has a probability of 1/6. For a pack of 52 cards each individual card has a 1/52 chance of being drawn. The perfectly weighted coin gives a one in two chance of heads or tails. Such a uniform distribution could be applied to choosing musical objects; with seven distinct diatonic notes, set each to have a one in seven chance of arising.

The real world is a bit messier, and this is why I was careful to mention ideal and perfect dice rather than biased equipment. In actual examples of tonal musical pieces, you might suspect that the tonic or the dominant in a diatonic scale appears far more often than the supertonic; statistical evidence from large folk song corpuses would bear this suspicion out. Perhaps we should allocate a greater chance of choosing the tonic than the supertonic, creating an unequal probability density function?[19]

Composers can choose whatever probability distribution they like over a set of musical objects, and need not be bound by modeling traditional musical practice (the selection of one note at a time, free of the context of previous choices, is not the most natural model, anyway). The only restriction is that the total of the probabilities sum to 1. Let's give another discrete example for an unequal scale in C major:

$$C\ (0.5)\ D\ (0.1)\ E\ (0.05)\ F\ (0.2)\ G\ (0.05)\ A\ (0.07)\ B\ (0.03)$$

This is rather a non-standard model, since the dominant G might be expected to be far more likely than the supertonic D or submediant A. Further, the act of using this distribution time and time again pays no attention to the previous draw, so the note that follows the leading note is not restricted in any different way from the note that follows the tonic, for example. This can be fixed by a higher-order transition distribution, discussed below.

How does this non-uniform distribution get used in practice? We first create a uniformly drawn random number between 0 and 1. There are always routines available in programming to provide such a value, typically using a Lehmer pseudo-random number generator or similar process. We can then look at a table of cumulative probabilities to see which event

---

[19] There is an intimate link with information theory (see Section 9.6), since equal outcomes equate to maximal entropy (heat death).

actually gets selected. The **cumulative distribution function** (CDF) is created as a running total of the successive probabilities from the probability density function; the cumulative distribution in our notes case looks like:

$$C\ (0.5)\ D\ (0.6)\ E\ (0.65)\ F\ (0.85)\ G\ (0.9)\ A\ (0.97)\ B\ (1)$$

So if we 'rolled' a 0.7, we get an F, and if we 'drew' a 0.93 we take an A (each number is the maximum value allotted to that option in the range; the minimum comes from the previous value, where for the first option there is always an implicit understanding of starting at 0.0). Any events that had zero probability in the original probability density function would be smoothly missed out in the cumulative distribution function, by the way.

The same sort of constructions can be carried out for continuous distributions, since we do not always employ discrete objects; we might want to work with frequency continua for glissandi, or control timbral features, or generate other continuous sound model data. There is a wonderful variety of named probability distributions to select from for these purposes, from the Beta to the Myhill distributions and beyond, as well as the opportunity to use any function of your own devising [Lorrain, 1980; Ames, 1991]. Note, however, that unless an analytical formula can be provided for the cumulative distribution function, we will require some form of sampling to make a table that a computer can use; this table can be a very good approximation to an underlying continuous function, of course (the famous normal distribution is treated in a sidebar, and see Figure 8.7).

The distributions are used to form the decision making primitives that increase the number of routes a program can actually take on its course, rather than always settling for a known path. In practice, distributions are often conveniently packaged up in 'sequence generators', which return a new number each time they are called according to the underlying distribution.[20]

In order to go beyond independent draws, here is a further probability refresher. Consider a discrete state space, where each state has an associated probability. If $states = \{a, b, c\}$, perhaps representing three rhythmic values, or the choice between three instruments, or any three musical objects we wish to select among, we can write out the probabilities of each occurrence:

$$P(x = a) = 0.2$$
$$P(x = b) = 0.2$$
$$P(x = c) = 0.6$$

Probabilities over all states sum to 1, because there must always be some state as the outcome. We can now introduce dependencies that go beyond a single immediate 'roll of

---

[20]Charles Ames in particular has been concerned to control the speed at which the overall shape of a distribution is revealed in such sampling [Ames, 1995].

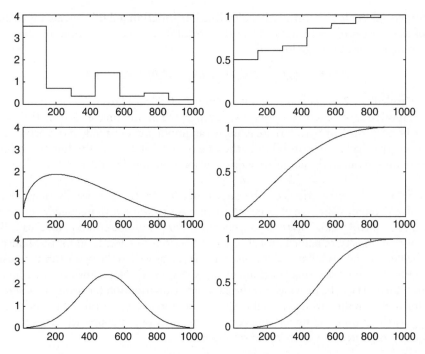

Figure 8.7   Three probability distributions, with probability density function (left column) and cumulative distribution function (right column). The top row shows the seven-item discrete distribution discussed in the text. The bottom row is the normal distribution, here plotted between minus and plus three standard deviations. The middle row is a special distribution called the beta distribution, essentially characterized for an input x between 0 and 1 by $Cx^{\alpha}(1-x)^{\beta}$ where C is a normalization constant to make sure the final distribution adds up to 1.0 when summed [Ames, 1991, p. 63]. In this figure, $\alpha = 0.5$ and $\beta = 2$.

the computerized dice'. Conditional probabilities can be expressed:

$$P(x_n = a \mid x_{n-1} = a) = 0.2$$
$$P(x_n = b \mid x_{n-1} = a) = 0.4$$
$$P(x_n = c \mid x_{n-1} = a) = 0.4$$

These equations express that given the previous state at time point $n-1$, x_{n-1}, as being a, the choice of new state x_n is twice as likely to be b or c than a again. We would need three equations each for the cases $x_{n-1} = b$ and $x_{n-1} = c$ too. Given prior state, conditional probabilities also sum to 1. This mechanism allows us to introduce the promised 'transition table', which takes into account previous results in determining what happens next. If the current state depends on k prior states, we have a kth order Markov chain. This can cause a combinatorial explosion in the size of the transition table, because of the number of probabilities required to cover all cases:

3 states, 0th order: 3 probabilities

3 states, 1st order: 9 probabilities

3 states, 2nd order: 27 probabilities

3 states, kth order: 3^k probabilities

In practice, many of the transitions are zero, making a sparse array. From this point on, the whole machinery of mathematical probability theory, including the Bayesian formalisms based around conditional probability, could be brought in. In practice, quite a lot has been done in computer music just using basic probability distributions and low-order ($k = 1$–5, say) Markov chains.

Rather than directly specifying every event, generative works are often characterized by the controlled use of probability distributions. This does not make them 'random' in a pejorative sense, for the composer-designers are almost always immensely careful about the extent of variation allowed, which can be employed to very subtle effect rather than producing overt changeability. Probability distributions thus contribute in a refined way to undermine the notion of a fixed work, without losing compositional control of character. Probability theory can also form the foundation of an aesthetic, as in Xenakis's stochastic music, and statistical mechanics is a very good way of handling the overall behavior of dense clouds of sound.

Further Techniques

We now review various alternative methods investigated in algorithmic composition. While any artificial intelligence method can be employed, particularly at the scientific modeling end – we shall discuss this more in Chapter 9 – it is perfectly possible to create effective algorithmic works using only a small subset of techniques. Many works are founded on the controlled use of some basic probability distributions, to select among options or to provide values to test. Another aspect of a 'typical' generative music program is the necessary coding of some music representation and musical rules. These form the substance of the operating theory of music for a particular work within which probabilities can guide choices or be tested. A basic example is a conditional rule; if condition x is met, do y. Condition x might be a test on the current value of a random variable (drawn from a probability distribution). The Illiac Suite used a 'generate and test' procedure, which kept generating random numbers until a number turned up that could make it through a sieve of musical context-specific rules [Hiller and Isaacson, 1959]. Thus, in various ways, probability theory can drive musical decisions, and add generative spice to the mix.

Dealing with a continuous probability distribution in practice: the example of the normal distribution

The lowest row of Figure 8.7 shows the normal distribution, named incorrectly but irrevocably after Gauss (hence Gaussian) when de Moivre and Laplace might have been better candidates. This is an unequal but symmetrical distribution also dubbed the 'bell curve'. How would we use this in practice?

The mathematical definition of the 'Gaussian' is parameterized by two variables, the mean μ (center point of the distribution) and the standard deviation σ (intuitively, how 'spread out' the distribution is). Its formula is:

$$\frac{1}{\sigma \sqrt{2\pi}} e^{-(x-\mu)^2/2\sigma^2}$$

which can be simplified to a standard form by taking $\mu = 0$ (center on origin) and $\sigma = 1$:

$$\frac{1}{\sqrt{2\pi}} e^{-x^2/2}$$

This gives the probability density function.

In order to generate a sequence of normally distributed values, and also to use a Gaussian to select from a set of discrete options, we need a method to create the corresponding cumulative distribution function, for which there are several approaches. It is usual to model the CDF for the normal form with zero mean and unit standard deviation, and results can be transferred to any μ and σ using the transformation $\sigma x + \mu$ for a drawn x. Possible approaches are:

1. Use a numerically calculated table of the cumulative distribution, as provided by textbooks on statistics (essentially, sampling). Linear or higher order curve fitting can be applied over segments.

2. Apply an approximation based on the central limit theorem (if lots of distributions are summed, they tend in the limit to a normal distribution). An example is

$$\sum_{i=1}^{12} u_i - 6$$

where each u_i is a uniform continuous random number from 0.0 to 1.0 (which is easily provided by the computer's standard random number generator; call it 12 times) [Lorrain, 1980, p. 74].

3. Adopt an exact analytical reframing, such as the polar method [Ames, 1991, pp. 64–5]. There are some refinements such as the Box–Muller transform, and the Ziggurat algorithm, for the interested reader to explore.

Table lookup is probably the most practical choice, with guaranteed efficiency. Although the Gaussian can extend out to positive and negative infinity, in practice it is sufficient to cover the distribution up to three standard deviations (−3 to 3 for the normal form), which accounts for 99.7% of values.

Yet we don't have to use probability at all.[21] Consider the notion of a sequence generator again, as introduced above. While we can take a statistical view of any generated data, a sequence generator does not have to be probabilistic, and could also be created by an entirely deterministic process. The Lehmer psuedo-random number generator is actually deterministic, but you wouldn't think so when its parameters are well chosen, for then its statistics over time allow it to approximate white noise. One further example is a nonlinear iterative map like the Logistic map. Here, successive values are generated from the equation:

$$x(n+1) = \lambda x(n)(1 - x(n)), \quad 0 \leq x(n) \leq 1 \tag{8.2}$$

where λ is a special parameter, usually from 0.0 to 4.0, and values from 3.57 upwards to 4 can cause chaotic behavior in the output. The invocation of chaos is an indication of richness even within seemingly simple deterministic procedures.

Data can be sourced, then, from many places, including probabilistic and deterministic equations, or drawn simply from measurements of some real-world phenomena. Indeed, any of the signal synthesis methods we have examined could provide discrete data points, and

---

[21]For the case of generate and test, it might seem strange to have a sieve of tests and wait for the right random number to come along; why not always generate exactly what you need in the current conditions? In fact, this leads to a consideration of the best search tactic, whether you seek optimal decisions, whether any fitting solution would do, or whether you can even specify well all conditions in advance. Random numbers may give one practical method to try a diversity of routes without exhaustively enumerating them.

conversely, any of the probabilistic methods could be applied at the audio signal level. For example, different kinds ('colors') of noise source can be created by filtering white noise.[22] Now, one subtlety is that, in the case of events, the next value is often drawn on demand, at a non-uniform rate, and the theories of sampling we have encountered require evenly spaced values. The logistic map nevertheless provides an example of a source that has been used both for algorithmic composition of events and for algorithmic synthesis of waveforms.

So we can take inspiration from any mathematical or other field, perhaps translating from esoteric numerical functions to musical parameters (see also the coverage in Section 9.5). The drawback of this sort of sonification of data, or mapping from mathematics, is that the domains are not always comparable. Using geomagnetic data to control sound synthesis or running a Lorenz attractor to determine a sequence of notes is an interesting artistic conceit, but, for the various psychological reasons outlined in this chapter, it may not always prove the most valid tactic unless some care is taken. Unfortunately it is all too easy to end up with a cheap way out of the dilemma, by running the mapping using some basic default, such as to control diatonic scale note selection, where any source of data might work and the individuality of the source is lost.[23] Even given a 'no chance of failure' mapping, it is in the longer term that these structures often fall down, but this is not to deny that other domains can supply rich and invigorating sources of data. When we consider models of information that liken musical content to a $1/f$ distribution (we shall investigate this more in Section 9.6), or fractal maps, there may be structural features that translate well because they already capture some properties of music. Composers have carried out many experiments here already and a fund of knowledge is developing, if much mediated by the particularities of individual works [Doornbusch, 2002].

Returning to rules, Good Old-Fashioned Algorithmic Composition parallels Good Old-Fashioned Artificial Intelligence. Symbolic logic is the order of the day, and logical deduction proceeds from facts and rules to solutions to compositional problems. The necessity of encoding musical knowledge is called the 'knowledge acquisition' problem [Roads, 1996, p. 904], and is what makes expert system building rather difficult; it is hardly trivial to write out rules for producing musical fugues, for instance. One related and celebrated example is Kemal Ebcioğlu's expert system for harmonizing chorales in the manner of J.S. Bach, which employs 350 rules expressed in a first-order predicate calculus [Ebcioğlu, 1990]. More recent AI work has concentrated far more on machine learning, where not every facet of a system has to be specified in advance (some probability theory becomes incorporated in training the learning system, which uses inductive rather than deductive reasoning). Such efforts often employ 'sub-symbolic' connectionist architectures [Todd and Loy, 1991; Leman,

---

[22] One method would be a windowed process, using the inverse FFT and overlap add. Each window starts with its own spectrum of white noise, by generating random amplitudes and phases for each bin in the discrete Fourier spectrum. The coloring is then applied by using a particular weighting for the amplitude of the bins, for example, flat (no filtering) for white noise, $1/f$ for pink noise or $1/f^2$ for brown noise (Brownian motion). The inverse Fourier transform is used to get back to the time domain where the output sequence is to be constructed. See also Section 9.6.

[23] An example is provided by the WolframTones website, http://tones.wolfram.com/, which explores the sounds made by cellular automata; but note how much of the work is done in the choice of mapping and representation itself, with highly quantized pitch and time.

1993; Toiviainen, 2000; Griffith and Todd, 1999], but the problem of interpreting inputs and outputs remains for modeling the problem space.

Many computer applications in music revolve around different search algorithms, such as hunting for an elusive 'ultimate melody' within specified bounds according to a set of rules [Ames, 1987; Russell and Norvig, 2003]. Indeed, searches inevitably arise in computation, but not all searches are practicable. The combinatorial nature of music can make it impossible to run a real-life computer in finite time and space to carry out a search through all possible configurations. To hunt through all conceivable 80-note monodies, where each note can have 10 possible pitches, we reach a search space the size of the number of atoms in the observable universe – we can't build a computer that could accomplish this exhaustive search. The combinations are quickly explosive, for we won't always just have a single pitch defining a note. For example, M parameters defining an M-dimensional space where any one parameter has N options leads to a search space of size N^M just to select *one* musical object. Imagine ten features, each of which is represented by a seven-bit number – ten MIDI parameters, if you will; this gives 127^{10} straight off for one event. Choose nine and you've again exceeded the observable universe limit. In practice, all searches must be constrained in some way; this involves the use of **heuristics** as 'rules of thumb' that limit the number of paths that have to be explored. There are many refined techniques to make search tractable, including **back-tracking**, a method to jump back to earlier decision points when the current avenue proves unworkable. By defining a cost function, and then keeping track of how successful certain search directions are proving, **dynamic programming** techniques can restrict attention to the most beneficial routes. Of course, the numerical attribution of what constitutes a successful path becomes another site of rules for the algorithm. In general, approximate rather than total searches are all that is possible, and we may find local maxima rather than a global best solution; but that is the price of getting some sort of answer in a reasonable time.

There is no 'finally' paragraph here, but the beginning of a journey through all the algorithmic apparatus at our disposal in our rich computer culture. Figure 8.8 shows a screenshot from AthenaCL, a Python-built algorithmic composition tool with extensive algorithm libraries. Other examples range from Symbolic Composer and AC Toolbox to extensions for any of the major computer music languages from Pd to SuperCollider. Figure 8.2 showed a program built by Karlheinz Essl on top of Max/MSP. Further interesting options range from constraints programming, as particularly exhibited by Torsten Anders's *Strasheela* program [Anders, 2007], to the formal modeling of musical grammars, following computational linguistics [Roads, 1985b]. David Cope's work on Experiments in Musical Intelligence is a good exemplar of statistical analysis of large corpuses used to generative compositional ends [Cope, 2001], driving the creation of new pastiche works. Machine learning gives us some hope that a database of influence can be surpassed and new creative works can emerge. As you learn AI techniques, you can consider how they might be applied to modeling musical style and automating musical composition, and further topics along these lines appear in Chapter 9. Other surveys of techniques can be pursued in the further reading for this chapter.

Figure 8.8   AthenaCL is a powerful open-source algorithmic composition environment, built with and extending Python, and freely available from http://www.athenacl.org. The screenshot shows program text as well as the outputs of various parameter generators. Shown here are values derived from a random walk through a Xenakisian sieve (a kind of non-uniform scale structure), a dynamically remapped sine oscillator (the boundaries for wrapping are being moved around over time), a beta distribution, a cellular automaton (local rules over change in a one-dimensional array), the logistic map, fractional noise of the form $1/f^3$, and a Markov chain. Image reproduced by permission of Christopher Ariza.

8.4 SUMMARY

This chapter could have been much longer. There are still many forms and styles of musical creativity we've hardly touched on, and I hope the subjectivities of composition are apparent. We've encountered the contrasting pulls of intuition and formalism, of time spent developing technology and time spent using technology. We have explored many aspects of music, at various timescales, connecting up to the psychological literature for some primary musical parameters, as well as seeing some of the interactions that make everything more complicated. We've also dug into the possibilities of the computer, particularly where programming allows the automatic generation and manipulation of music in algorithmic composition. Other chapters of this book give a further wealth of possibilities, from interactive musical scenarios to network music making. Never be dissuaded, but embrace the compositional joys and compromises of the real world. There might be limited rehearsal time or access to gallery space for set-up, awkward collaborators, small and indifferent or large and hostile audiences ... but most of us keep on trying because music making is such a strong and delicious human compulsion!

8.5 EXERCISES

1. Try to write down a list of musical styles that are furthest from 'computer music'. Now go back through the list, considering how each one might inspire new computer music, or find a new hybrid with computer involvement.

2. The melodic minor scale in 12TET has a direction-dependent pattern (upwards, the offsets from a starting note in multiples of a semitone are $[0, 2, 3, 5, 7, 9, 11, 12]$, and back down again $[12, 10, 8, 7, 5, 3, 2, 0]$). Consider 19TET, in the conventional form of fitting 19 equally spaced steps to one octave. How large is one step as a frequency ratio? Working in 19TET, consider how you could generalize this conditional behavior, creating dependencies of the scale shape on the starting note, direction of travel, current contour and target pitch, and more to taste. Create a pitch-based study to explore this notion.

3. Start with a complex tone, with significant amplitude at least for the first ten harmonics, synthesizing this tone directly using additive synthesis (add up ten or more sine waves; you could even do this manually in a sound editor if you aren't already familiar with a computer music package, but the next step will be tougher). Over time, reduce the strength of the odd harmonics to zero (the first, third and so forth). What happens to the pitch? Now experiment with detuning a subset of the harmonics to create inharmonic components. When can you hear out individual components and when do they become more fused? You might pursue this further using a sinusoidal modeling tool for the analysis of existing sound (such as SPEAR, see Chapter 3), applying it to a relatively simple strongly pitched source sound and manipulating partial tracks.

4. Create your own taxonomy of timbre. Begin by listening carefully through your personal libraries of samples (or delve through an online archive like Freesound, at www.freesound.org). What aspects of sound seem most prominent to you? What compromises do you have to make to create a manageable taxonomy? Once you have a draft, you might like to compare another system [Schaeffer, 2005; Smalley, 1997; Schafer, 1994]. What did you miss out?

5. Multichannel composition is sometimes dependent on access to more expensive systems, but you can often experiment with space composition using headphone-based listening, transaural systems which seek to work over a stereo speaker set-up, and 5.1-style home cinema. Create a short spatial sound test of around a minute, monitoring only by headphones (you might explore filtering, delays and panning laws, as applied to source material). Now listen back over loudspeakers. Repeat the exercise, but preparing the material with stereo monitoring out loud, before hearing the final test over headphones.

6. Use the human hand as the inspiration for a composition. You may want to explore the physiology of the hand, cultural associations, hand gestures, mime and sign language, performance footage of musicians' hands and many more. The constraints of the fingers are interesting in themselves, especially when interacting with the layout of a musical instrument (compare the guitar fretboard and the piano keyboard, for example). Could you write a computer program that generates music based on some form of physical constraint relating to the hand, driving computer music from a model of physicality, without necessarily falling into common practice Western tonality? You might also investigate Fitt's law from psychology, which gives a measure of how quickly a musician can move over a distance to a given target . . . .

7. Where does inspiration come from? Go and compose something with your favorite (or for an alternative challenge, your least favorite) computer music software as a break from reading this book. A time limit might be an interesting constraint; set an alarm clock to ring after 17 minutes. Perhaps try to represent your anger at all the information in the world? If your piece was in free time, the next day repeat the exercise taking advantage of metrical structures and expectancy. Conversely, if you created a very rhythmic work, your next creation should be as free of metrical association as you can make it!

8. Practice layering sound within different durations, using a DAW package. Load up ten different musical extracts, which might vary from monophonic instrumental recordings, through speech, to complex soundscapes and polyphonic musical works. Use only ten tracks (one per layer), volume envelopes, basic spatialization and cut and paste, and create mixes of three seconds, ten seconds, 30 seconds and three minutes. Note that not all layers have to sound at once the whole time! But you must use each source once within the duration. What sorts of musical setting, motion and transition can you discover? You will of course find a great dependence on your choice of materials; you can repeat this as many times as you like with different starting materials.

9. It is an interesting fact that many electronic music compositions have a single author. Many animated films, however, have whole casts of creators. Discuss and

then produce a collaborative piece with your peers. What compromises must you make? What advantages are there to such work? Try to keep records during the compositional process itself, such as a rough journal of decisions, structural plans and revisions, various draft versions. After creation, discuss the process again, and the nature of your contributions.

10. Sample the normal distribution for $\mu = 0$ and $\sigma = 1$ by calculating 1000 evenly spaced steps over the input range $[-3$ to $3]$. By using a running total and iterating over the 1000 values, create the corresponding cumulative distribution function in a new array of size 1000. Armed with this, create a small algorithmic work where draws from the normal distribution are used to control all choices of parameter (one suggestion might be to make a generative version of an earlier study, perhaps the one from Exercise 3, drawing harmonic amplitudes and detuning factors at successive steps from the normal distribution to shape control envelopes). You can rescale to new mean and standard deviation using $\sigma u + \mu$ but be careful with ranges; the table you have sampled goes out to three standard deviations, so will create values in the range $[\mu - 3\sigma, \mu + 3\sigma]$.

8.6

FURTHER READING

Ames, C. (1987). Automated composition in retrospect 1956–1986. *Leonardo*, 20(2):169–186.

Ariza, C. (2009). Extensive web-based bibliography of algorithmic composition resources: http://www.flexatone.net/algoNet/

Bailey, D. (1993). *Improvisation: Its Nature And Practice In Music*, 2nd Edition. Da Capo Press, New York, NY.

Cope, D. (2001). *Virtual Music: Computer Synthesis of Musical Style*. MIT Press, Cambridge, MA.

Emmerson, S. (ed) (1986). *The Language of Electroacoustic Music*. Macmillan, London.

Erickson, R. (1975). *Sound Structure in Music*. University of California Press, Berkeley, CA.

Hiller, L. and Isaacson, L. (1979, original 1959). *Experimental Music: Composition with an Electronic Computer*. Greenwood Press, Westport, CT.

Licata, T. (ed) (2002). *Electroacoustic Music: Analytical Perspectives*. Greenwood Press, Westport, CT.

Miranda, E. (2001). *Composing with Computers*. Focal Press, Oxford.

Nierhaus, G. (2009). *Algorithmic Composition: Paradigms of Automated Music Generation.* Springer-Verlag/Wien, New York, NY.

Pellman, S. (1994). *An Introduction to the Creation of Electroacoustic Music.* Wadsworth Publishing Co., Belmont, CA.

Roads, C. (ed) (1985). *Composers and the Computer.* William Kaufmann, Inc., Los Altos, CA.

Roads, C. (2009). *Composing Electronic Music.* Oxford University Press, Oxford.

Schafer, R. M. (1994, original 1977). *The Soundscape: Our Sonic Environment and the Tuning of the World.* Destiny Books, Rochester, VT.

Schafer, R. M. (1986). *The Thinking Ear.* Arcana Editions, Toronto, Canada.

Schwarz, E. and Childs, B. (eds) (1998). *Contemporary Composers On Contemporary Music,* Expanded Edition. Da Capo Press, New York, NY.

Simoni, M. (ed) (2006). *Analytical Methods of Electroacoustic Music.* Routledge, New York, NY.

Tenney, J. (2006). *Meta-Hodos: A Phenomenology of 20th Century Musical Materials and a Approach to the Study of Form, and META Meta-Hodos,* 2nd Edition. Frog Peak Music, Lebanon, NH.

Truax, B. (1999). *Handbook of Acoustic Ecology,* 2nd Edition. Online book: http://www. sfu.ca/sonic-studio/handbook/

Wilkins, M. L. (2006). *Creative Music Composition: The Young Composer's Voice.* Routledge, New York, NY.

Wishart, T. (1994). *Audible Design: A Plain and Easy Introduction to Practical Sound Composition.* Orpheus the Pantomime, York.

Wishart, T. (1996). *On Sonic Art,* Revised edition (ed. S. Emmerson). Routledge, New York, NY.

Zorn, J. (ed) (2000). *Arcana: Musicians on Music.* Granary Books, Inc., New York, NY (First of a series: *Arcana II* and *Arcana III* are also available).

Chapter 9

■ Modeling

'Only art and science can raise men to the level of the Gods.'

Beethoven [Hamburger, 1984, p. 26]

OBJECTIVES

This chapter covers:

- the many faces of musical modeling;
- computational musicology;
- modeling of musical expression;
- sonification – translating real-world data to sound;
- information theory and music.

9.1 THE ACT OF MODELING

We have already encountered auditory models, physical models, spectral models, algorithmic composition as outlining a particular music theory, and more; so the use and concept of a 'model' is not especially novel. This chapter uses the topic of modeling as a way to collect together some interesting issues, from artificial intelligence in music to musical expression and computer-based musicology. It is an opportunity to present a snapshot of work at the intersection of music and the sciences, of computational applications in the humanities, and of more involved explorations proceeding out of computer science, which bring a diverse set of methodologies. Computer programs always necessitate strict modeling; this is one of their strengths, in that they force us to be explicit about all aspects of a problem. It can be a real challenge to elucidate all stages of a musical process in sufficient detail to actually make it operational. We are prompted to reflect deeply on our basic assumptions. A necessary prelude to the instantiation of any working computational system is a choice of representation for the musical data, so there are always immediate demands to meet in computer music modeling.

From David Huron's theory of anticipation [Huron, 2006], through the Generative Theory of Tonal Music (GTTM) [Lerdahl and Jackendoff, 1983] back to historical treatises from Aristoxenus to Zarlino, there is no shortage of theories on how music might be modeled. In many cases the unadorned theories are not mechanizable, but it is interesting to consider computational implementation even if computer realization was not an original concern of the theorists! GTTM was not itself put into operation by its authors, though subsequent investigators have attempted to extend the theory to cope [Temperley, 2001; Hamanaka *et al.*, 2006]. As we have discussed in previous parts of this book, it may be that no one theory is enough to cover such a divergent cultural domain as music. GTTM's remit is clearly Western classical tonal music, and though David Temperley [2001] has tried to extend this to cover some aspects of popular and of African musical cultures, the question of the universality of any one theory of music is a dangerous territory we will continue to tread lightly around!

As an example of different approaches to musical modeling, Table 9.1 is adapted from work by Pearce *et al.* [2002]. It demonstrates the variety of disciplines, motivations and hence evaluation criteria involved in modeling the act of composition. There are perspectives here that may seem far flung from the practical act of composition – such as investigation of the mental states of a composer as explored within the framework of cognitive science – but nevertheless may have very interesting things to reveal about the subject.

Table 9.1 Methodologies in automated composition.

Domain	Activity	Motivation
Composition	Algorithmic composition	Expansion of compositional repertoire
Software engineering	Design of compositional tools	Development of tools for composers
Musicology	Computational modeling of musical styles	Proposal and evaluation of theories of musical styles
Cognitive science	Computational modeling of music cognition	Proposal and evaluation of cognitive theories of musical composition

Because of the overlap in this chapter with more scientific approaches to the study of music, it is worth briefly mentioning the methods of science. In scientific terms, a successful theory must offer some measure of prediction about future phenomena that fall within its remit, and the more powerful theories offer greater generalization, that is, more predictions over a wider range of phenomena. In the iterative design cycle of experiment and theory, a theory is only as good as its next result, and always open to revision by a more powerful tool. Just as the generalization ability of an algorithm must be tested in machine learning to prove that it can cope with unseen future cases that were not part of its training, useful scientific theories are validated by the success of their own predictions.

In this setting, the computer is a natural aide to calculating predictions, such as running a simulation of an acoustical model to compare its output to the measurement of a real instrument. For example, Bruyns [2006] validates a physical model based on modal synthesis for arbitrary shapes, by recording the sound of a metal plate in the shape of the letter 'G' being struck in an anechoic chamber. The computer is also often intimately involved in running the experiments themselves, for instance when programming the data collection and processing routines for experiments in music psychology and psychoacoustics [Deutsch, 1999; Clarke and Cook, 2004; Hallam *et al.*, 2009]. Aside from laboratory studies, there is also a further class of scientific modeling work with computers that investigates the 'computationally empowered thought experiment' [Wheeler *et al.*, 2002]. Here, the computer is a simulator which is fed with as much uncontested scientific data as possible, but which then assists an investigator in the generation of new speculative theories, even where there is little chance of immediately obtaining concrete data to attempt falsification. We see this in particular in some work in evolutionary modeling or artificial life, where virtual agents are programmed to act in putatively lifelike ways [Miranda and Biles, 2007].

At many points in this book we have seen how music can intersect with advanced work in artificial intelligence (AI), and this provides an example of how models are imported from one field to another application area. From the virtual brains of interactive music systems (Section 6.4.3 also provides complementary coverage to that here) to machine learning algorithms in music information retrieval (Section 7.2), there is scope to employ sophisticated algorithms. As argued previously, music is a challenging real-life test domain. Fashions in AI are reflected in computer music research, with the same shift from an emphasis on the symbolic to sub-symbolic connectionist architectures around the late 1980s [Leman, 1993]. Engineering interest in Bayesian statistical signal processing, or the data mining techniques of MIR, equally reflect how technologies cross fields, and that AI is a treasure house of useful tools for computer music.

Computer music research is also closely influenced by the related field of computational linguistics, as we saw with the early (1960) physical model of the voice by Kelly and Lochbaum, or can find reflected in discussion of generative grammars as models in algorithmic composition [Roads, 1985b], or Hidden Markov Models in automatic accompaniment [Orio and Déchelle, 2001], to give two examples. Pattern recognition algorithms developed for searching text strings have been utilized in musical pattern analysis [Pearce and Wiggins, 2004].

New paradigms are constantly evolving. A new subfield of AI, **computational creativity**, has begun to explicitly tackle the simulation of human creativity by machine [Boden, 2003; Sternberg, 1999; Deliège and Wiggins, 2006]. Human creativity turns out to be a rather tangled web of social attribution and political maneuvering, co-discovery, trial and error and happenstance. 'Genius' has been, if not entirely debunked, knocked down a peg or put in a wider context. But work in this area can potentially provide new insights into the creative process, which support the construction of more human-like algorithmic composition systems (though perhaps this work also reveals the missing social web, real-world embodiment and auditory power of the typical computer program). The purest aims of computational creativity are perhaps interlinked with the modeling of music cognition mentioned in Table 9.1, but are of potential importance for the whole field.

With many domains influencing computer music, and with the potential for any successful model to impact back on other disciplines, you might be forgiven for feeling a little overwhelmed sometimes by all the things you could do. It is usually found, though, that specific musical tasks require relatively specific solutions, and general theories of music are hampered by the subjectivities of the domain.[1] We are extremely fortunate if we can find relatively general rules underlying a large sector of musical culture, and it is fascinating to theorize, and attempt to corroborate theories, concerning such a rich part of human life.

9.2 REPRESENTATIONS

Computer manipulation of music offers the calculating power of the untiring machine, and thereby many fantastic tools for the analyst. Yet it has the consequence of demanding formalization of a notoriously subjective domain. The difficulty of selecting an appropriate **representation** is acknowledged by anyone who has attempted to code up a musical example for processing [de Poli *et al.*, 1991; Marsden and Pople, 1992; Leman, 1993; Wiggins *et al.*, 1993; Selfridge-Field, 1997; Roads *et al.*, 1997]. Decisions at this first but fundamental stage impact on all later work, since they determine what inferences can be made over the representation, and it is a prime site for the introduction of the prior biases of an analyst. We may even be starting from an existing abstraction, which already encapsulates decisions as to what it is pertinent to encode within a given musical culture. Examples would be a Western classical score or the psuedo-onomatopoeic bol notation of tabla strokes [Huron, 1992, p. 20]; [Kippen and Bel, 1992]. This does not mean that a historically derived representation captures everything about the music: an opera aria might be written in a highly quantized score, but any expressive performance is full of micro-deviations in timing and in pitch [Gabrielsson, 1999]. If we have a recording of the final music, we

---

[1]See also the discussion of 'generalize versus specialize' by Wilson [2008, p. 193].

still have the audio analysis problem of transcription, where decisions must be taken on what to manually annotate, or for computer automation – a situation whose profound difficulties were already encountered in Section 3.6. It is sometimes claimed that music theory mathematics is an adequate investigative tool alone, but this is to accept the initial premises of the representational encoding (such as the octave equivalence and inversion equivalence steps in pitch class set analysis). Furthermore, if we are seeking a close match to human information processing, there is an allied issue of how music is neurally and cognitively encoded [Howell *et al.*, 1991; Peretz and Zatorre, 2003].

We saw the difficulties again in Chapter 8 when confronting various aspects of music and auditory perception. Indeed, the conflict of discrete and continuous, analog and digital representation has been a recurring motif of electronic music:

> The computer gives access to the continuum of sound and provides a ductile and seemingly neutral material. Does continuum imply indifferentiation? Are discrete categories, quantizing processes, scales, and familiar prototypes essential to nonvague perception and hence to a music capable of stimulating cognition? Is sonic space homogeneous and unbounded – or will perception reveal sharp edges, preferred dimensions, and deeply anchored constraints? [Risset, 1985, p. 135]

The tension between low- and high-level description is prevalent. Wiggins *et al.* [1993] differentiate what they call 'expressive completeness' as representing any musical source, and 'structural generality' as having the capacity to manipulate higher-level aspects of music. A raw recorded waveform could potentially store any type of music, but without any further processing has no high-level handles for that data; it is expressively complete, but not structurally general. MIDI is more structurally general, in that it is a higher-level representation to start with, but its assumptions restrict the types of music it can easily represent, showing a lack of expressive completeness. The design of good representational systems would seek to maximize both factors.

To give a further example which links well to music information retrieval research, consider the notion of contour [Adams, 1976; Morris, 1993]. From an original solo vocal line full of complex timbral information such as vibrato, microtonal embellishment and glissando, the line might be reduced to a series of discrete pitch direction tokens chosen from as few as three possibilities: same, up or down.[2] So, sidestepping rhythmic information, the first line of 'Baa Baa Black Sheep' can be represented as successive intervals from the start note, same-up–same–up–up–up–down–down. This encoding can still be a valuable feature in navigating a large space of potential melodies, because it significantly reduces the dimensionality of the problem,[3] but has lost essential information on the exact musical line (imagine replacing

---

[2]Themefinder (www.themefinder.org) calls this 'gross contour', and it is also referred to as Parsons code. The references in Section 7.2 will quickly lead you to more information on the use of contour representations in query by singing and other MIR tasks.
[3]Over a longer sequence of events, the uniqueness of a particular melody becomes more pronounced. But substituting different intervals for any given contour description should illustrate the basic combinatoriality of music!

each of the contour steps with an appropriate interval of your own choosing). There are many more refined contour descriptions, from using five, seven or more step sizes, working back up towards the original more continuous notion of pitch. If we now factor in the various ways any given human being might encode the music themselves, from the implicit mental models of non-specialist listeners to the formal preferences of highly trained analysts, all highly culturally contingent, we get a good sense of the dilemmas of representations.

In practical work, we still need to make a decision in order to proceed, and we can do so as long as we are clear about our assumptions. Even if an unanticipated consequence of a choice of representation comes back to haunt us later on, it is sometimes possible to convert between formats post-hoc, or patch up a hole for an emerging data need. Even where the representational assumptions are later proven restrictive, we often had to set out on a given path to find this out. The revisionism that can plague large-scale projects is just a natural consequence of human authors not being able to anticipate every consequence of a given knowledge representation, yet being required to work on some system in the meantime.

That there is no one best solution is also reflected in a wide variety of choices of encoding format. Perhaps fortunately, MIDI is not the only option for representing music! For standard music notation, a short list of formats might mention Digital Alternate Representation of Musical Scores (DARMS), Notation Interchange File Format (NIFF), MuseData, abc, MusicXML or MusiXTeX, though not all of these are directly editable as ASCII text [Selfridge-Field, 1997]. The sidebar demonstrates a simple score encoding, created via the Lilypond scoring software and its own mark-up language.

The influence of representational decisions is keenly felt by any end-user of a program [Magnusson, 2009]. For example, how often have you used a particular audio package and wanted to obtain the data at some stage of your workflow, only to find that data inaccessible, locked into the internals of that system? System and programming language designers should be acutely aware of the influence they can have over the work practices of users of their systems [Sears and Jacko, 2008]. A flexible program may have to offer multiple ways to achieve a musical aim, to suit the different cognitive styles of users [Eaglestone et al., 2008]. Often different users seek out different packages to suit them (for example, choosing a visual programming environment over a textual one).

The issue is also not just the nature of musical data, but what operations are available to manipulate that data. Representation becomes critical to the design of new programming languages and other systems for computer music, which must anticipate the consequences of any given transformation [Dannenberg, 1993; Honing, 1993]. A classic example is how best to deal with the vibrato for an event that is being time stretched; should the vibrato remain at the same rate but elongate in time, or should it be stretched as an envelope is stretched, slowing down as it is extended? Although an operator of a computer music system could be given the option to choose, each new option multiplies the amount of work the system designer must put in, and the potential complexity for the end-user. Sometimes the neatness of particular representations from a computer science point of view distracts computer music software creators from the actual musical needs of their user base. Finding the right balance of specific task-oriented functionality and customizability is one of the fundamental tradeoffs of software design.

9.3 AUTOMATING MUSICOLOGICAL ANALYSIS

Much early work in computer music concerned applications of computers in musicological analysis [Lincoln, 1970]. Here, the capability of the computer to handle large volumes of data became freely apparent, giving musicologists access to new tools for analysis, from the statistical properties of individual works to trends spanning the currents of musical style [Manning *et al.*, 2009; Selfridge-Field, 1993]. We have seen a contemporary equivalent in the efforts in music information retrieval to provide efficient ways to access and catalog the huge numbers of audio recordings available online (Section 7.2). In neither case is the computer a magical panacea; much hard work goes into preparing data and into investigating appropriate algorithms for analysis, and work remains at the mercy of the initial choice of encoding or features to extract. A basic problem of musical analysis is the decision as to what constitutes an important event or subsequence to be extracted from the musical surface, determining the segmentation [Forte, 1973; Cook, 1994; Pople, 2004]. The computer only reinforces the need to be explicit about this.

This section will deal predominantly with symbolic musical data, already encoded via some representational decision, rather than audio files. This may bring us perilously close to putting the classical score on a pedestal, since a majority of Western scholarship is about the Western classical tradition, though there are many alternative representations among the world's musics. It is worth pointing out, however, some further avenues of computational analysis based on audio recordings, as productive alternatives. The methods of MIR are being increasingly applied to non-Western musics, and there is a history of the analysis of recordings in ethnomusicological research [Tzanetakis *et al.*, 2007]. Further, in investigating electronic music, audio analysis tools often prove highly pertinent, as the digital musician's signal manipulation tools are turned back on the analysis of works!

Sidestepping any controversy about the best encoding of music, the payoff of preparing data in a computer-friendly format is being able to run as many evaluations of a data set as desired, prodigiously faster than working with pen and paper [Manning *et al.*, 2009]. However, claims of automation should be taken with a pinch of salt here. In most musicological applications, the computer is a tool used under the careful guidance of a human musicologist for specific repetitive tasks, and the analyst does not give much interpretative autonomy to the machine. Nevertheless, there are algorithms that can assist the process of hunting out significant aspects of a large data set from a more unbiased statistical perspective, as long as the bias of initial encoding decisions and choice of algorithm are acknowledged.[4]

---

[4]Some work discussed in this chapter seeks universal principles to guide decisions, such as a basis in information theoretic criteria, and seemingly more neutral statistical and machine learning techniques can be applied. Yet the basic problem of initial encoding cannot be circumvented even if pushed a step further back. The pragmatic hope is that all assumptions can be laid bare, and the most general theories constructed from minimal axioms; here, the computer is an indispensable tool, and the bias of the human analyst potentially minimized.

Lilypond

Lilypond is an open-source score typesetting software for Western common practice notation, and well worth trying out (http://lilypond.org). It has its own internal '.ly' format for representing music, and the user can write descriptions of scores directly in this language. There are also various auxiliary programs supporting MIDI input, graphical user interfaces and other file formats that can convert output to the Lilypond format.

Figure 9.1   A measure of music typeset by Lilypond.

Figure 9.1 is a non-trivial if undeveloped score, corresponding to the following format instructions:

```
\version "2.10.33"
\include "english.ly"
\relative c' {
\time 3/2
<<
\new Staff {\clef treble c8.(\pp fs16 c'4)
          \times 4/5 { r8 ef16\< e f8\f\>-> d, g\! } d8( g) r4}
\new Staff {\clef bass r2 <a,, bf' >2 r4 \acciaccatura b8 ef-. cs-.}
>>
}
```

The Lilypond format is meant to be humanly editable, and you should be able to find in this text the commands that designate each staff, clef types, an acciaccatura or possibly dynamics (look for pp). The encoding is English language format, where a to g are the standard pitch names and s is for sharp and f for flat. A rest is denoted by r, and note durations are marked with numbers: 8 would be an eighth note, 16 a sixteenth and so forth. A dot after a duration value makes a dotted note, and \times is a construction for bringing in a tuplet. The notations for articulation, slurs or the crescendo and diminuendo are a little more concealed but involve accent and staccato dot marks, parentheses for slur start and end positions and \< and \> for the hairpins.

Lilypond supports much more complicated scores, and is relatively tweakable; this example is designed to give you an insight into the mark-up process, an alternative way of depicting Western note-based music. You might like to think about what information is being lost by this discrete note-based encoding, and how the encoding is specific to a particular style of music (for example, could you use the methods here to encode a work in 19 notes per octave?).

To help conduct studies in this area, there are many existing collections of musical works in symbolic formats ready for processing, and tools to tackle them.[5] One famous and much-analyzed data set is the Essen folksong collection (currently maintained by Ewa Dahlig at www.esac-data.org), now comprising 20 000 monophonic melodies mainly of German, Polish and Chinese origin, and encoded in a straightforward ASCII format. As one example of a computational study that takes advantage of this collection, Toiviainen and Eerola [2001] used a Self-Organizing Map in order to automatically cluster 6000 entries, as part of an investigation of melodic similarity. Aside from resources created by musicologists, the Internet contains innumerable MIDI files and alternative score-like representations, many created by enthusiastic hobbyists, some of high quality and others of doubtful veracity. Just as in the use of metadata for audio recordings, a certain amount of care will be required, but there are plenty of files out there for a web scraping program to obtain. As for analysis tools, you could write your own programs directly in your favorite environment, which is perfectly feasible for parsing some of the friendlier ASCII formats, or with the assistance of standard MIDI file reading libraries. Alternatively, a number of pre-created frameworks and extensions for symbolic music analysis are detailed in Table 9.2. One of the most well known is David Huron's Humdrum software, and its associated kern score format. There is an affiliated and well-stocked download site offering mainly classical scores

---

[5]At the time of writing, two useful starting points for finding data sets are http://www.informatics.indiana.edu/donbyrd/ MusicTestCollections.HTML, where Donald Byrd maintains a long list of resources taking in multiple proprietary and public file formats, and links compiled by Georg Holzmann containing both audio and symbolic resources (http://grh.mur.at/misc/ mir_datasets.html).

in multiple formats called Kern Scores (http://kern.humdrum.net/). This website also includes many pre-rendered analyses for each piece, illuminating different aspects including voicings, metrical structure and changing key.

Table 9.2   A selection of symbolic music analysis tools.

Software	Description	Link
MIDIToolbox	MATLAB extension library for MIDI file processing, which contains many analysis tools from metrical analysis to key detection	http://www.jyu.fi/hum/laitokset/musiikki/en/ research/coe/materials/miditoolbox/
Humdrum	A suite of command-line tools for symbolic score processing and analysis	http://musiccog.ohio-state.edu/Humdrum/
jSymbolic	Java tool for symbolic data feature extraction and analysis, developed for music information retrieval applications but equally applicable to musicological analysis	http://jmir.sourceforge.net/
The Melisma Music Analyzer	Analysis tools relating to work by Temperley [2001] including meter, harmony, key, grouping and stream segregation	http://www.link.cs.cmu.edu/music-analysis/

Symbolically formatted data tends to give certain information for free, such as a single pitch for each note event, a clear onset time and duration, and pre-quantized rhythms, though all discrete precision is at the expense of loss of some expressive and continuous data. But, even where the data is supposedly clear, the analysis of music is not suddenly made trivial; there are significant challenges remaining [Rowe, 2001; Temperley, 2001]. We have noted already the issue of segmentation as a classic problem of musical analysis, computer or no computer. To encounter the problem of segmentation in a practical setting, let's consider how a MIDI file of a conventional Western classical work – say, a Beethoven symphony – could be broken up into units for analysis. Assuming your MIDI file provides bar boundary information, should you work by measure boundaries? By beat boundaries? By changing harmonies? Even identifying the current chord can be problematic, for not all contributing notes to a given harmony are playing with the same rhythm (real compositions don't tend to use strict first species counterpoint!). Perhaps the beat boundaries aid spotting the most significant harmonic events, and we should prioritize the contribution of those notes falling on a beat? But is there not a danger of being confused by suspensions, or losing sight of passing notes? If we had access to an original score in encoding a work, some assignments of voices might be unambiguous. But in contrapuntal piano music, for instance, how would you find the different voices if you weren't supplied with this information in the original encoding? (Figure 9.2 gives a marked-up example.) How would you deal with the extraction of musical phrases and sections at various timescales, when phrase marks are not always available, and composers are not averse to the specification of joined and ambiguous phrases that end and start on the same note? The answer to all this is that it depends a great deal on what you are seeking in the first place.

Figure 9.2   The three voices in the third fugue from J.S. Bach's 48. Note the overlaps of register and the difficulty that would arise in automatically separating the voices; segregation of the lines requires thematic analysis to fully disambiguate cases, though allocating voice by register or order would provide a baseline. Reproduced by permission of © Craig Sapp.

So, just as for audio analysis, computer algorithms can be written to extract salient features from symbolically encoded data, and there is a healthy literature on these investigations. One example is the problem of symbolic key finding. Figure 9.3 shows a **keyscape**, a diagram of the key of a work according to the timescale of investigation. Lower levels of the diagram correspond to smaller windows of notes for analysis, with the window shifted in position through the work; the top level is the whole piece, so there is only one window and result here. This diagram is a neat depiction of the problem of assigning a single unambiguous key at any point in time, because of the substantial problem of resolving the exact pertinence of global versus local context. It is likely that short-term memory (around ten seconds) and the perceptual present (around three seconds) would form the most important interpretative timescales for a realtime listener (compare Section 8.2.5), though this is not to say that a composer preparing a work is bound by the same criteria, nor that an analyst like Heinrich Schenker would agree. The algorithm used here is based on key profiles, statistical measures of the salience of particular notes within each key. These can be used to score all possible keys against an input collection of pitch classes, to find the best-fitting key for that input. Algorithm 9.1 gives you an idea of how to search for a winning key, given profiles for each possibility. A profile is derived from a large corpus of example works, or from psychological experimentation [Krumhansl, 1990], and is simply an array of weights. One profile is the Krumhansl–Kessler profile, seen here in its form for a major key, with one weight for each semitone:

$$[0.152, 0.053, 0.083, 0.056, 0.105, 0.098, 0.06, 0.124, 0.057, 0.088, 0.055, 0.069]$$

You should see that the first (tonic) and then the eighth (dominant) entries have the largest weights. The profile would be rotated for each possible transposition to be tested, such that the large tonic 0.152 weight rests in turn on each key root to be tested.

Often co-constrained to key, but more particular in timescale and function, is the identification of harmony. This is a standard task[6] in (a)tonal analysis for which students of Western

---

[6]It might be a common assignment, but it is hardly free of ambiguity, and there are often multiple solutions in interpretation. It also gets harder as the harmonic resources of Western music become stretched through the later Romantic period.

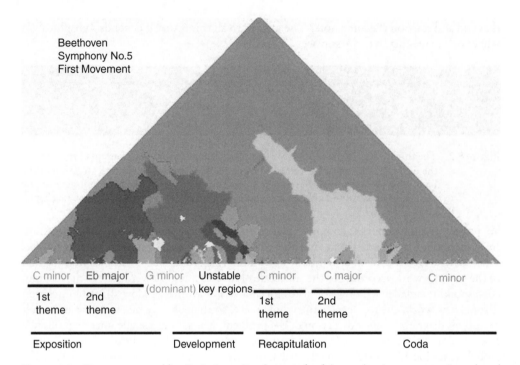

Figure 9.3   Keyscape created by Craig Sapp. Beethoven's fateful symphonic movement is analyzed using a symbolic key finding algorithm operating for window sizes from the whole piece down to a very local level. The analysis becomes increasingly 'noisy' as it becomes more local. The overall key is C minor, perhaps not surprisingly. Reproduced by permission of © Craig Sapp.

music often wish they had a computer program in order to relieve them of the drudgery! We might wish to operationalize Schoenberg's functional method of harmony, or Forte's pitch class set analysis. Again, many computational approaches have been offered [Kroger *et al.*, 2008], with classic early studies such as Terry Winograd's grammar of harmonic syntax [Winograd, 1986]. Gaining an assignment of chords can be a prelude to exploring their succession, and a recent investigation by Rohrmeier and Cross [2008] highlighted the asymmetrical nature of chord transitions (attributed to the goal-directed nature of harmonic progression) in another classic data set, J.S. Bach's chorale harmonizations (386 of them in this study).

Hopefully, this discussion, which has stopped short of the further issues of musical grouping, phrasing, sectional boundaries, metrical structure extraction and more, has been enough to convince you of the challenges and rewards of computer implementation. Think of how symbolic analysis procedures might inform an interactive music system based on live MIDI input [Rowe, 2001]. One further aspect of musicological investigation with computers is worth noting at this stage, which is the link to algorithmic composition,

---

Algorithm 9.1 Basic key finding algorithm; given a collection of pitches and key profiles, find the best matching key profile.

Input: Collection c of pitches as MIDI note numbers 0 to 127; set of key profiles k
Output: Key profile index for closest match, *maxindex*

1: $histogrampc = [0,0,0,0,0,0,0,0,0,0,0,0]$ // to form a histogram of pitch classes
2: **for** $n = 0$ to $size(c) - 1$ **do**
3:     $temp \leftarrow c[n]$ modulo 12   // Convert pitch to pitch class
4:     $histogrampc[temp] \leftarrow histogrampc[temp] + 1$ // Populate histogram
5: **end for**
6: $maxscore \leftarrow 0$ // Initialize variable for finding maximum score
7: $maxindex \leftarrow 0$ // Will give the final output
8: **for** $m = 0$ to $size(k) - 1$ **do**
9:     $profile \leftarrow k[m]$ // Get current key profile to test
10:     $tempscore \leftarrow 0$ // Initialize for finding current correlation
11:     **for** $n = 0$ to 11 **do**
12:         $tempscore \leftarrow tempscore + profile[n] * histogrampc[n]$ // Match pc count to profile strength
13:     **end for**
14:     **if** $tempscore > maxscore$ **then**
15:         $maxscore \leftarrow tempscore$
16:         $maxindex \leftarrow m$
17:     **end if**
18: **end for**

---

as anticipated in Table 9.1. Synthesis of music within a style is a method of obtaining good feedback on the success or failure of a stylistic analysis, potentially informing an experimental design cycle in musicology. The algorithmic composition techniques we began to explore in Section 8.3.1 are of note here, and as per Pearce *et al.* [2002], we would probably want to differentiate investigation of historical style as having separate evaluation criteria from the general use of the computer in free composition. One exemplary study is the work of Kippen and Bel [1992] in Hindustani tabla music and its instantiation in the Bol Processor software (http://bolprocessor.sourceforge.net/) as a generative grammar, developed in a tight feedback loop with expert tabla performers.

9.4 MODELING OF MUSICAL EXPRESSION

> Computer synthesis is not necessarily cursed with ice-cold perfection. [Risset, 1985, p. 119]

> [I]t is precisely these elements that are most difficult for the computer to generate, since they come not only from the context of the music, but from an emotional experience as well as a lifetime of making music. [Winkler, 1998, p. 8]

Since the use of score-like representations can mean treating symbolic abstractions of music that have shed much of their expressive fine detail, this section seeks to redress the balance. We engage with computer music's contributions to an active area of research in music psychology, musical performance and expression [Windsor, 2009; Juslin, 2009; Clarke, 2004; Gabrielsson, 1999]. But it is also possible to create generative models of those stylistically appropriate deviations from mechanical playback that characterize human musical performance and convey much emotional currency. This may go as far as modeling the personal expressive preferences of an individual musician. So, although to some observers machine music implies a harsh metronomicity – and some sectors of electronic dance music might be the stereotype here – computers can also be the means of investigating human expression. In some ways, the precision of computer analysis and playback[7] is the exact tool required for intensive investigation.

Computer-driven sensor technology has an important role to play in scientific and pedagogical work with musicians. In Chapter 6 we already encountered many tools that would be of help to those studying musical performance, from physiological sensors to computer vision. One example from the i-MAESTRO project is the use of multi-camera tracking of a performer in combination with sensors to create a three-dimensional animated model of a string player's movements. This is used to give feedback on posture and expressive gesture in music education [Ng *et al.*, 2008], as depicted in Figure 9.4. The InfoMus Lab at the University of Genoa have also been highly involved in computer vision and sensor techniques, with their own EyesWeb platform for the capture of expressive gestural information, and work with both dancers and musicians [Camurri *et al.*, 2005]. Such work is coupled to the general interface investigations of the NIME community. At the InfoMus Lab, they also explore the coding of expressive rules, as discussed below. A majority of studies of performance to date have been based around the piano, not just because some researchers might admire 19th-century piano repertoire, but because recording the physical control action on a piano is, if not unproblematic, at least less problematic than for more continuous control-based instruments like the violin. The velocity and timing of key strike is the essential information to be recorded, and has been accessible from early player pianos to more finely detailed modern MIDI and optical reproducing pianos [Windsor, 2009].

Where there is no auxiliary sensor data, it is still possible to annotate recordings. Computer-assisted audio analysis techniques in particular can help to explore a musical source directly [McAdams *et al.*, 2004]. Although there are some MIDI recordings containing useful expressive performance data, which are more immediately parsable, the realm of audio transcription is often unavoidable (for example, how would you otherwise investigate the expressive singing of Ella Fitzgerald?). To avoid laborious and potentially error-strewn manual work, computer analysis of audio is of great assistance, for example in the mark-up of event onsets and note substructure, and the detection of pitch and vibrato. Because

---

[7]Extreme precision allows a composer to create incredibly intricate rhythms; unfortunately, a human observer unfamiliar with such an idiom often fails to pick up on micro-timings, since they are interpreted at the level of expression rather than as the timing markers themselves. This can lead to the failure for a general audience of certain rhythmic studies, when their training essentially misinterprets the nature of the expressive content.

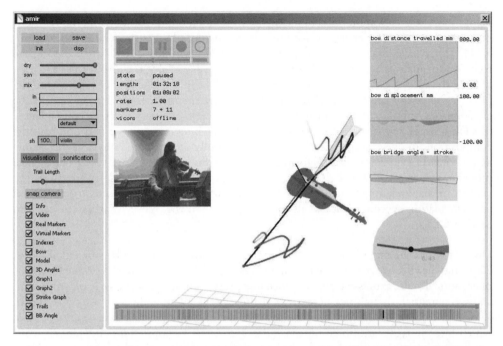

Figure 9.4   3-D augmented mirror: screenshot of performance capture software showing sensor data and virtual reconstruction gained from multiple cameras. Reproduced by permission of Dr Kia Ng, Project Coordinator of the i-Maestro EC IST project (www.i-maestro.org).

of the great challenges of automatic transcription, procedures may be most reliable for monophonic sources (see also Chapter 3). One example is provided by work at the Centre for the History and Analysis of Recorded Music (CHARM) into historical recordings, work which also falls within the remit of music information retrieval. In the Mazurka project, many available interpretations of Chopin mazurkas were analyzed side by side for their similarities and differences of interpretation [Sapp, 2008]. Because the score is known, it could be fitted to each audio recording, greatly assisting the accuracy of what would otherwise be a full polyphonic transcription problem. As another developed example of the benefits of computational analysis, a team at Pompeu Fabra have been applying Spectral Modeling Synthesis towards further understanding expressive performance in saxophone, Irish fiddle playing and tenor singing, to name three. Driven by computer analysis, the team have managed to introduce expressive transformations directly to a source audio signal [Ramirez and Hazan, 2005]. One impressive demonstration is the addition of mordents (a particular ornament) to a recording of Irish fiddle playing [Perez *et al.*, 2008].

Analysis informs attempts to generalize observed performance expression into rules for synthesis. Within the context of the saxophone modeling work just introduced, Ramirez *et al.* [2008] have used genetic algorithms (with sequential covering criteria to gradually explain all the data) to explore a space of possible performance rules. Such a methodology helps to minimize researcher bias in picking out the rules. On the other hand, the synthesis of expression has been energetically pursued for decades by researchers at Stockholm's KTH.[8] They have established a large rulebase for (Western) music performance using the technique of analysis by synthesis [Friberg *et al.*, 2000]; essentially, trying out rules and then judging the success of the result, in a design feedback loop just like that of Kippen and Bel [1992]. Out of this project, the Director Musices software provides one framework for the encoding of symbolic rules for musical expression. There can be very practical consequences of such research. Synthesis of expression can inform interactive music and non-realtime composition. In one example, Brad Garton has carefully incorporated physical constraints and idiomatic expression into algorithmic composition works in 'virtual performance modeling' [Garton, 1992]. It is also a practical area for commercial software, from the expressive playback functionality in a score editing program like Sibelius to the phrase and articulation specific choice of playback segments in the Synful synthesizer (see also Section 5.1.5).

Discussion of expression links us back to studies of emotion in music [Juslin and Sloboda, 2001] and the affective computing paradigm discussed in Section 6.2.5. As a primary conduit of emotional state, expressive performance intersects with the personal style of a musician, and is a potential, though not necessarily definite, guide to an audience's response. Again, algorithmic composition can learn much from such studies, if the aim is to create music which hits the right emotional buttons [Riecken, 1992; Legaspi *et al.*, 2007]. Such work can help computer-generated music map onto factors of tension and release, which often underlie the appreciation of musical form at intermediate timescales [Farbood, 2006]. David Cope [2001], with his SPEAC analysis, has experimented with marking up database material with indications of tension and release at multiple hierarchical levels, in order to get a better understanding of the original emotional context of musical information. Models of emotion, connecting musical attributes to particular emotional significations, have found their way into research directed towards effective computer game music, which can reflect the drama of a character's situation [Livingstone and Brown, 2005; Eladhari *et al.*, 2006]. A recurring model plots emotional states using the two dimensions of valence (positive or negative affect, judged as good or bad) and activation (from unstimulated to energetic) [Sloboda and Juslin, 2001]. Although this obscures certain distinctions – anger and fear are both states of high arousal and negative affect – it has proved a good starting point for computational models. Yet, because emotion is a high-level and subjective reaction to music, it is hardly a solved topic in cognitive neuroscience, and computational modeling of affect and expression remains an active and open arena.

9.5 SONIFICATION

We change tack now to approach computer music from another direction, motivated by the needs of interpreting and modeling data. **Sonification** is the translation of any general

---

[8] http://www.speech.kth.se/music/performance/

data into the auditory domain, to take advantage of the ear's acuity in investigating its properties [Brewster, 2008; Kramer and Walker, 2005; Kramer, 1994b]. Because of the distracting power of language, non-speech sounds are usually favored. It is a theme that may seem parallel to 'modeling', in that it is putatively data driven, but the choice of mapping itself becomes the working model. While various currents can be distinguished in this work, basic examples of sonification in action might include auditory displays used for monitoring equipment status or providing software feedback, audio counterparts to visualization tools (equivalents of graphs, animations), or a method of sound synthesis from real-world data. One justification for carrying out such translation between domains – say, from neutron scattering experiment data to a synthesized soundscape – is that presentation of data in a novel modality may give new and valuable insights to the experimenter. In neural terms, the temporal resolution of the ear is higher than that of the eye, and the ear may (arguably) be better developed to cope with simultaneous streams of information [Chion, 1994; Fitch and Kramer, 1994].

Sonification experiments can also inform some other topics in computer music, such as the act of mapping from physical action to audio output in instrument design, where the auditory modality directly supports another sense. On the other hand, the process is subject to abuse, if the mapping itself introduces spurious artefacts and the interpretation of the original data is skewed. Finding an effective mapping for any given context may be a delicate tightrope walk, and the best psychoacoustic attributes of sound to exploit are a subject of research: 'formal psychometric testing is necessary in order to learn how to restrict the universe of possible sound attributes to those most effective for data representation' [Kramer, 1994b, p. xxxi]. In the worst case, it may be a leap too far to claim any effective analogy between the audio and the original data. Interestingly, composers have been well aware of such issues, and of the impact on the apprehension of musical form. 'As Varèse often remarked, genuine success in architecture results from a genuine understanding of the building material, not from imposing structures developed with other materials' [Risset, 1985, p. 126]. It is important to bear in mind the level of intermediary processing between original data and aural manifestation [Kramer, 1994b, pp. 186–188]; Gregory Kramer distinguishes **audification** as the direct use of data in a time-domain waveform, as might be pertinent to earthquake data. Sonification involves the data being used as control signals for some sound synthesis process. It is possible to explore those sound synthesis algorithm features best matched to features of data sets [Scarletti, 1994]. High-dimensional data must be mapped to many synthesis model parameters, raising the danger of limited attentional bandwidth. Spatialization algorithms can help create high-dimensional spaces for immersive virtual environments [Wenzel, 1994]. Work must be highly task specific: 'a neutral, unbiased, auditory display is, in our experience, just not achievable … [we] set our sights on working with whatever artful means we can muster in order to create the most comprehensible output possible' [Kramer, 1994b, p. 202].

Sonification is being taken seriously, not only in terms of auditory design for user interfaces, but in scientific institutes. NASA itself distributes the xSonify Java application, which offers a few data transformations to control MIDI synthesizer playback. An Austrian research project investigated a general platform for sonification research in the SonEnvir software environment (http://sonenvir.at/). Their collaborations include data from the physics of baryon spectra, the chaotic double pendulum, lattice quantum chromodynamics, EEG, juggling, the explorer Magellan's route around the globe represented as social geographic data, air pollution, and an election! Most of this research (and a theoretical model based on these sonifications) is described in Alberto de Campo's PhD thesis [de Campo, 2009]. Figure 9.5 depicts an application that sonifies EEG data in real time.

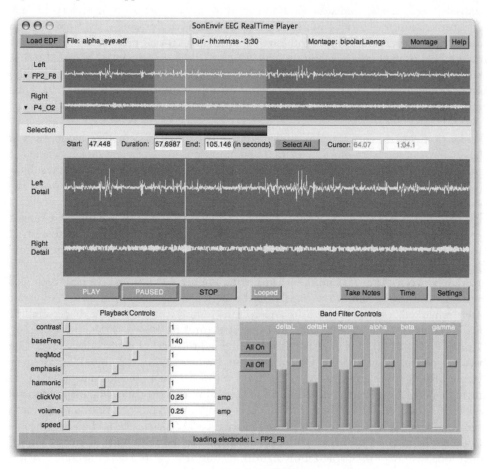

Figure 9.5   EEG sonification. The top section is for choosing a data file and selecting which of the electrodes (mounted on the subject's head) to listen to, and a time range within the file. The EEG signal is sonified in six separate bands; relative volumes of these bands and other playback parameters can be adjusted during playback. Reproduced by permission of © Alberto de Campo.

While sonification can be a scientific tool, composers' ears may be pricking up at the thought of taking advantage of interesting and exotic structures from other domains. Many composers do find inspiration by drawing from the data of the natural sciences. Examples include Charles Dodge's *Earth's Magnetic Field* (1970), Natasha Barrett's installation *Displaced: Replaced II* (2002), based on audiovisualization of live meteorological data from sensors, and Bob Sturm's *Music From the Ocean* (2002), based on tidal data from an array of ocean buoys off the coast of California. Mention of these works links back to the topic of mapping in algorithmic composition, with a negotiation of process and product. Motivations may diverge in many ways from the strictly scientific; see Section 8.3.2 and [Doornbusch, 2002].

9.6 THE INFORMATION CHARACTERISTICS OF MUSIC

Following the publication and popularization of Claude Shannon's 1948 foundational work on information theory, many early investigations in computational musicology and algorithmic composition were inspired by these principles [Pierce, 1968; MacKay, 2003]. This section is an opportunity to take a specific look at some modeling of music inspired by information theory. We shall also encounter a specific application of Zipf's law, that attempts to fit certain global properties of music to the form of $1/f$ noise. Such attempts to provide universal laws or basic axioms of musical content are illuminating for the negotiation of local and global detail they involve. They represent an honest attempt to sidestep the assumptions and social negotiations we usually bring to music, even though by the same avoidance of subjectivity they can find it difficult to provide the final word on music's makeup.

Let's treat information theory first. Probabilities run on the scale from 0 (impossible) to 1 (definite); the information content of an individual event is naturally described by the (negative) logarithm to the base 2 of its probability. I'll now try to justify that statement. Consider a fair coin; there is a 50% chance, or a probability of 0.5, that the coin will come up heads on a single throw. How much information do we gain from this outcome? There are two possibilities, so the coding of this outcome only requires two states, and $-\log_2(0.5) = 1$, or one bit of information, one bit giving us two states. If that seems too trivial, consider a fair six-sided dice. There are six possible outcomes, and sure enough $-\log_2(1/6) = \log_2(6)$ tells us that it takes about 2.6 bits to encode each throw of the dice. These examples actually only work for equal probability distributions. The generalization is to consider, for an exhaustive set of outcomes X, the equation:

$$\sum_{x \in X} -P(x) \log_2(P(x)) \tag{9.1}$$

which is known as the **entropy**, the weighted average of the information content of each possible outcome, and hence in the long run the best estimator to measure the information content per event.[9] Information content tells us about the unexpectedness of a particular outcome, whereas entropy signifies the uncertainty over the range of possible outcomes.

Now, the English language might be next on our list of targets. MacKay [2003, p. 22] cites probabilities for the vowels of the English language, as extracted from a computing textbook. Let's instead work on the probabilities of pitches appearing in the first movement of Beethoven's fatefully important Fifth Symphony. Figure 9.6 plots the probability and the information value of each discrete pitch. This was generated using a MIDI file from the kernscores website, and the MIDI Toolbox in MATLAB; I would have been a diligent musicologist indeed to obtain these statistics without a computer! The diagram can give an appreciation of the relation between the rarity of an occurrence and the information content it brings.

Two extremes of information are provided by white noise, and by continual repetition of the same event. White noise has a flat spectral profile; it's impossible to predict what will come next at any scale. The repeating note is *too* predictable. In the former case, information content is maximally high, and the latter is highly redundant, because only a little information is necessary to encode basic repetition [Loy, 2007a; Snyder, 2000]. Music tends to play a game between these extremes, using repetition to reinforce a musical statement but retaining processes of change, where all of this can happen over multiple timescales and parameters. Perhaps some atonal composition or free improvisation falls a little closer to white noise (on the edge of our perceptual abilities, toying with the amount from which we can make sense without information overload), and some minimalism deliberately overdoes the repetition (perhaps to strengthen the contrast when a change does eventually occur after a trance-like state of overfulfilled expectancy).

Voss and Clarke [1978] have shown that musical audio tends to fit the same spectral power distribution as $1/f$ noise, at form bearing timescales longer than a second (thus not at the level of local audio signal or faster rhythmic event rates). Whilst white noise is flat, $1/f$ noise falls off in inverse proportion to increasing frequency; that's what the $1/f$ means, after all. Although not illuminating the fine detail, or high level significations, this seems to correspond to 'just enough' correlation of events to be a baseline of musical preference. Generation based on $1/f$ noise has been used in algorithmic composition as an alternative to overly random white noise ($1/f^0 = 1$), and overly correlated Brownian noise ($1/f^2$, also corresponding to a random walk), showing a pleasing balance of return and novelty [Moore, 1990; Roads, 1996; Dodge and Jerse, 1997]. The $1/f$ form also turns up in studies of frequencies of word use in language corpora, and in other musicological studies, counts of musical attributes have been observed to fit variants of Zipf's law, that is, fitting a curve of the form $1/f^n$ for some n, usually for n from 1 to 2 [Zanette, 2006]. Rohrmeier and Cross [2008] demonstrate that the frequencies of use of chords by Bach in a large corpus

---

[9]Just to dispense with one technicality, note that for zero probability events, their information is infinite (they're *that* unexpected), but their contribution to the entropy is zero since $0 \log_2(0) = 0$, because a linear function goes to zero faster than a log function can diverge to infinity.

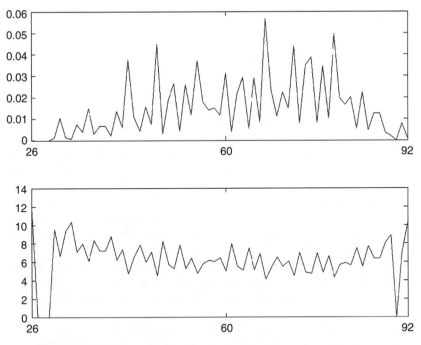

Figure 9.6   Probability and information graphs for notes in the first movement of Beethoven's Fifth
Symphony. The top graph gives the probability of each note in the piece's range, from
MIDI note 26 (a low D) up to 92 (a high C). There is an inverse relationship to the
lower graph of information content for each note. For clarity and to avoid perturbing
the graph, the information content of non-appearing notes (probability zero events) has
been set artificially to zero, though it is actually infinite. The entropy is the notewise
inner product of the two plotted data arrays.

of his chorales follows $1/f^2$, a situation where some chords (major, minor and dominant
seventh) are highly significant options within the style.

Though the analysis so far may give a sense of the information value of any pitch within
the global context of the whole piece, or a typical profile of musical token use, there is
more insight into local structure to be gained in terms of common transition sequences
that appear in a work or corpus. Analyzing this is a matter of expanding the dictionary of
possible tokens. Where we previously had only monograms, uncontextualized, a first-order
Markov chain might look at all digrams, that is, transitions from any one pitch to any other.

Consider the contrived sequence:

$$c\;d\;f\;g\;e\;f\;g\;a\;d\;f\;a\;g\;g\;g\;b$$

This is really just a sequence of letters, which could stand for any musical events we wished
to tag with them; but you're possibly already thinking just of a diatonic melody (without

rhythmic values).[10] To consider all transitions might be to make a table of transition counts for all the appearing digrams:

$$c \to d : 1, \quad d \to f : 2, \quad e \to f : 1, \quad f \to g : 2$$
$$f \to a : 1, \quad g \to e : 1, \quad g \to g : 2, \quad g \to a : 1$$
$$g \to b : 1, \quad a \to d : 1, \quad a \to g : 1$$

The counts add up to 14, one less than the 15 original tokens, because there is no transition from the final event. A generative procedure, starting from any token a to f, could follow available options based on the relative frequencies in this tiny corpus. Starting at g, there are four options, e, g, a and b, with relative probabilities $1/6, 2/6, 2/6$, and $1/6$. Note how there is no transition *starting* at b, and it could be possible to get stuck at such a terminating token. In practice, you can jump to a new point, or at least relax criteria. It is possible to create a cyclic graph to represent all the paths, which can end up with a number of different loops and sections [Ames, 1989]. Markov models appear frequently in musical modeling work, and orders from three to four tend to work well as a tradeoff between capturing local rules of transition, but avoiding direct citation of the original piece [Hiller and Isaacson, 1959; Pierce, 1968; Ames, 1989]. More complicated models may involve variable-order Markov models and other refinements of these ideas [Dubnov *et al.*, 2003; Pearce and Wiggins, 2004].

It is also possible to take the perspective of the onwards flow of expectancy at any given moment in time for a listener, with local confirmation and surprise. Modeling of **dynamic expectancy** can combine expectations from prior knowledge of a style with the local detail of the specific stimulus, and has been productively approached by some researchers [Pearce *et al.*, 2008]. In this setting, information theory has been taken as a good basis on which to create a relatively neutral segmentation algorithm for musical works; Potter *et al.* [2007] demonstrate such a structural analysis for Philip Glass's *Gradus* (1968), which aligns well with the judgments on form boundaries made independently by expert musicologists, though extensions to less strictly minimalist works remain an open question.

Early adopters of algorithmic composition were very aware of information theory [Pierce, 1968], and a fascination with information-theoretic ideas has given rise to a number of compositions. Lejaren Hiller, whose research work had engaged with the application of information-theoretic ideas in algorithmic composition, also explored them to structure musical works. In his *Algorithms I* the first movement, 'The Decay of Information', drops from 100% to 50% information content by modifying the order of a Markovian model [Hiller, 1989, p. 80]. A more recent example is Laurie Spiegel's *The Unquestioned Answer* (1997), where she establishes a realtime control for introducing noise into otherwise stable loops, creating an intervention against the gradual increase of redundancy that otherwise occurs with every repetition [Spiegel, 1997].

---

[10] As observed already, general string processing algorithms can be applied to any sequence of tokens [Pearce and Wiggins, 2004]. Typically, polyphonic music is a more complicated venture! Meredith *et al.* [2002] develop geometrically motivated algorithms to spot repeating patterns in polyphonic music, rather than relying on string processing, which would distort voice leading.

9.7 SUMMARY

This chapter confronted a range of topics through the theme of modeling. The motivations ranged from scientific concerns in data analysis and psychology to musicological investigation across large corpuses of data. The computer has become a central tool for testing out theories by crunching musical data. We saw how critical the choice of representation could be to any of these pursuits. Symbolic representations such as MIDI or various encoded score formats are convenient ways of handling data, though they always embody starting assumptions. Audio analysis tools also have application here, for instance, in the examination of musical expression, though yet again an analysis model must be selected in order to proceed. There may exist some universal principles that can assist in analyzing music from a minimal set of assumptions, for example by drawing upon information theory, but the most effective general models may remain elusive in the face of the specificity of music's many cultural manifestations. Nonetheless, artists and scientists can find much more to occupy them in exploring models of music, assisted by the computer.

9.8 EXERCISES

1. How would you classify the work of David Cope, with respect to Table 9.1? You might consider how he actually evaluates his work, whether by the reaction of general audiences, or by the feedback of expert musicologists and computer scientists (see also [Cope, 2001; Wiggins, 2007]). Can someone contribute to more than one field of research simultaneously?

2. Research the origins of music in prehistory, and recent publications concerning this (see for example [Mithen, 2006; Hallam *et al.*, 2009]). How can computer modeling contribute to these debates in the absence of extensive archaeological data? Can you create a simple model of evolutionary processes where basic agents 'sing' to each other [Griffith and Todd, 1999; Miranda and Biles, 2007]? How much anthropomorphic thinking is your simulation guilty of?

3. Having seen the problems of representation, how would you now evaluate the successes and failures of MIDI? You may wish to refer back to Chapter 2 and further references therein as well.

4. Imagine you are designing your own computer music tool or language. How neutral a scheme can you create, which supports as wide a set of music making activities as possible? Does all useful functionality equate to specific assumptions

about musical content? If so, what aspects of music would you emphasize? (Note: this makes a good group exercise, so you may want to compare your design with that of a friend, or consult and negotiate on a design that supports more than one person's view of music.)

5. Manual annotation: take a ten-second excerpt of a recording of a singer, and mark up what you consider to be the most important musical events and features *by hand* (you may use a sound editor to help you, but should not run any automatic detection algorithms). Now compare this experience to using an annotation tool with built-in feature extraction (such as Sonic Visualizer, see Section 7.2). Which was more convenient, and which more accurate? Do you trust your ears or the computer's? How much were you distracted by visual representations of audio, and how much did you work with your ears alone?

6. Take last season's statistics for your favorite sports team, or concert schedule for your favorite musical ensemble. Sonify this data, so as to attempt to reveal trends in the data (how you do this is up to the software you have access to; you may wish to download a general environment such as xSonify, or build your own in a computer music package). Once the sonification is constructed, try to find an aspect of the data that is *not* well represented in the audio output. You can then attempt a second sonification that improves or contrasts with the first, giving a different viewpoint on the data set.

7. Create a music program that takes a rigidly timed and absolutely pitch quantized input (such as a MIDI file that has been quantized in a sequencer to a strict grid), and adds expression. You might want to subtly modify timing, perhaps with respect to important structural boundaries, and substitute careful vibrato and glissando to avoid expressionless and uniform holding of pitch. This is analogous to the work on analysis by synthesis of Friberg *et al.* [2000].

8. Build a music generating program with a single control, a slider on a one-dimensional scale from happy to sad. One quick trick to achieve this might be to equate a major key with happy and a minor with sad, though such a choice is highly culturally constrained. Can you find any other attributes of music to control that help to reinforce your evocation of a particular mood? What are the dangers of such an approach to modeling emotional affect?

9. Firmly in the domain of Western classical music, analyze a (long) monophonic melody of discrete pitches for the component trigrams, making a histogram of the frequency of occurrence. Note that there could be a large set of possibilities; for N pitches, there are potentially N^3 possible transitions (though a sequence of M notes won't necessarily have the chance to contain all of these, and a musical work with any redundancy wouldn't want to do so). Make a generative program that uses the trigrams to construct output musical sentences; does your program ever get stuck for a continuation? Consider strategies to get around this.

10. Create a musical composition inspired by the formula for entropy given above (Equation 9.1). Can you manipulate information content on the fly?

9.9

FURTHER READING

Balaban, M., Ebcioglu, K. and Laske, O. (eds) (1992). *Understanding Music with AI: Perspectives on Music Cognition*. The AAAI Press/MIT Press, Menlo Park, CA.

Clarke, E. and Cook, N. (eds) (2004). *Empirical Musicology: Aims, Methods, Prospects*. Oxford University Press, Oxford.

Computing in Musicology series: Center for Computer Assisted Research in the Humanities, Stanford University (http://www.ccarh.org).

Haus, G. (ed) (1993). *Music Processing*. Oxford University Press, Oxford.

Howell, P., West, R. and Cross, I. (eds) (1991). *Representing Musical Structure*. Academic Press, London.

Kramer, G. (ed) (1994). *Auditory Display: Sonification, Audification, and Auditory Interfaces*. Addison-Wesley Publishing Company, Reading, MA.

Marsden, A. and Pople, A. (eds) (1992). *Computer Representations and Models in Music*. Academic Press, London.

Pope, S. T. (ed) (1991). *The Well Tempered Object: Musical Applications of Object-Oriented Software Technology*. MIT Press, Cambridge, MA.

Proceedings of the International Conference on Auditory Display (ICAD) and further resources from the International Community for Auditory Display (http://www.icad.org/).

Schwanauer, S. M. and Levitt, D. A. (eds) (1993). *Machine Models of Music*. MIT Press, Cambridge, MA.

Temperley, D. (2001). *Basic Cognition of Musical Structure*. MIT Press, Cambridge, MA.

Chapter 10

Conclusions

'[W]ill anyone ever discover that much desired
meta-language by which music could be fully described?'

Pierre Schaeffer [2005, p. 81]

The rise of computer technology has promoted applications in all walks of life. Music cannot help but have been influenced, and has been closely involved with developments in computer science since the 1950s. Realtime audio signal processing, interactive music systems, online music search and computational musicology are just a few examples of the many application areas where music itself provides great challenges for digital technology.

In the early years of mainframes, access was only in the hands of a few institutions, with rental costs for an hour's work prohibitive. Now, mobile phones and laptops are everywhere, and an age of ubiquitous computing is upon us. Computer literacy is taken for granted, and musicians have embraced the many positive benefits of digital technology, even as they continue to push the boundaries of possibility.

Could there be an end of computer music? That is, at what point would we consider that all the main advances in the field had been achieved, and all that remained was to employ them? This question is intimately tied to the ultimate remit and capacity of technology and of the human mind. Music itself is a cultural institution of startling fecundity, and it only takes a few tweaks and hybridizations of existing styles to set up new musical circumstances. Musicologists are likely to remain chasing musical culture to the end of time-based media.

To help discuss the many unsolved issues in computer music, and to help guide you to some promising directions in computer music research, some themes are listed here which may stimulate ideas for research projects, or at least get you dreaming about the future.[1]

After a whole book, a little speculation as to the future of computer music is forgivable, and such provocations help to clarify our ultimate goals. An element of science fiction easily creeps in, but it makes it fun even when predictions may inevitably be proven well off target. I am not the only one to have engaged in computer music futurology; for example, Leigh Landy [2001] provides an entertaining list of 26 alphabetically organized predictions and Richard Moore [1996] reviews pioneering dreams that inspired or continue to inspire computer music. Research consortiums have also created roadmaps of how they perceive the state of the art and potentially fruitful directions.[2] Most appropriately of all, Max Mathews recently released a short story detailing the musical experiences in the year 2164 of a relativistic time traveler from 2001. In his tale, the most important music making has become guided ensemble improvisation within computer-enhanced Audio Performances, but the art of recording the 'classics' has also survived in a transfigured form, and he touches with poignancy and humor on issues including spatial sound and sound synthesis [Mathews, 2008].

Now to the list. Many of these ideas are being anticipated and pondered by computer music researchers as you read, are already on their way, or admit many precedents. For the sake of readability, and for the looser style of this final chapter, forgive my missing out specific references; but you can pursue any one of these categories and start to find large further literatures, guided by other information in this book:

1. **Ubi-music-comp** – ubiquitous musical computing. This could include mobile phone music applications and highly socially integrated computer music.

2. **Non-standard interfaces for all users** Examples might include audio applications for visually impaired people, tactile vibrational music for the deaf, and music therapy through interactive music systems.

3. **Overcoming the semantic gap** MIR research has made apparent the gulf between computational audio analysis and human perception, particularly in high-level interpretation of music; how close can we bring human and computer auditory faculties?

4. **Realtime auditory models** available as DSP chips and in standard audio interfaces. Could an accurate simulation ever run faster than realtime? This would have a great influence on algorithmic composition and interactive music systems.

---

[1] I've avoided outlining 23 problems. This number could have been chosen in homage to Hilbert, a great mathematician whose own research themes stimulated mathematics at the dawn of the 20th century. Hilbert found that some of his questions were quickly solved, while others remain unsolved to this day. Perhaps lists compiled in the field of computer music could be termed Hillerbert Problems, in homage to Lejaren Hiller?

[2] See, for example, the UK Roadmap for Digital Music Research (http://music.york.ac.uk/dmrn/roadmap/documents.html) or the S2S2 Consortium's *A Roadmap for Sound and Music Computing* (Version 1.0, 2007, http://smcnetwork.org/roadmap).

5. **Computer music languages based on auditory perception** Can a new generation of languages be designed, which are built from the ground up based on computational auditory scene analysis?

6. **The limits of human musicality and a consideration of musical universals** While acknowledging the dangers of painting everything with the same brush, how far is it possible to map out the space of musical styles? What are the possible music theories of computer music?

7. **Interdependent parameters in composition** Can composers create musical syntax that respects the multidimensional qualities of sound, and allows for the complex interactions of parameters?

8. **Spatial sound, at last** Commercial take-up of surround sound remains driven by home cinema systems; can any further 3D sound standard break through, perhaps based around more natural sound radiation designs for loudspeakers?

9. **Personal projection, body integrated sound** Our future clothing may incorporate the ability to make personal audiovisual displays, to control the surrounding acoustic environment. Should we anticipate noise terrorists and personally directed advertising clamor, and will our own individual anti-sound bubbles be ready in defense?

10. **Virtual assistants for recording engineers, composers and producers** Without making grand claims for AI, expert systems can advise human work, distilling knowledge particularly to benefit newcomers to a field, or as friendly reference manuals. There is nothing absolute about advice, which can always be disregarded by human whim. Mastering assistants and other tools to support recording engineers are already being built, and these advisory systems extend to composition, production and other preserves of human endeavor.

11. **The universal learning synthesizer** Given an input sound, the universal synthesizer can recreate it, not just by the trivial mode of digital playback, but by finding an appropriately and engagingly parameterized expressive model, and immediately enabling generalizing sound transformations. No doubt the control interface would support natural language specification of desired sound timbre.

12. **A prediction on prediction** Prediction is the essential human survival skill, and computers must be made much better at stylistically informed musical anticipation to fit in with human music making.

13. **Your own musical companion to grow up with** On a Utopian note, imagine a generative system that grows up with you, interacts with you, learns with you as a musician to whatever level you desire, and is the soundtrack of your life. It also interacts with other people and their own musical systems, accompanying you as a computer music familiar.

14. **Cybernetic and cyborg musicians** From neural implants and musical training upgrades to 17-fingered gloves and other delicate musical augmentations.

15. **Exotic physics and computer music** All hail the nanotube orchestra and tachyon detector music!

16. **New forms of computer** There are plenty of novel computing developments to come, and new computing technologies will continue to drive computer music developments. We are already seeing the impact of multicore architectures and the renewed interest in parallelism, but what further impact for quantum or biological computing?

17. **Retro computer music** Imagine the future spectacle of the historically informed mainframe orchestra, or a revivalist movement for old-style laptop ensembles.

18. **Digital archiving** We'll probably always have the problems of digital archiving, with version creep outdating old programs.

19. **Machine historians** Every day brings masses of new information. Informavores though we are, we are already unable to cope with keeping track of it all (you can always find musical examples I won't have heard of). Recommendation systems and information agents highly attuned to our information needs may assist in coping with the overwhelming mass of human history. Perhaps the machines will become our chief historians, archivists, librarians and cultural conduits, so we'd better make sure we engineer them carefully.

20. **Improvisation over composition** A museum culture supports a survival of the culturally fittest artifacts, chasing after the mass of data; we may make a conscious choice to throw off old things and prefer a process of constant renewal free of surveillance and recording. The new composers might be the designers of new improvisation frameworks and support systems.

21. **Computers without humans, or alien music** Perhaps only interesting as a reflection on our own deep involvement with computers, we can imagine modeling musical robots or programs that form their own ecosystems of producers and listeners, with auditory systems divergent from our own. Recall the Arthur C. Clarke quotation from the head of Chapter 8.

22. **New Venues** Finally, Stockhausen gets his wish for inherently spatial music-friendly new concert halls, only they're on the moon!

Possible futures swirl around us and we see technologies quickly debated, satirized, and turned to new creative uses. The release of Microsoft's Songsmith software was a case in point. A potentially useful and even impressive piece of software combining machine listening and generative music, pitch and beat tracking of input singing automatically drives harmonized and synchronized computer-generated accompaniment. Yet its initial publicity video was widely mocked, and much parodied. Since its release (last month at the time of writing), many YouTube videos have been posted showing the effect of running a cappellas sourced from pop session master tapes through the software, creating such humorous mash-ups as rock vocal set against lounge backing. Such an incident only shows how actively the future is constructed, and how much opportunity there is to contribute!

Music is a rich domain engaging both objective theoretical models and subjective personal experience. It is part of the lifeblood of human culture, and naturally supplies a wonderful domain for computational engagement, an engagement that transforms music itself in turn. New developments in computing automatically impact on computer music, and you can apply any computer science you like to musical problems. Many artists are fascinated by wherever science dares to tread, and often provide stimulating commentaries on new technologies. Here's to the continued healthy mutual interaction of music and computing!

10.1 EXERCISES

1. Imagine setting up an Academy of Computer Music. What topics would you teach, and why?

2. Can you justify the use of computers in music making and art? Imagine that computers are suddenly abandoned by humankind. What would we lose? Would we gain anything?

3. Choose one from the list of future possibilities above and consider how you would tackle it.

References

Adams, C. R. (1976). Melodic contour typology. *Ethnomusicology*, 20(2):179–215.

Addessi, A. R., Pachet, F. and Caterina, R. (2004). Children confronting an interactive musical system. In *Proceedings of the International Conference on Music Perception and Cognition*.

Adrien, J. M. (1991). The missing link: Modal synthesis. In de Poli *et al.* [1991], pp. 269–97.

Alderman, J. (2001). *Sonic Boom: Napster, P2P and the Future of Music*. Fourth Estate, London.

Allen, J. and Rabiner, L. (1977). A unified approach to short-time Fourier analysis and synthesis. *Proceedings of the IEEE*, 65(11):1558–64.

Álvaro Barbosa (2003). Displaced soundscapes: A survey of network systems for music and sonic art creation. *Leonardo Music Journal*, 13:53–9.

Amatriain, X. (2007). CLAM: A framework for audio and music application development. *IEEE Software*, 24(1):82–5.

Amatriain, X., Bonada, J., Loscos, A. and Serra, X. (2002). Spectral processing. In Zölzer [2002], pp. 373–438.

Ames, C. (1987). Automated composition in retrospect: 1956–1986. *Leonardo*, 20(2):169–85.

Ames, C. (1989). The Markov process as a compositional model: a survey and a tutorial. *Leonardo*, 22(2):175–87.

Ames, C. (1990). Artificial intelligence and musical composition. In Kurzweil, R. (ed.), *The Age of Intelligent Machines*, pp. 386–9. MIT Press, Cambridge, MA.

Ames, C. (1991). A catalog of statistical distributions: Techniques for transforming random, determinate and chaotic sequences. *Leonardo Music Journal*, 1(1):55–70.

Ames, C. (1995). Thresholds of confidence: An analysis of statistical methods for composition. *Leonardo Music Journal*, 5:33–8.

Ames, C. and Domino, M. (1992). Cybernetic Composer: an overview. In Balaban *et al.* [1992], pp. 186–205.

Anders, T. (2007). *Composing Music by Composing Rules: Design and Usage of a Generic Music Constraint System*. PhD thesis, Queen's University, Belfast.

Anderson, J. R. (2000). *Learning and Memory: An Integrated Approach*, 2nd Edition. John Wiley & Sons, New York, NY.

Arfib, D. (1979). Digital synthesis of complex spectra by means of multiplication of nonlinear distorted sine waves. *Journal of the Audio Engineering Society*, 27(10):757–68.

Arfib, D., Couturier, J. M., Kessous, L. and Verfaille, V. (2002a). Strategies of mapping between gesture data and synthesis model parameters using perceptual spaces. *Organised Sound*, 7(2):127–44.

Arfib, D., Keiler, F. and Zölzer, U. (2002b). Source-filter processing. In Zölzer [2002], pp. 299–372.

Ariza, C. (2009). The interrogator as critic: The Turing test and the evaluation of generative music systems. *Computer Music Journal*, 33(2):1–23.

Assayag, G., Bloch, G., Chemillier, M., Cont, A. and Dubnov, S. (2006). OMax brothers: a dynamic topology of agents for improvisation learning. In *AMCMM '06: Proceedings of the 1st ACM workshop on audio and music computing multimedia*, pp. 125–32.

Aucouturier, J.-J. (2006). *Ten Experiments on the Modelling of Polyphonic Timbre*. PhD thesis, University of Paris 6, France.

Aucouturier, J.-J. and Defreville, B. (2007). Differences in the cognition of urban soundscapes and polyphonic music: A pattern recognition point of view. In *Inter-noise*, Istanbul, Turkey.

Aucouturier, J.-J. and Pachet, F. (2003). Representing musical genre: A state of the art. *Journal of New Music Research*, 32(1):83–93.

Austin, L. and Field, A. (2001). Sound diffusion in composition and performance practice II: An interview with Ambrose Field. *Computer Music Journal*, 25(4):21–30.

Austin, L. and Smalley, D. (2000). Sound diffusion in composition and performance: An interview with Denis Smalley. *Computer Music Journal*, 24(2):10–21.

Bailey, D. (1980). *Improvisation: Its Nature and Practice in Music*. Moorland publishing Co Ltd, Ashbourne, Derbyshire, England.

Balaban, M., Ebcioğlu, K. and Laske, O. (eds) (1992). *Understanding Music with AI: Perspectives on Music Cognition*. The AAAI Press/MIT Press, Menlo Park, CA.

Balzano, G. J. (1980). The group-theoretic description of 12-fold and microtonal pitch systems. *Computer Music Journal*, 4(4):66–84.

Barragán, H. and Reas, C. (2007). Extension 8: Electronics. In Reas and Fry [2007], pp. 633–59.

Barrett, N. (2002). Spatio-musical compositional strategies. *Organised Sound*, 7(3):313–23.

Beauchamp, J. (ed.) (2007a). *Analysis, Synthesis and Perception of Musical Sounds*. Springer, New York, NY.

Beauchamp, J. W. (2007b). Analysis and synthesis of musical instrument sounds. In Beauchamp [2007a], pp. 1–89.

Begault, D. R. (1994). *3-D Sound for Virtual Reality and Multimedia*. Academic Press, Cambridge, MA.

Bello, J. P., Daudet, L., Abdallah, S., Duxbury, C., Davies, M. and Sandler, S. B. (2004). A tutorial on onset detection in music signals. *IEEE Transactions on Speech and Audio Processing*.

Bennett, G. and Rodet, X. (1989). Synthesis of the singing voice. In Mathews and Pierce [1989b], pp. 19–44.

Berlioz, H. (ed.) (1970). *Memoirs*. Panther Books Ltd/Granada Publishing Limited, Freymore, St Albans, Herts. Translated by David Cairns.

Biles, J. A. (2002). GenJam: Evolutionary computation gets a gig. In *Conference on Information Technology Curriculum*, Rochester, NY.

Bilmes, J. A. (1993). Techniques to foster drum machine expressivity. In *Proceedings of the International Computer Music Conference (ICMC)*.

Bischoff, J., Gold, R. and Horton, J. (1985). Music for an interactive network of microcomputers. In Roads and Strawn [1985], pp. 588–600.

Blauert, J. (1997). *Spatial Hearing: The Psychophysics of Human Sound Localization (Revised Edition)*. MIT Press, Cambridge, MA.

Boden, M. (2003). *The Creative Mind: Myths and Mechanisms*, 2nd Edition. Routledge, New York, NY.

Boersma, P. (1998). *Functional phonology: Formalizing the interactions between articulatory and perceptual drives*. PhD thesis, University of Amsterdam.

Bonada, J. (2000). Automatic technique in frequency domain for near-lossless time-scale modification of audio. In *Proceedings of the International Computer Music Conference (ICMC)*, pp. 396–9, Berlin.

Bongers, B. (2000). Physical interfaces in the electronic arts: Interaction theory and interfacing techniques for real-time performance. In Wanderley, M. M. and Battier, M. (eds), *Trends in Gestural Control of Music*, IRCAM, Paris.

Borin, G., Poli, G. D. and Sarti, A. (1992). Algorithms and structures for synthesis using physical models. *Computer Music Journal*, 16(4):30–42.

Boulanger, R. (1989). Interview with Roger Reynolds, Joji Yuasa and Charles Wuorinen. In Roads [1989], pp. 51–60.

Boulanger, R. (ed.) (2000). *The CSound Book*. MIT Press, Cambridge, MA.

Brandt, E. (2001). Hard sync without aliasing. In *Proceedings of the International Computer Music Conference (ICMC)*.

Brant, H. (1998). Space as an essential aspect of musical composition. In Schwartz, E. and Childs, B. (eds), *Contemporary Composers on Contemporary Music*, pp. 221–42. Da Capo Press, New York.

Bregman, A. S. (1990). *Auditory Scene Analysis: The Perceptual Organization of Sound*. MIT Press, Cambridge, MA.

Brewster, B. and Broughton, F. (2006). *Last Night a DJ Saved My Life*. Headline Book Publishing, London.

Brewster, S. (2008). Nonspeech auditory output. In Sears and Jacko [2008], pp. 247–64.

Bristow-Johnson, R. (1996). Wavetable synthesis 101, a fundamental perspective. In *101st AES Convention*.

Brown, C. and Bischoff, J. (2002). Indigenous to the net: Early network music bands in the San Francisco Bay Area.

Brown, J. C. and Puckette, M. S. (1992). An efficient algorithm for the calculation of a constant Q transform. *Journal of the Acoustical Society of America*, 92(5):2698–701.

Brown, J. C. and Puckette, M. S. (1993). A high-resolution fundamental frequency determination based on phase changes of the Fourier transform. *Journal of the Acoustical Society of America*, 94(2):662–7.

Bruyns, C. (2006). Modal synthesis for arbitrarily shaped objects. *Computer Music Journal*, 30(3):22–37.

Brăiloiu, C. (1984). *Problems of Ethnomusicology*. Cambridge University Press, Cambridge.

Camurri, A. (1993). Applications of artificial intelligence methodologies and tools for music description and processing. In Haus [1993], pp. 233–66.

Camurri, A., De Poli, G., Friberg, A., Leman, M. and Volpe, G. (2005). The MEGA project: Analysis and synthesis of multisensory expressive gesture in performing art applications. *Journal of New Music Research*, 34(1).

Camurri, A. and Leman, M. (1997). AI-based music signals applications – a hybrid approach. In Roads, C., Pope, S. T., Piccialli, A. and Poli, G. D. (eds), *Musical Signal Processing*, pp. 349–81. Svets and Zeitlinger, Lisse, the Netherlands.

Cann, R. (1985). An analysis/synthesis tutorial. In Roads and Strawn [1985], pp. 114–44.

Carlos, W. (1987). Tuning: At the crossroads. *Computer Music Journal*, 11(1):29–43.

Carlsson, A. (2008). Chip music: low-tech data music sharing. In Collins, K. (ed.), *From Pac-Man to Pop Music: Interactive Audio in Games and New Media*, pp. 153–62. Ashgate, Aldershot, Hampshire.

Cascone, K. (2000). The aesthetics of failure: Post-digital tendencies in contemporary computer music. *Computer Music Journal*, 24(4).

Casey, M. (2005). Acoustic lexemes for organizing Internet audio. *Contemporary Music Review*, 24(6):489–508.

Casey, M. and Slaney, M. (2006). Song intersection by approximate nearest neighbour search. In *Proceedings of the International Symposium on Music Information Retrieval*.

Casey, M., Veltkamp, R., Goto, M., Leman, M., Rhodes, C. and Slaney, M. (2008). Content-based music information retrieval: Current directions and future challenges. *Proceedings of the IEEE*, 96(4):668–96.

Chafe, C. (1999). A short history of digital sound synthesis by composers in the U.S.A. In *Creativity and the Computer, Recontres Musicales Pluridisciplinaires*, Lyon.

Chafe, C. (2004). Case studies of physical models in music composition. In *Proceedings of the 2004 International Congress on Acoustics*, Kyoto.

Chafe, C. and Gurevich, M. (2004). Network time delay and ensemble accuracy: Effects of latency, asymmetry. In *117th Convention of the Audio Engineering Society*, San Francisco, CA.

Chapman, N. and Chapman, J. (2006). *Web Design: A Complete Introduction*. John Wiley and Sons, Chichester, West Sussex.

Cheng, C. I. and Wakefield, G. H. (2001). Moving sound source synthesis for binaural electroacoustic music using interpolated head-related transfer functions (HRTFs). *Computer Music Journal*, 25(4):57–80.

Chion, M. (1994). *Audio-vision*. Columbia University Press, New York, NY.

Chowning, J. (1971). The simulation of moving sound sources. *Journal of the Audio Engineering Society*, 19(1):2–6.

Chowning, J. (1973). The synthesis of complex audio spectra by means of frequency modulation. *Journal of the Audio Engineering Society*, 21(7):526–34.

Chowning, J. (1989). Frequency modulation synthesis of the singing voice. In Mathews and Pierce [1989b], pp. 57–63.

Chowning, J. (1999). Perceptual fusion and auditory perspective. In Cook [1999], pp. 261–75.

Chowning, J. and Roads, C. (1985). Composition with John Chowning. In Roads [1985a], pp. 17–25.

Chuchacz, K., Woods, R. and O'Modhrain, S. (2008). Novel percussive instrument design – converting mathematical formulae into engaging musical instruments. In *Proceedings of the International Computer Music Conference (ICMC)*, Belfast.

Clarke, A. C. (1999a). Rocket to the renaissance. In Macauley, I. T. (ed.), *Greetings Carbon Based Bipeds!* Voyager, London.

Clarke, E. (1988). Generative principles in music performance. In Sloboda [1988], pp. 1–26.

Clarke, E. (1999b). Rhythm and timing in music. In Deutsch [1999], pp. 473–500.

Clarke, E. (2004). Empirical methods in the study of performance. In Clarke and Cook [2004], pp. 77–102.

Clarke, E. and Cook, N. (eds) (2004). *Empirical Musicology: Aims, Methods, Prospects*. Oxford University Press, Oxford.

Clayton, M. (2000). *Time in Indian Music: Rhythm, Metre and Form in North Indian Rāg Performance*. Oxford University Press, Oxford.

Collins, N. (2005). A comparison of sound onset detection algorithms with emphasis on psychoacoustically motivated detection functions. In *AES Convention 118*, Barcelona.

Collins, N. (2006a). Investigating computational models of perceptual attack time. In *Proceedings of International Conference on Music Perception and Cognition (ICMPC2006)*, Bologna.

Collins, N. (2006b). Towards a style-specific basis for computational beat tracking. In *Proceedings of International Conference on Music Perception and Cognition (ICMPC2006)*, Bologna.

Collins, N. (2006c). *Towards Autonomous Agents for Live Computer Music: Realtime Machine Listening and Interactive Music Systems*. PhD thesis, University of Cambridge.

Collins, N. (2007a). Audiovisual concatenative synthesis. In *Proceedings of the International Computer Music Conference (ICMC)*, Copenhagen.

Collins, N. (2007b). Musical robots and listening machines. In Collins and d'Escriván [2007], pp. 171–84.

Collins, N. (2008). Errant sound synthesis. In *Proceedings of the International Computer Music Conference (ICMC)*, Belfast.

Collins, N. and d'Escriván, J. (eds) (2007). *Cambridge Companion to Electronic Music*. Cambridge University Press, Cambridge.

Collins, N., McLean, A., Rohrhuber, J. and Ward, A. (2003). Live coding techniques for laptop performance. *Organised Sound*, 8(3):321–29.

Collins, N. and Olofsson, F. (2006). klipp av: Live algorithmic splicing and audiovisual event capture. *Computer Music Journal*, 30(2):8–20.

Cook, N. (1987). Musical form and the listener. *The Journal of Aesthetics and Art Criticism*, 46(1):23–9.

Cook, N. (ed.) (1994). *A Guide to Musical Analysis*. Oxford University Press, Oxford.

Cook, P. R. (1991). *Identification of Control Parameters in an Articulatory Vocal Tract Model with Applications to the Synthesis of Singing*. PhD thesis, CCRMA, Stanford.

Cook, P. R. (1996). Singing voice synthesis: History, current work, and future directions. *Computer Music Journal*, 20(3):38–46.

Cook, P. R. (ed.) (1999). *Music, Cognition and Computerized Sound*. MIT Press, Cambridge, MA.

Cook, P. R. (2002). *Real Sound Synthesis for Interactive Applications*. AK Peters, Wellesley, MA.

Cooper, M. and Foote, J. (2003). Summarizing popular music via structural similarity analysis. In *IEEE Workshop on Applications of Signal Processing to Audio and Acoustics*, pp. 127–30.

Cope, D. (ed.) (2001). *Virtual Music: Computer Synthesis of Musical Style*. MIT Press, Cambridge, MA.

Cox, C. and Warner, D. (eds) (2004). *Audio Culture: Readings in Modern Music*. Continuum, London.

Cross, I. (2003). Music as biocultural phenomenon. *Annals of the New York Academy of Sciences (The Neurosciences and Music)*, 999:106–11.

Cutler, C. (2004). Plunderphonia. In Cox and Warner [2004], pp. 138–56.

Dannenberg, R. (1989). Real-time scheduling and computer accompaniment. In Mathews and Pierce [1989b], pp. 225–61.

Dannenberg, R. (1993). Music representation issues, techniques and systems. *Computer Music Journal*, 17(3):20–30.

Dannenberg, R., Thom, B. and Watson, D. (1997). A machine learning approach to musical style recognition. In *Proceedings of the International Computer Music Conference (ICMC)*, pp. 344–7, Thessaloniki, Greece.

Dattorro, J. (1997). Effect design. part 2: Delay-line modulation and chorus. *Journal of the Audio Engineering Society*, 45(10):764–88.

Daudet, L. and Torrésani, B. (2006). Sparse adaptive representations for musical signals. In Klapuri and Davy [2006], pp. 65–98.

de Campo, A. (2009). *Science By Ear. An Interdisciplinary Approach to Sonifying Scientific Data*. PhD thesis, University for Music and Dramatic Arts Graz, Graz, Austria.

de Cheveigné, A. (2006). Multiple $F0$ estimation. In Wang and Brown [2006], pp. 45–79.

de Poli, G., Piccialli, A. and Roads, C. (eds) (1991). *Representations of Musical Signals*. MIT Press, Cambridge, MA.

Deliège, I. (1989). A perceptual approach to contemporary musical forms. *Contemporary Music Review*, 4(1):213–30.

Deliège, I. and Sloboda, J. (1996). *Musical Beginnings: Origins and Development of Musical Competence*. Oxford University Press, New York.

Deliège, I. and Wiggins, G. A. (eds) (2006). *Musical Creativity: Multidisciplinary Research in Theory and Practice*. Psychology Press, London.

Depalle, P., Garcia, G. and Rodet, X. (1995). The recreation of a castrato voice, Farinelli's voice. In *IEEE ASSP Workshop on Applications of Signal Processing to Audio and Acoustics*, pp. 242–5.

Desain, P. and Honing, H. (1992). *Music, Mind and Machine: Studies in Computer Music, Music Cognition and Artificial Intelligence*. Thesis Publishers, Amsterdam.

Desain, P. and Honing, H. (1993). Tempo curves considered harmful. *Contemporary Music Review*, 7(2):123–38.

Deutsch, D. (ed.) (1999). *The Psychology of Music*, 2nd Edition. Academic Press, San Diego, CA.

Dix, A. (2008). Network-based interaction. In Sears and Jacko [2008], pp. 265–94.

Dixon, S. (2001). An empirical comparison of tempo trackers. In *Proceedings 8th Brazilian Symposium on Computer Music*.

Dixon, S. (2006). Onset detection revisited. In *International Conference on Digital Audio Effects (DAFx)*, Montréal.

Dodge, C. (1989). On *Speech Songs*. In Mathews and Pierce [1989b], pp. 9–17.

Dodge, C. and Jerse, T. A. (1997). *Computer Music: Synthesis, Composition and Performance*, 2nd Edition. Schirmer Books, New York, NY.

Doornbusch, P. (2002). Composers' views on mapping in algorithmic composition. *Organised Sound*, 7(2):145–56.

Doornbusch, P. (2004). Computer sound synthesis in 1951: The music of CSIRAC. *Computer Music Journal*, 28(1):10–25.

Doraisamy, S., Adnan, H. and Norowi, N. M. (2006). Towards a MIR system for Malaysian music. In *Proceedings of the International Symposium on Music Information Retrieval*.

Downie, J. S. (2003). Music information retrieval. *Annual Review of Information Science and Technology*, 37:295–340.

Downie, J. S. (2008). The music information retrieval evaluation exchange (2005–2007): A window into music information retrieval research. *Acoustical Science and Technology*, 29(4):247–55.

Dubnov, S., Assayag, G., Lartillot, O. and Bejerano, G. (2003). Using machine learning methods for musical style modeling. *Computer*, pp. 73–80.

Eaglestone, B., Ford, N., Holdridge, P. and Carter, J. (2008). Are cognitive styles an important factor in design of electroacoustic music software? *Journal of New Music Research*, 37(1):77–85.

Ebcioğlu, K. (1990). An expert system for harmonizing chorales in the style of J.S. Bach. *Journal of Logic Programming*, 8:145–85.

Eladhari, M., Nieuwdorp, R. and Fridenfalk, M. (2006). The soundtrack of your mind: mind music – adaptive audio for game characters. In *Proceedings of the International Conference on Advances in Computer Entertainment Technology*, Hollywood, CA.

Ellis, D. P. (2006). Extracting information from music audio. *Communications of the ACM*, 49(8):32–7.

Emmerson, S. (2000a). Crossing cultural boundaries through technology? In Emmerson [2000c], pp. 115–37.

Emmerson, S. (2000b). 'Losing touch?': The human performer and electronics. In Emmerson [2000c], pp. 194–216.

Emmerson, S. (ed.) (2000c). *Music, Electronic Media and Culture*. Ashgate Publishing Limited, Aldershot, England.

Essl, G., Serafin, S., Cook, P. R. and Smith, J. O. (2004). Theory of banded waveguides. *Computer Music Journal*, 28(1):37–50.

Every, M. (2006). *Separation of Musical Sources and Structure from Single-Channel Polyphonic Recordings*. PhD thesis, University of Surrey, UK.

Farbood, M. (2006). *A quantitative, parametric model of musical tension*. PhD thesis, MIT.

Fellgett, P. (1975). Ambisonics. Part one: General system description. *Studio Sound*, 17(8):20.

Fields, B., Casey, M., Jacobs, K. and Sandler, M. (2008). Do you sound like your friends? exploring artist similarity via artist social network relationships and audio signal processing. In *Proceedings of the International Computer Music Conference (ICMC)*.

Fildes, J. (2008). 'Oldest' computer music unveiled.

Fitch, T. and Kramer, G. (1994). Sonifying the body electric: Superiority of an auditory over a visual display in a complex multi-variate system. In Kramer [1994a], pp. 307–26.

Florens, J.-L. and Cadoz, C. (1991). The physical model: Modeling and simulating the instrumental universe. In de Poli *et al.* [1991], pp. 227–68.

Föllmer, G. (2005). Lines of net music. *Contemporary Music Review*, 24(6):439–44.

Foote, J. and Uchihashi, S. (2001). The beat spectrum: A new approach to rhythm analysis. In *Proc. Int. Conf. on Multimedia and Expo (ICME)*.

Forsyth, D. A. and Ponce, J. (2003). *Computer Vision: A Modern Approach*. Prentice Hall, Upper Saddle River, NJ.

Forte, A. (1973). *The Structure of Atonal Music*. Yale University Press, New Haven, CT.

Freeman, J. (2008). Extreme sight-reading, mediated expression, and audience participation: Real-time music notation in live performance. *Computer Music Journal*, 32(3):25–41.

Freeman, J., Varnik, K., Ramakrishnan, C., Neuhaus, M., Burk, P. and Birchfield, D. (2005). Auracle: a voice-controlled, networked sound instrument. *Organised Sound*, 10(3):221–31.

Friberg, A., Colombo, V., Frydén, L. and Sundberg, J. (2000). Generating musical performances with Director Musices. *Computer Music Journal*, 24:23–9.

Fulop, S. A. and Fitz, K. (2006). Algorithms for computing the time-corrected instantaneous frequency (reassigned) spectrogram, with applications. *Journal of the Acoustical Society of America*, 119(1):360–71.

Gabrielsson, A. (1999). The performance of music. In Deutsch [1999], pp. 501–602.

Galloway, A. R. (2007). Extension 4: Network. In Reas and Fry [2007], pp. 563–77.

Gardner, W. G. (1995). Efficient convolution without input–output delay. *Journal of the Audio Engineering Society*, 43(3):127–36.

Garton, B. (1992). Virtual performance modeling. In *International Computer Music Conference*, San Jose.

Geekie, G. (2002). Carnatic ragas as music information retrieval entities. In *Proceedings of the International Symposium on Music Information Retrieval*.

Gerzon, M. (1974). Surround-sound psychoacoustics. *Wireless World*, 80:483–6.

Gerzon, M. (1975). Ambisonics. Part two: Studio techniques. *Studio Sound*, 17(10):60.

Gillespie, B. (1999). Haptics in manipulation. In Cook [1999], pp. 247–60.

Glasberg, B. R. and Moore, B. C. J. (2002). A model of loudness applicable to time-varying sounds. *Journal of the Audio Engineering Society*, 50(5):331–42.

Godsmark, D. and Brown, G. J. (1999). A blackboard architecture for computational auditory scene analysis. *Speech Communication*, 27:351–66.

Gold, B. and Morgan, N. (2000). *Speech and Audio Signal Processing: Processing and Perception of Speech and Music*. John Wiley and Sons, New York, NY.

Gómez, E. (2006). *Tonal Description of Music Audio Signals*. PhD thesis, Universitat Pompeu Fabra.

Gómez, E., Klapuri, A. and Meudic, B. (2003). Melody description and extraction in the context of music content processing. *Journal of New Music Research*, 32(1).

Goto, M. (2001). An audio-based real-time beat tracking system for music with or without drum-sounds. *Journal of New Music Research*, 30(2):159–71.

Goudeseune, C. (2002). Interpolated mappings for musical instruments. *Organised Sound*, 7(2):85–96.

Gouyon, F. (2005). *A Computational Approach to Rhythm Description: Audio Features for the Computation of Rhythm Periodicity Features and Their Use in Tempo Induction and Music Content Processing*. PhD thesis, Universitat Pompeu Fabra.

Gouyon, F. and Dixon, S. (2005). A review of automatic rhythm description systems. *Computer Music Journal*, 29(1):34–54.

Gouyon, F. and Meudic, B. (2003). Towards rhythmic content processing of musical signals: Fostering complementary approaches. *Journal of New Music Research*, 32(1):41–64.

Grella-Mozejko, P. (2007). Earle Brown – form, notation, text. *Contemporary Music Review*, 26(3):437–69.

Griffith, N. and Todd, P. M. (eds) (1999). *Musical Networks: Parallel Distributed Perception and Performance*. MIT Press, Cambridge, MA.

Hainsworth, S. W. (2004). *Techniques for the Automated Analysis of Musical Audio*. PhD thesis, University of Cambridge.

Hajda, J. M. (2007). The effect of dynamic acoustical features on musical timbre. In Beauchamp [2007a], pp. 250–71.

Hallam, S., Cross, I. and Thaut, M. (eds) (2009). *The Oxford Handbook of Music Psychology*. Oxford University Press, Oxford.

Hamanaka, M., Hirata, K. and Tojo, S. (2006). Implementing 'a generative theory of tonal music'. *Journal of New Music Research*, 35(4):249–77.

Hamburger, M. (ed.) (1984). *Beethoven: Letters, Journals and Conversations*. Thames and Hudson Ltd., London.

Hamer, M. (2005). Ivory encore for dead piano greats. *New Scientist*, 186(2496):27.

Hamming, R. W. (1989). *Digital Filters*, 3rd Edition. Prentice-Hall, Englewood Cliffs.

Harley, J. (2004). *Xenakis: His Life in Music*. Routledge, New York,NY.

Harris, F. J. (1978). On the use of windows for harmonic analysis with the discrete Fourier transform. *Proceedings of the IEEE*, 66(1):51–83.

Harrison, J. (1998). Sound, space, sculpture: some thoughts on the 'what', 'how' and 'why' of sound diffusion. *Organised Sound*, 3(2):117–27.

Harrower, A. (2005). Copyright issues in Internet music. *Contemporary Music Review*, 24(6):483–8.

Harvey, J. (2000). Spectralism. *Contemporary Music Review*, 19(3):11–14.

Haus, G. (ed.) (1993). *Music Processing*. Oxford University Press, Oxford.

Hayes, M. H. (1999). *Digital Signal Processing*. McGraw-Hill, New York, NY.

Hedges, S. A. (1978). Dice music in the eighteenth century. *Music and Letters*, 59(2):180–7.

Herrera-Boyer, P., Peeters, G. and Dubnov, S. (2003). Automatic classification of musical instrument sounds. *Journal of New Music Research*, 32(1):3–21.

Hiller, L. (1970). Music composed with computers – a historical survey. In Lincoln [1970], pp. 44–96.

Hiller, L. (1989). Composing with computers: A progress report. In Roads [1989], pp. 75–89.

Hiller, L. and Isaacson, L. (1959). *Experimental Music: Composition with an Electronic Computer*. Greenwood Press.

Hinckley, K. (2008). Input technologies and techniques. In Sears and Jacko [2008], pp. 161–76.

Hoffman, M. and Cook, P. R. (2007). Real-time feature-based synthesis for live musical performance. In *Proceedings of New Interfaces for Musical Expression (NIME)*, New York.

Honing, H. (1993). Issues in the representation of time and structure in music. *Contemporary Music Review*, 9(2):221–39.

Honing, H. (2001). From time to time: The representation of timing and tempo. *Computer Music Journal*, 25(3):50–61.

Howell, P., West, R. and Cross, I. (eds) (1991). *Representing Musical Structure*. Academic Press, London.

Hsu, W. (2005). Using timbre in a computer-based improvisation system. In *Proceedings of the International Computer Music Conference (ICMC)*, pp. 777–80, Barcelona, Spain.

Hsu, W. (2008). Two approaches for interaction management in timbre-aware improvisation systems. In *Proceedings of the International Computer Music Conference (ICMC)*, Belfast.

Hugill, A. (2005). Internet music: An introduction. *Contemporary Music Review*, 24(6):429–37.

Hugill, A. (2007). The origins of electronic music. In Collins and d'Escriván [2007], pp. 7–23.

Hunt, A. and Wanderley, M. M. (2002). Mapping performer parameters to synthesis engines. *Organised Sound*, 7(2):97–108.

Huron, D. (1992). Design principles in computer-based music representation. In Marsden and Pople [1992], pp. 5–39.

Huron, D. (2006). *Sweet Anticipation*. The MIT Press, Cambridge, MA.

Impett, J. (2001). *Computational Models for Interactive Composition/Performance Systems*. PhD thesis, University of Cambridge.

International Federation of the Phonographic Industry (2008). Digital music report 2008.

Ishii, H. (2008). Tangible user interfaces. In Sears and Jacko [2008], pp. 469–87.

Jaffe, D. A. (1985). Ensemble timing in computer music. *Computer Music Journal*, 9(4):38–48.

Jaffe, D. A. (1987a). Spectrum analysis tutorial, part 1: The discrete Fourier transform. *Computer Music Journal*, 11(2):9–24.

Jaffe, D. A. (1987b). Spectrum analysis tutorial, part 2: Properties and applications of the discrete Fourier transform. *Computer Music Journal*, 11(3):17–35.

Jaffe, D. A. and Smith, J. O. (1983). Extensions of the Karplus–Strong plucked-string algorithm. *Computer Music Journal*, 7(2):56–69.

Jehan, T. (2005). *Creating Music by Listening*. PhD thesis, Massachusetts Institute of Technology.

Jehan, T., Machover, T. and Fabio, M. (2002). Sparkler: An audio-driven interactive live computer performance for symphony orchestra. In *Proceedings of the International Computer Music Conference (ICMC)*, Göteborg, Sweden.

Johnson, S. (2000). The counterpoint of species. In Zorn [2000], pp. 18–58.

Jordà, S. (2005). *Digital Lutherie: Crafting Musical Computers for New Musics' Performance and Improvisation*. PhD thesis, Universitat Pompeu Fabra.

Jordà, S. (2007). Interactivity and live computer music. In Collins and d'Escriván [2007], pp. 89–106.

Juslin, P. N. (2009). Emotion in music performance. In Hallam *et al.* [2009], pp. 377–89.

Juslin, P. N. and Sloboda, J. A. (eds) (2001). *Music and Emotion: Theory and Research*. Oxford University Press, Oxford.

Kahn, D. (1999). *Noise, Water, Meat: A History of Sound in the Arts*. MIT Press, Cambridge, MA.

Kapur, A. (2005). A history of robotic musical instruments. In *Proceedings of the International Computer Music Conference (ICMC)*, Barcelona.

Kapur, A., Singer, E., Benning, M. S., Tzanetakis, G. and Trimpin (2007). Integrating hyperinstruments, musical robots & machine musicianship for North Indian classical music. In *Proceedings of New Interfaces for Musical Expression (NIME)*, pp. 238–41.

Karjalainen, M., Tolonen, T., Välimäki, V., Erkut, C., Laurson, M. and Hiipakka, J. (2001). An overview of new techniques and effects in model-based sound synthesis. *Journal of New Music Research*, 30(3):203–12.

Karjalainen, M., Valimaki, V. and Tolonen, T. (1998). Plucked-string models: From the Karplus–Strong algorithm to digital waveguides and beyond. *Computer Music Journal*, 22(3):17–32.

Karplus, K. and Strong, A. (1983). Digital synthesis of plucked-string and drum timbres. *Computer Music Journal*, 7(2):43–55.

Kassler, M. (1966). Towards musical information retrieval. *Perspectives of New Music*, 4(2):59–67.

Katz, B. (2007). *Mastering Audio: The Art and the Science*, 2nd Edition. Focal Press, Oxford.

Keller, D. (2008). The musician as thief: Digital culture and copyright law. In Miller, P. D. (ed.), *Sound Unbound: Sampling Digital Music and Culture*, pp. 135–50. MIT Press, Cambridge, MA.

Kiefer, C., Collins, N. and Fitzpatrick, G. (2008a). Evaluating the Wiimote as a musical controller. In *Proceedings of the International Computer Music Conference (ICMC)*, Belfast.

Kiefer, C., Collins, N. and Fitzpatrick, G. (2008b). HCI methodology for evaluating musical controllers: A case study. In *Proceedings of New Interfaces for Musical Expression (NIME)*, Genoa, Italy.

Kippen, J. and Bel, B. (1992). Modelling music with grammars: Formal language representation in the Bol Processor. In Marsden and Pople [1992], pp. 207–38.

Klapuri, A. (2004). Automatic music transcription as we know it today. *Journal of New Music Research*, 33(3):269–82.

Klapuri, A. (2006). Auditory model-based methods for multiple fundamental frequency estimation. In Klapuri and Davy [2006], pp. 229–65.

Klapuri, A. and Davy, M. (eds) (2006). *Signal Processing Methods for Music Transcription*. Springer, New York, NY.

Klingbeil, M. (2005). Software for spectral analysis, editing, and synthesis. In *Proceedings of the International Computer Music Conference*, Barcelona, Spain.

Koenig, G. M. (1971). Summary observations on compositional theory. Technical report, Institute of Sonology, Utrecht.

Kojs, J., Serafin, S. and Chafe, C. (2007). Cyberinstruments via physical modeling synthesis: Compositional applications. *Leonardo Music Journal*, 17:61–6.

Kramer, G. (ed.) (1994a). *Auditory Display: Sonification, Audification, and Auditory Interfaces*. Addison-Wesley Publishing Company, Reading, MA.

Kramer, G. (1994b). Some organizing principles for representing data with sound. In Kramer [1994a], pp. 185–221.

Kramer, G. and Walker, B. N. (2005). Sound science: Marking ten international conferences on auditory display. *ACM Transactions on Applied Perception*, 2(4):383–8.

Kroger, P., Passos, A., Sampaio, M. and Cidra, G. (2008). Rameau: A system for automatic harmonic analysis. In *International Computer Music Conference*, Belfast.

Krumhansl, C. L. (1990). *Cognitive Foundations of Musical Pitch*. Oxford University Press, New York.

LaBelle, B. (2007). *Background Noise: Perspectives on Sound Art*. Continuum, New York, NY.

Lai, J., Karat, C.-M. and Yankelovich, N. (2008). Conversational speech interfaces and technologies. In Sears and Jacko [2008], pp. 381–91.

Landy, L. (2001). From algorithmic jukeboxes to zero-time synthesis: a potential A-Z of music in tomorrow's world (a *conference provocation*). *Organised Sound*, 6:91–6.

Landy, L. (2007). *The Art of Sound Organisation*. MIT Press, Cambridge, MA.

Lansky, P. (1989). Compositional applications of linear predictive coding. In Mathews and Pierce [1989b], pp. 2–8.

Lansky, P. and Roads, C. (1989). Interview with Paul Lansky. In Roads [1989], pp. 35–43.

Laroche, J. (2003). Efficient tempo and beat tracking in audio recordings. *J. Audio. Eng. Soc.*, 51(4):226–33.

Lartillot, O. and Toiviainen, P. (2007). A MATLAB toolbox for musical feature extraction from audio. In *International Conference on Digital Audio Effects (DAFx)*, Bordeaux, France.

Laske, O. (1989). Composition theory in Koenig's project one and project two. In Roads [1989], pp. 119–30.

Lazzaro, N. (2008). Designing emotions for games, entertainment interfaces and interactive products. In Sears and Jacko [2008], pp. 679–700.

LeBrun, H. (1979). Digital waveshaping synthesis. *Journal of the Audio Engineering Society*, 27(4):250–66.

Lee, J. H., Downie, J. S. and Cunningham, S. J. (2005). Challenges in cross-cultural/multilingual music information seeking. In *Proceedings of the International Symposium on Music Information Retrieval*.

Legaspi, R., Hashimoto, Y., Moriyama, K., Kurihara, S. and Numao, M. (2007). Music compositional intelligence with an affective flavor. In *Proceedings of the 12th International Conference on Intelligent User Interfaces*, pp. 216–24, Honolulu, Hawaii.

Leider, C. (2004). *Digital Audio Workstation*. McGraw-Hill, New York, NY.

Leman, M. (1993). Symbolic and subsymbolic description of music. In Haus [1993], pp. 119–64.

Lerdahl, F. (1987). Timbral hierarchies. *Contemporary Music Review*, 2(1):135–60.

Lerdahl, F. and Jackendoff, R. (1983). *A Generative Theory of Tonal Music*. MIT Press, Cambridge, MA.

Levin, G. (2007). Extension 3: Vision. In Reas and Fry [2007], pp. 547–61.

Levine, S. N. and Smith, J. O. (2007). A compact and malleable sines+transients+noise model for sound. In Beauchamp [2007a], pp. 145–74.

Lewis, G. E. (1999). Interacting with latter-day musical automata. *Contemporary Music Review*, 18(3):99–112.

Lewis, G. E. (2000). Teaching improvised music: An ethnographic memoir. In Zorn [2000], pp. 78–109.

LeWitt, S. (1967). Paragraphs on conceptual art. *Artforum*, 5(10):79–83.

Li, F. (2007). Extension 7: Mobile. In Reas and Fry [2007], pp. 617–31.

Licht, A. (2007). *Sound Art: Beyond Music, Between Categories*. Rizzoli International Publications, Inc., New York, NY.

Lincoln, H. B. (ed.) (1970). *The Computer and Music*. Cornell University Press, Ithaca, NY.

Livingstone, S. R. and Brown, A. R. (2005). Virtual performance modelling. In *Proceedings of the Second Australasian Conference on Interactive Entertainment*, pp. 105–11, Sydney, Australia.

Logan, B. (2000). Mel frequency cepstral coefficients for music modeling. In *Proceedings of the International Symposium on Music Information Retrieval*, Plymouth, MA.

London, J. (2004). *Hearing in Time: Psychological Aspects of Musical Meter*. Oxford University Press, New York.

Lorrain, D. (1980). A panoply of stochastic 'cannons'. *Computer Music Journal*, 41(1):53–81.

Loy, G. (1989a). Composing with computers – a survey of some compositional formalisms and programming languages for music. In Mathews and Pierce [1989b], pp. 291–396.

Loy, G. (1989b). Musicians make a standard: The MIDI phenomenon. In Roads [1989], pp. 181–98.

Loy, G. (2007a). *Musimathics, Volume 1*. MIT Press, Cambridge, MA.

Loy, G. (2007b). *Musimathics, Volume 2*. MIT Press, Cambridge, MA.

Lyon, E. (2002). Dartmouth symposium on the future of computer music software: A panel discussion. *Computer Music Journal*, 26(4):13–30.

MacKay, D. J. C. (2003). *Information Theory, Inference, and Learning Algorithms*. Cambridge University Press, Cambridge.

Madden, T., Smith, R. B., Wright, M. and Wessel, D. (2001). Preparation for interactive live computer performance in collaboration with a symphony orchestra. In *Proceedings of the International Computer Music Conference (ICMC)*, Havana, Cuba.

Magnusson, T. (2009). *Epistemic Tools: The Phenomenology of Digital Musical Instruments*. PhD thesis, University of Sussex.

Magnusson, T. and Hurtado, E. (2007). The acoustic, the digital and the body: A survey on musical instruments. In *Proceedings of New Interfaces for Musical Expression (NIME)*, New York, NY.

Makhoul, J. (1975). Linear prediction: A tutorial review. *Proceedings of the IEEE*, 63(4):561–80.

Mäki-Patola, T., Laitinen, J., Kanerva, A. and Takala, T. (2005). Experiments with virtual reality instruments. In *Proceedings of New Interfaces for Musical Expression (NIME)*, Vancouver, Canada.

Malham, D. G. (1998). Approaches to spatialisation. *Organised Sound*, 3(2):167–77.

Malham, D. G. (2001). Toward reality equivalence in spatial sound diffusion. *Computer Music Journal*, 25(4):31–8.

Malham, D. G. and Myatt, A. (1995). 3-D sound spatialization using ambisonic techniques. *Computer Music Journal*, 19(4):58–70.

Mallat, S. (1998). *A Wavelet Tour of Signal Processing*, 2nd Edition. Academic Press, San Diego, CA.

Mandryk, R. L., Atkins, M. S. and Inkpen, K. M. (2006). A continuous and objective evaluation of emotional experience with interactive play environments. In *Proceedings of Computer–Human Interaction (CHI)*, Montréal, Canada.

Manning, P., Selfridge-Field, E., Reily, S. A. and Pople, A. (2009). Computers and music. *Grove Music Online. Oxford Music Online*.

Marsden, A. and Pople, A. (eds) (1992). *Computer Representations and Models in Music*. Academic Press, London.

Martin, K., Scheirer, E. and Vercoe, B. (1998). Music content analysis through models of audition. In *ACM Workshop on Content Processing of Media for Multimedia Applications, Bristol*.

Mashinter, K. (2006). Calculating sensory dissonance: Some discrepancies arising from the models of Kameoka & Kuriyagawa and Hutchinson & Knopoff. *Empirical Musicology Review*, 1(2).

Matarić, M. J. (2007). *The Robotics Primer*. MIT Press, Cambridge, MA.

Mathews, M. V. (1969). *The Technology of Computer Music*. MIT Press, Cambridge, MA.

Mathews, M. V. (2008). Lektrowsky's will. *Array (Journal of the International Computer Music Association)*, pp. 110–20.

Mathews, M. V. and Moore, F. R. (1970). GROOVE – a program to compose, store, and edit functions of time. *Communications of the ACM*, 13(12):715–21.

Mathews, M. V. and Pierce, J. R. (1989a). The Bohlen–Pierce scale. In Mathews and Pierce [1989b], pp. 165–73.

Mathews, M. V. and Pierce, J. R. (eds) (1989b). *Current Directions in Computer Music Research*. MIT Press, Cambridge, MA.

Matossian, N. (1986). *Xenakis*. Kahn and Averill, London.

McAdams, S. (1989). Psychological constraints on form-bearing dimensions in music. *Contemporary Music Review*, 4(1):181–98.

McAdams, S. and Bregman, A. (1985). Hearing musical streams. In Roads and Strawn [1985], pp. 658–98.

McAdams, S., Depalle, P. and Clarke, E. (2004). Analyzing musical sound. In Clarke and Cook [2004], pp. 157–96.

McAulay, R. and Quatieri, T. (1986). Speech analysis/synthesis based on a sinusoidal representation. *IEEE Transactions on Acoustics, Speech, and Signal Processing*, 34(4):744–54.

McCartney, J. (2002). Rethinking the computer music language: SuperCollider. *Computer Music Journal*, 26(4):61–8.

McCormack, J. (2003). Evolving sonic ecosystems. *Kybernetes: The International Journal of Systems and Cybernetics*, 32(1):184–202.

McDermott, J., Griffith, N. J. and O'Neal, M. (2006). Target-driven genetic algorithms for synthesizer control. In *International Conference on Digital Audio Effects (DAFx)*, Montréal, Canada.

McEnnis, D., McKay, C. and Fujinaga, I. (2006). jAudio: Additions and improvements. In *Proceedings of the International Symposium on Music Information Retrieval*.

Meneghini, M. (2007). An analysis of the compositional techniques in John Chowning's *Stria*. *Computer Music Journal*, 31(3):26–37.

Meredith, D., Lemström, K. and Wiggins, G. A. (2002). Algorithms for discovering repeated patterns in multidimensional representations of polyphonic music. *Journal of New Music Research*, 31(4):321–45.

Minsky, M. and Laske, O. (1992). Understanding musical activities. In Balaban *et al.* [1992].

Miranda, E. R. (ed.) (2000). *Readings in Music and Artificial Intelligence*. Harwood Academic Publishers, Amsterdam.

Miranda, E. R. (2002). *Computer Sound Design: Synthesis Techniques and Programming*, 2nd Edition. Focal Press, Oxford.

Miranda, E. R. and Biles, J. A. (eds) (2007). *Evolutionary Computer Music*. Springer-Verlag, London.

Miranda, E. R. and Wanderley, M. M. (2006). *New Digital Musical Instruments: Control and Interaction Beyond the Keyboard*. A-R Editions, Inc., Middleton, WI.

Mitchell, T. (1997). *Machine Learning*. McGraw-Hill, Singapore.

Mithen, S. (ed.) (2006). *The Singing Neanderthal*. Phoenix, London.

Moore, B. C. (2004). *An Introduction to the Psychology of Hearing*, 5th Edition. Elsevier, London.

Moore, F. R. (1990). *Elements of Computer Music*. P T R Prentice Hall, Englewood Cliffs, NJ.

Moore, F. R. (1996). Dreams of computer music: Then and now. *Computer Music Journal*, 20(1):25–41.

Moorer, J. A. (1985). About this reverberation business. In Roads and Strawn [1985], pp. 605–39.

Morris, R. D. (1993). New directions in the theory and analysis of musical contour. *Music Theory Spectrum*, 15(2):205–28.

Morris, T. (2004). *Computer Vision and Image Processing*. Palgrave Macmillan, Houndmills, Hampshire.

Murray-Rust, D., Smaill, A. and Edwards, M. (2006). MAMA: An architecture for interactive musical agents. In *ECAI: European Conference on Artificial Intelligence*, pp. 36–40.

Neecham, J. and Ling, W. (1965). *Science and Civilisation in China*. Cambridge University Press, Cambridge.

Nettl, B. and Russell, M. (eds) (1998). *In the Course of Performance: Studies in the World of Musical Improvisation*. University of Chicago Press, Chicago.

Ng, K. (2002). Sensing and mapping for interactive performance. *Organised Sound*, 7(2):191–200.

Ng, K., Weyde, T. and Nesi, P. (2008). i-Maestro: Technology-enhanced learning for music. In *International Computer Music Conference*, Belfast.

Nilson, C. (2007). Live coding practice. In *Proceedings of New Interfaces for Musical Expression (NIME)*, New York.

Norman, K. (2004). *Sounding Art: Eight Literary Excursions Through Electronic Music*. Ashgate, Aldershot, Hampshire.

Nuttall, A. (1981). Some windows with very good sidelobe behavior. *IEEE Transactions on Acoustics, Speech and Signal Processing*, 29(1):84–91.

Nyman, M. (ed.) (1999). *Experimental Music: Cage and Beyond*. Cambridge University Press, Cambridge.

Ord-Hume, A. W. J. G. (1973). *Clockwork Music: An Illustrated History of Mechanical Musical Instruments*. George Allen and Unwin Ltd., London.

Orio, N. (2006). Music retrieval: A tutorial and review. *Foundations and Trends in Information Retrieval*, 1(1):1–90.

Orio, N. and Déchelle, F. (2001). Score following using spectral analysis and hidden Markov models. In *Proceedings of the International Computer Music Conference (ICMC)*, Havana, Cuba.

O'Sullivan, D. and Igoe, T. (2004). *Physical Computing*. Thomson Course Technology PTR, Boston, MA.

Oswald, J. (2004). Bettered by the borrower: The ethics of musical debt. In Cox and Warner [2004], pp. 131–7.

Otondo, F. and Barrett, N. (2007). An interview with Natasha Barrett. *Computer Music Journal*, 31(2):10–19.

Pachet, F. (2003). The Continuator: Musical interaction with style. *Journal of New Music Research*, 32(3):333–41.

Paine, G. (2002). Interactivity, where to from here? *Organised Sound*, 7(3):295–304.

Painter, T. and Spanias, A. (2000). Perceptual coding of digital audio. *Proceedings of the IEEE*, 88(4):451–513.

Pardo, B. and Birmingham, W. (2002). Improved score following for acoustic performances. In *Proceedings of the International Computer Music Conference (ICMC)*, Göteborg, Sweden.

Park, T. H., Li, Z. and Biguenet, J. (2008). Not just more FMS: Taking it to the next level. In *Proceedings of the International Computer Music Conference (ICMC)*, Belfast.

Parncutt, R. (1994). A perceptual model of pulse salience and metrical accent in musical rhythms. *Music Perception*, 11(4):409–64.

Patel, A. D. (2008). *Music, Language and the Brain*. Oxford University Press, New York, NY.

Pearce, M., Meredith, D. and Wiggins, G. (2002). Motivations and methodologies for automation of the compositional process. *Musicae Scientiae*, 6(2):119–47.

Pearce, M., Müllensiefen, D. and Wiggins, G. (2008). A comparison of statistical and rule-based models of melodic segmentation. In *Proceedings of the International Symposium on Music Information Retrieval*, pp. 89–94, Philadelphia.

Pearce, M. and Wiggins, G. (2004). Improved methods for statistical modelling of monophonic music. *Journal of New Music Research*, 33(4):367–85.

Peretz, I. and Zatorre, R. (eds) (2003). *The Cognitive Neuroscience of Music*. Oxford University Press, New York.

Perez, A., Maestre, E., Ramirez, R. and Kersten, S. (2008). Expressive Irish fiddle performance model informed with bowing. In *International Computer Music Conference*, Belfast.

Pickles, J. O. (1988). *Introduction to the Physiology of Hearing*, 2nd Edition. Academic Press, London.

Pierce, J. R. (1968). *Science, Art, and Communication*. Clarkson N. Potter, Inc., New York, NY.

Pierce, J. R. (1999). The nature of musical sound. In Deutsch [1999], pp. 1–23.

Pohlmann, K. C. (2005). *Principles of Digital Audio*, 5th Edition. McGraw-Hill, New York.

Pople, A. (2004). Modeling musical structure. In Clarke and Cook [2004], pp. 127–56.

Pöppel, E. (2004). Lost in time: a historical frame, elementary processing units and the 3-second window. *Acta Neurobiologiae Experimentalis*, 64:295–301.

Pöppel, E. and Wittman, M. (1999). Time in the mind. In Wilson, R. A. and Keil, F. (eds), *The MIT Encyclopedia of the Cognitive Sciences*, pp. 841–3. MIT Press, Cambridge, MA.

Potter, K., Wiggins, G. and Pearce, M. (2007). Towards greater objectivity in music theory: Information-dynamic analysis of minimalist music. *Musicae Scientiae*, 11(2):295–322.

Preece, J., Sharp, H., Benyon, D., Holland, S. and Carey, T. (1994). *Human–Computer Interaction*. Addison-Wesley, Wokingham, UK.

Prendegast, M. (2003). *The Ambient Century*. Bloomsbury, London.

Pressing, J. (1988). Improvisation: Methods and models. In Sloboda [1988], pp. 129–78.

Puckette, M. (2002). Max at seventeen. *Computer Music Journal*, 26(4):31–43.

Puckette, M. (2007). *The Theory and Technique of Computer Music*. World Scientific Publishing Co., Inc., Hackensack, NJ.

Pulkki, V. (1997). Virtual sound source positioning using vector base amplitude panning. *Journal of the Audio Engineering Society*, 45(6):456–66.

Rabenstein, R. and Petrausch, S. (2006). Digital sound synthesis by block-based physical modeling. In *2nd International Symposium on Communications, Control and Signal Processing (ISCCSP)*, Marrakech, Morocco.

Rabiner, L. and Juang, B.-H. (1993). *Fundamentals of Speech Recognition*. Prentice Hall, Englewood Cliffs, NJ.

Ramirez, R. and Hazan, A. (2005). Modeling expressive music performance in jazz. In *International Florida Artificial Intelligence Research Society Conference*.

Ramirez, R., Hazan, A., Maestre, E. and Serra, X. (2008). A genetic rule-based expressive performance model for jazz saxophone. *Computer Music Journal*, 32:38–50.

Raphael, C. (2001). Synthesizing musical accompaniments with Bayesian belief networks. *Journal of New Music Research*, 30(1):59–67.

Raphael, C. (2004). Aligning musical scores with audio using hybrid graphical models. In *Proceedings of the International Symposium on Music Information Retrieval*.

Reas, C. and Fry, B. (2007). *Processing: A Programming Handbook for Visual Designers and Artists*. MIT Press, Cambridge, MA.

Reich, S. (2002). *Writings on Music 1965–2000 (Paul Hillier (ed.))*. Oxford University Press, New York.

Reynolds, S. (2008). *Energy Flash: A Journey Through Rave Music and Dance Culture*, 2nd Edition. Picador, London.

Riecken, R. D. (1992). WOLFGANG – a system using emoting potentials to manage musical design. In Balaban *et al.* [1992], pp. 206–36.

Risset, J.-C. (1985). Digital techniques and sound structure in music. In Roads [1985a], pp. 114–38.

Risset, J.-C. (1989). Paradoxical sounds. In Mathews and Pierce [1989b], pp. 149–58.

Risset, J.-C. and Wessel, D. L. (1999). Exploration of timbre by analysis and synthesis. In Deutsch [1999], pp. 113–69.

Roads, C. (1985a). *Composers and the Computer*. William Kaufmann, Inc., Los Altos, CA.

Roads, C. (1985b). Grammars as representations for music. In Roads and Strawn [1985], pp. 403–42.

Roads, C. (1985c). Improvisation with George Lewis. In Roads [1985a], pp. 76–87.

Roads, C. (1985d). Research in music and artificial intelligence. *Computing Surveys*, 17(2).

Roads, C. (1985e). A tutorial on nonlinear distortion or waveshaping synthesis. In Roads and Strawn [1985], pp. 83–94.

Roads, C. (ed.) (1989). *The Music Machine*. MIT Press, Cambridge, MA.

Roads, C. (1996). *The Computer Music Tutorial*. MIT Press, Cambridge, MA.

Roads, C. (2001). *Microsound*. MIT Press, Cambridge, MA.

Roads, C., Pope, S. T., Piccialli, A. and de Poli, G. (eds) (1997). *Musical Signal Processing*. Swets & Zeitlinger, Lisse, Netherlands.

Roads, C. and Strawn, J. (eds) (1985). *Foundations of Computer Music*. MIT Press, Cambridge, MA.

Rocchesso, D. (2000). Fractionally addressed delay lines. *IEEE Transactions on Speech and Audio Processing*, 8(6):717–27.

Rocchesso, D. (2002). Spatial effects. In Zölzer [2002], pp. 137–200.

Rocchesso, D. and Fontana, F. (eds) (2003). *The Sounding Object*. Information Society Technologies Grant Report (IST-2000-25287).

Rodet, X. (1997). The diphone program: New features, new synthesis methods and experience of musical use. In *Proceedings of the International Computer Music Conference (ICMC)*, pp. 418–21, Thessaloniki, Hellas.

Rodet, X. (2002). Synthesis and processing of the singing voice. In *Proc. 1st IEEE Benelux Workshop on Model based Processing and Coding of Audio (MPCA-2002)*, Leuven, Belgium.

Rodet, X. and Lefevre, A. (1996). Macintosh graphical interface and improvements to generalized diphone control and synthesis. In *Proceedings of the International Computer Music Conference (ICMC)*, Hong Kong.

Rodet, X., Potard, Y. and Barrière, J. B. (1984). The CHANT project: From the synthesis of the singing voice to synthesis in general. *Computer Music Journal*, 8(3):15–31.

Rodet, X. and Schwarz, D. (2007). Spectral envelopes and additive+residual analysis/synthesis. In Beauchamp [2007a], pp. 175–227.

Roederer, J. G. (1995). *The Physics and Psychophysics of Music*, 2nd Edition. Springer-Verlag, New York.

Rohrhuber, J. (2007). Network music. In Collins and d'Escriván [2007], pp. 140–55.

Rohrmeier, M. and Cross, I. (2008). Statistical properties of harmony in Bach's chorales. In *Proceedings of the 10th International Conference on Music Perception and Cognition*, Sapporo, Japan.

Rosen, J. (2008). Researchers play tune recorded before Edison. *New York Times*.

Rosenboom, D. (1997). Extended musical interface with the human nervous system: Assessment and prospectus. *Leonardo Monograph Series*, 1.

Rossing, T. D. and Fletcher, N. H. (1998). *The Physics of Musical Instruments*, 2nd Edition. Springer Science+Business Media, Inc., New York, NY.

Rowe, R. (1993). *Interactive Music Systems*. MIT Press, Cambridge, MA.

Rowe, R. (2001). *Machine Musicianship*. MIT Press, Cambridge, MA.

Rumsey, F. and McCormick, T. (2006). *Sound and Recording: An Introduction*, 5th Edition. Focal Press, Oxford.

Russell, S. and Norvig, P. (2003). *Artificial Intelligence: A Modern Approach*, 2nd Edition. Prentice Hall, Upper Saddle River, NJ.

Ryan, J. (1991). Some remarks on musical instrument design at STEIM. *Contemporary Music Review*, 6(1):3–17.

Sapp, C. S. (2008). Hybrid numeric/rank similarity metrics for musical performance analysis. In *Proceedings of the International Symposium on Music Information Retrieval*, Philadelphia.

Scarletti, C. (1994). Sound synthesis algorithms for auditory data representations. In Kramer [1994a], pp. 223–51.

Schaeffer, P. (2005). *Solfège de l'Objet Sonore*. Institut National de l'Audiovisuel, Paris.

Schafer, R. M. (1986). *The Thinking Ear: Complete Writings on Music Education*. Arcana, Toronto.

Schafer, R. M. (1994). *The Soundscape: Our Sonic Environment and the Tuning of the World*. Destiny Books, Rochester, VT.

Schedel, M. (2007). Electronic music and the studio. In Collins and d'Escriván [2007], pp. 24–37.

Scheirer, E. D. (1996). Bregman's chimerae: Music perception as auditory scene analysis. In *Proceedings of the International Conference on Music Perception and Cognition*.

Scheirer, E. D. (1998). Tempo and beat analysis of acoustic musical signals. *Journal of the Acoustical Society of America*, 103(1):588–601.

Scheirer, E. D. (2000). *Music-Listening Systems*. PhD thesis, Massachusetts Institute of Technology, Cambridge, MA.

Scheirer, E. D. and Slaney, M. (1997). Construction and evaluation of a robust multifeature speech/music discriminator. In *International Conference on Acoustics, Speech, and Signal Processing*.

Schiemer, G. and Havryliv, M. (2006). Pocket gamelan: tuneable trajectories for flying sources in Mandala 3 and Mandala 4. In *Proceedings of New Interfaces for Musical Expression (NIME)*, pp. 37–42.

Schwarz, D. (2004). *Data-driven Concatenative Sound Synthesis*. PhD thesis, Université Paris 6.

Sears, A. and Jacko, J. A. (eds) (2008). *The Human–Computer Interaction Handbook*, 2nd Edition. Lawrence Erlbaum Associates, New York, NY.

Selfridge-Field, E. (1993). Music analysis by computer. In Haus [1993], pp. 3–24.

Selfridge-Field, E. (ed.) (1997). *Beyond MIDI: The Handbook of Musical Codes*. MIT Press, Cambridge, MA.

Serra, M.-H. (1997a). Introducing the phase vocoder. In Roads *et al.* [1997], pp. 31–90.

Serra, X. (1997b). Current perspectives in the digital synthesis of musical sounds. *Formats*, 1.

Serra, X. (2007). State of the art and future directions in musical sound synthesis. In *International Workshop on Multimedia Signal Processing*, Chania, Crete.

Serra, X. and Smith, J. O. (1990). Spectral modeling synthesis: A sound analysis/synthesis system based on a deterministic plus stochastic decomposition. *Computer Music Journal*, 14(4):12–24.

Sethares, W. A. (2005). *Tuning Timbre Spectrum Scale*, 2nd Edition. Springer Verlag, Berlin, Germany.

Simon, I., Morris, D. and Basu, S. (2008). MySong: Automatic accompaniment generation for vocal melodies. In *Computer Human Interaction (CHI)*, Florence, Italy.

Singer, E. (2008). The digital luthier: New musical instrument design in the 21st century. In Zorn, J. (ed.), *Arcana III: Musicians on Music*, pp. 204–14. Hips Road, New York, NY.

Slaney, M., Ellis, D. P. W., Sandler, M., Goto, M. and Goodwin, M. M. (2008). Introduction to the special issue on music information retrieval. *IEEE Transactions on Audio, Speech and Language Processing*, 16(2):253–4.

Slaney, M. and Lyon, R. F. (1990). A perceptual pitch detector. In *Proc. ICASSP*, pp. 357–60.

Sloboda, J. A. (1985). *The Musical Mind*. Oxford University Press, Oxford.

Sloboda, J. A. (ed.) (1988). *Generative Processes in Music: The Psychology of Performance, Improvisation and Composition*. Oxford University Press, Oxford.

Sloboda, J. A. and Juslin, P. N. (2001). Psychological perspectives on music and emotion. In Juslin and Sloboda [2001], pp. 71–104.

Smalley, D. (1986). Spectro-morphology and structuring processes. In Emmerson, S. (ed.), *The Language of Electroacoustic Music*, pp. 61–93. The MacMillan Press Ltd, Basingstoke, England.

Smalley, D. (1997). Spectromorphology: explaining sound shapes. *Organised Sound*, 2(2):107–26.

Smalley, D. (2007). Space-form and the acousmatic image. *Organised Sound*, 12(1):35–58.

Smallwood, S., Trueman, D., Cook, P. R. and Wang, G. (2008). Composing for laptop orchestra. *Computer Music Journal*, 32(1):9–25.

Smith, J. O. (1991). Viewpoints on the history of digital synthesis. In *Proceedings of the International Computer Music Conference (ICMC)*, pp. 1–10.

Smith, J. O. (1992). Physical modeling using digital waveguides. *Computer Music Journal*, 16(4):74–91.

Smith, J. O. (1996). Physical modeling synthesis update. *Computer Music Journal*, 20(2):44–56.

Smith, L. S. (1994). Sound segmentation using onsets and offsets. *Journal of New Music Research*, 23:11–23.

Smoliar, S. W. (1999). Modelling musical perception: A critical view. In Griffith and Todd [1999], pp. 97–110.

Snyder, B. (2000). *Music and Memory: An Introduction*. MIT Press, Cambridge, MA.

Solis, J., Chida, K., Taniguchi, K., Hashimoto, S. M., Suefuji, K. and Takanishi, A. (2006). The Waseda flutist robot. *Computer Music Journal*, 30(4):12–27.

Sorensen, A. (2005). Impromptu: An interactive programming environment for composition and performance. In *Australasian Computer Music Conference*, pp. 149–53, Brisbane.

Sound, S. O. (1999). Recording Cher's 'Believe'.

Spiegel, L. (1997). An information theory based compositional model. *Leonardo Music Journal*, 7.

Spiegel, L. (1998). Graphical GROOVE: memorial for the VAMPIRE, a visual music system. *Organised Sound*, 3(3):187–91.

Sterling, M., Dong, X. and Bocko, M. (2008). Representation of solo clarinet music by physical modeling synthesis. In *Proceedings of the International Conference on Acoustics, Speech and Signal Processing*, Las Vegas.

Sternberg, R. J. (ed.) (1999). *Handbook of Creativity*. Cambridge University Press, Cambridge.

Stilson, T. and Smith, J. (1996). Alias-free digital synthesis of classic analog waveforms. In *Proceedings of the International Computer Music Conference (ICMC)*.

Stobart, H. and Cross, I. (2000). The Andean anacrusis? Rhythmic structure and perception in Easter songs of Northern Potosí, Bolivia. *British Journal of Ethnomusicology*, 9(2):63–94.

Stockhausen, K. (ed.) (1989). *Towards a cosmic music*. Element Books Limited, Longmead, Shaftesbury, Dorset.

Stockhausen, K. and Barkin, E. (1962). The concept of unity in electronic music. *Perspectives of New Music*, 1(1):39–48.

Stowell, D. and Plumbley, M. D. (2008). Characteristics of the beatboxing vocal style (Tech. Rep. C4DM-TR-08-01). Technical report, Dept. of Electronic Engineering, Queen Mary, University of London.

Stowell, D., Robertson, A., Bryan-Kinns, N. and Plumbley, M. D. (2009). Evaluation of live human-computer music-making: quantitative and qualitative approaches. *International Journal of Human-Computer Studies*, Forthcoming.

Strogatz, S. H. (1994). *Nonlinear Dynamics and Chaos*. Addison-Wesley, Reading, MA.

Sturm, B. L. (2006a). Adaptive concatenative sound synthesis and its application to micromontage composition. *Computer Music Journal*, 30(4):46–66.

Sturm, B. L. (2006b). Concatenative sound synthesis and intellectual property: An analysis of the legal issues surrounding the synthesis of novel sounds from copyright-protected work. *Journal of New Music Research*, 35(1):23–33.

Sturm, B. L., Roads, C., McLeran, A. and Shynk, J. J. (2008). Analysis, visualization, and transformation of audio signals using dictionary-based methods. In *Proceedings of the International Computer Music Conference (ICMC)*, Belfast.

Sundberg, J. (1989). Synthesis of singing by rule. In Mathews and Pierce [1989b], pp. 45–55.

Sundberg, J. (1991). Synthesizing singing. In de Poli *et al.* [1991], pp. 299–324.

Sundberg, J. (1999). The perception of singing. In Deutsch [1999], pp. 171–214.

Taube, H. (2004). *Notes from the Metalevel: An Introduction to Computer Composition*. Routledge, New York, NY.

Temperley, D. (2001). *The Cognition of Basic Musical Structures*. MIT Press, Cambridge, MA.

Thaut, M. (2005). *Rhythm, Music, and the Brain*. Routledge, New York.

Thom, B. (2003). Interactive improvisational music companionship: A user-modeling approach. *User Modeling and User-Adapted Interaction Journal*, 13(1-2):133–77.

Tillmann, B. and Bigand, E. (2004). The relative importance of local and global structures in music perception. *The Journal of Aesthetics and Art Criticism*, 62(2):211–22.

Timoney, J., Lysaght, T., Schoenweisner, M. and Manus, L. M. (2004). Implementing loudness models in MATLAB. In *International Conference on Digital Audio Effects (DAFx)*.

Todd, P. M. and Loy, D. G. (eds) (1991). *Music and Connectionism*. MIT Press, Cambridge, MA.

Toiviainen, P. (2000). Symbolic AI versus connectionism in music research. In Miranda [2000], pp. 47–68.

Toiviainen, P. and Eerola, T. (2001). A method for comparative analysis of folk music based on musical feature extraction and neural networks. In *VII International Symposium on Systematic and Comparative Musicology, III International Conference on Cognitive Musicology*, Jyväskylä, Finland.

Tolonen, T., Välimäki, V. and Karjalainen, M. (1998). Evaluation of modern sound synthesis methods. TR48. Technical report, Helsinki University of Technology.

Traub, P. (2005). Sounding the net: Recent sonic works for the internet and computer networks. *Contemporary Music Review*, 24(6):459–81.

Truax, B. (1988). Real-time granular synthesis with a digital signal processor. *Computer Music Journal*, 12(2):14–26.

Truax, B. (1998). Composition and diffusion: space in sound in space. *Organised Sound*, 3(2):141–6.

Trueman, D. (2007). Why a laptop orchestra? *Organised Sound*, 12(2):171–9.

Tzanetakis, G. and Cook, P. (2000). Marsyas: a framework for audio analysis. *Organised Sound*, 4:169–75.

Tzanetakis, G., Kapur, A., Schloss, W. A. and Wright, M. (2007). Computational ethnomusicology. *Journal of Interdisciplinary Music Studies*, 1:1–24.

Ulyate, R. and Bianciardi, D. (2002). The interactive dance club: Avoiding chaos in a multi participant environment. *Computer Music Journal*, 26(3):40–49.

Välimäki, V. and Takala, T. (1996). Virtual musical instruments – natural sound using physical models. *Organised Sound*, 1(2):75–86.

van Dinther, R. and Patterson, R. (2005). The domain of tonal melodies: Physiological limits and some new possibilities. *Nova Acta Leopoldina: Science and Music – The Impact of Music*, 92(341):17–31.

van Kranenburg, P., Garbers, J., Volk, A., Wiering, F., Grijp, L. and Veltkamp, R. C. (2007). Towards integration of MIR and folk song research. In *Proceedings of the International Symposium on Music Information Retrieval*.

van Noorden, L. and Moelants, D. (1999). Resonance in the perception of musical pulse. *Journal of New Music Research*, 28(1):43–66.

Verfaille, V. and Arfib, D. (2001). A-DAFx: Adaptive digital audio effects. In *International Conference on Digital Audio Effects (DAFx)*, Limerick.

Verma, T. S. and Meng, T. H. Y. (2000). Extending spectral modeling synthesis with transient modeling synthesis. *Computer Music Journal*, 24(2):47–59.

Virtanen, T. (2006). *Sound Source Separation in Monaural Music Signals*. PhD thesis, Tampere University of Technology, Finland.

Voss, R. F. and Clarke, J. (1978). '1/f noise' in music: Music from 1/f noise. *Journal of the Acoustical Society of America*, 63(1):258–63.

Walker, W. F. (1997). A computer participant in musical improvisation. In *Proc. Computer–Human Interaction (CHI)*.

Wanderley, M. M. and Orio, N. (2002). Evaluation of input devices for musical expression: Borrowing tools from HCI. *Computer Music Journal*, 26(3):62–76.

Wang, D. and Brown, G. J. (eds) (2006). *Computational Auditory Scene Analysis: Principles, Algorithms, and Applications*. John Wiley and Sons/IEEE Press, Hoboken, NJ.

Wang, G. (2008). *The ChucK Audio Programming Language: A Strongly-timed and On-the-fly Environ-/mentality*. PhD thesis, Princeton University.

Wang, G. and Cook, P. R. (2004). On-the-fly programming: Using code as an expressive musical instrument. In *Proceedings of New Interfaces for Musical Expression (NIME)*, Hamamatsu, Japan.

Watkinson, J. (2001). *The Art of Digital Audio*, 3rd Edition. Focal Press, Oxford.

Weinberg, G. (2005). Interconnected musical networks: Toward a theoretical framework. *Computer Music Journal*, 29(2):23–39.

Weinberg, G. and Driscoll, S. (2006). Towards robotic musicianship. *Computer Music Journal*, 30(4):28–45.

Weisberg, A. (1993). *Performing Twentieth Century Music: a Handbook for Conductors and Instrumentalists*. Yale University Press, New Haven.

Wenzel, E. M. (1994). Spatial sound and sonification. In Kramer [1994a], pp. 127–50.

Wessel, D. (1979). Timbre space as a musical control structure. *Computer Music Journal*, 3(2):45–52.

Wessel, D. and Wright, M. (2002). Problems and prospects for intimate musical control of computers. *Computer Music Journal*, 26(3):11–22.

Wheeler, M., Bullock, S., Paolo, E. D., Noble, J., Bedau, M., Husbands, P., Kirby, S. and Seth, A. (2002). The view from elsewhere: Perspectives on ALife modeling. *Artificial Life*, 8:87–100.

Wiggins, G. (2007). Review of *Computer Models of Musical Creativity* by David Cope. *Literary and Linguistic Computing*.

Wiggins, G., Miranda, E., Smaill, A. and Harris, M. (1993). A framework for the evaluation of music representation systems. *Computer Music Journal*, 17(3):31–42.

Will, U. and Ellis, C. (1996). A re-analyzed Australian western desert song: Frequency performance and interval structure. *Ethnomusicology*, 40(2):187–222.

Wilson, A. O. (2008). Sensor- and recognition-based input for interaction. In Sears and Jacko [2008], pp. 177–99.

Wilson, S. (2002). *Information Arts: Intersections of Science, Art and Technology*. MIT Press, Cambridge, MA.

Windsor, L. (2000). Through and around the acousmatic: The interpretation of electroacoustic sounds. In Emmerson [2000c], pp. 7–35.

Windsor, L. (2009). Measurement and models of performance. In Hallam *et al.* [2009], pp. 323–31.

Winkler, T. (1998). *Composing Interactive Music: Techniques and Ideas Using Max*. MIT Press, Cambridge, MA.

Winograd, T. (1986). Linguistics and the computer analysis of tonal harmony. *Journal of Music Theory*, 12:2–59.

Wishart, T. (1994). *Audible Design: A Plain and Easy Introduction to Practical Sound Composition*. Orpheus the Pantomime Ltd, York.

Wishart, T. (1996). *On Sonic Art (revised edition, edited by Simon Emmerson)*. Routledge, New York, NY.

Witten, I. H. and Frank, E. (2005). *Data Mining: Practical Machine Learning Tools and Techniques*, 2nd Edition. Morgan Kaufmann Publishers, San Francisco.

Wright, M. (2005). Open sound control: an enabling technology for musical networking. *Organised Sound*, 10(3):193–200.

Wright, M. (2008). *The Shape of an Instant: Measuring and Modeling Perceptual Attack Time with Probability Density Functions*. PhD thesis, CCRMA, Stanford, CA.

Wright, M., Beauchamp, J., Fitz, K., Rodet, X., Rödet, A., Serra, X. and Wakefield, G. (2000). Analysis/synthesis comparison. *Organised Sound*, 5(3):173–89.

Xenakis, I. (1994). La crise de la musique sérielle. In Galliari, A. and Xenakis, I. editors, *Kéleütha*, pp. 39–43. L'Arche, Paris.

Xenakis, I. (1985). Music composition treks. In Roads [1985a], pp. 172–92.

Xenakis, I. (1992). *Formalized Music*. Pendragon Press, Stuyvesant, NY.

Yavelow, C. (1989). Music and microprocessors: MIDI and the state of the art. In Roads [1989], pp. 199–234.

Yost, W. A. (2007). *Fundamentals of Hearing: An Introduction*, 5th Edition. Academic Press, Burlington, MA.

Zadel, M. and Fujinaga, I. (2004). Web services for music information retrieval. In *Proceedings of the International Symposium on Music Information Retrieval*, Barcelona, Spain.

Zanette, D. H. (2006). Zipf's law and the creation of musical context. *Musicae Scientiae*, 10:3–18.

Zicarelli, D. (2002). How I learned to love a program that does nothing. *Computer Music Journal*, 26(4):44–51.

Zils, A. and Pachet, F. (2001). Musical mosaicing. In *International Conference on Digital Audio Effects (DAFx)*.

Zölzer, U. (ed.) (2002). *DAFX – Digital Audio Effects*. John Wiley and Sons, Chichester, England.

Zorn, J. (ed.) (2000). *Arcana: Musicians on Music*. Granary Books, Inc., New York, NY.

Index